FRANCIS MCCAFFERY

Network Architecture with Cisco

Comprehensive Cisco Guide to Network Architectures for Efficient Data Traffic Management

Copyright © 2024 by Francis McCaffery

All rights reserved. No part of this publication may be reproduced, stored or transmitted in any form or by any means, electronic, mechanical, photocopying, recording, scanning, or otherwise without written permission from the publisher. It is illegal to copy this book, post it to a website, or distribute it by any other means without permission.

First edition

*This book was professionally typeset on Reedsy.
Find out more at reedsy.com*

Contents

Introduction to Network Architecture	1
Cisco's Networking Ecosystem	33
The Hierarchical Network Design Model	67
Scalable Network Design Principles	98
Optimizing Data Traffic Flow	129
Ensuring Redundancy and High Availability	171
Software-Defined Networking (SDN) with Cisco	202
Cisco SD-WAN: The Future of Wide Area Networking	240
Cisco Meraki: Simplified Network Management	277
Implementing Zero Trust Architecture with Cisco	316
Firewalls and Intrusion Prevention with Cisco	348
Case Studies in Network Architecture	388
Multi-Vendor Environments and Cisco Integration	419
The Future of Network Architecture with Cisco	451
Practice Labs and Configuration Examples	476
Troubleshooting and Network Optimization	514
Appendices	547

Introduction to Network Architecture

Defining Network Architecture

Network architecture refers to the design and structure of a network, including the arrangement of its components, the communication protocols it employs, and the methods used to ensure the network operates efficiently and securely. It is the blueprint that governs how devices and systems within a network connect, communicate, and function together. Essentially, network architecture provides a comprehensive framework for building, managing, and optimizing network infrastructure to meet the needs of an organization, whether it's a small business or a global enterprise.

At its core, network architecture encompasses both the physical layout of network devices (such as routers, switches, and servers) and the logical structure that dictates how data flows through the network, as well as the protocols and services that ensure smooth operation. A well-designed network architecture is crucial for ensuring reliable performance, security, scalability, and ease of management, which are all vital for the seamless functioning of modern IT systems.

The term "network architecture" is often used interchangeably with terms like **network design** or **network infrastructure**, but it is broader in scope. Network architecture is not just about how the network is built, but also about how it is optimized and maintained over time. In this section, we'll break down the key elements that define network architecture, its importance, and the factors that influence its design.

Key Components of Network Architecture

There are several key components and principles that define a network architecture. These include:

Physical Layer (Hardware Infrastructure)

The physical infrastructure of the network includes all the hardware devices that make up the network, such as:

- **Routers:** Devices that forward data packets between different networks. Routers manage traffic, ensuring data packets find their optimal path to reach their destination.
- **Switches:** These operate within a local area network (LAN), directing data between devices within the same network segment, often based on MAC addresses.
- **Cabling:** Whether copper cables (Ethernet) or fiber optics, cabling provides the physical medium for data transmission.
- **Access Points:** Wireless access points provide network connectivity to wireless devices like laptops, smartphones, and IoT devices.
- **Servers and Storage Systems:** These provide centralized services, including file storage, databases, application hosting, and more.

The physical components are the tangible elements that create the "bones" of the network. Their arrangement and the technologies used determine much of the network's performance and reliability.

Logical Layer (Network Topology and Protocols)

Beyond the physical infrastructure, the logical layer defines the **topology** (the network's layout) and the protocols that allow devices to communicate across the network. The key aspects of the logical layer include:

- **Network Topology:** The layout or arrangement of different devices

within the network. Common topologies include bus, ring, star, mesh, and hybrid models. The choice of topology depends on factors like scalability, fault tolerance, and performance.
- **IP Addressing and Subnetting:** The IP address scheme defines how devices within the network are identified and how traffic is routed. Subnetting allows for the efficient allocation of IP addresses across the network.
- **Routing Protocols:** Protocols like **OSPF** (Open Shortest Path First) and **BGP** (Border Gateway Protocol) determine how data packets travel from one network to another and how they navigate around the network.
- **Network Services:** Essential services like DNS (Domain Name System), DHCP (Dynamic Host Configuration Protocol), and NAT (Network Address Translation) help manage traffic and ensure smooth communication across devices.

These logical constructs define how data flows through the network, how it is directed to its destination, and how the network can efficiently handle large volumes of traffic without congestion.

Security Architecture

A critical part of network architecture is ensuring that the network is secure against external threats and internal vulnerabilities. The security architecture encompasses:

- **Firewalls and Intrusion Detection Systems (IDS):** Firewalls control incoming and outgoing network traffic, while IDS monitor traffic for signs of suspicious activity.
- **Virtual Private Networks (VPNs):** VPNs encrypt data and create secure tunnels for remote users to connect to the network.
- **Access Control Lists (ACLs):** ACLs define which devices and users can access specific parts of the network, ensuring only authorized access.

- **Encryption:** Data encryption protects sensitive information from being intercepted or accessed by unauthorized users.

Security is woven into every layer of the network, from the physical devices to the protocols used for communication. The goal is to prevent unauthorized access, protect sensitive data, and ensure network integrity.

The Importance of Network Architecture

A well-thought-out network architecture is vital for any organization, as it has a direct impact on several aspects of business operations. Here are a few of the most critical reasons why network architecture is so important:

Performance and Efficiency

The architecture of a network significantly affects its performance. A poorly designed network may face bottlenecks, causing slow speeds, delays, and packet loss. A strong architecture ensures that data flows smoothly, minimizing latency and maximizing throughput. By optimizing the routing paths, leveraging load balancing, and using Quality of Service (QoS) techniques, network architects can guarantee that critical applications perform efficiently even under high traffic loads.

Scalability

As businesses grow and technology advances, network demands change. A robust network architecture allows for easy scalability. It ensures that the network can accommodate the addition of new devices, locations, or services without significant redesigns. Whether scaling up data centers or adding new branches to a corporate network, the architecture must be flexible enough to grow with the business.

Security

Security is a paramount concern in any network. With increasing cyber threats, designing a network with strong security measures is essential. The architecture must incorporate firewalls, encryption, segmentation, and access control mechanisms to protect against unauthorized access, data breaches, and attacks. Security must be integrated from the ground up, not treated as an afterthought.

Reliability and Redundancy

Network downtime can severely impact productivity, customer satisfaction, and revenue. A strong network architecture includes redundancy and failover mechanisms that ensure high availability. Redundant links, servers, and data paths can take over automatically if a primary link fails, keeping the network running smoothly even during hardware failures.

Cost Efficiency

Well-planned network architecture can help organizations save money by avoiding costly downtime and over-provisioning of resources. Efficient use of resources, coupled with scalable and flexible designs, allows businesses to only invest in what they need at any given time. Additionally, network optimization can help reduce operating costs by improving performance and utilizing resources more effectively.

Factors Influencing Network Architecture

Designing network architecture is a complex task that requires considering numerous factors to ensure the network meets organizational needs and expectations. Some of the key factors influencing network architecture include:

Business Requirements

The nature of the business dictates the network's architecture. For example, a multinational corporation with offices around the world may require a distributed network design with high levels of redundancy and disaster recovery capabilities, while a small retail business may have simpler, centralized networking needs.

Data Traffic Patterns

Understanding the types of data traffic that will flow through the network—such as voice, video, and file sharing—is essential for designing a network that can handle those loads efficiently. High-traffic applications, like cloud-based services, may require specialized configurations to ensure minimal latency and maximum throughput.

Budget Constraints

Budget limitations often influence the selection of network components, the complexity of the design, and the choice of technologies used. Balancing performance, security, and cost is a critical aspect of network architecture. Choosing the right balance of on-premises versus cloud-based solutions can help businesses stay within budget while still achieving their desired performance.

Future Growth and Technological Advancements

As technology evolves, network architects must design with future advancements in mind. Technologies such as 5G, IoT (Internet of Things), and AI-driven applications will place new demands on network infrastructure. Planning for these changes and ensuring that the architecture is flexible enough to incorporate them is crucial.

Compliance and Regulatory Requirements

Many industries, such as healthcare and finance, have strict compliance and regulatory requirements regarding data storage, transmission, and access. These regulations can influence network design, such as the use of encryption, segmentation, and data redundancy to ensure compliance.

In conclusion, network architecture is not just about wiring together a collection of devices. It is the design and implementation of a system that needs to be both functional and future-proof, scalable, secure, and cost-effective. A well-designed network architecture not only meets the current demands of the business but is also flexible enough to adapt to future changes, technological advancements, and new business requirements. Whether an organization is managing a small office network or a large-scale enterprise system, understanding the principles and best practices of network architecture is essential for building a resilient, efficient, and secure network infrastructure.

As businesses continue to rely on digital technologies, network architecture will remain a key element in enabling success. The ability to create an effective network architecture—one that supports performance, growth, and security—can make the difference between a thriving business and one that struggles to keep up with the pace of change.

The Role of Network Architecture in Modern Enterprises

In the rapidly evolving landscape of modern business, network architecture has become more than just a technical necessity—it is a fundamental driver of operational success, competitiveness, and innovation. As enterprises grow more dependent on digital technologies, the robustness, scalability, and flexibility of their network architecture directly impact their ability to function efficiently and respond to market demands. Network architecture is the underlying framework that supports everything from day-to-day operations to strategic initiatives, enabling the flow of data, communication, and services across various channels.

In this section, we'll explore the crucial role network architecture plays in modern enterprises, covering its influence on business performance, efficiency, collaboration, and future growth. The integration of network architecture into the business strategy allows organizations to not only meet their current needs but also prepare for future technological advancements and shifts in the business environment.

Enabling Seamless Communication and Collaboration

One of the primary roles of network architecture in any modern enterprise is to enable seamless communication between employees, departments, and external partners. In today's business world, communication isn't limited to just emails or phone calls—organizations are increasingly reliant on collaborative tools, video conferencing, instant messaging, and cloud-based file sharing, all of which demand a fast, reliable, and secure network infrastructure.

Effective network architecture ensures that these communication channels remain uninterrupted, with the ability to handle a large number of simultaneous connections and applications. For example:

- **Video Conferencing**: Applications like Zoom, Microsoft Teams, and Google Meet depend heavily on a low-latency, high-bandwidth network to deliver smooth, real-time video and audio communication. Poor network design can lead to dropped calls, lagging video, or audio delays, which hinder productivity and can damage an organization's reputation.
- **VoIP (Voice over IP)**: With businesses increasingly using VoIP for internal communication and customer service, ensuring that voice traffic is prioritized over less time-sensitive traffic (like email or file downloads) is essential. A well-designed network using **Quality of Service (QoS)** policies can ensure that VoIP traffic receives high priority, avoiding issues like jitter and call dropouts.
- **Instant Messaging and File Sharing**: Services like Slack, Microsoft Teams, and Dropbox require fast, reliable access to cloud services. If the network architecture isn't robust enough to handle high levels of data transfer, employees may experience slow uploads/downloads, resulting in delays and frustration.

A well-architected network allows organizations to scale their communication infrastructure seamlessly, ensuring that as the workforce grows or the business enters new markets, these communication services continue to function without degradation in quality.

Supporting Business Operations and Data-Driven Decision-Making

Network architecture plays a critical role in supporting the business operations that drive day-to-day activities. Beyond communication, it facilitates access to business-critical systems, including ERP (Enterprise Resource Planning), CRM (Customer Relationship Management), and other internal software applications. These applications rely on a solid network foundation to ensure they can operate efficiently, handle large volumes of data, and provide real-time insights to decision-makers.

The increasing use of **big data** and **data analytics** tools has amplified the need for powerful network architecture that can handle the sheer volume of data being generated, stored, and analyzed. Many enterprises now use cloud-based data platforms (e.g., AWS, Microsoft Azure, or Google Cloud) to process and store vast amounts of business data. Network architecture must be designed to support:

- **High-Speed Data Transfer**: Whether it's retrieving sales data from a CRM, accessing inventory systems, or analyzing customer insights, businesses need a network that can handle large data transfers with minimal delay.
- **Cloud Access and Hybrid Networks**: As enterprises adopt cloud computing and hybrid environments, the network architecture must support seamless integration between on-premises infrastructure and remote cloud-based services. This means managing traffic between local data centers, remote branches, and cloud providers efficiently.
- **Real-Time Analytics**: With the growing importance of data-driven decision-making, real-time analytics platforms require high-throughput, low-latency networks to provide instant insights to executives, managers, and operational teams.

Without a reliable and fast network, businesses risk losing valuable time, productivity, and even market share. Data-driven decision-making requires fast access to relevant data, and network performance directly influences how quickly this can happen.

Enabling Scalability and Growth

One of the key reasons modern enterprises prioritize network architecture is its ability to scale as the organization grows. As businesses expand into new markets, increase their customer base, or develop new products and services, the demands on the network increase. An adaptable and scalable network architecture allows an enterprise to grow without disrupting its operations.

In terms of **scalability**, network architecture supports growth in several ways:

- **Modular Network Design**: A modular design allows businesses to scale their infrastructure in a step-by-step, predictable manner. This means adding new devices, offices, or branches can be done incrementally without the need to overhaul the entire network. With Cisco's **Enterprise Campus Architecture**, for example, new devices or buildings can be integrated into an existing network with minimal disruption.
- **Cloud Integration and Hybrid Models**: As businesses grow, many choose to leverage the cloud for additional computing power or storage. Cloud solutions are inherently scalable, and modern network architecture enables seamless integration between on-premises data centers and cloud platforms, providing the flexibility to scale on-demand.
- **Software-Defined Networking (SDN)**: SDN technologies, such as Cisco's **ACI** (Application Centric Infrastructure) or **DNA**, provide flexibility by decoupling the network control plane from the data plane. This allows for rapid adjustments to the network, without the need for manual reconfiguration of devices, making scaling a much smoother process.

For businesses, the ability to grow without experiencing network bottlenecks or performance issues is essential. A well-architected network can accommodate increases in traffic, new users, and additional services while maintaining optimal performance.

Ensuring Security and Compliance

INTRODUCTION TO NETWORK ARCHITECTURE

Security is no longer just an IT concern—it is a critical component of overall business strategy. Cybersecurity threats are evolving rapidly, and a breach can have far-reaching consequences, including financial loss, data theft, and damage to the company's reputation. Effective network architecture integrates security into the fabric of the network, protecting data at every point of transmission, ensuring compliance with industry standards, and safeguarding against both external and internal threats.

Key elements of network security architecture include:

- **Firewalls and Intrusion Prevention Systems (IPS)**: Modern firewalls go beyond simple packet filtering; they are designed to protect against sophisticated attacks, including those targeting specific applications and services. Cisco's **ASA (Adaptive Security Appliance)** and **Firepower** firewall systems integrate advanced security features like threat intelligence, malware detection, and application visibility.
- **Zero Trust Architecture**: The Zero Trust security model assumes no user or device can be trusted by default, whether inside or outside the network. This model requires continuous authentication and verification for every access request. Cisco's **Identity Services Engine (ISE)** helps enforce policies based on user roles, devices, and behaviors, ensuring that only authorized users and devices gain access to sensitive information.
- **Network Segmentation and Access Control**: By segmenting the network into smaller, isolated zones (e.g., separate networks for finance, HR, or R&D departments), businesses can limit the impact of a breach. This can be achieved through VLANs, access control lists (ACLs), and segmentation techniques. Cisco's **TrustSec** technology allows businesses to enforce security policies based on roles rather than physical network locations, providing an additional layer of security.
- **Compliance**: Many industries, such as healthcare (HIPAA), finance (PCI-DSS), and government (FISMA), have strict regulatory require-

ments for data protection. A strong network architecture ensures compliance with these regulations by providing mechanisms for secure data transmission, access control, and encryption.

In a world where data breaches and cyberattacks are prevalent, building security into the network architecture is essential for safeguarding an organization's data, operations, and reputation.

Supporting Remote Work and Global Operations

In the wake of the COVID-19 pandemic, remote work became a necessity for many businesses, and now it has become a permanent part of the corporate landscape. As a result, network architecture must support not only traditional in-office operations but also the needs of remote employees, contractors, and global operations.

Network design must allow for:

- **Virtual Private Networks (VPNs)**: VPNs create secure tunnels between remote users and the corporate network, ensuring sensitive data is encrypted while in transit. With remote work on the rise, VPNs have become a crucial component of any enterprise network.
- **Cloud-Based Applications**: Many businesses have shifted to cloud-based collaboration tools (e.g., Google Workspace, Microsoft 365) that require strong, reliable connectivity to the internet. Modern network architecture must ensure that employees can access these applications without disruption, no matter their location.
- **SD-WAN (Software-Defined Wide Area Networking)**: SD-WAN technology allows businesses to dynamically manage and optimize traffic between remote sites and data centers, ensuring efficient use of bandwidth. Cisco's **Viptela SD-WAN** solution offers secure, high-performance connectivity to remote offices, enhancing productivity for remote workers while maintaining security.

For multinational companies, network architecture also ensures that global offices are connected securely and can access centralized resources

INTRODUCTION TO NETWORK ARCHITECTURE

without significant performance issues. With global teams and remote workers becoming the norm, a flexible, secure, and efficient network is essential to maintain business continuity and productivity.

Network architecture is a critical element that underpins every aspect of a modern enterprise's IT infrastructure. It enables seamless communication, supports business operations, facilitates data-driven decision-making, and ensures security and compliance. A well-designed network architecture is not just about connecting devices—it's about creating a flexible, scalable, and resilient foundation that can grow and adapt to meet the changing needs of the business.

In today's fast-paced and increasingly digital business environment, the role of network architecture extends beyond technical considerations. It is a strategic asset that allows organizations to remain competitive, embrace new opportunities, and ensure they can scale securely and efficiently. As businesses continue to innovate and embrace new technologies like cloud computing, IoT, and AI, the role of network architecture will become even more critical in driving business success and ensuring operational continuity in an interconnected world.

Key Principles of Network Design

Effective network design is foundational to ensuring that an organization's network infrastructure is reliable, secure, scalable, and efficient. Network design is more than just connecting devices or ensuring traffic flows from one point to another—it is about creating a holistic system that aligns with business goals, user needs, and technological advancements. When designing a network, there are several key principles that guide architects in building robust, sustainable, and adaptable infrastructures.

In this section, we will delve into the fundamental principles of network design that every network architect should consider. These principles apply whether the network is designed for a small business or a large-scale enterprise and ensure that the network is capable of handling future growth, unforeseen challenges, and evolving technologies.

1. Scalability

Scalability is the ability of a network to handle increased load or to be easily expanded as demand grows. When designing a network, scalability is critical because the needs of the organization will change over time, often in ways that were not immediately foreseeable at the time of the initial design. A network that cannot scale will quickly become a bottleneck as traffic, devices, and services grow, leading to performance degradation, increased downtime, and higher costs.

To ensure scalability:

- **Modular Design**: Adopt a modular network architecture, where components can be easily added or upgraded without disrupting the entire system. For example, Cisco's **Enterprise Campus Architecture** offers a modular approach to network design, where new devices and additional network capacity can be added incrementally.
- **Cloud Integration**: Many modern networks are hybrid—combining on-premises infrastructure with cloud-based services. Leveraging cloud resources (e.g., AWS, Azure, Google Cloud) allows businesses to scale compute and storage capabilities without the need for extensive hardware upgrades.
- **Future-Proofing**: When choosing devices and infrastructure, consider emerging technologies and growth predictions. For instance, investing in **10G or 100G Ethernet** may be necessary for networks that anticipate heavy data traffic in the near future.

Scalable network architecture allows an organization to grow without needing a complete overhaul. This principle ensures that businesses can expand their network efficiently and cost-effectively.

2. Redundancy and High Availability

Network redundancy refers to the practice of duplicating critical components within the network to ensure that the network remains operational in case of failure. High availability (HA) is the ability of a system or component to continue functioning even in the event of hardware failure, network outages, or other disruptions. This principle is essential for ensuring that an enterprise network has minimal downtime, which is particularly important for mission-critical applications and services.

To achieve redundancy and high availability:

- **Redundant Paths**: Design the network with multiple paths for data to travel, allowing traffic to automatically reroute in case one path fails. This can be done using technologies like **Spanning Tree Protocol (STP)** for Ethernet networks or **MPLS (Multiprotocol Label Switching)** in wide-area networks (WANs).
- **Load Balancing**: Distribute network traffic across multiple devices or links to prevent any single component from becoming a bottleneck. **Cisco's Application Control Engine (ACE)** or other load balancing solutions can be used to improve the availability and performance of applications by distributing requests efficiently.
- **Failover Systems**: Implement automatic failover solutions that detect hardware or link failures and reroute traffic to backup systems. For example, **HSRP (Hot Standby Router Protocol)** or **VRRP (Virtual Router Redundancy Protocol)** can be used to provide router redundancy.
- **Data Replication**: For critical data, use replication mechanisms that ensure data is available even if one storage system or server fails. Techniques like **RAID (Redundant Array of Independent Disks)** and **data mirroring** help ensure data resilience.

High availability is a non-negotiable principle for modern networks. A network that can continue to function even when parts of it fail ensures business continuity, enhances productivity, and protects the organization's reputation.

3. Security

Network security is a fundamental principle of network design that spans all aspects of the infrastructure. Security involves protecting the network from internal and external threats, ensuring data confidentiality, integrity, and availability. With cyber threats becoming increasingly sophisticated, network design must integrate security into every layer, rather than bolting it on as an afterthought.

Key security considerations in network design include:

- **Perimeter Defense**: Implement firewalls, intrusion detection/prevention systems (IDS/IPS), and VPNs at the network's perimeter to filter and monitor incoming and outgoing traffic. **Cisco's ASA Firewalls** and **Firepower** series offer robust perimeter protection.
- **Segmentation and Micro-Segmentation**: Divide the network into smaller segments to reduce the potential impact of a breach. For example, separate user data from sensitive financial systems using VLANs or **Cisco TrustSec** segmentation to enforce policies based on identity rather than just physical location.
- **Zero Trust Architecture**: Adopting a Zero Trust model means assuming that no user or device, whether inside or outside the network, is trusted by default. This principle necessitates continuous authentication, granular access control, and continuous monitoring.
- **Encryption**: Encrypt data both in transit and at rest to ensure that sensitive information cannot be intercepted or accessed by unauthorized parties. For instance, use **IPsec VPNs** for encrypting traffic over untrusted networks or **SSL/TLS** for securing web applications.
- **Access Control**: Implement **Role-Based Access Control (RBAC)** or **Network Access Control (NAC)** to ensure that only authorized users and devices can access specific resources. Tools like **Cisco ISE (Identity Services Engine)** help enforce access control policies.

Designing with security in mind is not only essential for protecting sensitive data but also for ensuring compliance with regulatory standards, such as GDPR, HIPAA, and PCI-DSS.

4. Performance Optimization

Network performance is critical for ensuring that users and applications receive the data they need with minimal delay and in a reliable manner. Performance optimization in network design involves considering both the hardware and software elements of the network to ensure low latency, high throughput, and efficient traffic management.

Key performance principles include:

- **Traffic Prioritization**: Use **Quality of Service (QoS)** to prioritize time-sensitive traffic like VoIP, video conferencing, or online gaming over less critical data like file downloads. This ensures that critical applications are always given priority when network congestion occurs.
- **Bandwidth Management**: Ensure that there is sufficient bandwidth to meet the organization's needs. Tools like **Cisco's WAN Optimization** can be used to optimize data transfer and reduce bandwidth consumption through techniques like data compression and caching.
- **Network Monitoring and Analytics**: Continuously monitor network performance using tools like **Cisco DNA Center** or **SolarWinds** to identify bottlenecks, unusual traffic patterns, or potential failure points. Proactive network monitoring ensures that issues are addressed before they affect performance.
- **Traffic Shaping**: Apply traffic shaping policies to smooth out bursts of traffic that could overwhelm the network. By controlling the rate at which data packets are sent, the network can avoid congestion and maintain optimal performance for all users.

Ensuring high performance across a network requires careful attention to how traffic is managed, how devices communicate, and how to optimize the network's capacity to handle workloads efficiently.

5. Flexibility and Adaptability

Flexibility and adaptability are critical principles for designing networks that can evolve over time. Modern enterprises face rapidly changing demands, whether driven by new business initiatives, technological innovations, or external factors such as the COVID-19 pandemic. A flexible network architecture allows organizations to adapt quickly to changes in the business environment without significant disruptions or expensive upgrades.

To build flexibility into a network:

- **Software-Defined Networking (SDN)**: SDN enables more dynamic and flexible management of network resources. Through a centralized controller, network administrators can quickly adjust network configurations and policies without needing to manually reconfigure each device. This reduces operational complexity and allows faster responses to business needs.
- **Virtualization**: Network virtualization allows the physical network to be abstracted, creating multiple virtual networks on the same physical infrastructure. This flexibility enables businesses to deploy new services quickly, without the need to invest in additional hardware.
- **Hybrid Cloud Models**: As more businesses adopt hybrid cloud environments, network design must be flexible enough to integrate on-premises resources with cloud infrastructure. This enables organizations to use cloud services for scalability while retaining critical data and systems on-premises for security or compliance reasons.

A flexible network architecture can accommodate future changes, whether that means adding new services, adopting new technologies, or responding to business shifts. It allows organizations to be agile and responsive to market and technological changes.

6. Cost Efficiency

Cost efficiency is a balancing act in network design. While the temptation may be to invest in cutting-edge technology, it's important that network architects design with the organization's budget in mind. Over-engineering a network can lead to excessive capital expenditures (CapEx) and increased operational costs (OpEx) without yielding proportional benefits. On the other hand, under-engineering may result in performance issues, security vulnerabilities, and scalability limitations.

To achieve cost-efficient design:

- **Right-Sizing Hardware**: Ensure that the network infrastructure is appropriately scaled to meet current and projected demand. Over-investing in expensive equipment that exceeds the current needs may be wasteful, while under-investing may lead to performance issues.
- **Cloud and Hybrid Models**: Consider leveraging cloud infrastructure where appropriate. Cloud-based solutions can often provide cost savings by reducing the need for extensive on-premises hardware, while allowing for on-demand scaling.
- **Energy Efficiency**: Modern network equipment is designed to be energy-efficient, reducing operational costs over time. For example, **Cisco's Catalyst 9000 series switches** use energy-saving technologies like **Energy Efficient Ethernet (EEE)**, reducing power consumption.

A cost-efficient network is one that delivers the required performance and scalability without unnecessary expenditures. Network architects must balance performance, security, and flexibility while keeping the organization's budget in mind.

Designing a network that meets the needs of a modern enterprise requires careful consideration of multiple principles. Scalability, redundancy, security, performance, flexibility, and cost efficiency all play critical roles in ensuring that the network can support business operations, adapt to future needs, and protect against disruptions. By adhering to these principles, network architects can create robust, reliable, and future-proof networks that support the dynamic needs of modern businesses.

The Cisco Approach to Network Architecture

As one of the most prominent leaders in the networking industry, Cisco has revolutionized the way enterprises approach network design, security, and management. Cisco's network architecture is built upon decades of expertise, innovation, and a deep understanding of the challenges and opportunities that modern enterprises face. The Cisco approach combines cutting-edge technology, industry best practices, and scalable solutions, enabling organizations to build networks that are not only efficient but also secure, flexible, and future-ready.

In this section, we will explore the Cisco approach to network architecture, including the frameworks, technologies, and philosophies that guide the design and implementation of enterprise networks. Cisco's solutions cover every layer of the network, from physical infrastructure to cloud integration, and offer enterprises a comprehensive suite of tools to build, manage, and optimize their networks.

1. Cisco's Intent-Based Networking (IBN)

At the heart of Cisco's modern network architecture is **Intent-Based Networking (IBN)**, a concept that represents a shift from traditional network management to a more intelligent, automated approach. With IBN, the focus moves from manually configuring and managing network devices to defining high-level business objectives or "intent" and allowing the network to automatically translate these into actionable policies and configurations.

IBN is built on Cisco's **DNA Center**, a centralized network management platform that uses automation, analytics, and machine learning to optimize network performance and simplify operations. By using IBN, businesses can:

- **Define Business Intent**: Rather than configuring individual network devices and links, administrators define the desired outcomes (e.g., "All sales team devices should be prioritized for bandwidth" or "Ensure secure access for remote workers"). Cisco's IBN system then

INTRODUCTION TO NETWORK ARCHITECTURE

automates the application of policies that meet these objectives.
- **Achieve Automation**: With IBN, network tasks such as provisioning, monitoring, and troubleshooting are automated. This reduces human error, minimizes downtime, and accelerates the deployment of new services or infrastructure.
- **Use Analytics for Continuous Optimization**: Cisco DNA Center continuously analyzes network performance, user behavior, and traffic patterns to ensure that the network is always optimized. This is particularly beneficial for detecting and responding to issues before they impact end-users.

Intent-Based Networking is not only a more efficient way of managing networks, but it also allows for greater alignment between IT and business objectives. As a result, the network becomes a strategic asset that actively supports the goals of the organization, rather than just a passive conduit for data traffic.

2. Cisco Digital Network Architecture (DNA)

Cisco Digital Network Architecture (DNA) is an integrated architecture that spans the entire enterprise network, from the campus and branch offices to the data center and cloud. Cisco DNA combines software, hardware, and services to provide a comprehensive solution for simplifying network design, deployment, and management. DNA embraces a **software-driven, open architecture** approach, allowing for greater flexibility, automation, and security.

Key components of Cisco DNA include:

- **DNA Center**: Cisco's DNA Center is the central management platform that serves as the brain of the DNA architecture. It provides a single pane of glass for managing, automating, and securing the entire network. DNA Center allows for intuitive network design, policy automation, real-time monitoring, and integrated security enforcement.
- **Network Automation**: Cisco DNA automates critical tasks such as

configuration, provisioning, and monitoring, reducing the complexity and manual effort traditionally required for network management. Automation increases efficiency and ensures consistency across the entire network.

- **SD-Access (Software-Defined Access)**: Cisco's SD-Access simplifies network segmentation, improving security and traffic management across campuses and branch offices. By abstracting the physical network into a virtual overlay, SD-Access allows administrators to apply policies across the network based on user roles, device types, and application needs rather than the underlying physical topology.
- **Security Integration**: Cisco DNA also incorporates security at every level of the network. Through technologies like **Cisco Identity Services Engine (ISE)**, **Cisco TrustSec**, and **Enforcement Points** at the network's edge, DNA ensures that security policies are enforced dynamically based on user identity and device posture.
- **Analytics and Insights**: Through Cisco's DNA Assurance and Analytics, the network continually monitors traffic, performance, and user behavior to provide insights and optimization suggestions. This data helps network administrators make informed decisions about network adjustments, upgrades, or new service deployments.

With Cisco DNA, enterprises can reduce complexity, improve security, and ensure that the network is agile enough to adapt to changing business demands. It enables a more proactive approach to network management, one that continuously adjusts to optimize performance and efficiency.

3. Cisco's SD-WAN (Software-Defined Wide Area Network)

As businesses increasingly rely on cloud applications and remote workers, traditional WAN architectures often become inefficient and expensive. Cisco's **SD-WAN** solution provides a more flexible, scalable, and cost-effective approach to connecting remote offices, branch locations, and cloud services.

Cisco SD-WAN allows businesses to replace traditional MPLS (Multiprotocol Label Switching) connections with broadband internet or hybrid solutions, while maintaining secure, high-performance connectivity. Cisco SD-WAN is integrated with Cisco's broader **Viptela** platform, providing a centralized control plane that simplifies the management of WAN traffic.

Key benefits of Cisco SD-WAN include:

- **Cost Savings**: By leveraging lower-cost internet connections instead of expensive MPLS links, businesses can significantly reduce the cost of WAN connectivity.
- **Optimized Application Performance**: Cisco SD-WAN uses **Application-Aware Routing** to automatically prioritize traffic based on application needs. For example, voice or video traffic can be prioritized over general web browsing, ensuring the best performance for business-critical applications.
- **End-to-End Security**: With built-in **Zero Trust** security, Cisco SD-WAN ensures that all traffic is encrypted, regardless of whether it travels across the public internet or private networks. Additionally, SD-WAN can dynamically route traffic over secure, high-performance paths, minimizing risk while maintaining reliability.
- **Simplified Management**: Through the centralized Cisco vManage platform, administrators can configure, monitor, and troubleshoot the SD-WAN network from a single interface, reducing operational complexity and improving troubleshooting speed.

SD-WAN represents a powerful evolution in the way enterprises build and manage their wide-area networks. It allows businesses to embrace digital transformation and cloud adoption while ensuring their networks remain secure, reliable, and cost-efficient.

4. Cisco ACI (Application Centric Infrastructure)

Cisco ACI (Application Centric Infrastructure) is Cisco's next-generation network architecture for the data center. Unlike traditional networking models that are device-centric, ACI focuses on **applications** and their requirements, creating a network that is highly optimized for application performance, agility, and security.

ACI enables a unified, automated data center network that integrates both physical and virtual environments. It decouples the network's control plane and data plane, allowing for dynamic, application-aware policies that optimize traffic flow and improve network resource utilization.

Key features of Cisco ACI include:

- **Application-Aware Networking**: ACI enables administrators to define policies based on the specific needs of applications. For example, if an application requires low latency or high throughput, ACI can automatically adjust the network to meet those requirements without manual intervention.
- **Unified Management**: Cisco ACI integrates the network's physical and virtual components, providing a single point of management through the **Cisco Application Policy Infrastructure Controller (APIC)**. This unified approach reduces complexity and improves the agility of data center operations.
- **Policy-Driven Automation**: With ACI, network provisioning and configuration are automated based on policies defined by the applications. This ensures that the network is always in sync with application demands, reducing the time spent on manual configurations and enabling faster service delivery.
- **Security and Segmentation**: ACI integrates advanced network segmentation and security features, allowing for granular control over traffic flows. Using **Cisco's TrustSec** technology, ACI enforces security policies at the application level, ensuring that sensitive data is protected throughout the network.

Cisco ACI transforms the data center network from a static, hardware-centric model to a dynamic, application-aware infrastructure that is optimized for modern workloads. With ACI, businesses can achieve greater agility, improve operational efficiency, and ensure that their networks are aligned with the evolving needs of their applications.

5. Cisco Meraki: Cloud-Managed Networking

Cisco Meraki offers a cloud-managed network solution that simplifies the deployment and management of networking devices, such as routers, switches, firewalls, and wireless access points. Meraki's ease of use, combined with robust functionality, makes it an ideal solution for businesses that need scalable, secure, and simple-to-manage networks.

Key benefits of Cisco Meraki include:

- **Cloud Management**: Meraki devices are managed entirely from the cloud, enabling administrators to configure and monitor their network from anywhere, using a simple, intuitive interface. There's no need for on-site management or complex configurations, making Meraki ideal for distributed teams or businesses with remote locations.
- **Integrated Security**: Cisco Meraki integrates security features, including firewalls, intrusion detection, and VPN support, directly into the hardware. This provides end-to-end security without requiring separate devices or services.
- **Scalability**: Meraki allows businesses to scale their networks easily, whether they are expanding a single location or deploying a network across multiple offices worldwide. The cloud-based management makes it easy to add new devices, configure settings, and deploy new sites with minimal effort.
- **Analytics and Reporting**: Meraki's cloud dashboard provides rich analytics and reporting on network performance, user behavior, and application usage, helping administrators optimize network operations and troubleshoot issues quickly.

Meraki represents Cisco's commitment to providing simple yet powerful networking solutions for businesses of all sizes, with the flexibility to meet both small-scale and enterprise-level needs.

Cisco's approach to network architecture is comprehensive, flexible, and highly scalable. With innovations like **Intent-Based Networking**, **Cisco DNA**, **SD-WAN**, and **Cisco ACI**, Cisco provides enterprises with the tools they need to build networks that are agile, secure, and optimized for performance. Whether an organization is looking to automate network management, integrate cloud services, or improve the security and efficiency of its data center, Cisco offers a wide array of solutions that are tailored to meet the demands of modern enterprises.

Through its commitment to innovation and forward-thinking technologies, Cisco has cemented itself as a trusted partner for enterprises looking to stay ahead in a rapidly evolving digital landscape. By adopting Cisco's network architecture, organizations can ensure they have the infrastructure they need to support business growth, drive digital transformation, and maintain a competitive edge in an interconnected world.

The Importance of Efficient Data Traffic Management

Efficient data traffic management is a critical element in the design and operation of modern networks. As businesses and organizations become more reliant on technology, data traffic—whether generated by employees, customers, devices, or applications—has grown exponentially. Managing this traffic efficiently is no longer a luxury; it is a necessity for ensuring that networks remain functional, responsive, and scalable. Without effective data traffic management, networks can become congested, performance can degrade, and users can experience delays or downtime, all of which can significantly impact business operations, user satisfaction, and ultimately, the bottom line.

In this section, we will explore the importance of efficient data traffic management in enterprise networks, its key components, and the benefits it offers to organizations. By implementing the right strategies and tools for traffic management, businesses can ensure that their networks are optimized for performance, security, and scalability.

1. Optimizing Network Performance

The primary objective of data traffic management is to ensure that network resources are used optimally, with minimal delays or congestion. Unmanaged traffic or poorly prioritized data can lead to network bottlenecks, latency, and a general degradation in performance, particularly for real-time applications like VoIP, video conferencing, and interactive online services.

Key strategies for optimizing network performance include:

- **Traffic Prioritization**: By categorizing traffic based on its importance or time-sensitivity, network administrators can ensure that critical applications are always given priority. For instance, **Quality of Service (QoS)** can be used to prioritize voice and video traffic over less time-sensitive data, such as file transfers or system updates. By ensuring that latency-sensitive traffic is given the necessary resources, the network will perform efficiently even under heavy load.
- **Load Balancing**: Load balancing involves distributing network traffic across multiple links or devices to prevent any single link or device from becoming a bottleneck. This not only helps improve the overall performance of the network but also ensures that no single point of failure can disrupt service. For example, Cisco's **Application Control Engine (ACE)** provides intelligent load balancing that automatically distributes traffic based on real-time network conditions, ensuring optimal resource utilization.
- **Bandwidth Management**: Effective bandwidth management ensures that the network's available bandwidth is distributed according to the needs of various applications. For example, certain types of traffic, such as cloud applications or enterprise resource planning (ERP) systems, may require higher bandwidth allocation than standard browsing. Tools like Cisco's **WAN Optimization** can help ensure

that bandwidth is utilized efficiently by optimizing data transfer and reducing unnecessary traffic.

By optimizing network performance, organizations can ensure that their network operates at peak efficiency, regardless of the volume of data or the complexity of the applications in use.

2. Minimizing Network Congestion

Network congestion occurs when the demand for network resources exceeds the capacity of the network, leading to delays, packet loss, and increased latency. This is particularly problematic in environments where real-time applications are in use, such as voice and video conferencing, as well as in networks supporting mission-critical operations.

Effective traffic management strategies can help prevent or mitigate network congestion:

- **Traffic Shaping and Policing**: Traffic shaping is a technique used to control the flow of data packets into the network, ensuring that traffic does not exceed certain thresholds. By regulating the rate at which traffic is sent, traffic shaping helps smooth out bursts of data and prevents congestion. **Traffic policing** can also be used to enforce bandwidth usage limits, dropping or marking packets that exceed predefined limits.
- **Congestion Control Mechanisms**: Protocols such as **TCP Congestion Control** and **Explicit Congestion Notification (ECN)** can be employed to detect and react to congestion on the network. These protocols dynamically adjust the rate at which data is transmitted to avoid congestion and maintain stable performance. Cisco's **MPLS (Multiprotocol Label Switching)** and **QoS** technologies offer traffic management solutions that can dynamically adjust routing paths to avoid congested areas of the network.
- **Link Aggregation**: Link aggregation, also known as **Ethernet bonding**, involves combining multiple physical links into a single logical link to increase overall bandwidth and reduce the risk of

congestion. For example, **Cisco's EtherChannel** technology allows administrators to combine multiple Ethernet interfaces into a single high-speed virtual link, effectively increasing the available bandwidth and balancing traffic across multiple paths.

By preventing network congestion, businesses can ensure that their networks remain responsive and that performance does not degrade, even as the volume of data traffic increases.

3. Ensuring Security and Compliance

Data traffic management is not just about improving performance and reducing congestion; it is also a crucial aspect of securing network resources and ensuring compliance with regulatory standards. Without effective traffic management, networks are vulnerable to security breaches, data leaks, and attacks, which can compromise sensitive information and disrupt operations.

Key security benefits of efficient traffic management include:

- **Segmentation and Isolation**: Traffic management allows for the segmentation of the network into different zones based on security requirements. For example, sensitive data can be isolated from less critical traffic using **VLANs (Virtual Local Area Networks)** or **firewall policies**. This reduces the attack surface and ensures that if one part of the network is compromised, the rest of the network remains secure.
- **Application-Level Security**: By managing traffic at the application level, network administrators can ensure that malicious traffic is blocked before it reaches critical applications. **Application-layer firewalls** and **intrusion detection systems (IDS)** can be used to inspect and filter traffic, ensuring that only legitimate traffic is allowed access to the network.
- **Data Encryption**: Traffic management tools can also enforce encryption for sensitive data, ensuring that all traffic between devices and servers is secure. Technologies like **IPsec** VPNs, **SSL/TLS**

encryption, and **MACsec (Media Access Control Security)** can be implemented to protect data both in transit and at rest.
- **Compliance with Regulatory Standards**: Many industries are subject to regulatory requirements that mandate the secure handling of data, including **HIPAA, GDPR,** and **PCI-DSS**. Effective data traffic management helps organizations ensure compliance with these standards by providing tools to monitor, control, and secure network traffic in real time.

Efficient traffic management, therefore, plays a critical role in not only protecting the network from threats but also ensuring that the organization adheres to regulatory and security best practices.

4. Supporting Scalability and Flexibility

As organizations grow, so too does the volume of data traffic that their networks must handle. Efficient data traffic management helps ensure that the network can scale to meet the increased demands of new users, devices, and applications, without compromising performance or reliability.

Key strategies for supporting scalability include:

- **Cloud Integration**: Many organizations are moving to cloud environments or adopting hybrid cloud models to scale their operations. By managing traffic efficiently between on-premises data centers and cloud platforms, businesses can ensure that resources are used effectively. Cisco's **SD-WAN** solution enables businesses to securely extend their networks to the cloud, optimizing data transfer and ensuring that the network can scale with business needs.
- **Elastic Traffic Management**: Elasticity refers to the network's ability to automatically scale resources up or down based on demand. **Cisco's Application Centric Infrastructure (ACI)** and **SDN (Software-Defined Networking)** technologies enable dynamic resource allocation, allowing businesses to adjust their networks in real-time based on traffic patterns and user demands. This ensures

that the network remains flexible and can easily adapt to changing needs.
- **Multi-Path Routing**: Multi-path routing techniques allow traffic to be routed along multiple paths, ensuring that no single link is overwhelmed by high traffic volumes. By implementing intelligent routing protocols like **BGP (Border Gateway Protocol)** or **OSPF (Open Shortest Path First)**, network administrators can ensure that the network can efficiently manage increased traffic load without degrading performance.

By ensuring that the network is scalable and flexible, data traffic management helps businesses meet their growing needs without requiring a complete overhaul of the network infrastructure.

5. Enhancing User Experience

Ultimately, the success of any network lies in the experience of its users. Whether it's employees working within an organization or customers accessing cloud-based services, the speed, reliability, and responsiveness of the network have a direct impact on user satisfaction. Efficient data traffic management helps ensure that users have a seamless experience, regardless of network load.

Key strategies for improving user experience include:

- **Low Latency for Real-Time Applications**: Many modern applications, such as video conferencing, VoIP, and online gaming, are highly sensitive to latency. Effective traffic management ensures that these applications receive the bandwidth and priority they need to function properly, even under heavy network load. Tools like **Cisco's WAN Optimization** can help reduce latency by compressing traffic, caching frequently accessed data, and optimizing protocol overhead.
- **Minimizing Packet Loss**: Packet loss, which occurs when network devices drop packets due to congestion or errors, can severely impact application performance. Efficient traffic management helps minimize packet loss by controlling the flow of data and ensuring

that the network has enough capacity to handle the traffic load.
- **Traffic Prioritization for Critical Applications**: By giving priority to critical applications (e.g., customer-facing services, financial transactions, or essential business tools), organizations ensure that users experience the best performance for their most important tasks. This is particularly important in environments where performance directly impacts revenue, productivity, or customer satisfaction.

Efficient data traffic management is an essential practice for any organization that relies on a network to drive its business operations. By ensuring optimal network performance, minimizing congestion, enhancing security, supporting scalability, and improving the user experience, effective traffic management helps businesses maintain a competitive edge in today's fast-paced digital world.

As organizations continue to adopt cloud services, expand globally, and rely on data-intensive applications, the need for advanced traffic management solutions will only increase. Leveraging technologies like **SD-WAN**, **QoS**, **traffic shaping**, and **SDN** can help businesses manage data traffic efficiently and build networks that are resilient, secure, and adaptable to future needs.

Ultimately, efficient traffic management is not just about optimizing the flow of data—it's about creating a network that supports the organization's goals, delivers a superior user experience, and ensures that the network can evolve with the ever-changing demands of modern business.

Cisco's Networking Ecosystem

Overview of Cisco's Product Portfolio: Routers, Switches, Firewalls, and Wireless

Cisco is a global leader in networking technology, offering a comprehensive suite of products and solutions that cater to every aspect of modern enterprise networks. Whether an organization is building a small office network or managing a global, cloud-enabled infrastructure, Cisco provides the essential tools to optimize, secure, and scale the network. Cisco's portfolio spans a wide range of technologies, including routers, switches, firewalls, and wireless solutions, each of which plays a crucial role in ensuring network performance, security, and reliability.

In this section, we will explore the key components of Cisco's networking ecosystem, examining the purpose and capabilities of their routers, switches, firewalls, and wireless products. We will highlight how these solutions integrate with one another and support the diverse needs of businesses in today's digital landscape.

1. Cisco Routers: The Backbone of Network Connectivity

Routers are critical devices that direct data traffic between different networks, ensuring seamless communication across local area networks (LANs), wide area networks (WANs), and the internet. Cisco's router portfolio is designed to meet the performance, security, and scalability requirements of organizations ranging from small businesses to large enterprises and service providers.

Key Features of Cisco Routers:

- **Routing Protocols**: Cisco routers support a broad range of dynamic routing protocols, including **OSPF (Open Shortest Path First)**, **EIGRP (Enhanced Interior Gateway Routing Protocol), BGP (Border Gateway Protocol)**, and **IS-IS (Intermediate System to Intermediate System)**. These protocols enable Cisco routers to automatically determine the most efficient path for data, ensuring optimal network performance and fault tolerance.
- **Advanced Security**: Cisco routers come with integrated security features such as **VPN (Virtual Private Network)** support, **firewall protection**, and **intrusion detection systems (IDS)**. With technologies like **Cisco IOS XE** and **Cisco IOS XR**, routers can provide deep packet inspection, traffic filtering, and end-to-end encryption, ensuring secure communication across corporate networks.
- **WAN Optimization**: Cisco's **WAN Optimization** solutions, such as the **Cisco 4000 Series Integrated Services Routers (ISR)**, help improve the performance of wide area networks by reducing bandwidth usage, minimizing latency, and enhancing application delivery. Cisco's **SD-WAN** solutions further extend WAN capabilities, allowing businesses to optimize connectivity between branch offices and cloud services with greater flexibility.
- **Scalability**: Cisco routers are designed to scale, accommodating the growing demands of enterprises. With modular architectures, businesses can easily expand their routing capacity by adding additional interfaces or upgrading their existing hardware, allowing the network to grow without requiring a complete overhaul.
- **Cloud Integration**: As cloud adoption continues to rise, Cisco routers are engineered to work seamlessly with cloud environments. The **Cisco 8000 Series Routers**, for example, are optimized for cloud-scale networking and enable businesses to connect their on-premises data centers with public and private cloud environments, supporting

hybrid cloud strategies.

Use Cases for Cisco Routers:

- **Branch Connectivity**: Cisco routers provide secure and reliable connectivity for branch offices, supporting a wide variety of WAN protocols and technologies to connect remote locations to the corporate network.
- **Data Center Connectivity**: High-performance Cisco routers enable seamless communication between data centers and the broader network, ensuring that mission-critical applications can operate efficiently and securely.
- **Service Provider Networks**: Cisco's high-capacity routers, such as the **ASR Series**, are designed to meet the needs of service providers, offering scalability and resilience to handle vast amounts of traffic while supporting service delivery.

2. Cisco Switches: Enabling Efficient Network Communication

Switches are fundamental to building the local area networks (LANs) that connect devices within a building or campus. Cisco's switching portfolio includes a wide range of products that cater to different network sizes, from small businesses to large enterprises, providing the performance, flexibility, and scalability needed to support a variety of applications and devices.

Key Features of Cisco Switches:

- **Layer 2 and Layer 3 Switching**: Cisco offers both **Layer 2** (Data Link layer) and **Layer 3** (Network layer) switches. **Layer 2 switches**, such as those in the **Cisco Catalyst Series**, forward data based on MAC addresses and are typically used for basic LAN setups. **Layer 3 switches**, such as the **Cisco Catalyst 9000 Series**, can perform routing functions in addition to traditional switching, enabling them to route traffic between different subnets and VLANs within a

network.
- **Power over Ethernet (PoE)**: Many of Cisco's switches support **Power over Ethernet (PoE)**, allowing them to deliver both data and power to connected devices over a single Ethernet cable. This is particularly useful for powering devices like **IP phones, wireless access points**, and **security cameras**.
- **High Performance and Low Latency**: Cisco switches are built for high throughput and low latency, ensuring that data is transmitted across the network quickly and efficiently. This is particularly important in environments where real-time applications, such as video conferencing or VoIP, require low delays and stable connections.
- **Network Segmentation and VLANs**: Cisco switches enable administrators to segment network traffic using **Virtual Local Area Networks (VLANs)**. VLANs allow for better traffic management and security by isolating different types of traffic or groups of users on separate networks, without requiring physical network separation. Cisco's **Cisco Identity Services Engine (ISE)** enhances VLAN management by providing identity-based access control.
- **Stacking and Redundancy**: Cisco switches support stacking technology, which allows multiple physical switches to be interconnected and managed as a single logical unit. This provides greater redundancy, simplified management, and scalability. The **Cisco Catalyst 9000** series supports **StackPower** technology, which enables power sharing across stacked switches, ensuring continuous operation in case of power failure.
- **Network Automation and Management**: With **Cisco DNA Center** and **Cisco Meraki**, Cisco switches can be managed and automated centrally. These platforms enable network administrators to deploy, monitor, and troubleshoot switches from a single interface, reducing manual configuration tasks and improving network efficiency.

Use Cases for Cisco Switches:

CISCO'S NETWORKING ECOSYSTEM

- **Enterprise Campus Networks**: Cisco's switches are widely used to build large-scale enterprise LANs, providing the high-performance backbone needed to support critical business applications.
- **Data Centers**: Cisco's **Nexus Series** switches are designed specifically for high-density, high-performance environments like data centers, supporting the efficient transfer of large volumes of data.
- **SMB Networks**: Cisco offers simpler, more cost-effective switch solutions for small and medium-sized businesses that require reliable, secure network connectivity without the complexity of enterprise-level systems.

3. Cisco Firewalls: Protecting the Network Perimeter

Firewalls are essential for protecting an organization's network from unauthorized access, cyber threats, and external attacks. Cisco's firewall solutions provide robust security features to safeguard both on-premises and cloud-based environments, ensuring that only legitimate traffic is allowed to pass while blocking malicious activity.

Key Features of Cisco Firewalls:

- **Next-Generation Firewall (NGFW)**: Cisco's **Firepower** series firewalls offer advanced threat protection by combining traditional firewall capabilities with integrated **intrusion prevention systems (IPS)**, **malware defense**, and **application control**. This multi-layered approach provides more granular control over traffic and can detect and block advanced threats, such as zero-day attacks, ransomware, and botnets.
- **Application Awareness**: Cisco NGFWs are application-aware, meaning they can identify and control traffic based on the specific applications generating it. This allows businesses to enforce policies that prioritize business-critical applications, while blocking non-essential applications that may consume bandwidth or introduce security risks.
- **VPN Support**: Cisco firewalls provide robust VPN capabilities,

including **IPsec** and **SSL VPN**, to ensure secure communication for remote workers and branch offices. These firewalls can establish encrypted tunnels for traffic, protecting sensitive data as it moves across the internet.
- **Integrated Threat Intelligence**: Cisco's firewalls leverage **Cisco Talos**, one of the largest threat intelligence networks in the world, to provide real-time updates on emerging threats. This ensures that Cisco firewalls are always equipped with the latest intelligence to protect against new and evolving cyberattacks.
- **Centralized Management**: Cisco offers centralized management of firewalls through platforms such as **Cisco Firepower Management Center (FMC)** and **Cisco Meraki Dashboard**. These platforms allow network administrators to configure, monitor, and analyze firewall policies and events from a single interface, streamlining security operations and response.

Use Cases for Cisco Firewalls:

- **Perimeter Security**: Cisco firewalls are often deployed at the network perimeter to protect an organization from external threats, ensuring that only legitimate traffic is allowed into the network.
- **Cloud Security**: With the growing shift to cloud computing, Cisco's firewalls are designed to protect workloads in the cloud, offering security controls for hybrid and multi-cloud environments.
- **Remote Access**: Cisco's VPN-enabled firewalls provide secure access for remote workers, ensuring that employees can connect to the corporate network securely from anywhere in the world.

4. Cisco Wireless Solutions: Ensuring Seamless Connectivity

Wireless networks are essential for modern enterprises, offering the flexibility and mobility needed to support a wide variety of devices, from smartphones to laptops to IoT devices. Cisco's wireless solutions provide high-performance, secure, and scalable wireless connectivity, whether

for small offices or large campus deployments.
Key Features of Cisco Wireless Solutions:

- **Wi-Fi 6 (802.11ax)**: Cisco's **Wi-Fi 6** access points, such as the **Cisco Catalyst 9100 Series**, are built to deliver faster speeds, higher capacity, and better performance in dense environments. Wi-Fi 6 provides enhanced support for devices that require high throughput, such as HD video streaming, gaming, and augmented reality applications.
- **Secure Wireless Networking**: Cisco provides a range of security features for wireless networks, including **WPA3 encryption**, **802.1X authentication**, and **Cisco Identity Services Engine (ISE)** for policy-based access control. These solutions ensure that wireless networks are protected from unauthorized access and security breaches.
- **Network Automation and Management**: Cisco's wireless solutions are integrated with **Cisco DNA Center** and **Cisco Meraki**, enabling automated deployment, centralized monitoring, and seamless troubleshooting. These platforms simplify the management of large-scale wireless networks and provide insights into network performance and usage.
- **Scalability**: Cisco's wireless solutions are designed to scale with the needs of the business, from small office deployments to large campus environments. The **Cisco Meraki MR Series** offers cloud-managed wireless solutions that can scale with ease, while the **Catalyst 9100 Series** is ideal for large enterprise networks, offering robust performance and support for thousands of devices.

Use Cases for Cisco Wireless Solutions:

- **Enterprise Campus Networks**: Cisco wireless access points provide high-speed, secure wireless connectivity throughout large campuses, supporting mobile devices, laptops, and mission-critical

applications.
- **Remote Work and Hybrid Offices**: With the rise of remote work, Cisco's wireless solutions offer secure and reliable connectivity for employees working from home or satellite offices.
- **Internet of Things (IoT)**: Cisco wireless solutions provide the bandwidth and connectivity needed to support the growing number of IoT devices in enterprise networks.

Cisco's product portfolio—encompassing routers, switches, firewalls, and wireless solutions—forms the backbone of enterprise networks across industries. By offering high-performance, scalable, and secure networking products, Cisco enables businesses to build and manage reliable, efficient networks that meet the needs of modern applications and users.

Whether it's providing seamless connectivity across global offices with routers and switches, securing the network perimeter with advanced firewalls, or enabling mobility with cutting-edge wireless solutions, Cisco's ecosystem is designed to support the growth and transformation of businesses in today's digital-first world. Through innovation, integration, and exceptional support, Cisco remains a key player in shaping the future of enterprise networking.

Cisco IOS, NX-OS, and Other Operating Systems

Cisco's network operating systems—**Cisco IOS, NX-OS**, and other specialized systems—are integral to the functionality, management, and optimization of Cisco network devices. These operating systems enable network professionals to configure, monitor, secure, and maintain routers, switches, firewalls, and other Cisco devices, ensuring that the network operates smoothly and efficiently. Each operating system is designed with specific use cases and environments in mind, offering tailored features and capabilities to address the unique needs of different network infrastructures.

In this section, we will explore Cisco's key operating systems—IOS, NX-OS, and other specialized platforms—understanding their distinctions, strengths, and how they integrate into the broader Cisco ecosystem.

1. Cisco IOS (Internetwork Operating System)

Cisco IOS is one of the most widely used operating systems in the world, running on the majority of Cisco's networking hardware, including routers and some switches. It provides the core software infrastructure that enables Cisco's devices to function and support a wide range of network services. IOS is known for its robustness, security, and the ability to support a variety of network protocols, including those that enable routing, switching, security, and network management.

Key Features of Cisco IOS:

- **Routing Protocols**: IOS supports a comprehensive array of routing protocols such as **RIP (Routing Information Protocol), OSPF (Open Shortest Path First)**, **BGP (Border Gateway Protocol)**, and **EIGRP (Enhanced Interior Gateway Routing Protocol)**. These protocols allow Cisco devices to determine the most efficient path for traffic, providing flexibility and fault tolerance in the network.
- **Security**: IOS includes integrated security features like **Access Control Lists (ACLs), VPN support**, and **firewall capabilities**. **IOS Zone-Based Firewall** (ZBFW) and **IPS/IDS** (Intrusion Prevention/Detection Systems) are commonly used in security-sensitive deployments. IOS also integrates with **Cisco Identity Services Engine (ISE)** for policy enforcement and device authentication.
- **Network Management**: Cisco IOS supports a range of network management protocols, including **SNMP (Simple Network Management Protocol), NetFlow**, and **Syslog**, which allow administrators to monitor and manage the health and performance of the network. Cisco's **Embedded Event Manager (EEM)** and **Cisco Prime** offer

automation capabilities to reduce administrative overhead.
- **Quality of Service (QoS)**: IOS includes robust **QoS** capabilities to ensure that time-sensitive traffic (such as VoIP and video) is prioritized over other types of data. By defining policies for traffic classification, marking, and scheduling, IOS ensures that mission-critical applications receive the bandwidth they need.
- **IOS Licensing**: Cisco IOS supports various feature sets depending on the device model and licensing level. These feature sets range from basic routing and switching capabilities to advanced features like network virtualization, security, and high availability.

Use Cases for Cisco IOS:

- **Enterprise Networks**: Cisco IOS is widely used in enterprise networks for routing and switching, supporting a range of devices that form the core of an organization's IT infrastructure.
- **Service Providers**: Service providers use IOS-based routers for high-performance, secure, and scalable networking solutions, leveraging its ability to support a broad range of protocols and configurations.
- **Small and Medium-Sized Businesses (SMBs)**: IOS offers an affordable and flexible solution for SMBs, providing reliable network routing and security with the ability to scale as the business grows.

2. Cisco NX-OS (Nexus Operating System)

NX-OS is Cisco's specialized operating system designed for data center environments, particularly for Cisco's **Nexus** series switches. It is optimized for high-performance, high-availability, and low-latency networking, making it ideal for large-scale data center operations and cloud environments. NX-OS is built to handle the complex needs of modern data centers, including virtualization, automation, and robust security features.

Key Features of Cisco NX-OS:

- **Data Center Optimized**: NX-OS is specifically engineered for data center networking, supporting high-density 10/40/100-Gigabit Ethernet ports and providing advanced features like **FCoE (Fibre Channel over Ethernet)** and **virtual SAN (VSAN)** support, which is essential for modern data center infrastructures that rely on both storage and networking convergence.
- **Virtualization**: One of the standout features of NX-OS is its native support for **network virtualization**. Through **Virtual Device Contexts (VDCs)**, **Virtual Port Channels (vPCs)**, and **FabricPath**, NX-OS enables data center administrators to create logically separated network environments, increasing flexibility and security. **VXLAN (Virtual Extensible LAN)** is supported for network overlays, providing the foundation for modern cloud and hybrid IT architectures.
- **High Availability and Scalability**: NX-OS is designed for high-availability environments, supporting **N+1** redundancy, **Stateful Switchover (SSO)**, and **Non-Stop Forwarding (NSF)** to ensure minimal downtime and continuous service. The operating system also supports **line-rate performance** with low latency, making it suitable for mission-critical data center operations that require real-time data processing.
- **Automation and Orchestration**: NX-OS integrates with Cisco's **Data Center Network Manager (DCNM)** and supports **Cisco ACI (Application Centric Infrastructure)**, enabling network automation, policy-based management, and orchestration of the data center network. Administrators can automate complex workflows and ensure consistency across large-scale networks.
- **Security Features**: NX-OS includes strong security mechanisms like **MACsec (Media Access Control Security)** for link-layer encryption, as well as **Secure Boot** and **Role-Based Access Control (RBAC)** to restrict administrative access. **Dynamic ARP Inspection (DAI)** and **Control Plane Policing (CoPP)** further harden the system against unauthorized access and attacks.

Use Cases for Cisco NX-OS:

- **Data Center Networking**: NX-OS is deployed in data centers to provide high-performance, scalable, and secure switching capabilities. It supports a range of data center technologies, from traditional 3-tier architectures to modern spine-leaf designs.
- **Cloud Environments**: With its strong support for network virtualization and automation, NX-OS is well-suited for hybrid and multi-cloud environments, enabling seamless integration between on-premises data centers and cloud platforms.
- **Large-Scale Enterprises**: Large enterprises with complex, high-traffic environments benefit from the advanced features of NX-OS, ensuring that their data centers can scale to meet the demands of cloud computing, big data, and enterprise applications.

3. Cisco IOS XE: Extending IOS with Modular Architecture

Cisco IOS XE is an advanced version of Cisco IOS that extends its capabilities with a modular, service-oriented architecture. Unlike traditional IOS, which is monolithic, IOS XE separates the system and application software, allowing for enhanced flexibility and more efficient resource utilization. It runs on Cisco's **CSR 1000V Series** routers and other devices designed for high-performance, cloud-ready networking.

Key Features of Cisco IOS XE:

- **Modular Architecture**: The modular design of IOS XE allows network services such as routing, security, and QoS to run in separate processes, improving system stability and reliability. This architecture supports faster updates and better isolation of failures.
- **Cloud Integration**: IOS XE is optimized for hybrid cloud and multi-cloud environments, providing integration with Cisco's **SD-WAN** solutions and other cloud networking technologies. It is designed to deliver secure, high-performance connectivity for cloud applications and services.

- **Advanced Security**: Like traditional IOS, IOS XE offers robust security features, including **next-generation firewalls**, **VPN support**, and **network segmentation**. The separation of control and data planes enhances security by allowing traffic inspection and policy enforcement at multiple layers.
- **Network Automation and Management**: IOS XE supports **Network Function Virtualization (NFV)**, enabling network functions to be virtualized and deployed as software services. Integration with **Cisco DNA Center** and other automation platforms allows administrators to manage, monitor, and optimize the network more efficiently.
- **Flexibility and Scalability**: IOS XE supports both traditional on-premises network architectures and modern software-defined networks (SDN). It's designed to meet the needs of enterprises transitioning to next-generation networks that require flexibility and scalability.

Use Cases for Cisco IOS XE:

- **Edge and Branch Offices**: IOS XE is used in branch routers and edge devices where cloud and SD-WAN connectivity are essential. It provides high-performance routing, security, and automation for remote offices.
- **Enterprise WAN**: IOS XE enhances the performance and scalability of enterprise WANs by providing seamless connectivity to cloud services and offering robust management tools for hybrid and multi-cloud environments.
- **Service Providers**: Service providers use IOS XE to deploy virtualized network functions, such as routers, firewalls, and VPNs, as software services, reducing hardware dependencies and improving operational flexibility.

4. Other Cisco Operating Systems

Beyond IOS, NX-OS, and IOS XE, Cisco also offers several other specialized operating systems designed for specific applications or network environments:

- **Cisco CatOS**: This operating system was originally used in Cisco's Catalyst Series switches before being superseded by IOS and NX-OS. While CatOS is no longer in active development, it still supports older models and configurations in some legacy environments.
- **Cisco Meraki OS**: Cisco Meraki is a cloud-managed IT platform that uses a proprietary operating system designed to support Meraki devices like switches, routers, and wireless access points. Meraki OS offers a simple, intuitive web-based interface for managing devices and services, ideal for businesses with limited IT resources or those looking for an easy-to-manage cloud solution.
- **Cisco Unified Communications Manager (CUCM):** For organizations deploying VoIP solutions, Cisco CUCM is the operating system used in their unified communications solutions. It provides call control, management, and routing for IP telephony systems, integrating with other Cisco products to support a comprehensive collaboration environment.

Cisco's diverse operating systems—**IOS, NX-OS, IOS XE**, and others—form the foundation of its networking ecosystem. Each system is designed to address specific needs, whether it's the high-performance demands of data centers (NX-OS), the versatility and security of enterprise routing and switching (IOS), or the cloud-readiness and automation of modern networks (IOS XE). Together, they offer network professionals the tools necessary to build, manage, and scale networks that are secure, efficient, and aligned with the future of digital business.

By understanding the strengths and features of each operating system, organizations can select the right Cisco platform for their network environment, ensuring optimal performance, security, and scalability. As networks continue to evolve, Cisco's operating systems will remain at the heart of modern networking, enabling businesses to embrace the future of IT infrastructure.

Introduction to Cisco Digital Network Architecture (DNA)

In the rapidly evolving landscape of IT, businesses are constantly challenged to build and manage networks that are agile, scalable, secure, and capable of supporting a diverse array of applications and users. Cisco's **Digital Network Architecture (DNA)** is a transformative solution that helps enterprises meet these challenges by providing a comprehensive, intent-based networking platform. Cisco DNA leverages automation, analytics, and cloud-based management to deliver a network that is both intelligent and responsive, enabling businesses to stay competitive in the digital age.

Cisco DNA is designed to support organizations as they transition to a more dynamic and flexible network environment, integrating modern technologies such as **Software-Defined Networking (SDN)**, **Network Function Virtualization (NFV)**, and **Artificial Intelligence (AI)** into a cohesive, automated, and highly adaptable networking solution. Through its focus on automation, simplicity, security, and analytics, Cisco DNA is able to significantly reduce the complexity of network management while improving operational efficiency, security, and agility.

In this section, we will provide a comprehensive introduction to Cisco DNA, including its key components, how it integrates with Cisco's existing network products, and the benefits it offers to enterprises looking to optimize their network infrastructures.

What is Cisco Digital Network Architecture (DNA)?

At its core, **Cisco DNA** is a blueprint for building and managing next-generation networks that can adapt to business needs, deliver high-performance connectivity, and protect critical data and applications. It is a complete framework that combines software, hardware, and services to create an intelligent, secure, and automated network. Cisco DNA provides an integrated approach to network design, operation, and optimization, with a focus on three main pillars:

Automation and Intent-Based Networking

Cisco DNA leverages **intent-based networking (IBN)**, a paradigm where network administrators specify the desired outcomes (or "intent") for the network, rather than manually configuring individual devices and components. Cisco DNA then automates the configuration and management of the network to achieve these outcomes, ensuring that policies are applied consistently across the entire infrastructure. This helps eliminate human error, reduces configuration time, and ensures faster deployment of new services and applications.

Advanced Analytics and Insights

Cisco DNA incorporates **analytics and machine learning** to continuously monitor network performance and generate insights that help organizations optimize their network. Using technologies like **Cisco DNA Center** and **Cisco Stealthwatch**, businesses can gain real-time visibility into network traffic, application performance, and security events. These analytics allow for predictive insights, such as identifying potential issues before they affect network performance, enabling proactive maintenance and troubleshooting.

Security and Policy Automation

Security is a foundational element of Cisco DNA. The architecture integrates **Cisco's security portfolio**—including **Cisco Identity Services Engine (ISE)**, **Cisco Umbrella**, and **Cisco SecureX**—to provide end-to-end protection across the network. Cisco DNA allows businesses to automate security policies based on user, device, and application context, ensuring consistent enforcement of security measures. Furthermore, it can dynamically adjust security configurations based on network activity, adapting to evolving threats in real time.

By combining these three pillars—automation, analytics, and security—Cisco DNA enables businesses to create a network that is both intelligent and agile, capable of supporting a variety of use cases and business objectives, while minimizing manual intervention and operational complexity.

Key Components of Cisco DNA

Cisco DNA is composed of several interconnected components, each playing a critical role in realizing the benefits of an intelligent, software-driven network. These components include **Cisco DNA Center**, **Cisco SD-WAN**, **Cisco Wireless Solutions**, and **Cisco Network Security**, all working together to automate, secure, and optimize the network.

1. Cisco DNA Center: The Network Management Platform

Cisco DNA Center is the central platform for managing, automating, and analyzing Cisco networks. It provides a single interface to configure and monitor network devices, deploy network policies, and gain insights into network performance. Cisco DNA Center simplifies network management by centralizing tasks like configuration, monitoring, troubleshooting, and security policy enforcement.

Key Features of Cisco DNA Center:

- **Network Automation**: DNA Center automates device provisioning, configuration, and policy enforcement across the network. Using templates and workflows, administrators can quickly deploy new devices or services without needing to manually configure each device.
- **Intent-Based Networking**: With DNA Center, administrators define network policies based on business intent rather than manual device configuration. This means specifying the desired outcome (e.g., "secure guest access," "prioritize voice traffic," or "isolate IoT devices") and allowing DNA Center to automatically implement the necessary network configurations to achieve that goal.
- **Real-Time Analytics and Insights**: DNA Center provides actionable insights through network telemetry and analytics, allowing IT

teams to monitor network health, track application performance, and quickly troubleshoot issues. This is supported by **AI-powered analytics** that can predict network behavior and suggest optimizations.
- **Policy and Security Management**: With **Cisco Identity Services Engine (ISE)** and **Cisco Stealthwatch**, DNA Center enables granular network access policies, automates security compliance, and provides advanced threat detection capabilities.

2. Cisco SD-WAN: Software-Defined Wide Area Networking

Cisco SD-WAN is an essential component of Cisco DNA that delivers secure, reliable, and scalable wide area network (WAN) connectivity. It uses software-driven automation to manage traffic across branch offices, remote locations, and cloud applications, enabling businesses to take advantage of cheaper internet connections and optimize traffic flow between locations.

Key Features of Cisco SD-WAN:

- **Cloud-First WAN Architecture**: Cisco SD-WAN is built for cloud-first environments, enabling direct-to-cloud traffic from branch offices, eliminating the need to backhaul traffic through a central data center.
- **Advanced Security**: Cisco SD-WAN integrates with Cisco's security portfolio to provide end-to-end encryption, secure access to cloud services, and real-time threat intelligence.
- **Application Performance Optimization**: SD-WAN optimizes application traffic by prioritizing business-critical apps and dynamically routing traffic based on network conditions, improving user experience and application performance.
- **Centralized Management and Policy Enforcement**: SD-WAN simplifies the management of distributed networks through centralized control, enabling administrators to define policies, monitor performance, and ensure compliance from a single dashboard.

CISCO'S NETWORKING ECOSYSTEM

3. Cisco Wireless Solutions: High-Performance Wi-Fi for the Digital Workplace

Cisco's **wireless solutions** are a cornerstone of Cisco DNA, providing high-performance, secure wireless networking to support a wide range of devices, from smartphones and laptops to IoT devices. Cisco's **Wi-Fi 6 (802.11ax)** access points and **Meraki cloud-managed wireless** solutions are designed to meet the growing demands of mobile-first and cloud-first enterprises.

Key Features of Cisco Wireless Solutions:

- **Wi-Fi 6**: Cisco's Wi-Fi 6 access points offer faster speeds, better performance in high-density environments, and improved battery life for connected devices. They support **OFDMA (Orthogonal Frequency Division Multiple Access)** and **MU-MIMO (Multi-User Multiple Input Multiple Output)** to ensure efficient communication with multiple devices simultaneously.
- **Cloud-Managed Wireless**: Cisco Meraki provides a simple, cloud-based interface for managing wireless networks. With Meraki, businesses can easily deploy, monitor, and troubleshoot wireless networks, reducing the complexity associated with traditional on-premises solutions.
- **Security**: Cisco's wireless solutions come with integrated security features such as **WPA3 encryption**, **802.1X authentication**, and **Cisco ISE** for advanced identity and access management, ensuring that only authorized users and devices can connect to the network.

4. Cisco Network Security: Protecting the Network with Intelligence

Cisco DNA includes robust security capabilities that protect the network from threats at every layer, from the perimeter to the endpoint. Security is integrated throughout the network, using both **static** and **dynamic** methods to identify and mitigate risks.

Key Features of Cisco Network Security:

- **Cisco SecureX**: Cisco SecureX is an open security platform that integrates security tools, processes, and policies across Cisco's entire security portfolio. It provides a unified interface to manage security incidents, enforce policies, and gain insights into potential threats.
- **Next-Generation Firewalls**: Cisco's next-generation firewalls, such as the **Firepower Series**, provide deep visibility and granular control over network traffic. They offer advanced features like intrusion prevention, malware protection, and URL filtering, ensuring that only legitimate traffic is allowed into the network.
- **Cisco Umbrella**: Cisco Umbrella provides cloud-delivered security to protect users from threats on the internet. It uses DNS-layer security to block malicious traffic before it reaches the network, helping to secure users regardless of their location.

Benefits of Cisco DNA

Cisco DNA offers a wide range of benefits that can help organizations reduce complexity, improve network performance, and adapt to the demands of modern IT environments. Some of the key advantages include:

- **Simplified Network Management**: By automating key network management tasks, Cisco DNA reduces the need for manual intervention, freeing up IT resources and allowing network administrators to focus on strategic tasks. DNA Center's intent-based automation and policy-driven approach streamline network deployment and operation.
- **Faster Service Deployment**: With network automation and policy-based configuration, businesses can deploy new network services and applications more quickly. Changes to the network are automatically propagated, ensuring consistency and reducing deployment time.
- **Improved Network Security**: By integrating security directly into the network, Cisco DNA enables businesses to enforce consistent security policies across the entire network. Advanced threat detection

and real-time analytics help identify and mitigate potential risks before they impact operations.
- **Enhanced Network Agility**: Cisco DNA enables businesses to respond quickly to changing network requirements. With cloud integration, SD-WAN capabilities, and network automation, companies can easily adapt to new technologies, applications, or business models.

Cisco's **Digital Network Architecture (DNA)** represents the next step in the evolution of enterprise networking. By combining automation, analytics, and security into a unified framework, Cisco DNA helps businesses create networks that are smarter, more secure, and more adaptable to the needs of the digital age. With Cisco DNA, organizations can optimize their network operations, reduce complexity, and ensure that their networks are ready to support the demands of tomorrow's technologies. As businesses continue to embrace cloud computing, IoT, and other digital innovations, Cisco DNA provides the tools needed to build networks that can scale, perform, and protect in an increasingly complex and dynamic environment.

Cisco Meraki: Cloud-Managed Networking

Cisco Meraki is a leader in cloud-managed IT solutions, providing a suite of networking, security, and IT management tools designed to simplify the deployment and management of network infrastructure. Meraki's cloud-first approach enables organizations to manage their entire network—including routers, switches, firewalls, wireless access points, security cameras, and mobile devices—from a single, intuitive dashboard. This cloud-driven model is particularly well-suited for businesses looking to scale their network with minimal complexity while maintaining high levels of performance, security, and flexibility.

In this section, we will explore the key features of **Cisco Meraki** and examine how it leverages cloud technology to transform traditional network management. We'll also look at how Meraki fits within the broader Cisco ecosystem and how its solutions benefit organizations of all sizes, from small businesses to large enterprises.

What is Cisco Meraki?

Cisco Meraki is a cloud-based network management platform that offers a wide range of hardware and software products for building, deploying, and managing networks. The central idea behind Meraki is to simplify network management by centralizing control through the cloud, removing the need for on-site configuration, and providing an intuitive web-based interface. This cloud-managed approach allows network administrators to easily monitor network health, configure devices, apply security policies, and troubleshoot issues without needing physical access to the network devices themselves.

Meraki provides a full suite of networking solutions, including:

- **Meraki MX Series**: Security appliances that deliver comprehensive threat protection, SD-WAN, and secure internet access.
- **Meraki MS Series**: Managed switches that provide enterprise-grade network switching, enabling the configuration of VLANs, link aggregation, and Power over Ethernet (PoE).
- **Meraki MR Series**: Wireless access points that deliver high-performance Wi-Fi with cloud management, and advanced features like **Wi-Fi 6** support, **mesh networking**, and integrated security.
- **Meraki MV Series**: Cloud-managed security cameras that offer scalable video surveillance with cloud storage, motion detection, and advanced analytics.
- **Meraki Management Platform**: A centralized, cloud-based dashboard that simplifies network management and configuration, providing real-time monitoring, analytics, and troubleshooting tools.

What makes Meraki unique is the ability to manage all of these devices and services from a single cloud dashboard, without needing to install software on local servers or dedicated network management hardware. The devices themselves are designed to be plug-and-play, minimizing the complexity typically associated with network deployment.

Key Features of Cisco Meraki

Meraki's cloud-managed networking platform offers several features that are designed to make network management simpler, more secure, and more scalable. Below are some of the key features that set Cisco Meraki apart from traditional network management solutions.

1. Cloud-Based Management

The primary advantage of Cisco Meraki is its **cloud-first** approach. The Meraki dashboard allows network administrators to monitor and manage their entire network infrastructure remotely. Because everything is cloud-managed, administrators can access the dashboard from anywhere with an internet connection, giving them the flexibility to monitor network performance, troubleshoot issues, and make changes in real-time, without being physically on-site.

- **Remote Management**: Administrators can access and manage all Meraki devices—routers, switches, access points, security cameras, etc.—from a single cloud-based dashboard.
- **Zero-Touch Provisioning**: New devices are automatically discovered and configured once they connect to the internet. This eliminates the need for complex manual configuration and enables faster deployment, especially in large-scale environments.
- **Simplified Configuration**: The web-based interface simplifies device configuration with easy-to-understand menus and tools, even for network managers with limited technical expertise.

2. Scalability

Meraki's cloud-based architecture makes it incredibly easy to scale a network as the organization grows. Whether expanding to new office locations or increasing the number of devices, Meraki networks can grow without needing significant changes to the underlying infrastructure.

- **Add New Locations with Ease**: New Meraki devices can be added to an existing network seamlessly, with all settings, policies, and configurations automatically applied.
- **Cloud-Based Updates**: Meraki devices receive firmware updates and feature enhancements directly from the cloud, ensuring that all devices across the network are running the latest software with minimal administrative effort.
- **Flexible Hardware Options**: Meraki offers a wide range of hardware, from small, cost-effective solutions for SMBs to high-performance options for large enterprises and data centers. This flexibility allows businesses to grow their networks without needing to replace existing hardware.

3. Network Visibility and Analytics

Meraki's dashboard provides real-time visibility into the network's performance and usage, offering detailed insights into the health of the entire infrastructure. This includes data on network traffic, application usage, user activity, security events, and more.

- **Real-Time Monitoring**: The dashboard displays real-time metrics on network health, device status, traffic patterns, and security events, allowing administrators to quickly identify and address issues.
- **Deep Analytics**: Meraki's platform includes powerful analytics tools that allow administrators to understand network behavior at a granular level. Detailed reports can be generated for things like bandwidth usage, user activity, and application performance, helping IT teams make data-driven decisions for optimizing the network.
- **Customizable Dashboards**: Network admins can customize their dashboard to display key metrics and performance indicators that matter most to their specific use case.

4. Simplified Security and Policy Management

Security is a critical aspect of any network, and Meraki includes several features designed to simplify and strengthen network security. The cloud-managed approach ensures that security updates and policies are consistently applied across all devices and locations.

- **Built-In Security Features**: Meraki's security appliances (Meraki MX) provide built-in **next-generation firewall (NGFW)** capabilities, including intrusion detection and prevention (IDS/IPS), VPN support, content filtering, and malware protection. Meraki also includes advanced threat protection, such as **Cisco Advanced Malware Protection (AMP)** and **DNS-layer security** with **Cisco Umbrella**.
- **Policy-Based Access Control**: Administrators can set up policies to control access based on user, device type, or application. Meraki supports **802.1X authentication** for granular control over network access and integration with **Active Directory** or **RADIUS** for identity management.
- **Centralized Security Management**: Through the Meraki dashboard, administrators can configure security settings, monitor security events, and implement policies across the entire network. This centralized approach makes it easier to ensure consistent security practices are in place.

5. Simplified Troubleshooting and Support

Meraki's cloud management platform makes troubleshooting network issues much easier than traditional on-premises solutions. The intuitive dashboard provides diagnostic tools, logs, and real-time data that help administrators identify the root cause of issues and resolve them quickly.

- **Diagnostic Tools**: Meraki's platform offers built-in diagnostic tools such as **Ping**, **Tracert**, and **Speed Test**, which help IT teams quickly isolate connectivity issues.

- **Event Logs**: The dashboard logs network activity and security events, allowing administrators to trace issues or identify malicious activity across the network.
- **Automated Alerts**: Meraki can send real-time alerts for specific network events, such as a drop in performance, security threats, or device failures. This helps administrators react to potential issues before they impact network performance or security.

6. Meraki's Integration with Cisco Ecosystem

One of the key benefits of Cisco Meraki is how it seamlessly integrates with Cisco's broader networking ecosystem, including **Cisco DNA** and **Cisco Security Solutions**. This integration helps create a unified, end-to-end networking platform that combines the best of cloud-based management with traditional networking technologies.

- **Cisco SD-WAN Integration**: Meraki integrates with Cisco's SD-WAN solutions, enabling organizations to securely and intelligently route traffic across the wide-area network (WAN), optimizing application performance and security across branch offices, data centers, and remote users.
- **Cisco Umbrella Integration**: Meraki's security offerings are enhanced by Cisco Umbrella, providing additional DNS-layer security and proactive protection against malicious internet traffic.
- **Cisco Identity Services Engine (ISE)**: Meraki integrates with Cisco ISE to deliver enhanced access control and network segmentation, ensuring that only authorized users and devices can connect to the network.

Benefits of Cisco Meraki

Meraki's cloud-managed platform offers a range of benefits for businesses looking to simplify and optimize their networking operations:

- **Ease of Use**: The intuitive Meraki dashboard and zero-touch

provisioning make it easy for organizations of any size to deploy, manage, and scale their networks, regardless of technical expertise.
- **Cost Efficiency**: Meraki's cloud-first approach eliminates the need for dedicated on-site management infrastructure, reducing capital expenses and the ongoing costs of managing complex network systems.
- **Security and Compliance**: With built-in security features and centralized management, Meraki ensures that networks are secure and compliant with industry standards, reducing the risk of security breaches and data loss.
- **Scalability**: Meraki's cloud-based management and flexible hardware options make it easy to scale networks to meet the growing needs of a business, from adding new locations to increasing the number of devices.
- **Remote Management**: With cloud-based access, network administrators can manage their networks from anywhere in the world, allowing for greater flexibility and responsiveness to network issues or configuration changes.

Cisco Meraki offers a powerful, cloud-managed solution that simplifies network management, enhances security, and provides actionable insights across the entire network. Its intuitive, cloud-based platform is designed to meet the needs of modern businesses, whether they are small organizations or large enterprises with complex, distributed networks. By leveraging Meraki's hardware and cloud services, companies can deploy, manage, and scale their networks with ease, while ensuring high levels of performance and security.

With its ability to integrate seamlessly into Cisco's broader networking ecosystem and its focus on simplicity, scalability, and security, Cisco Meraki is well-positioned to drive the future of cloud-managed networking.

Cisco ACI: Application Centric Infrastructure

As networks become more complex and organizations increasingly rely on applications to drive business operations, the need for a more agile, scalable, and efficient approach to data center networking has never been more critical. Cisco's **Application Centric Infrastructure (ACI)** is a revolutionary architecture that addresses these challenges by aligning network policies and operations with the needs of applications. By shifting from traditional network-centric models to an **application-centric** approach, Cisco ACI enables organizations to build a more flexible, automated, and scalable network that meets the demands of modern IT environments, such as hybrid cloud, DevOps, and microservices.

In this section, we will explore Cisco ACI, its key features, how it works, and the benefits it offers for businesses looking to modernize their data center networking infrastructure. We'll also delve into how ACI integrates with Cisco's broader portfolio of solutions, including **Cisco Nexus switches**, **Cisco UCS (Unified Computing System)**, and **Cisco Application Policy Infrastructure Controller (APIC)**.

What is Cisco ACI?

Cisco ACI is an advanced **SDN (Software-Defined Networking)** solution designed to optimize the management of data center networks by focusing on the needs of applications. ACI's application-centric approach shifts the focus of network management from individual devices (e.g., switches, routers, firewalls) to the requirements of applications themselves, enabling more agile, automated, and scalable networking operations.

At the heart of Cisco ACI is the **Application Policy Infrastructure Controller (APIC)**, which serves as the centralized management and policy enforcement point. Through ACI, network administrators define policies based on application requirements, rather than manually configuring devices based on static network attributes. The ACI architecture automatically enforces these policies across the entire network, enabling faster provisioning, improved security, and enhanced performance.

ACI is designed to support **modern workloads** such as virtualized environments, hybrid clouds, and microservices, making it particularly suitable for enterprises undergoing digital transformation.

Key Components of Cisco ACI

Cisco ACI is built around several key components that work together to create a comprehensive, policy-driven application-aware network. These components include the **ACI fabric, APIC, Cisco Nexus switches**, and **ACI endpoints**.

1. Cisco ACI Fabric

The **ACI fabric** is the physical and logical network infrastructure that connects data center resources (such as compute, storage, and network devices) and allows them to communicate with each other. The ACI fabric provides a flexible, high-performance foundation for implementing policies across the network and supports multi-tenancy, enabling organizations to isolate workloads and ensure that each application has the necessary resources to perform optimally.

The fabric is designed to be scalable, supporting everything from small to large data center environments. It is built around a **leaf-spine** architecture, where **leaf switches** connect to both **spine switches** and endpoint devices (such as servers or virtual machines). This architecture ensures high availability, redundancy, and low-latency communication, which is essential for modern application workloads.

2. Application Policy Infrastructure Controller (APIC)

The **APIC** is the central management platform for Cisco ACI. It serves as the policy controller and provides the administrative interface through which network administrators configure and manage the ACI fabric. The APIC is responsible for translating business intent into network policies, automating network provisioning, and ensuring that policies are consistently enforced across the ACI fabric.

Key features of the APIC include:

- **Centralized Policy Management**: Administrators can define policies based on application requirements (e.g., security, performance, or availability) rather than individual device configurations.
- **Automation and Orchestration**: The APIC automates the provisioning of network resources and can integrate with external orchestration systems (such as VMware vCenter, OpenStack, and Kubernetes) for end-to-end automation.
- **Real-Time Analytics and Monitoring**: APIC provides deep visibility into application performance, network health, and security events, enabling administrators to troubleshoot and optimize the network in real time.

3. Cisco Nexus Switches

Cisco's **Nexus switches** are the hardware that forms the backbone of the ACI fabric. These switches are specifically designed to support the high bandwidth, low latency, and scalability requirements of modern data center environments. The Nexus switches work with the APIC to implement the network policies defined by administrators and ensure that traffic flows efficiently and securely through the fabric.

Key Cisco Nexus switches for ACI include the **Nexus 9000 series**, which provide high-density, low-latency connectivity for both physical and virtual environments. These switches are available in both **modular** and **fixed-port** configurations to meet the needs of various data center sizes and use cases.

4. ACI Endpoints

Endpoints in the Cisco ACI fabric refer to the devices (servers, virtual machines, containers, etc.) that are connected to the network and consume or provide application services. Endpoints can be physical or virtual, and ACI treats both equally, enabling organizations to build hybrid environments that span physical and virtual resources.

ACI automatically learns and tracks endpoints as they move throughout the network, ensuring that policies are dynamically applied regardless of where the endpoint resides within the fabric. This capability is particularly important for environments where workloads are frequently moved, such as virtualized or containerized applications.

How Cisco ACI Works: An Application-Centric Approach

Cisco ACI's application-centric approach to network management is centered around **application policies**, which define the behavior and requirements of an application. These policies are expressed in terms of **application network profiles**, which consist of several key elements:

- **Application Network Profiles (ANPs)**: These profiles define the application's network requirements, including security, quality of service (QoS), and connectivity. By defining an ANP, administrators can ensure that the network is configured to meet the specific needs of the application, without worrying about configuring individual devices or ports.
- **End-Point Groups (EPGs)**: EPGs are logical groups of endpoints (servers, virtual machines, etc.) that share common network policies. For example, all servers hosting a specific application could be grouped into an EPG, and policies such as security rules and traffic prioritization can be applied to the entire group rather than to each endpoint individually.
- **Contracts**: Contracts define the rules for communication between different EPGs. For example, a contract could specify that web servers in one EPG are allowed to communicate with database servers in another EPG, but with specific restrictions (such as only allowing traffic on certain ports or protocols). Contracts enforce application-level policies, enabling a highly granular and secure method of controlling communication between workloads.
- **ACI End-Point Learning**: ACI automatically learns and tracks endpoint identities and their associated policies as they connect to the fabric. This eliminates the need for manual device or IP address configurations and ensures that endpoints can move freely within

the fabric without disrupting application performance or security.

By using a policy-driven approach that aligns network behavior with the needs of applications, ACI simplifies network management, reduces human error, and improves agility. Policies are automatically enforced, ensuring that applications receive the appropriate resources and security protections, regardless of where they are located in the data center.

Benefits of Cisco ACI

Cisco ACI offers a variety of benefits that make it an attractive solution for organizations looking to modernize their data center networking:

1. Improved Agility and Flexibility

With ACI, organizations can respond more quickly to changing application needs, whether they are scaling up or deploying new services. The automated provisioning of network resources and the application of policies based on application requirements allows businesses to deploy new applications or update existing ones faster, without waiting for manual configurations or network changes.

- **Automated Workload Provisioning**: With ACI, workloads can be automatically provisioned, configured, and connected based on the policies defined by the application. This reduces manual intervention and accelerates service deployment.
- **Seamless Application Mobility**: ACI allows applications and workloads to move freely within the data center without disrupting network connectivity or performance. This is critical in virtualized or containerized environments where workloads can shift rapidly.

2. Simplified Management and Operational Efficiency

By shifting from a device-centric to an application-centric model, Cisco ACI simplifies network management and reduces complexity. Network administrators no longer need to configure individual devices or manage static IP addresses; instead, they can define application policies that

CISCO'S NETWORKING ECOSYSTEM

automatically configure the network as needed.

- **Centralized Management**: The APIC provides a single point of control for the entire network, streamlining management and troubleshooting. Administrators can view the entire network topology, including endpoint connections, application profiles, and policy enforcement, in one intuitive interface.
- **Policy-Driven Automation**: ACI automates network configuration and provisioning based on business policies, ensuring that security, compliance, and performance requirements are met consistently across the network.

3. Enhanced Security

Cisco ACI provides strong security capabilities by segmenting applications and workloads based on policy-driven access controls. This approach not only secures traffic between endpoints but also ensures that applications are protected from unauthorized access.

- **Micro-Segmentation**: ACI enables granular control over traffic between application components, even within the same network segment. This reduces the attack surface and limits lateral movement in case of a security breach.
- **Integrated Security Policies**: Security policies can be applied at the application level, ensuring that all endpoints are subject to the same rules regardless of their location in the fabric.

4. Scalability

Cisco ACI is designed to support the scaling needs of modern data centers, whether they are growing to handle more traffic or expanding to support more applications and workloads.

- **High-Performance Fabric**: ACI's leaf-spine architecture ensures that the fabric can scale to support high bandwidth and low-latency

traffic, even as the number of endpoints and workloads increases.
- **Support for Hybrid and Multi-Cloud Environments**: ACI can integrate with public cloud providers, allowing businesses to extend their data center networks into hybrid cloud environments. This enables businesses to scale their network infrastructure seamlessly as they adopt more cloud services.

Cisco ACI represents a fundamental shift in how data center networks are designed, deployed, and managed. By focusing on the needs of applications rather than individual network devices, ACI enables organizations to build more agile, scalable, and secure infrastructures that can support modern workloads like virtualized applications, microservices, and hybrid cloud environments. With its policy-driven architecture, automation, and centralized management, ACI simplifies network operations while ensuring that applications receive the performance and security they require. As businesses continue to embrace digital transformation, Cisco ACI provides a critical foundation for building the next-generation networks that will power their growth and innovation.

The Hierarchical Network Design Model

Core, Distribution, and Access Layers

The **Hierarchical Network Design Model** is a widely recognized framework for designing scalable, efficient, and reliable networks. This model is structured into three distinct layers: **Core**, **Distribution**, and **Access**, each serving a specific purpose in the network. This approach ensures that networks can handle high volumes of traffic, provide fault tolerance, and support complex, dynamic applications, while maintaining performance and scalability.

In this section, we will examine the roles and responsibilities of each layer in the hierarchical network design, explaining how they work together to create a robust network infrastructure that meets the needs of modern enterprises. We'll explore the specific tasks handled by each layer, the technologies commonly employed at each stage, and how Cisco implements this model to build high-performance, reliable networks.

Core Layer

The **Core Layer** is the backbone of the network, responsible for providing high-speed, high-capacity connectivity between various parts of the network. Its primary function is to facilitate fast and reliable data transfer between distribution layers and provide optimal paths for traffic routing. In large, enterprise-level networks, the core layer serves as the point of aggregation for multiple data center switches, internet gateways, and inter-network connections.

Functions and Responsibilities

1. **High-Speed Data Transport**: The core layer is designed for maximum throughput, ensuring fast, uninterrupted data flow between different parts of the network. As the primary traffic path, it is expected to carry large amounts of data and support the entire infrastructure.
2. **Redundancy and Fault Tolerance**: Core layer devices are often configured with high availability in mind. They include multiple connections, redundant links, and failover mechanisms to ensure that the network remains operational even in the event of hardware failures.
3. **Traffic Aggregation**: The core layer aggregates traffic from various sources, including different distribution switches or data centers. It acts as a central hub through which data flows to its final destination. A well-designed core layer can ensure that bottlenecks do not occur, providing optimal network performance.
4. **Routing and Path Selection**: Although the distribution layer is responsible for determining the best route for traffic, the core layer plays a critical role in providing the fastest possible paths for inter-network communication. Core routers use advanced routing protocols to dynamically adjust and reroute traffic in response to network conditions.

Core Layer Technologies and Equipment

The core layer typically employs high-performance **core switches** or **routers** that can handle large-scale traffic efficiently. These devices need to support fast forwarding rates, large table sizes, and advanced routing protocols.

- **Core Switches**: Cisco's **Catalyst 9000 series** switches are commonly

THE HIERARCHICAL NETWORK DESIGN MODEL

used at the core layer. These switches are designed for high throughput and provide Layer 3 (routing) functionality, offering advanced features like **Quality of Service (QoS)** and **Multicast** support.
- **Core Routers**: Cisco's **ASR (Aggregation Services Routers)** and **ISR (Integrated Services Routers)** are commonly used at the core layer to ensure the network can support a range of traffic types and applications, such as voice, video, and data.
- **Redundant Links and High Availability**: Technologies like **Virtual Routing and Forwarding (VRF)**, **Equal-Cost Multi-Path (ECMP)** routing, and **Hot Standby Router Protocol (HSRP)** are used to ensure that the core layer is both scalable and highly resilient.

Best Practices for Core Layer Design

1. **High-Speed, Low-Latency Links**: Ensure that links between core switches are fast and capable of handling heavy traffic loads without causing delays.
2. **Scalability**: The core should be designed to support future network expansion. It should be able to accommodate additional distribution or access switches as needed.
3. **Redundancy**: Implement redundant hardware, including links, power supplies, and paths, to ensure that the network remains operational even in the event of hardware failures.
4. **Minimal Complexity**: Keep the core layer design simple by avoiding unnecessary services or configurations. The focus should be on speed, reliability, and ease of management.

Distribution Layer

The **Distribution Layer** serves as the intermediary between the access layer and the core layer, responsible for directing traffic between devices within the access layer and ensuring that data is forwarded to the appropriate destinations within the core layer. In essence, the distribution layer is where network policies, routing, and security measures are implemented.

Functions and Responsibilities

1. **Routing and Forwarding**: The distribution layer acts as the point of aggregation for different segments of the network. It performs Layer 3 routing between VLANs (Virtual Local Area Networks) and subnets, ensuring that traffic from one part of the network is efficiently forwarded to another. Routing protocols like **OSPF (Open Shortest Path First), EIGRP (Enhanced Interior Gateway Routing Protocol)**, and **BGP (Border Gateway Protocol)** are commonly used at this layer.
2. **Policy Enforcement**: This layer is responsible for applying network policies related to security, traffic prioritization, access control, and Quality of Service (QoS). **ACLs (Access Control Lists), firewall policies**, and **NAT (Network Address Translation)** are commonly configured at the distribution layer to secure the flow of traffic between different parts of the network.
3. **Traffic Control and Load Balancing**: The distribution layer ensures that traffic is efficiently distributed across the network by using load-balancing techniques. It manages how data is routed between different devices, balancing traffic across multiple links to prevent network congestion and ensure optimal performance.
4. **Network Segmentation**: The distribution layer helps segment the network into different logical parts, such as different **VLANs** or **subnets**, improving both security and performance by isolating traffic types and applications.

Distribution Layer Technologies and Equipment

At the distribution layer, high-performance switches and routers are used to aggregate traffic, implement policies, and route traffic to the core. Cisco's **Catalyst 9000 series** switches and **Nexus 5000 series** switches are commonly deployed in the distribution layer, offering both Layer 3 routing and Layer 2 switching capabilities.

- **Layer 3 Switches**: Cisco's **Catalyst 9300** and **Catalyst 9400** series switches offer robust routing capabilities, advanced security features, and the ability to handle large volumes of traffic while maintaining low latency.
- **Router Integration**: Distribution layer devices often serve as aggregators for WAN connections and inter-network routing. Cisco's **ISR** and **ASR** routers are typically deployed to ensure high throughput, load balancing, and failover capabilities.

Best Practices for Distribution Layer Design

1. **Simplified Routing**: Ensure that routing at the distribution layer is as efficient as possible, using appropriate protocols and technologies to minimize complexity and improve convergence times.
2. **Redundancy**: Redundant connections between the distribution and core layers should be established to ensure continued network availability in case of hardware failure.
3. **Network Segmentation**: Use VLANs and subnets to logically separate different network segments, ensuring that traffic is isolated according to business or security needs.
4. **Implement Security Policies**: The distribution layer should enforce security policies by implementing access control lists (ACLs), firewalls, and traffic filtering to prevent unauthorized access or attacks.

Access Layer

The **Access Layer** is the layer closest to end-user devices and provides connectivity to the network. Its role is to enable devices such as computers, printers, IP phones, wireless access points, and IoT devices to access network resources. The access layer is responsible for **port-level security**, **QoS management**, and **user authentication**.

Functions and Responsibilities

1. **Device Connectivity**: The primary function of the access layer is to provide physical and logical connections to the network for user devices. This includes managing user traffic from devices like desktops, laptops, mobile phones, and IoT devices.
2. **Network Access Control**: The access layer enforces policies related to user authentication, ensuring that only authorized devices and users can access the network. This often involves technologies like **802.1X** for port-based authentication and **MAC address filtering**.
3. **Traffic Forwarding**: The access layer forwards traffic to the distribution layer for further routing, but it may also perform local switching for traffic within the same VLAN or subnet. The access layer's primary job is to forward traffic efficiently while applying local policies (such as QoS and security controls).
4. **Support for Wireless and Wired Devices**: The access layer handles both wired connections (via **Ethernet switches**) and wireless connections (via **wireless access points**). It ensures seamless access for users regardless of whether they are connected to the network via physical cables or Wi-Fi.

Access Layer Technologies and Equipment

At the access layer, **Ethernet switches** and **wireless access points (APs)** are deployed to provide device connectivity. Cisco's **Catalyst 2000 series** and **Catalyst 3000 series** switches are commonly used in the access layer to provide reliable, high-speed connectivity to devices.

- **Switches**: The **Catalyst 9300** and **Catalyst 3650** series switches support Power over Ethernet (PoE), which is essential for providing power to devices such as IP phones and access points.
- **Wireless Access Points**: Cisco's **Meraki MR** series and **Aironet** APs provide wireless connectivity, ensuring that devices can connect to the network wirelessly with support for Wi-Fi standards like **Wi-Fi 5 (802.11ac)** and **Wi-Fi 6 (802.11ax)**.

THE HIERARCHICAL NETWORK DESIGN MODEL

Best Practices for Access Layer Design

1. **Simplified Configuration**: Configure access layer switches and wireless access points to provide easy and reliable connectivity for end-users, ensuring minimal downtime and simplified troubleshooting.
2. **Security**: Implement strong authentication measures (e.g., **802.1X**) to prevent unauthorized access, and use **MAC address filtering** to control which devices can connect to the network.
3. **Support for IoT Devices**: As the Internet of Things (IoT) becomes more prevalent, the access layer should be designed to support a growing number of IoT devices, providing both security and performance management.

The **Core**, **Distribution**, and **Access** layers form the foundation of the hierarchical network design model, ensuring that networks are scalable, efficient, and secure. Each layer has a distinct role that contributes to the overall performance and reliability of the network. Cisco's products and technologies, including the **Catalyst series switches**, **Nexus series switches**, and **Meraki cloud-managed devices**, play a crucial role in implementing the hierarchical design model, providing organizations with the tools they need to build modern, high-performance networks that can meet the demands of today's business environment. Whether it's providing high-speed routing at the core, enforcing policies at the distribution layer, or ensuring reliable user connectivity at the access layer, Cisco's solutions are designed to support networks at every level.

Modular Network Design Concepts

In modern networking, flexibility, scalability, and ease of management are essential. The **modular network design** concept plays a key role in ensuring that networks can grow, adapt, and evolve in response to new business needs, technological advancements, and increasing traffic demands. By segmenting network functions into distinct, logically defined modules, modular design allows for a more organized, resilient, and scalable approach to building and managing network infrastructures.

In this section, we will explore the core principles of modular network design, the benefits it provides, and how it aligns with the **Hierarchical Network Design Model**. Additionally, we will examine the essential components of a modular design and how Cisco's technologies and tools enable the implementation of modular network architectures.

What is Modular Network Design?

Modular network design is a strategic approach that divides a network into smaller, manageable functional blocks (or "modules") that can be independently developed, deployed, and scaled. The primary goal of modular design is to simplify network planning and management by providing flexibility to add, remove, or upgrade network components without disrupting the overall network performance or operation.

A modular network design follows a **layered** approach that aligns well with the **Hierarchical Network Design Model**. Each module is optimized for specific tasks, such as routing, security, or data center management, and is designed to integrate seamlessly with other modules. This modularity allows organizations to address specific needs as they arise, ensuring that network resources can be allocated dynamically based on performance requirements, cost constraints, or business priorities.

Core Principles of Modular Network Design

There are several key principles that define modular network design. These principles help ensure that the network is efficient, scalable, and resilient.

1. Scalability

A modular network design is built with scalability in mind, allowing for easy expansion as the network grows. Each module can be independently scaled to accommodate more devices, more traffic, or more services, without having to redesign the entire network. This capability is crucial for businesses that experience rapid growth or need to quickly respond to changing market conditions.

For example, in a **data center network**, additional switches or routers can be added to the **distribution layer** to handle more traffic as the network expands. Similarly, more **access layer switches** can be deployed to provide additional connectivity to end-users.

2. Redundancy and High Availability

Redundancy is an essential feature of modular design, ensuring that critical network functions continue to operate even in the event of hardware failures or network issues. By introducing redundancy at multiple layers of the network, such as in the core, distribution, and access layers, modular design minimizes the risk of downtime and enhances overall network reliability.

Each module should be designed with failover mechanisms in place, such as **dual power supplies**, **redundant links**, and **automated traffic rerouting** in the event of a failure. Cisco's **HSRP (Hot Standby Router Protocol)** and **VRRP (Virtual Router Redundancy Protocol)**, for example, provide failover capabilities that ensure continuous service availability, even if one router or switch fails.

3. Flexibility and Modularity

The modular design approach allows network administrators to choose the right combination of modules to meet specific needs. Different modules can serve different purposes, such as providing routing, security, access control, or data storage. Modules can be deployed in various configurations based on business requirements, allowing for flexibility in how the network is built and managed.

This flexibility extends to the types of devices used within each module.

For instance, a modular design can incorporate a mix of **physical devices** (such as routers and switches) and **virtual devices** (such as virtual routers and firewalls), enabling seamless integration with hybrid and multi-cloud environments.

4. Simplified Management and Troubleshooting

A modular approach simplifies network management by reducing complexity. With distinct modules, administrators can easily isolate and troubleshoot problems within specific areas of the network. This not only reduces the time and effort spent diagnosing and resolving issues, but it also enables more effective maintenance, as changes or updates to one module can be made without disrupting other parts of the network.

For example, if there is a connectivity issue in the access layer, it can be addressed without affecting the distribution or core layers, leading to faster resolution times and minimized impact on overall network performance.

5. Security and Policy Enforcement

Security can be managed at the modular level, allowing for more granular control over different segments of the network. Each module can enforce specific security policies, ensuring that sensitive data is protected and that only authorized traffic is allowed to pass through the network.

In a modular design, the **distribution layer** may enforce access control policies for different types of users or devices, while the **core layer** focuses on ensuring secure communication between different parts of the network. Cisco's **Identity Services Engine (ISE)** and **Cisco Secure Firewall** provide comprehensive security capabilities that can be applied to each layer of the modular network design.

Modules in a Modular Network Design

To understand how modular network design works, it's important to explore the main modules that typically form the foundation of the network. These include the **Core Module**, the **Distribution Module**, the **Access Module**, and other specialized modules such as the **Data Center Module** and **Edge Module**.

THE HIERARCHICAL NETWORK DESIGN MODEL

1. Core Module

The **Core Module** is the high-performance backbone of the network, designed for high-capacity routing and data forwarding. This module connects the distribution modules and ensures fast, reliable communication across the entire network. It is typically composed of high-end routers or switches that provide minimal latency and maximum throughput.

In a Cisco network, **Cisco Nexus 9000** series switches and **ASR routers** are commonly deployed in the core module to support high-performance routing and ensure that data flows seamlessly through the network.

2. Distribution Module

The **Distribution Module** serves as the intermediary between the access and core layers, performing important tasks such as routing, traffic filtering, policy enforcement, and security. The distribution module ensures that traffic is directed to the correct destination and that network policies (such as Quality of Service and security rules) are applied.

In this module, **Cisco Catalyst 9000** series switches or **Cisco Nexus 5000/7000** series switches provide routing and switching services, as well as advanced policy and security features.

3. Access Module

The **Access Module** is the layer closest to end-user devices. It provides physical and logical connectivity to users, workstations, wireless access points, and other networked devices. The access module is responsible for providing secure and reliable connectivity while enforcing policies related to user access, security, and quality of service.

Cisco Catalyst 1000/3000/9000 series switches and **Meraki Wireless Access Points** are commonly used in the access module to deliver the necessary connectivity and services to users.

4. Data Center Module

The **Data Center Module** is specifically designed to support high-performance data center operations, such as virtualization, storage, and cloud services. This module includes devices and technologies that enable data center infrastructure to operate efficiently, including storage area networks (SANs), hyper-converged systems, and compute resources.

Cisco's **UCS (Unified Computing System)** and **Nexus 5000/7000** series switches are often deployed in the data center module to ensure that applications and services run smoothly, with the ability to scale and meet growing demands.

5. Edge Module

The **Edge Module** is the point where the network connects to external entities, such as the internet, remote offices, or external partners. This module provides connectivity to external networks, ensures secure communication, and typically includes **firewalls**, **VPNs**, and **WAN optimization** solutions.

Cisco's **ASR routers** and **Cisco Secure Firewall** are common components of the edge module, ensuring secure and reliable connections between the enterprise network and the outside world.

Benefits of Modular Network Design

The benefits of adopting a modular network design are numerous and directly impact the performance, scalability, and reliability of the network. Here are the key advantages:

1. Scalability

A modular network design allows businesses to scale their network in a flexible and cost-effective manner. As demand grows, new modules (such as additional access switches, routers, or storage units) can be added without disrupting existing infrastructure.

2. Flexibility

With modularity, businesses can mix and match different technologies and services to create a custom solution that best fits their needs. The ability to swap out or upgrade individual modules also allows the network to evolve with changing business requirements.

3. Fault Tolerance and Redundancy

Redundant components at each module ensure that the network is resilient to failures. If one module fails, traffic can be rerouted through another, minimizing downtime and ensuring business continuity.

4. Simplified Management

By isolating network functions into distinct modules, network management becomes simpler. Troubleshooting can be done at the module level, and changes or upgrades to one module can occur without impacting others, leading to improved efficiency and reduced risk.

5. Improved Security

Modular design enables the implementation of security policies at each level of the network. For instance, each module can have its own security controls, such as firewalls, intrusion detection systems, or access control lists, helping to protect the network from internal and external threats.

Modular Network Design offers a powerful approach for building scalable, flexible, and resilient networks. By segmenting the network into functional modules, organizations can enhance their ability to grow, adapt, and optimize their network infrastructure in response to changing needs. This approach aligns with Cisco's broader strategy of providing businesses with advanced, customizable solutions that can evolve with technology trends and business demands. Whether it's adding more capacity, improving security, or integrating new technologies, modular network design offers the agility and performance needed for the modern enterprise.

Designing for Scalability and Redundancy

When it comes to building a robust, high-performance network, scalability and redundancy are two fundamental principles that ensure the network can accommodate growing demands while maintaining uninterrupted service. **Scalability** allows a network to expand smoothly and efficiently, adapting to new users, applications, and services, while **redundancy** ensures that the network remains resilient to failures, offering continuous service even when components go down.

In the context of Cisco networking solutions, scalability and redundancy are achieved through careful design considerations and the deployment of advanced technologies. In this section, we will delve into the principles of designing for scalability and redundancy, discuss how these principles apply in a modular network design, and explore the Cisco tools and technologies that enable the creation of scalable, fault-tolerant networks.

Understanding Scalability in Network Design

Scalability refers to the ability of a network to grow without compromising its performance or reliability. As businesses expand, their network needs also increase. Scalability ensures that the network can handle more users, more devices, more traffic, and more applications while maintaining optimal performance and without requiring a complete overhaul of the existing infrastructure.

Types of Scalability

1. **Vertical Scalability (Scale-Up)**: This refers to increasing the capacity of individual devices or components in the network. For instance, upgrading a router or switch to a higher-performance model with more ports or faster processing power is a form of vertical scalability. This approach works well when a specific device or module reaches its capacity limit, but it has its limitations, such as the maximum hardware capacity or performance of a device.
2. **Horizontal Scalability (Scale-Out)**: This refers to adding more devices or components to the network to distribute the load across multiple resources. Rather than relying on a single device to handle all traffic, horizontal scaling involves deploying additional routers, switches, or access points. Horizontal scalability is typically the preferred method for large-scale networks because it provides a more flexible and cost-effective solution to growing demands.

In a Cisco network, **stackable switches** such as the **Cisco Catalyst 9300** or **Meraki MX** can be deployed to scale the network horizontally. Additionally, **Cisco's SD-WAN solutions** allow for the easy expansion of WAN connectivity across multiple branch locations or remote sites.

Designing for Scalability

1. **Modular Architecture**: One of the most effective ways to achieve scalability is by adopting a **modular network architecture**. By breaking the network into functional modules (core, distribution, and access layers), each layer can be independently scaled to meet specific needs. For example, additional distribution switches can be added as more users or services are integrated into the network, and additional core devices can be deployed to handle more significant traffic flows.
2. **High-Capacity Core Layer**: The **core layer** should be designed with scalability in mind. Core switches and routers should be capable of handling large amounts of traffic and supporting high-speed links to accommodate future growth. Cisco's **Nexus 9000** series and **Catalyst 9500** switches are commonly used in the core layer for their ability to handle high-throughput and support large-scale routing.
3. **Traffic Segmentation and Load Balancing**: To maintain performance as the network grows, **traffic segmentation** and **load balancing** should be implemented to distribute traffic efficiently across network resources. Technologies like **Virtual Local Area Networks (VLANs)** and **Equal-Cost Multi-Path (ECMP)** routing can be used to segregate traffic and balance the load among multiple devices, ensuring that no single device becomes a bottleneck.
4. **Cloud Integration**: Cloud environments provide excellent scalability opportunities, allowing organizations to extend their network infrastructure without the need for additional on-premises hardware. Cisco's **Meraki cloud-managed solutions** and **Cisco ACI** allow for cloud-based networking, enabling businesses to scale their network seamlessly across on-premises and cloud environments.

Understanding Redundancy in Network Design

Redundancy is the practice of duplicating critical components of a network to prevent single points of failure. Redundant components, such as routers, switches, and links, ensure that if one part of the network fails, there is an alternative path or device that can take over, preventing network outages and minimizing downtime.

Types of Redundancy

1. **Device Redundancy**: This involves deploying multiple devices to handle the same tasks, so if one device fails, another can take over. For example, in a router or switch pair, protocols like **HSRP (Hot Standby Router Protocol)** or **VRRP (Virtual Router Redundancy Protocol)** can be used to provide device redundancy. If the active router fails, the standby router automatically takes over the routing duties.
2. **Link Redundancy**: Redundant links between devices ensure that if one link goes down, traffic can be rerouted over another. Technologies such as **Spanning Tree Protocol (STP)** and **Rapid Spanning Tree Protocol (RSTP)** help ensure that redundant links do not create loops in the network while providing automatic failover.
3. **Power Redundancy**: Redundant power supplies and backup power solutions, such as **UPS (Uninterruptible Power Supply)** systems, are essential for maintaining network availability in the event of power failures. Many Cisco devices come with dual power supplies, ensuring that if one power source fails, the other can take over without interrupting service.
4. **Path Redundancy**: Path redundancy involves having multiple network paths to ensure that data can be rerouted in the event of a link failure. **Cisco's MPLS (Multiprotocol Label Switching)** and **SD-WAN** solutions offer path redundancy by intelligently routing traffic through multiple paths based on current network conditions, ensuring the best possible performance and reliability.

Designing for Redundancy

THE HIERARCHICAL NETWORK DESIGN MODEL

1. **Dual-Homed Devices**: Redundant devices should be connected to different switches or routers to prevent a single failure from affecting the entire network. A **dual-homed design** connects devices to two separate network segments, increasing fault tolerance by ensuring that if one segment fails, the other remains operational.
2. **Redundant Network Links**: To prevent disruptions caused by link failures, multiple network links should be implemented between critical devices. Cisco's **EtherChannel** technology allows multiple physical links between switches or routers to act as a single logical link, providing higher bandwidth and redundancy.
3. **Resilient Routing Protocols**: Implementing dynamic routing protocols like **OSPF**, **EIGRP**, and **BGP** helps ensure that traffic is automatically rerouted if a failure occurs. For example, BGP allows for path diversification and failover across multiple ISPs or data centers, while OSPF and EIGRP provide fast convergence and re-routing capabilities within the enterprise network.
4. **Automated Failover and Load Balancing**: Using technologies like **Cisco's Intelligent Traffic Director** and **Nexus 7000** series switches, networks can automatically failover and load balance across multiple paths or devices to maintain continuous service in case of a failure.

Best Practices for Designing Scalable and Redundant Networks

1. **Plan for Future Growth**: When designing for scalability, always consider the potential for future expansion. Design the core and distribution layers with enough headroom to handle increased traffic and added devices. Plan for future bandwidth needs by considering current usage patterns and predicting growth over time.
2. **Avoid Single Points of Failure**: Ensure that critical components such as routers, switches, and links have redundant counterparts in place. Using technologies like **HSRP**, **VRRP**, and **Cisco StackWise** can eliminate single points of failure in the network.

3. **Leverage Virtualization and Cloud Services**: Virtualized devices, cloud-managed solutions, and software-defined networking (SDN) provide flexibility and scalability. Cisco's **ACI** and **Meraki** solutions allow businesses to scale their networks quickly without the need for additional on-premises hardware.
4. **Test Failover Mechanisms**: Regularly test the failover mechanisms to ensure that redundancy measures are functioning correctly. This includes simulating link or device failures to verify that the network automatically reroutes traffic and maintains service availability.
5. **Monitor and Optimize Performance**: Continuously monitor network performance using Cisco's **Network Assurance Engine** or **Cisco DNA Center**. By keeping track of traffic patterns and device health, you can proactively address potential bottlenecks and ensure that the network remains optimized for both scalability and redundancy.

Designing for scalability and redundancy is essential for building a network that can grow with your organization and continue to function reliably, even in the face of failures. Through careful planning and the use of Cisco's advanced technologies and protocols, businesses can create networks that offer high performance, fault tolerance, and adaptability. By focusing on horizontal scalability, redundant devices and links, and resilient routing, businesses can ensure that their networks are capable of handling future demands and challenges, all while maintaining uninterrupted service and supporting the business's critical applications and services.

THE HIERARCHICAL NETWORK DESIGN MODEL

Cisco's Enterprise Campus Architecture

Cisco's **Enterprise Campus Architecture** is a highly scalable and flexible network design framework tailored for large enterprises. It provides a structured approach to designing a network that can meet the performance, security, and operational needs of an enterprise, while also being adaptable to future growth. The campus architecture is focused on providing reliable, high-performance networking within the enterprise environment, which typically includes areas like headquarters, branch offices, remote locations, and data centers.

The **Enterprise Campus Architecture** is based on Cisco's **Hierarchical Network Design Model**, which divides the network into distinct layers and modules that perform specific functions. This modular approach allows organizations to scale their network infrastructure as needed while maintaining efficient management, strong security, and high availability. In this section, we will delve deeper into Cisco's Enterprise Campus Architecture, exploring the key components, design principles, and how it enables organizations to optimize their networks for performance, security, and future scalability.

Overview of Cisco's Enterprise Campus Architecture

The Cisco Enterprise Campus Architecture provides a holistic and comprehensive design for building enterprise networks. It is divided into multiple layers, each performing distinct roles. These layers are designed to work together cohesively to deliver the optimal balance of performance, scalability, and resilience across the entire campus network.

The main components of the **Enterprise Campus Architecture** include:

1. **Core Layer**: This layer provides the high-speed backbone of the campus network, ensuring fast and efficient data forwarding between the distribution layer and other core network components. The core layer is responsible for ensuring minimal latency and supporting high-bandwidth traffic flows across the network.

2. **Distribution Layer**: The distribution layer acts as an intermediary between the core and access layers. It is responsible for routing, traffic management, and policy enforcement. This layer includes high-performance devices such as routers and distribution switches, which handle traffic segmentation, Quality of Service (QoS), security policy enforcement, and routing protocols.
3. **Access Layer**: The access layer provides end-user connectivity to the network. It is where devices such as laptops, workstations, wireless access points, and IP phones connect to the network. Access layer switches provide local connectivity and enforce network access policies for users and devices.
4. **Edge Layer (Optional)**: The edge layer connects the enterprise network to the outside world, such as the internet or external partner networks. It typically includes **firewalls, VPN gateways**, and **WAN optimization devices** to manage the connection between the enterprise and external networks.

Core Layer: High-Performance Backbone

The **core layer** is the foundation of Cisco's Enterprise Campus Architecture. This layer is designed to provide high-speed data transfer with minimal latency, connecting the distribution layers to other core components of the network, such as data centers, remote locations, or external networks. It plays a crucial role in delivering the high-throughput required for large-scale enterprise networks.

Key Functions of the Core Layer

- **High-Speed Routing and Switching**: The core layer performs high-speed routing and switching for all traffic that passes through the network. Cisco devices like the **Nexus 9000** series switches are typically deployed at the core layer to ensure minimal latency and maximum throughput.
- **Fault Tolerance**: The core layer should be designed to be fault-tolerant, with redundant devices and links to ensure continuous ser-

THE HIERARCHICAL NETWORK DESIGN MODEL

vice availability. Features like **HSRP** (Hot Standby Router Protocol) and **VRRP** (Virtual Router Redundancy Protocol) are used to provide router redundancy, while **EtherChannel** ensures link redundancy.
- **Scalability**: The core layer is designed to handle high traffic volumes and scale as the network grows. Cisco's **Catalyst 9500** and **Nexus** series switches are specifically engineered for high-density environments, supporting large numbers of ports and high-speed connections.
- **Minimal Access Control**: While some access control and security policies may be applied at the core layer, its primary function is to pass data between distribution switches. Complex policy enforcement typically happens at the **distribution** or **access** layers.

Best Practices for Core Layer Design

- Use high-performance switches such as the **Cisco Catalyst 9600** or **Nexus 9000** for minimal latency and fast forwarding speeds.
- Implement redundancy in the core layer to ensure high availability and fault tolerance.
- Optimize core switches for throughput and traffic management using **Cisco IOS XR** or **NX-OS**, depending on your requirements.

Distribution Layer: Traffic Management and Policy Enforcement

The **distribution layer** is responsible for controlling data traffic between the access and core layers. It is a crucial point for managing policies, implementing security measures, and routing traffic efficiently across the campus network. Devices in the distribution layer perform advanced routing functions, manage inter-VLAN traffic, enforce security policies, and apply Quality of Service (QoS) settings to ensure that different types of traffic receive the appropriate levels of priority.

Key Functions of the Distribution Layer

- **Routing**: The distribution layer is responsible for routing traffic

between different VLANs and subnets. This layer may also manage inter-site routing for multiple campus locations or remote offices.
- **Policy Enforcement**: The distribution layer is often where network security policies (e.g., **Access Control Lists (ACLs)**) and QoS policies are enforced. This ensures that traffic is prioritized based on its type and application, improving performance for mission-critical applications.
- **Traffic Segmentation**: Devices at the distribution layer segment the traffic into different VLANs and apply appropriate routing protocols (such as **OSPF, EIGRP,** or **BGP**) for efficient forwarding.
- **Security**: The distribution layer applies security measures such as **firewalls, intrusion detection/prevention systems (IDS/IPS)**, and **802.1X authentication** to control access to the network and protect against unauthorized access.

Best Practices for Distribution Layer Design

- Utilize Cisco's **Catalyst 9300** or **Nexus 7000** series switches in the distribution layer for efficient traffic management and policy enforcement.
- Leverage **Cisco Identity Services Engine (ISE)** for policy-based access control and security enforcement at the distribution layer.
- Implement **multilayer switches** that can handle both Layer 2 switching and Layer 3 routing to simplify the design and reduce latency.

Access Layer: End-User Connectivity and Network Access

The **access layer** is where devices connect to the network, such as desktops, laptops, wireless access points, and IP phones. The access layer's primary responsibility is to provide reliable connectivity for end-users while ensuring the security and performance of the network. This layer typically involves the deployment of **access switches** and **wireless access points**.

THE HIERARCHICAL NETWORK DESIGN MODEL

Key Functions of the Access Layer

- **End-User Connectivity**: The access layer provides the physical and logical connection points for end-user devices. It connects workstations, laptops, and IoT devices to the enterprise network.
- **Authentication and Security**: The access layer enforces security policies, such as **802.1X authentication** and **MAC address filtering**, to ensure that only authorized devices can access the network. **Network Access Control (NAC)** technologies are also commonly implemented at the access layer.
- **Wireless Connectivity**: In modern campuses, wireless connectivity is a critical part of the access layer. **Cisco Meraki** or **Cisco Aironet** wireless access points provide reliable Wi-Fi coverage across campus locations, integrating seamlessly with wired network access.
- **PoE (Power over Ethernet)**: Access layer switches often provide **PoE** capabilities to power connected devices such as IP phones, security cameras, and wireless access points, eliminating the need for separate power supplies.

Best Practices for Access Layer Design

- Use **Cisco Catalyst 9200** or **Meraki MS** switches for reliable, high-speed access layer connectivity.
- Deploy **Cisco Wireless Access Points** in the access layer to provide comprehensive, reliable wireless coverage across campus locations.
- Implement **802.1X** for secure authentication and enforce security policies at the access layer.

Edge Layer (Optional): Connecting to External Networks

While not always a mandatory component for all organizations, the **edge layer** connects the enterprise campus network to external networks, such as the internet, remote sites, or external partners. The edge layer typically includes components like **firewalls**, **VPN gateways**, and **WAN**

optimization devices. It helps manage external traffic and ensure that the enterprise network remains secure from outside threats.

Key Functions of the Edge Layer

- **Firewall and Security**: The edge layer often includes firewalls that control the flow of traffic between the enterprise network and external networks, ensuring that only authorized traffic is allowed to enter or exit the network.
- **VPN and Remote Access**: If remote employees or branch offices need to access the enterprise network securely, the edge layer often includes VPN gateways or remote access devices that facilitate encrypted connections to the network.
- **WAN Optimization**: **WAN optimization appliances** at the edge layer help improve performance for remote locations by reducing latency and compressing data traffic traveling over wide-area networks (WANs).

Best Practices for Edge Layer Design

- Use **Cisco Secure Firewall** and **Cisco Umbrella** for robust security and threat prevention at the network perimeter.
- Deploy **Cisco AnyConnect VPN** for secure remote access to the campus network.
- Implement **Cisco SD-WAN** for optimized connectivity and performance across geographically distributed locations.

Cisco's **Enterprise Campus Architecture** provides a powerful framework for designing scalable, secure, and high-performance networks for large enterprises. By organizing the network into distinct layers—core, distribution, access, and edge—Cisco's campus architecture ensures that each network component is optimized for its specific role. Whether it's ensuring high-speed connectivity at the core, enforcing security policies at the distribution layer, or providing end-user access at the access layer, Cisco's comprehensive suite of products and technologies offers organizations the tools they need to build reliable, resilient networks that can scale to meet the demands of the modern enterprise.

Cisco's Best Practices for Network Hierarchy

When designing and implementing network architectures, particularly for large enterprises, **network hierarchy** plays a crucial role in ensuring efficiency, scalability, and manageability. Cisco's best practices for network hierarchy are designed to help organizations build networks that are not only resilient and secure but also flexible enough to handle future growth. Following a hierarchical design approach ensures that the network is structured in a way that maximizes performance while reducing complexity.

The hierarchical network design model divides the network into distinct layers, each with specific functions and responsibilities. Cisco's approach to **network hierarchy** follows this layered model, typically involving **Core**, **Distribution**, and **Access** layers, which help organize the network based on traffic flow, function, and scalability needs.

In this section, we will explore Cisco's best practices for creating a network hierarchy, how to design each layer effectively, and the practical strategies you can use to achieve a high-performing, scalable, and fault-tolerant network architecture.

The Hierarchical Network Model: An Overview

Cisco's hierarchical model is built around the principle of dividing the network into different functional layers, each of which performs a specific role within the overall network infrastructure. By using a tiered approach, network complexity is reduced, and each layer can be optimized for its specific tasks, providing clear delineation of responsibilities and simplifying network management.

The **three main layers** in Cisco's hierarchical network model are:

1. **Core Layer**: The core layer is the backbone of the network and provides high-speed, low-latency connectivity between different parts of the network. It is designed for speed and redundancy, and its primary function is to carry large amounts of traffic between distribution layers, data centers, remote locations, and other critical network components.
2. **Distribution Layer**: The distribution layer acts as an intermediary between the core and access layers. It is responsible for routing traffic between VLANs (Virtual LANs), enforcing policies, and providing segmentation. The distribution layer also handles tasks like traffic filtering, load balancing, and providing interconnection between the core and access layers.
3. **Access Layer**: The access layer is where end-user devices (such as desktops, laptops, IP phones, and wireless access points) connect to the network. This layer is responsible for providing user connectivity, enforcing security policies, and controlling network access at the device level.

Each of these layers must be designed with specific considerations in mind to ensure optimal performance, security, and scalability. Cisco's best practices for network hierarchy emphasize the importance of clear separation between the layers to prevent bottlenecks and inefficiencies while ensuring that traffic flows smoothly and securely.

Best Practices for Core Layer Design

The **Core Layer** is the high-speed backbone of the network, responsible for efficiently transporting data across the network. Cisco's best practices for the core layer revolve around ensuring that it remains highly available, fault-tolerant, and scalable. Here are key design principles for building a robust core layer:

1. Use High-Performance, Resilient Devices

THE HIERARCHICAL NETWORK DESIGN MODEL

- **Core switches** such as the **Cisco Catalyst 9500** or **Cisco Nexus 9000** series are designed to deliver ultra-low latency and high throughput. These switches support high-density ports, 10/25/40/100GbE speeds, and are optimized for large-scale data forwarding.
- Ensure that the core layer devices are redundant and have no single points of failure. This is typically achieved by using **stacked switches** (for redundancy) or **dual devices** with **link aggregation** (using technologies like **EtherChannel**).

2. Minimize Complexity

- The core layer should focus on fast, simple data forwarding. Avoid complex features such as extensive ACLs, firewall rules, or deep packet inspection at this layer. Complex operations should be handled at the **distribution layer**, where they can be applied in a more manageable and scalable way.
- Implement **spine-leaf** topologies in data center networks to ensure efficient, non-blocking connectivity. This design enables optimal load balancing, lower latency, and increased scalability.

3. Focus on Scalability

- The core layer must be designed to handle future traffic growth without compromising performance. Cisco devices like the **Nexus 7000** series offer modular designs that can scale as traffic demands increase.
- Implement **Software-Defined Networking (SDN)** technologies like **Cisco ACI (Application Centric Infrastructure)** to help manage and scale traffic flows dynamically across the core layer.

4. Ensure High Availability

- Implement **hot standby protocols** such as **HSRP** (Hot Standby

Router Protocol) or **VRRP** (Virtual Router Redundancy Protocol) to ensure that if one router or switch fails, another can immediately take over.
- **Dual-homed connections** and **multiple fiber paths** should be deployed to prevent outages due to a single physical link failure.

Best Practices for Distribution Layer Design

The **Distribution Layer** connects the core layer with the access layer and is responsible for handling routing, policy enforcement, traffic management, and inter-VLAN communication. Cisco's best practices for this layer focus on scalability, redundancy, and efficient traffic management.

1. Centralize Routing and Policy Enforcement

- The distribution layer should be the primary location for routing between VLANs and enforcing network security policies. Cisco's **Catalyst 9300** or **Nexus 3000** series are excellent choices for these tasks.
- Leverage **Layer 3 switches** in the distribution layer to handle **routing** between different segments of the network (e.g., inter-VLAN routing). This approach reduces traffic at the access layer and ensures efficient management of broadcast traffic.

2. Implement Redundancy and Load Balancing

- Use **redundant routers** and **switches** to ensure that the distribution layer remains fault-tolerant. Redundant links between the core and distribution layers, as well as between distribution and access layers, help to ensure continuous service.
- Utilize **ECMP (Equal-Cost Multi-Path)** routing and **link aggregation** (such as **LACP**) to load-balance traffic across multiple paths, improving performance and fault tolerance.

THE HIERARCHICAL NETWORK DESIGN MODEL

3. Enforce Security and Quality of Service (QoS)

- Enforce security policies such as **Access Control Lists (ACLs)**, **802.1X authentication**, and **VPN segmentation** at the distribution layer. This layer acts as a control point for determining which devices and users can access the network.
- Apply **QoS policies** to prioritize traffic based on application type, ensuring that critical applications such as voice or video get priority over less time-sensitive data.

4. Manage Traffic Segmentation

- Use **VLANs** to logically segment traffic between different departments or business units, thereby enhancing security and reducing unnecessary traffic. Additionally, implement **policy-based routing** (PBR) to direct traffic flows based on specified criteria, such as source, destination, or application type.

Best Practices for Access Layer Design

The **Access Layer** is the point at which end devices, such as computers, IP phones, and wireless access points, connect to the network. Best practices for this layer emphasize performance, security, and ease of management.

1. Provide Reliable End-User Connectivity

- Use **Cisco Catalyst 9200** or **Meraki MS** switches at the access layer to ensure high-speed connectivity for end-user devices. These switches should be capable of handling **Power over Ethernet (PoE)** to support devices like IP phones and access points.
- Implement **802.1X** port-based authentication to control device access at the access layer, ensuring that only authorized devices can connect to the network.

2. Enhance Wireless Coverage and Connectivity

- **Wireless Access Points (APs)** should be strategically deployed across the access layer to provide robust Wi-Fi coverage for end-users. Cisco's **Aironet** or **Meraki** access points provide seamless connectivity and integration with the wired network.
- Configure **Wi-Fi networks** using proper **SSID segmentation** and ensure that **Quality of Service (QoS)** policies are applied to ensure that high-priority applications like voice and video maintain optimal performance.

3. Implement Network Access Control (NAC)

- At the access layer, use Cisco's **Identity Services Engine (ISE)** to enforce security policies. NAC allows for the dynamic enforcement of security policies based on user identity, device type, and location, ensuring that the network remains secure while providing seamless access to authorized users.

4. Maintain Scalability with Flexible Architectures

- The access layer should be designed for flexibility, allowing for easy expansion as the organization grows. Consider deploying **stackable switches** at the access layer to simplify management and ensure that capacity can be easily expanded without disrupting network operations.

Best Practices for Network Hierarchy Integration

To ensure that the **Core**, **Distribution**, and **Access layers** work together seamlessly, Cisco recommends several overarching best practices for the integration of the hierarchical network model:

1. **Ensure Clear Layer Boundaries**: Maintain clear functional bound-

aries between layers to prevent performance bottlenecks. Keep the core layer focused on high-speed forwarding, the distribution layer on policy enforcement and routing, and the access layer on end-user connectivity.
2. **Monitor and Optimize Network Performance**: Use tools like **Cisco DNA Center** and **Cisco Prime Infrastructure** for proactive monitoring and optimization. Regular network assessments allow for early identification of potential issues, ensuring that the network remains highly performant as it scales.
3. **Leverage Virtualization**: Use **network virtualization** technologies like **Cisco ACI** and **SD-WAN** to abstract the physical network infrastructure and simplify management. These technologies enable more flexible and scalable network architectures that are easier to manage and grow.
4. **Security Across All Layers**: Security should be consistently enforced across all layers of the network. Cisco's security solutions, such as **Cisco Secure Firewall**, **Identity Services Engine (ISE)**, and **Cisco Umbrella**, should be implemented across the network hierarchy to provide comprehensive, multi-layered security.

Cisco's best practices for network hierarchy offer a proven, structured approach for building highly scalable, efficient, and secure networks. By focusing on the separation of concerns between the core, distribution, and access layers, and applying principles such as redundancy, scalability, and security, organizations can create networks that are resilient, future-proof, and capable of supporting modern enterprise needs. Following these best practices ensures that the network not only meets current requirements but also provides the foundation for continued growth and innovation.

Scalable Network Design Principles

Understanding Scalability in Network Design

In the world of networking, **scalability** is one of the most critical attributes that a design must incorporate to ensure it can meet the evolving needs of an organization. At its core, scalability refers to the capacity of a network to handle an increase in workload, accommodate new users, or expand to support new locations or technologies without requiring a complete redesign. For enterprises, scalability is not just about handling more data or more devices; it's about ensuring that growth is seamless, cost-effective, and can be executed with minimal disruption to business operations.

This section will explore what scalability in network design truly means, the factors that contribute to a scalable network, and best practices for building networks that can grow alongside the organization's demands.

What is Scalability in Network Design?

Scalability in network design refers to the network's ability to accommodate future growth in terms of traffic, users, and devices, without a corresponding increase in complexity, cost, or degradation of performance. This growth can be in various forms:

1. **Traffic Scalability**: The ability of the network to handle increased traffic volumes without bottlenecks, slowdowns, or the need for significant re-engineering of network components.

2. **User Scalability**: The capacity to support more users, whether by adding additional devices, expanding to remote or branch offices, or increasing the number of connected devices, such as IoT sensors, mobile phones, and smart devices.
3. **Geographical Scalability**: The ability of the network to extend across multiple locations, such as additional offices, campuses, or even regions, while maintaining uniform performance and manageability.
4. **Technological Scalability**: The ability to integrate new technologies or services (such as cloud computing, software-defined networking (SDN), or high-definition video conferencing) into the existing network architecture without disrupting existing services or requiring a complete overhaul.

Scalability is not just about adding capacity, it is about maintaining **performance**, **security**, and **manageability** as the network grows. A scalable network can add resources and users dynamically, without having to manually redesign the infrastructure every time the organization's needs change.

Key Characteristics of a Scalable Network

A scalable network must exhibit certain key characteristics to be effective over time. These include:

1. **Elasticity**: A scalable network should be able to grow or shrink in response to demand. Elasticity allows a network to automatically adjust its resources based on the current load, ensuring that traffic can be efficiently distributed without overloading certain components. This is particularly important in cloud-based or hybrid networking environments.
2. **Modularity**: A modular approach to network design allows components to be added or replaced easily as needed. For example, **modular routers** and **switches**, such as the **Cisco Catalyst 9000** series or **Cisco Nexus** platforms, allow you to add additional ports

or capabilities as the network grows. This avoids the need for a complete redesign and ensures that the network can evolve with minimal disruption.

3. **Redundancy**: As networks grow, redundancy becomes essential. A scalable network design must have built-in redundancy to prevent failures from affecting performance or availability. This includes multiple paths for data, redundant power supplies, and failover mechanisms that ensure continuous availability.

4. **Performance Optimization**: A scalable network must be designed in a way that ensures its performance remains consistent even as it scales. This can involve traffic prioritization using **Quality of Service (QoS)**, **load balancing** across multiple paths, and ensuring low-latency paths for critical applications.

5. **Simplified Management**: As the network expands, management complexity increases. A scalable network should incorporate tools and techniques to ensure that network management remains streamlined and efficient. Technologies like **Cisco DNA Center**, **Software-Defined Networking (SDN)**, and **network automation** can provide centralized control and simplified management as the network grows.

Why Scalability Matters in Network Design

The importance of scalability in network design cannot be overstated. Here are several reasons why scalability should be a top priority in any network architecture:

1. **Growth Flexibility**: As organizations expand, their network requirements will increase. A scalable design ensures that the network can grow to accommodate new business units, additional data, and increased traffic without requiring a major overhaul or complete replacement of network infrastructure.

2. **Cost Efficiency**: Building a scalable network from the outset allows organizations to avoid costly, disruptive network upgrades

in the future. Rather than constantly needing to upgrade hardware or redesign the architecture to accommodate growth, a scalable network ensures that investments made early on will continue to pay off as the network expands.

3. **Business Continuity**: A scalable network supports business continuity by ensuring that as demand increases, the network can support it. In the event of an increase in traffic, users, or devices, a scalable network will allow the organization to expand its capacity without service interruptions.
4. **Future-Proofing**: With the rapid evolution of technologies like cloud computing, IoT, and AI-driven applications, the need for a network to be agile and adaptable has never been greater. Scalability ensures that the network is flexible enough to support these emerging technologies without requiring a full redesign. This future-proofs the network and helps the organization remain competitive in an ever-changing technological landscape.
5. **Improved User Experience**: A well-designed scalable network can maintain high levels of performance as the user base grows. Whether it's ensuring minimal latency for voice and video communications or providing sufficient bandwidth for data-heavy applications, scalability helps ensure that users experience consistent, reliable service even as the network expands.

Key Considerations for Achieving Scalability in Network Design

To build a truly scalable network, there are several key considerations and best practices that must be followed during the design phase. These include:

1. Hierarchical Network Design

Using a **hierarchical network design model** (as outlined earlier with Cisco's approach) is essential for scalability. By dividing the network into distinct layers—**Core**, **Distribution**, and **Access**—each with specific functions, the network can grow in a structured, predictable way. This approach allows additional devices or users to be added without overloading any one layer.

- **Core Layer**: Handles high-speed traffic forwarding across the network backbone. It should be able to scale to accommodate increasing traffic as the network grows.
- **Distribution Layer**: Handles routing and policy enforcement between different segments of the network. As the number of segments grows, the distribution layer should support additional routes and policies without performance degradation.
- **Access Layer**: Provides connectivity to end-user devices. Scalability here involves ensuring that the network can support an increasing number of devices, especially IoT devices and mobile endpoints.

2. Modular and Redundant Components

Modular design is a fundamental principle of scalability. By using modular components (such as Cisco's **Catalyst 9400** and **Nexus 7000** series), network administrators can add new modules to the network as needed, whether that's more bandwidth, additional interfaces, or support for new features. This approach ensures that the network can scale vertically (by adding more resources to existing devices) and horizontally (by adding more devices to the network).

Redundancy is also crucial in maintaining performance as the network grows. **Redundant links**, **multiple switches/routers**, and **load balancing** ensure that if one part of the network fails, there is always an alternative path for data. This improves network reliability and ensures uptime as the network scales.

3. Traffic Segmentation and Load Balancing

To maintain scalability, traffic must be managed efficiently. This involves segmenting traffic by **VLANs**, applying **Quality of Service (QoS)** policies, and implementing **load balancing** across multiple paths. **Cisco's ACI (Application Centric Infrastructure)**, for example, provides an integrated approach to traffic management that allows for optimized data flows, minimizing congestion and latency while improving overall performance.

Load balancing technologies like **Equal-Cost Multi-Path (ECMP)** routing or **Cisco's SD-WAN** solutions enable traffic to be evenly distributed across multiple paths, ensuring that no single link becomes overloaded as the network grows.

4. Automation and Software-Defined Networking (SDN)

As networks grow in complexity, **automation** becomes a key enabler of scalability. Cisco's **SDN** technologies, such as **Cisco DNA Center** and **ACI**, allow network configurations, management, and provisioning to be automated, reducing manual intervention and the risk of errors. Automation helps ensure that as the network scales, changes can be applied consistently and quickly, without overburdening network administrators.

For example, **Cisco DNA Center** offers a **single pane of glass** for managing network policies, automating device configurations, and monitoring performance. This centralized management platform helps scale networks efficiently by allowing administrators to deploy changes and monitor network health across a growing infrastructure.

5. Cloud Integration

A scalable network must also be able to integrate seamlessly with cloud environments. With more organizations relying on cloud computing, it is critical that the network can handle the increased demand for cloud services without compromising performance. **Cisco Meraki** and **Cisco SD-WAN** are two technologies that enable organizations to extend their network to the cloud while maintaining centralized control and management.

By integrating cloud services into the network design, companies can scale their network infrastructure flexibly and take advantage of cloud-native tools that automatically adjust to changes in workload, user base, or geographic reach.

Understanding scalability in network design is fundamental for building networks that will support an organization's growth in both the short and long term. A scalable network allows an organization to grow, adapt, and remain competitive in a rapidly changing technology landscape, while avoiding expensive, disruptive upgrades or complete redesigns. By following best practices like **hierarchical design**, **modular components**, **traffic management**, and embracing **automation** and **cloud integration**, organizations can create a network architecture that meets both current demands and future needs, all while maintaining high levels of performance, reliability, and security.

Choosing the Right Topology: Star, Mesh, and Hybrid

One of the foundational decisions in network design is the selection of the appropriate **network topology**. The topology of a network determines how the different components (such as routers, switches, devices, and servers) are connected to each other, which influences factors such as performance, reliability, scalability, and cost. **Topology selection** is crucial because it directly impacts the network's ability to handle traffic efficiently, maintain uptime, and scale as demands increase.

The three most commonly used network topologies in enterprise environments are **Star**, **Mesh**, and **Hybrid**. Each of these topologies offers distinct advantages and disadvantages, making them more suitable for different types of networks and organizational needs. In this section, we will explore the characteristics, benefits, and considerations for each topology to help guide the decision-making process when designing a network architecture.

Star Topology: Simple and Centralized

In a **Star topology**, all network devices are connected to a central **hub** or **switch**, which serves as the point of communication for the entire network. This central device acts as a mediator, forwarding traffic between devices, and plays a critical role in ensuring network connectivity.

Key Features of Star Topology:

- **Centralized Communication**: Every device communicates through a single point, the central hub or switch.
- **Simplicity**: The topology is relatively simple to design and implement, making it a popular choice for small to medium-sized networks.
- **Scalability**: It is relatively easy to add new devices to the network by simply connecting them to the central hub or switch.

Advantages of Star Topology:

1. **Simplicity and Ease of Management**: The star topology is easy to manage because all devices are connected to a single central device. Troubleshooting is also simplified because network administrators can quickly isolate the point of failure by checking the central hub or switch.
2. **Fault Isolation**: If one device fails or becomes disconnected, it does not impact the rest of the network. Only the affected device will lose connectivity, which increases overall reliability.
3. **Scalability**: Adding more devices to the network is relatively simple and does not require major changes to the existing network infrastructure. Additional switches or hubs can be added to accommodate more devices.
4. **Centralized Control**: Centralized management can simplify monitoring, security enforcement, and policy application.

Disadvantages of Star Topology:

1. **Single Point of Failure**: The central hub or switch represents a **single point of failure**. If the central device goes down, the entire network becomes inoperable. To mitigate this, redundancy (such as redundant switches or power supplies) may be necessary for high-availability environments.
2. **Performance Bottleneck**: The central hub or switch must handle all network traffic, which could become a bottleneck as the network

grows in size. High-performance devices are required to ensure the network does not slow down with increasing traffic.

When to Use Star Topology:

Star topology is most suitable for **small to medium-sized networks** or environments where network growth is expected but should remain manageable. It is commonly used in **local area networks (LANs)**, office buildings, and branch offices, where a central switch can handle a moderate amount of traffic and provide centralized management.

In a Cisco-based network, **Catalyst 1000** or **Catalyst 9000** series switches are often used as the central devices in a star topology, providing high throughput and efficient traffic management.

Mesh Topology: Highly Redundant and Resilient

A **Mesh topology** is a network design in which every device is directly connected to every other device in the network. This creates a highly redundant network where multiple paths exist between devices, ensuring that data can be rerouted through different paths in case of failures.

Key Features of Mesh Topology:

- **Direct Connectivity**: Every device is connected to every other device, forming a web-like structure.
- **High Redundancy**: Multiple physical paths exist between devices, which provides excellent fault tolerance.
- **Load Balancing**: Traffic can be distributed evenly across the multiple links, optimizing network performance and reducing congestion.

Advantages of Mesh Topology:

1. **Fault Tolerance and High Availability**: Mesh networks are highly resilient because there are multiple paths for data to travel. If one link fails, traffic can be rerouted through another link without impacting the overall network performance.
2. **Improved Performance**: Since multiple paths exist for communica-

SCALABLE NETWORK DESIGN PRINCIPLES

tion, mesh topologies can distribute network traffic more efficiently, reducing congestion and bottlenecks.

3. **No Single Point of Failure**: Unlike star topology, a mesh network does not have a central point of failure. This ensures that the network can remain operational even if one or more devices or connections fail.
4. **Scalable and Flexible**: Mesh topologies are inherently scalable. New devices can be added to the network by simply connecting them to other devices in the mesh, without affecting existing connections.

Disadvantages of Mesh Topology:

1. **Complexity**: Designing and managing a mesh network is complex due to the number of direct connections required between devices. This complexity can lead to higher costs for setup and maintenance.
2. **Cost**: The sheer number of connections in a full mesh design can be expensive, as each device needs to be connected to every other device. This can result in significant costs for cabling, routers, and switches.
3. **Difficult to Scale Large Networks**: Although mesh networks can be scaled, adding many devices can result in a highly complex configuration that is difficult to manage.

When to Use Mesh Topology:

Mesh topology is ideal for **large, mission-critical networks** where **high availability, fault tolerance**, and **redundancy** are required. This makes it suitable for **data center environments, wide area networks (WANs)**, and **backbone networks** where network uptime is crucial, and high-volume traffic demands can be spread across multiple paths.

Cisco's **Nexus 7000** or **Nexus 9000** series are excellent choices for building a mesh network in data centers, providing robust support for high-availability features, including **multi-chassis link aggregation** and **virtual port channels (vPC)** for redundancy.

Hybrid Topology: Flexibility and Balance

A **Hybrid topology** combines elements of different topologies to create a network design that leverages the strengths of each while mitigating their weaknesses. For example, a hybrid topology might combine the simplicity and centralized management of a star topology with the redundancy and fault tolerance of a mesh topology. Hybrid networks are highly flexible and can be customized to meet the specific needs of an organization.

Key Features of Hybrid Topology:

- **Combination of Topologies**: Hybrid networks combine features of multiple topologies (such as star, mesh, or tree topologies) to create a network that meets the specific needs of the organization.
- **Adaptable**: Hybrid topologies are adaptable to different environments and can evolve over time to accommodate changes in network requirements.

Advantages of Hybrid Topology:

1. **Flexibility**: Hybrid topologies offer a high degree of flexibility. They can be tailored to meet the needs of an organization by combining the advantages of multiple topologies.
2. **Cost-Effective**: By selectively incorporating mesh or star features, hybrid networks can achieve fault tolerance and scalability without the high cost of a full mesh design.
3. **Scalability and Manageability**: Hybrid networks can be easily scaled as the organization grows, and management is often simpler than in a full mesh design.

Disadvantages of Hybrid Topology:

1. **Complex Design and Implementation**: While hybrid topologies offer flexibility, their design can be complex. Careful planning is

required to ensure that the network remains efficient, scalable, and manageable.
2. **Potential for Increased Latency**: In some cases, hybrid designs may introduce latency due to the need for traffic to pass through multiple layers or components, particularly if the design incorporates elements of a mesh topology.

When to Use Hybrid Topology:

Hybrid topologies are best suited for **large enterprises** or **complex environments** that require a balance between scalability, redundancy, and cost-efficiency. For example, a hybrid design might be ideal for an organization with multiple regional offices, where the **star topology** is used for local office connections, while a **mesh** or **partial mesh** topology is used for the headquarters or data centers to provide higher redundancy and performance.

Cisco's **ACI** and **SD-WAN** solutions allow for the creation of hybrid network designs that integrate both on-premise and cloud resources, ensuring that performance and security are maintained across diverse environments.

Choosing the right network topology is a critical decision in designing a scalable, efficient, and reliable network. **Star topology** is ideal for simpler, smaller networks where ease of management is paramount, but scalability and redundancy are somewhat secondary. **Mesh topology**, on the other hand, offers high availability and fault tolerance, making it suitable for mission-critical, large-scale networks, though at a higher cost and complexity. **Hybrid topology** provides the flexibility to combine the best aspects of both, offering scalability and cost-efficiency while balancing complexity.

Ultimately, the decision depends on the size, scope, and specific needs of the organization. Whether you're building a small office network, a resilient data center, or a complex enterprise-wide infrastructure, Cisco's diverse product suite, such as the **Catalyst**, **Nexus**, and **Meraki** series, can help you implement the right topology for your business goals.

High Availability and Fault Tolerance in Design

In today's fast-paced business environment, network downtime is more than just an inconvenience—it can result in significant financial losses, disrupted operations, and damaged customer relationships. **High availability (HA)** and **fault tolerance (FT)** are essential concepts in network design that help ensure continuous service, even in the face of hardware failures, power outages, or other disruptions.

Building a network that guarantees high availability and fault tolerance requires a combination of architectural decisions, proactive monitoring, redundancy strategies, and disaster recovery plans. Cisco offers a variety of solutions and best practices to help businesses design and maintain networks that are resilient and capable of maintaining operations despite failures.

In this section, we'll explore the core concepts of **high availability** and **fault tolerance**, discuss the strategies for achieving these goals in network design, and highlight Cisco's technologies that make it easier to implement these solutions.

Understanding High Availability (HA) and Fault Tolerance (FT)

High Availability (HA) refers to the ability of a network or system to remain operational and accessible for the maximum possible amount of time. It is typically measured in terms of **uptime**, and is often expressed as a percentage (e.g., **99.9%** uptime, which translates to about 8.77 hours of downtime per year). The goal of high availability is to minimize service interruptions by ensuring that there is **no single point of failure** in the network, so that if one component fails, the system can continue to operate without noticeable disruption to users.

Fault Tolerance (FT), on the other hand, refers to the network's ability to continue functioning correctly in the event of a failure, often without any downtime at all. A fault-tolerant system is designed so that the failure of one or more components does not affect the overall operation of the network. This can be achieved through redundant components, load balancing, and real-time failover mechanisms.

Together, **high availability** and **fault tolerance** create a network environment where services are consistently available, resilient, and able to handle failures without causing major disruptions.

Key Strategies for Achieving High Availability and Fault Tolerance

To achieve high availability and fault tolerance in network design, the following strategies and best practices are typically implemented:

1. Redundancy in Critical Components

The most fundamental strategy for ensuring HA and FT is the use of **redundancy**. Redundancy involves duplicating critical components so that if one fails, another can immediately take over, preventing service disruption. Redundancy can be implemented in various parts of the network:

- **Redundant Routers and Switches**: Using multiple routers and switches within the core and distribution layers ensures that if one device fails, the other can continue routing traffic without interruption.
- **Dual Power Supplies**: Many enterprise-grade devices (such as Cisco Catalyst or Nexus switches) come with **dual power supplies**. If one power supply fails, the other can take over seamlessly, preventing a complete system shutdown.
- **Redundant Network Links**: Using **multiple physical paths** for data between devices ensures that if one link fails, traffic can be rerouted through another path.

2. Load Balancing and Traffic Distribution

Load balancing is the process of distributing incoming network traffic across multiple resources—such as servers, network links, or data centers—to ensure no single resource becomes overwhelmed. In the event of a failure, traffic can be automatically rerouted to healthy resources, preventing downtime and ensuring that network services remain accessible.

- **Cisco's ACI (Application Centric Infrastructure)** provides an intelligent, scalable solution for load balancing, helping ensure that traffic is optimally distributed based on current network conditions and availability.
- **Cisco SD-WAN** also offers built-in load balancing across multiple WAN connections, allowing enterprises to balance traffic between MPLS, broadband, and LTE connections, while ensuring seamless failover.

3. Link Aggregation and High-Speed Redundant Links

Link aggregation, or **EtherChannel** in Cisco terminology, allows multiple physical links to be combined into a single logical connection. This approach not only increases the overall bandwidth of the network but also provides redundancy. If one link in the aggregation fails, the others continue to carry traffic without any noticeable impact on performance.

- **Cisco's EtherChannel** technology can be used between switches or between switches and routers to provide both bandwidth expansion and fault tolerance. When designed correctly, EtherChannel ensures high availability and ensures minimal traffic disruption in case of a failure.

4. Hot Standby Router Protocol (HSRP) and Virtual Router Redundancy Protocol (VRRP)

HSRP (Hot Standby Router Protocol) and **VRRP** (Virtual Router Redundancy Protocol) are two Cisco protocols that enable router redundancy and ensure that there is no single point of failure in the network's routing

SCALABLE NETWORK DESIGN PRINCIPLES

path. These protocols allow multiple routers to work together, with one acting as the **active router** and the others as **standby routers**. If the active router fails, the standby router takes over, ensuring that routing is still available with minimal downtime.

- **HSRP** is commonly used in Cisco networks to provide redundancy at the gateway level. It ensures that a virtual IP address is always reachable, even if the physical device that typically handles routing becomes unavailable.
- **VRRP** works similarly to HSRP, but with support for multiple routers. It allows for better scaling and flexibility, as it can provide redundancy for both IPv4 and IPv6 traffic.

5. Redundant Internet Connections and WAN Paths

In a distributed, cloud-connected world, ensuring redundancy at the **WAN** and **Internet** connection level is equally important. Enterprises often rely on multiple Internet Service Providers (ISPs) to ensure that if one provider experiences an outage, traffic can be rerouted through another connection.

- **Cisco SD-WAN** allows for the seamless failover of WAN links, providing a cost-effective way to build redundancy without relying solely on MPLS links.
- **Dual ISPs** with automatic failover configurations ensure that the organization remains connected to the Internet and remote sites, even in the event of an ISP failure.

6. Data Backup and Disaster Recovery

While high availability focuses on minimizing service interruptions through redundancy, **disaster recovery (DR)** plans focus on the recovery of critical data and services after a catastrophic event, such as a data center failure or natural disaster. Cisco offers several solutions to help businesses with data backup, replication, and disaster recovery.

- **Cisco's HyperFlex** is a software-defined storage solution that helps to back up data in real time and replicate it to remote locations. This ensures that critical business data is always available, even if primary systems fail.
- **Cloud-based backup** and **disaster recovery solutions** such as **Cisco Umbrella** and **Cisco Meraki** can automatically synchronize critical data and applications to cloud environments, ensuring that in the event of a physical failure, the services can quickly be restored.

7. Monitoring, Alerts, and Predictive Analytics

Effective **network monitoring** is essential for identifying potential failures before they occur. Proactive monitoring of network devices, performance metrics, and traffic patterns can help administrators detect issues early and take corrective actions before they lead to network outages.

- **Cisco DNA Center** provides a centralized platform for monitoring, managing, and troubleshooting the network. With its advanced analytics and **AI-driven insights**, it can predict potential failures, enabling network engineers to take preventive measures.
- **Cisco Prime Infrastructure** offers network-wide visibility and health monitoring, providing real-time alerts about issues such as device failures, link congestion, or configuration changes that may impact network availability.

8. Geo-Redundancy and Distributed Data Centers

In large-scale, mission-critical environments, **geo-redundancy** (the practice of spreading resources across multiple geographical locations) ensures that if one data center or location experiences failure or natural disaster, services can be quickly restored from another location.

- **Cisco's ACI** and **SD-WAN** solutions are designed to integrate with distributed data centers and cloud environments. These tools allow for geo-redundancy and high availability across multiple sites, ensuring that services are always accessible, even in the face of regional disruptions.

Cisco Solutions for High Availability and Fault Tolerance

Cisco provides a comprehensive suite of products and technologies to support high availability and fault tolerance in enterprise network designs. Some of the key solutions include:

- **Cisco Catalyst Series**: Offers high availability with features such as redundant power supplies, stacking, and EtherChannel support, making it ideal for access and distribution layers in the network.
- **Cisco Nexus Series**: Designed for high-density, high-availability environments, the Nexus series includes features like **vPC (Virtual Port Channel)**, **multi-chassis link aggregation**, and **hot-swappable components** that ensure minimal disruption during hardware failure.
- **Cisco ACI (Application Centric Infrastructure)**: Provides an integrated solution that automates network and application traffic management, offering built-in fault tolerance and rapid failover between data centers.
- **Cisco SD-WAN**: Offers secure, reliable connectivity across distributed locations, with automatic WAN failover and traffic prioritization to ensure business continuity.
- **Cisco Meraki**: For cloud-managed networks, Meraki provides real-time monitoring, automated failover, and simplified management to maintain high availability without requiring on-site IT intervention.

Building a highly available and fault-tolerant network is essential to ensuring uninterrupted service and protecting against failures that could disrupt business operations. High availability focuses on keeping services online by minimizing downtime, while fault tolerance ensures that a network continues to function seamlessly even in the event of component failures. Through strategies like redundancy, load balancing, and real-time monitoring, combined with Cisco's enterprise-grade solutions like **Catalyst, Nexus, ACI, SD-WAN**, and **Meraki**, organizations can design networks that are resilient, scalable, and capable of delivering continuous uptime, even in the most demanding environments.

Using Cisco's Solutions for Scalable Networks

As businesses grow and evolve, their networks must keep pace with increasing demands for performance, capacity, and flexibility. Scalability is a fundamental characteristic of modern network design, enabling organizations to adapt to new technologies, more users, and higher data throughput without a complete redesign of their infrastructure. Achieving scalability requires not only the right architecture but also the right tools and solutions to expand capacity in a seamless and cost-effective manner.

Cisco, as one of the leading networking providers in the world, offers a comprehensive suite of products and technologies designed to help businesses build scalable networks that can evolve with their needs. Cisco's solutions address scalability across a range of network layers, from access to core, and offer flexibility in how networks can grow while maintaining performance, security, and reliability.

In this section, we'll explore how Cisco's solutions can be used to build scalable networks, covering key technologies such as **Cisco Catalyst, Cisco Nexus, Cisco SD-WAN, Cisco Meraki, Cisco ACI**, and more. We will also discuss how Cisco's cloud-managed offerings, automation capabilities, and network architectures help businesses achieve scalability without compromising efficiency.

1. Cisco Catalyst Series: Building Scalable Access and Distribution Layers

The **Cisco Catalyst Series** of switches is one of the most popular solutions for building scalable enterprise networks. Catalyst switches are ideal for the **access** and **distribution** layers of the network, providing high performance and flexibility for growing network environments. Whether you are expanding the number of users, devices, or applications on your network, Cisco Catalyst solutions offer scalability, advanced features, and support for future growth.

Key Features for Scalability:

- **Modular and Stackable Design**: Cisco Catalyst switches offer modular designs, allowing businesses to expand their network without replacing existing hardware. For example, the **Catalyst 9000** series supports **stacking**, enabling multiple switches to operate as a single logical unit, simplifying management while increasing capacity.
- **PoE+ (Power over Ethernet)**: With the ability to deliver power to devices such as IP phones, wireless access points, and cameras, Catalyst switches provide the flexibility to scale your network's edge devices without the need for additional power infrastructure.
- **Support for Multigigabit Ethernet (mGig)**: As businesses adopt higher-speed applications like video streaming and cloud services, **multigigabit** Ethernet ports on Catalyst switches support speeds of 2.5G, 5G, or 10G, ensuring your network can handle future bandwidth demands.
- **Advanced Security Features**: As networks scale, maintaining security becomes increasingly important. Cisco Catalyst switches integrate **Cisco Identity Services Engine (ISE)**, **802.1X authentication**, and **MACsec encryption** to secure user and device access while enabling network scalability.

Cisco Catalyst switches are designed for **flexible scaling**, allowing businesses to increase capacity as needed without disrupting operations. For large campuses or data centers, scaling can be done by adding additional stackable switches or using **Virtual Switching System (VSS)** technology to support high availability and better resource management.

2. Cisco Nexus Series: Scalable Core and Data Center Networks

The **Cisco Nexus Series** of switches is designed for data centers and large-scale enterprise networks, offering exceptional scalability and performance. With the increase in cloud services, virtualization, and massive data growth, the core and data center layers of enterprise networks require robust solutions that can handle high volumes of traffic without sacrificing performance or reliability.

Key Features for Scalability:

- **High-Density Ports**: The Cisco Nexus 9000 series switches are designed with high-density 10/40/100GbE ports, making them ideal for large-scale environments like **data centers** or high-performance compute clusters. This provides the capacity to handle massive data flows that are common in cloud environments, large campuses, and enterprise networks.
- **NX-OS Operating System**: Cisco's **NX-OS** is a robust, high-performance operating system built for scalability, offering features such as **virtualization**, **automation**, and **multitenancy**, which are critical for scalable data center networks.
- **Clos Fabric Architecture**: The Nexus series supports **Clos fabric architecture**, which is designed to optimize traffic flow and reduce congestion by using multiple paths for data, ensuring consistent performance as traffic demands increase. This is particularly important for **leaf-spine** designs in modern data center networks, allowing for easy scaling without bottlenecks.
- **Virtual Port Channels (vPC)**: Cisco Nexus supports **vPC** technology, which allows for the aggregation of links across two Nexus switches to provide active-active forwarding, increasing fault tolerance while simplifying network scaling.

With Cisco Nexus solutions, businesses can scale their data center networks quickly, securely, and with minimal disruption to existing operations. These solutions are optimized for **high-performance computing, cloud infrastructure**, and **enterprise applications** that demand flexible, reliable connectivity.

3. Cisco SD-WAN: Scalable Wide Area Network (WAN) Connectivity

With the rise of cloud computing, mobile devices, and remote work, businesses are increasingly looking for ways to extend their networks beyond the traditional perimeter. Cisco **SD-WAN** (Software-Defined WAN) provides a scalable solution for connecting branch offices, remote workers, and cloud applications, while maintaining performance, security, and flexibility across the WAN.

Key Features for Scalability:

- **Centralized Management**: Cisco SD-WAN allows businesses to centrally manage and orchestrate wide-area network configurations, ensuring that as new locations or devices are added, they can be easily integrated into the network.
- **Dynamic Path Selection**: Cisco SD-WAN uses dynamic path selection to route traffic based on real-time performance metrics. This ensures that critical applications have access to the optimal network path, improving performance and ensuring scalability as demand grows.
- **Cloud and Hybrid WAN Support**: Cisco SD-WAN is ideal for businesses adopting **cloud-first** strategies. The solution supports a hybrid WAN model that can seamlessly connect branch offices to both private MPLS networks and public internet connections, offering scalability for global networks without relying on expensive MPLS links.
- **Zero-Touch Provisioning**: With zero-touch provisioning, new branches and remote locations can be added to the network quickly, reducing the time and complexity involved in network expansion.

Cisco SD-WAN is an ideal solution for organizations with distributed branches, cloud services, and remote users who need secure, reliable, and scalable connectivity across wide-area networks.

4. Cisco Meraki: Cloud-Managed Networking for Scalable Edge Connectivity

Cisco Meraki is a cloud-managed networking solution that is ideal for organizations seeking scalable, easy-to-manage network infrastructure for their **branch offices, retail locations**, and **remote work environments**. Meraki products—ranging from wireless access points to security appliances and switches—are designed for **scalability** while being simple to deploy and manage through a centralized cloud dashboard.

Key Features for Scalability:

- **Cloud Management**: Meraki's cloud-managed approach allows network administrators to scale the network quickly by deploying devices to new locations and managing them centrally through the Meraki dashboard. This centralized control simplifies network administration and allows businesses to expand their networks without complex configurations.
- **Instant Deployment**: Meraki devices can be deployed in minutes using **zero-touch provisioning**, enabling businesses to scale by adding new devices (access points, switches, firewalls) quickly without requiring on-site IT expertise.
- **Scalable Wireless Networks**: Cisco Meraki offers high-density **wireless access points** that support modern Wi-Fi standards such as **Wi-Fi 6 (802.11ax)**, allowing organizations to scale wireless connectivity to accommodate growing numbers of devices.
- **Integrated Security**: Cisco Meraki integrates advanced security features, including **firewall protection, intrusion detection, content filtering**, and **VPN support**, ensuring that scalable network expansions remain secure.

Meraki is particularly well-suited for organizations with multiple branches, remote offices, or those using cloud-based applications. Its ease of deployment and centralized management capabilities make it a powerful tool for scaling networks at the edge, ensuring consistent performance and security as the business grows.

5. Cisco ACI (Application Centric Infrastructure): Scalable Data Center Automation

Cisco's **ACI** (Application Centric Infrastructure) is an architecture that integrates **software-defined networking (SDN)** with network infrastructure, providing a highly scalable solution for data center networks. ACI is designed to simplify network operations and automate provisioning, which is essential for large-scale data centers that need to quickly adapt to changing demands.

Key Features for Scalability:

- **Automation and Orchestration**: ACI automates network provisioning, configuration, and management, enabling faster, more scalable deployments. With **ACI fabric**, businesses can scale their data center networks efficiently, applying policies and configurations automatically to all devices within the fabric.
- **Policy-Driven Architecture**: ACI's policy-driven model allows businesses to scale their networks by defining business policies (e.g., security, bandwidth, and application priority) that automatically apply as the network grows, ensuring that the performance and security requirements are consistently met.
- **Application-Centric Design**: Cisco ACI's focus on applications ensures that network resources are allocated dynamically based on application demand, improving the scalability of critical applications and services.

Cisco ACI is perfect for **large-scale data centers, multi-cloud environments**, and **enterprises with complex application requirements**. Its programmability, automation, and scalability make it an ideal solution for growing network infrastructures.

Scalable networks are no longer a luxury—they are a necessity for businesses looking to stay competitive in an increasingly connected, data-driven world. Cisco's suite of solutions, including **Catalyst**, **Nexus**, **SD-WAN**, **Meraki**, and **ACI**, provide the tools and technologies needed to build scalable, high-performance networks that can evolve with changing business demands. By leveraging Cisco's innovations in **automation**, **cloud management**, **load balancing**, and **redundancy**, organizations can expand their networks seamlessly and cost-effectively, ensuring that their IT infrastructure remains agile and resilient as they grow. Whether you are scaling the access layer with Catalyst, extending the WAN with SD-WAN, or automating the data center with ACI, Cisco provides the comprehensive solutions needed to meet the demands of a scalable, modern enterprise network.

Case Study: Scaling a Global Enterprise Network with Cisco

In this case study, we will explore how a global enterprise can leverage Cisco's solutions to scale its network infrastructure across multiple regions, improving performance, security, and operational efficiency. As businesses expand across geographies and digital services increase, their networks must evolve to meet higher demands. A scalable network design becomes a key enabler for maintaining agility, reducing operational complexity, and ensuring consistent service delivery worldwide.

In this scenario, we focus on a fictional **global enterprise** called **Globex Corp.**, which operates in over 30 countries. With a growing number of employees, expanding cloud services, and an increasing reliance on real-time data, Globex Corp. faces the challenge of scaling its network infrastructure to support its global operations.

We will examine the steps taken by Globex Corp. to design, deploy, and scale their network with Cisco solutions, with particular emphasis on **Cisco SD-WAN**, **Cisco Meraki**, **Cisco ACI**, and **Cisco Catalyst and Nexus** switches. We will also explore the role of **automation**, **cloud integration**, and **network segmentation** in building a future-proof, scalable enterprise network.

1. The Challenge: Scaling the Network for Global Operations

Globex Corp. started as a small regional company but has grown rapidly over the past decade. As the company expanded its operations internationally, it faced several networking challenges:

- **Disparate Networks**: With offices in multiple regions, each location had a different set of networking technologies and configurations. There was no consistent standard across the company's global network, leading to inefficiencies and performance bottlenecks.
- **Increased Cloud Adoption**: As Globex Corp. moved more applications and services to the cloud, the company needed to ensure that remote locations and branch offices had reliable, high-speed access to cloud-based resources.
- **WAN Limitations**: The company's reliance on expensive MPLS circuits for wide-area connectivity was limiting the flexibility and scalability of the network. WAN congestion and network latency were increasingly becoming issues as more users and devices connected remotely.
- **Security and Compliance**: With offices in various countries, Globex Corp. needed to ensure compliance with local data privacy laws and enhance security across a vast, distributed network.

Given these challenges, the company needed a solution that could scale the network efficiently, reduce costs, improve performance, and ensure secure connectivity across regions, all while being easy to manage from a centralized point.

2. Cisco Solutions for Scaling a Global Network

To meet its growing demands, Globex Corp. turned to Cisco's suite of solutions, with a particular focus on **Cisco SD-WAN, Meraki cloud management, Cisco ACI for data center networking**, and **Cisco Catalyst and Nexus switches**. By leveraging these technologies, the company was able to implement a **scalable, reliable, and secure network architecture** that would support its global operations and growth for years to come.

Cisco SD-WAN for WAN Optimization and Flexibility

The first step in scaling the network was to address the limitations of the company's existing **WAN** infrastructure. Globex Corp. had been relying heavily on **MPLS** links for connecting its branch offices to headquarters and cloud resources, but the high cost and limited flexibility of MPLS were becoming significant barriers to scaling the network. Additionally, the MPLS links were not ideal for the increasing volume of cloud-based applications.

- **Solution**: **Cisco SD-WAN** was chosen to replace MPLS and provide greater flexibility, cost-effectiveness, and improved performance across the wide-area network. With SD-WAN, Globex Corp. could route traffic across multiple WAN connections, including broadband internet, LTE, and MPLS, without compromising on security or performance.
- **Benefits**:
- **Cost Efficiency**: By leveraging broadband internet and LTE connections as part of the SD-WAN design, Globex Corp. reduced its reliance on costly MPLS circuits, cutting WAN costs by 30%.
- **Dynamic Path Selection**: Cisco SD-WAN automatically routes traffic over the best-performing path in real-time, ensuring low

latency for critical applications and better performance for cloud services.
- **Centralized Management**: The SD-WAN solution was centrally managed via the **Cisco vManage** dashboard, which enabled the network operations team to monitor and manage traffic, configure policies, and apply security controls across all locations from a single interface.
- **Scalability**: As new branch offices were added, Cisco SD-WAN provided the flexibility to scale the WAN quickly, allowing for seamless integration of new sites without the need for complex configurations.

Cisco Meraki for Scalable, Cloud-Managed Edge Networking

Globex Corp. needed a solution that would allow them to scale and manage the network at the edge, particularly as the company continued to expand its remote work model and opened new branch offices around the world. **Cisco Meraki**, with its cloud-managed approach to networking, was the ideal choice for managing edge devices like wireless access points, switches, and security appliances.

- **Solution**: The company deployed **Meraki access points** to provide high-performance Wi-Fi in branch offices, **Meraki switches** to connect end-user devices, and **Meraki security appliances** to protect the network and ensure secure remote access.
- **Benefits**:
- **Zero-Touch Provisioning**: New offices and remote locations could be brought online quickly, with devices shipped pre-configured to be easily deployed and managed remotely via the **Meraki dashboard**.
- **Centralized Cloud Management**: All network devices were managed from a centralized cloud interface, making it easy to apply consistent configurations, monitor network health, and enforce security policies across a growing global network.
- **Scalable Wireless Networks**: As the company expanded, the Meraki

Wi-Fi 6 access points allowed Globex Corp. to scale its wireless network to accommodate growing numbers of devices and increasing bandwidth demands in crowded office environments.
- **Security and Compliance**: Meraki's **advanced security features** such as **site-to-site VPN**, **content filtering**, and **advanced firewall protection** helped ensure that remote offices and branch locations were secure and compliant with regional regulations.

Cisco ACI for Data Center Scalability and Automation

As Globex Corp. continued to grow, the company's data center infrastructure also needed to scale to meet increasing demands. The company relied on its data centers to host core applications, services, and customer data. The complexity of managing network policies, traffic flow, and security at the data center layer was becoming a challenge.

- **Solution**: **Cisco ACI** (Application Centric Infrastructure) was deployed in the company's primary data centers to automate network provisioning and management, providing the scalability needed to accommodate more applications and services.
- **Benefits**:
- **Automation**: Cisco ACI automated network provisioning, which allowed the network team to deploy new applications and services faster. ACI also simplified the management of complex network policies across multiple data centers.
- **Policy-Driven Architecture**: With **policy-based management**, Globex Corp. could define business policies (such as application priorities, security settings, and traffic routing) that were automatically enforced throughout the entire data center network.
- **Seamless Cloud Integration**: Cisco ACI's integration with **public cloud platforms** enabled Globex Corp. to extend its network seamlessly to hybrid cloud environments, ensuring consistent performance and security across on-premises and cloud resources.

Cisco Catalyst and Nexus Switches for Scalable Core and Access Layers

Globex Corp. deployed **Cisco Catalyst 9000 series switches** at the **distribution and access layers** to provide high-performance, secure connectivity across its offices. For the **core layer** of the network, **Cisco Nexus switches** were used to handle high-density, high-bandwidth requirements and ensure that the network could scale to accommodate future growth.

- **Solution**: Cisco Catalyst switches were deployed in regional offices and branch locations, while Nexus switches were used in the data center and core layers of the network.
- **Benefits**:
- **Stackable and Modular Design**: The Catalyst 9000 switches allowed Globex Corp. to add additional capacity as needed without disrupting operations, while the **modular design** of Nexus switches provided flexibility for future upgrades.
- **High-Speed Connectivity**: The **10GbE** and **40GbE** ports on the Nexus switches ensured the core network could handle increasing data traffic without bottlenecks, providing high-speed connectivity to data centers, remote offices, and cloud platforms.
- **Security and Segmentation**: Cisco's **TrustSec** and **Segmentation** technologies helped the company implement secure segmentation policies to protect sensitive data and ensure compliance across various regions and regulatory environments.

3. Results: A Scalable, Secure, and Efficient Global Network

After implementing Cisco's suite of solutions, Globex Corp. achieved the following results:

- **Cost Savings**: By replacing MPLS circuits with SD-WAN, the company reduced its WAN costs by 30% while maintaining high

performance and flexibility.
- **Improved Performance**: SD-WAN provided dynamic path selection and intelligent traffic routing, ensuring that users had optimal access to cloud applications and internal resources, even as the network expanded globally.
- **Simplified Network Management**: Cisco Meraki's cloud-managed platform allowed the company to scale its network easily, with centralized control over devices, security, and configurations across offices worldwide.
- **Greater Security**: With the integration of Meraki security appliances, Cisco ACI's policy-driven architecture, and SD-WAN's encrypted connections, Globex Corp. was able to enhance its network security and ensure compliance with local regulations.
- **Scalability for the Future**: The modular nature of Cisco's solutions, including the Catalyst and Nexus switches, as well as Cisco ACI's data center automation, positioned the company to continue expanding its network in the years ahead without the need for a complete redesign.

This case study demonstrates how **Cisco's solutions**, such as **SD-WAN, Meraki, ACI**, and **Catalyst/Nexus switches**, can help organizations scale their networks efficiently and securely. By leveraging Cisco's comprehensive portfolio, Globex Corp. was able to meet the demands of a rapidly growing, global enterprise network while improving performance, reducing costs, and ensuring robust security. Whether for branch office expansion, cloud adoption, or data center scalability, Cisco's solutions provide the flexibility, automation, and security needed for the modern enterprise network.

Optimizing Data Traffic Flow

Network Traffic Patterns and Bottlenecks

In modern enterprise networks, optimizing data traffic flow is crucial for ensuring efficient communication, maintaining high performance, and delivering seamless user experiences. As organizations increasingly rely on data-driven applications, cloud-based services, and real-time communications, understanding network traffic patterns and identifying potential bottlenecks becomes a vital aspect of network design and management. By recognizing and addressing these bottlenecks, network administrators can improve overall network efficiency, enhance productivity, and reduce costs associated with performance degradation or downtime.

This section delves into the intricacies of **network traffic patterns**, their impact on network performance, and how to identify and mitigate **traffic bottlenecks**. We'll explore common traffic behaviors, the causes of bottlenecks, and best practices for optimizing data traffic flow. Furthermore, we'll look at how **Cisco's network optimization solutions**, including **QoS (Quality of Service)**, **Traffic Shaping**, and **Load Balancing**, can help mitigate bottlenecks and enhance network performance.

1. *Understanding Network Traffic Patterns*

Before diving into bottlenecks and optimization strategies, it's essential to understand the various types of **network traffic patterns** that affect data flow across the network. Network traffic patterns describe the way data moves through a network, the direction it flows, and the intensity of the traffic load at any given time.

Types of Network Traffic

Network traffic can generally be categorized into three main types:

- **Unicast Traffic**: This refers to data sent from one source to one destination, typically used in client-server communications or between network devices. Most enterprise network traffic is unicast, such as requests from a user's device to access a web application hosted on a server.
- **Multicast Traffic**: This type of traffic is sent from one source to multiple destinations. It is commonly used for streaming media, live events, video conferencing, or multicast DNS services. Multicast traffic requires special network protocols to ensure data is efficiently delivered to all intended recipients without overloading the network.
- **Broadcast Traffic**: Broadcast traffic is sent from one source to all devices on the network. While broadcast traffic is useful for certain types of discovery services (such as DHCP or ARP), it can quickly consume bandwidth if not carefully managed, especially in large networks.

Traffic Flow Patterns

Understanding how traffic flows across the network is fundamental for identifying potential bottlenecks. Here are the key traffic flow patterns:

- **Local Traffic**: This traffic stays within a local network or LAN (Local Area Network) and does not traverse wide-area networks (WANs). Local traffic patterns are typically more predictable and easier to

optimize since it is confined to fewer devices and network segments.
- **Remote Traffic**: Traffic that traverses from a local network to a remote network, often involving a WAN or cloud infrastructure. Remote traffic typically has higher latency, and its flow needs to be carefully managed to avoid congestion or slowdowns.
- **Asymmetric Traffic**: This occurs when data flows predominantly in one direction, for example, when a server sends large amounts of data to multiple clients (download-centric applications). This type of traffic can create significant load on upstream or core network links, potentially causing bottlenecks if not appropriately balanced.
- **Symmetric Traffic**: Symmetric traffic refers to balanced data flow between the source and destination. Common in applications such as video conferencing or collaborative file sharing, symmetric traffic demands equal bandwidth in both directions and can cause congestion if the network is not properly provisioned.
- **Bursty Traffic**: Some applications generate traffic in bursts, with periods of low activity followed by sudden spikes. **Video streaming** or **large file transfers** are typical examples of bursty traffic. Such spikes can overwhelm network resources if not managed effectively, especially if the network lacks sufficient bandwidth during peak demand periods.

2. Identifying Network Traffic Bottlenecks

A **network bottleneck** occurs when a specific point in the network (e.g., a device, link, or segment) becomes overloaded with traffic, slowing down data transmission and causing delays. Bottlenecks can arise in various places across the network and can significantly impact performance and user experience. The ability to identify and address these bottlenecks is critical for maintaining a high-performance network.

Common Causes of Bottlenecks

- **Limited Bandwidth**: One of the most common causes of network bottlenecks is insufficient bandwidth. If network links (such as a WAN connection or internal link between switches) are unable to handle the volume of data being transmitted, traffic is forced to queue, leading to delays. Bandwidth limitations are particularly noticeable during peak usage times or when a new application demands more resources than are available.

- **Network Congestion**: Congestion occurs when the volume of traffic exceeds the capacity of the network infrastructure. This can happen due to the overloading of routers, switches, or links with more data than they can handle. Congestion often leads to **packet loss**, **latency**, and **jitter**—all of which degrade application performance.
- **Latency and High Round-Trip Times**: **Latency** refers to the delay between sending a packet and receiving a response. Long latency can occur due to the physical distance between endpoints, network devices with limited processing power, or inefficient routing. Applications sensitive to delay, such as VoIP or online gaming, are significantly affected by high latency and may exhibit poor performance when bottlenecks occur in the network path.
- **Insufficient Processing Power**: Devices such as routers, firewalls, and switches have finite processing power. When network traffic is high, or when security protocols (such as deep packet inspection or encryption) are applied, these devices may struggle to keep up, leading to bottlenecks. Insufficient CPU or memory resources on networking devices can also cause delays in packet forwarding.
- **Misconfigured Network Devices**: Incorrect configurations on switches, routers, or firewalls can introduce bottlenecks. For example, **incorrect Quality of Service (QoS)** settings may prioritize less-critical traffic over more important business-critical applications, causing delays in the transmission of important data.
- **Network Interface Saturation**: When a network interface (e.g., a server's NIC, router port, or switch port) becomes saturated with traffic, it cannot process additional packets, causing delays and packet loss. This is common in data-intensive applications such as file

transfers or video streaming, where high throughput demands can quickly saturate an interface if not properly provisioned.
- **Suboptimal Routing**: Inefficient or suboptimal routing, especially in complex network topologies, can cause longer path lengths for data. This increases network latency and exacerbates congestion on certain links or network segments. Poorly designed routing protocols or misconfigured routing tables are often responsible for such bottlenecks.

3. Best Practices for Optimizing Data Traffic Flow

Once the causes of bottlenecks are identified, network engineers can implement best practices to optimize traffic flow and alleviate congestion. Several techniques can be employed to ensure data is transmitted efficiently across the network.

Quality of Service (QoS) for Prioritization

QoS is a key mechanism for optimizing traffic flow by ensuring that high-priority applications receive the necessary bandwidth and low-latency access they require to function optimally. By classifying and marking network traffic based on its priority, QoS allows administrators to enforce traffic policies that prioritize mission-critical applications over less important traffic.

- **Implement Traffic Classes**: Define traffic classes based on application types (e.g., VoIP, video, HTTP) and allocate different levels of service to each class. High-priority applications like VoIP and video conferencing should be given priority over bulk traffic like file transfers or backup operations.
- **Apply Traffic Policing**: Traffic policing can be used to control traffic flow by limiting the bandwidth allocated to certain types of traffic or by discarding excess traffic. For example, during peak periods, non-essential applications may have their bandwidth throttled to ensure mission-critical applications are not impacted.

- **Configure Buffering and Queueing**: Implement buffer management strategies to store packets temporarily during periods of congestion. **Queueing** allows high-priority packets to be processed first, while lower-priority traffic is held in a separate queue, helping to avoid packet loss and delays.

Traffic Shaping and Load Balancing

- **Traffic Shaping**: Traffic shaping smooths out bursty traffic patterns by delaying the transmission of non-essential traffic during periods of congestion. This helps in balancing the flow of traffic and prevents sudden spikes from overwhelming the network.
- **Load Balancing**: **Load balancing** distributes incoming traffic across multiple servers, links, or network paths, preventing any single device or link from becoming overloaded. Load balancing can be done at the application level (e.g., DNS load balancing) or at the network level (e.g., link load balancing using ECMP or **Equal-Cost Multi-Path** routing).

Network Segmentation and Redundancy

- **Network Segmentation**: Divide the network into smaller segments or subnets to reduce the impact of local bottlenecks and contain traffic flows. For example, separating traffic into **VLANs** (Virtual Local Area Networks) allows you to isolate broadcast traffic and prioritize critical data streams.
- **Redundancy and Failover**: Design the network with redundancy in mind to avoid single points of failure. Using **dual links**, **redundant routers**, and **failover mechanisms** ensures that traffic can still flow even if a network device or link becomes congested or fails.

4. Cisco Solutions for Optimizing Traffic Flow

Cisco offers a range of technologies that can help organizations optimize data traffic flow and address bottlenecks:

- **Cisco SD-WAN**: Optimizes WAN traffic by selecting the best available path for each application based on real-time performance data. SD-WAN reduces latency and congestion by dynamically routing traffic over the most efficient path, whether it's

MPLS, broadband, or LTE.

- **Cisco Meraki**: Provides centralized traffic management with deep visibility into network traffic patterns. With Meraki's cloud-based dashboard, network administrators can easily apply QoS policies and monitor application performance to optimize data flow.
- **Cisco Catalyst and Nexus Switches**: Offer advanced features like traffic shaping, QoS, and load balancing. These switches provide the scalability needed to handle high volumes of traffic and optimize traffic flow within both campus and data center networks.
- **Cisco ACI**: Application Centric Infrastructure (ACI) automates network provisioning and traffic management in data centers, enabling more efficient data flow and reducing bottlenecks in the data center core.

Optimizing data traffic flow is essential for ensuring a network performs efficiently, especially in modern enterprises where the demands on bandwidth and real-time communication continue to grow. By understanding **network traffic patterns** and the causes of **bottlenecks**, network professionals can identify weaknesses in their network infrastructure and apply the right techniques to improve performance. Cisco's **SD-WAN**,

Meraki, **ACI**, and **Catalyst/Nexus switches** provide powerful tools for optimizing traffic flow, enabling businesses to scale efficiently, reduce latency, and enhance overall network performance. Through careful traffic management, proactive network design, and the right solutions, organizations can ensure that their networks run smoothly, even as they grow.

Quality of Service (QoS) for Traffic Prioritization

In the world of network management, **Quality of Service (QoS)** plays a pivotal role in ensuring that critical data traffic is delivered with the appropriate level of priority and reliability. QoS refers to a set of technologies and practices that manage and control the flow of data across a network, enabling prioritization of certain types of traffic, reducing delays, and ensuring optimal performance for high-priority applications. With the increasing reliance on applications that demand low latency and high bandwidth (such as VoIP, video conferencing, and cloud services), understanding and implementing QoS has become an essential task for network administrators.

This section will explore how QoS works, why it is important, and how to implement it effectively in a Cisco-based network. We'll cover the various techniques and tools used in QoS, such as **traffic classification**, **marking**, **queuing**, **traffic shaping**, and **policing**, and discuss how these can be utilized to ensure the right level of service for different types of traffic.

1. What is QoS and Why Is It Important?

Quality of Service (QoS) is a set of techniques used to manage network resources by prioritizing certain types of traffic, controlling bandwidth, minimizing latency, and reducing packet loss. The goal of QoS is to ensure that critical traffic, such as voice or video, gets preferential treatment over less time-sensitive traffic like email or file downloads. By managing network traffic, QoS helps prevent congestion, ensures network stability, and improves the user experience for performance-sensitive applications.

In an enterprise network, the demand for bandwidth is constantly growing. **Cloud applications**, **video conferencing**, and **collaboration tools** all require real-time, high-priority traffic to function effectively. Meanwhile, less critical services (like email or file transfers) do not need the same level of priority. Without proper QoS implementation, networks may experience congestion, high latency, jitter, or even packet loss, resulting in a poor user experience or failure of mission-critical applications.

QoS allows administrators to:

- **Guarantee bandwidth** for high-priority applications (e.g., VoIP, video calls).
- **Minimize delays and jitter** for real-time traffic.
- **Control congestion** by managing traffic during peak usage.
- **Ensure fair resource allocation** across different applications and users.
- **Prevent packet loss**, particularly for critical data flows.

2. Key QoS Concepts and Terminology

To effectively configure and implement QoS in a network, it's essential to understand the fundamental concepts and terminology that form the backbone of QoS management. These include traffic classification, traffic marking, scheduling, and policing.

Traffic Classification

Traffic classification is the process of categorizing network traffic based on its type and the needs of the application. By classifying traffic, network devices can treat different types of traffic according to their specific requirements. Classification is typically performed by examining packet headers and matching them to predefined policies or rules.

- **Layer 3 classification**: Uses the **IP address**, **protocol type**, or **port number** in the packet's IP header to classify traffic.
- **Layer 2 classification**: Relies on **MAC addresses** or **VLAN tags** in Ethernet frames to identify and classify traffic.

Traffic Marking

Once traffic is classified, it must be marked so that network devices (like routers and switches) can distinguish between different traffic classes. The most common method for marking packets is through the use of **Differentiated Services Code Point (DSCP)** values in the packet's IP header.

- **DSCP**: The DSCP field in the IP header (6 bits) is used to mark packets for QoS handling. Different DSCP values represent different priority levels, allowing devices to easily identify which packets are high priority (e.g., real-time voice or video) and which are lower priority (e.g., bulk data transfer).
- **IP Precedence**: An older method for marking traffic, with 3 bits available to prioritize traffic. While still in use, DSCP has largely replaced IP Precedence.

Queuing

After classification and marking, packets are placed into different queues based on their priority. The network devices then use **scheduling algorithms** to decide which packet to forward next. Packets in high-priority queues are transmitted first, while packets in lower-priority queues may experience delays, especially during periods of congestion.

- **FIFO (First-In-First-Out)**: A simple queuing mechanism where packets are forwarded in the order they arrive. This method does not prioritize traffic and is typically not ideal for QoS, as all packets are treated equally.
- **Priority Queuing (PQ)**: In priority queuing, traffic is divided into

multiple queues based on priority. High-priority traffic (e.g., VoIP) is placed in a queue that is serviced first, while lower-priority traffic is delayed or dropped when congestion occurs.
- **Class-Based Weighted Fair Queuing (CBWFQ)**: This is a more sophisticated approach where traffic is classified into different classes, and each class is given a portion of the available bandwidth. Within each class, traffic is treated according to its importance.

Traffic Shaping and Policing

- **Traffic Shaping**: Traffic shaping smooths out traffic flows by buffering packets and adjusting the rate at which packets are transmitted. It is typically used to prevent congestion by ensuring that data is sent at a consistent, manageable rate. Shaping is particularly useful for applications with bursty traffic patterns, as it helps prevent sudden spikes from overwhelming the network.
- **Traffic Policing**: Policing is used to monitor traffic flow and enforce traffic profiles by either **dropping packets** that exceed certain thresholds or **marking** them for lower priority handling. For instance, if a particular application exceeds its allocated bandwidth, policing can drop excessive packets, ensuring that the overall network performance remains stable.

3. Cisco QoS Solutions and Tools

Cisco provides a wide range of tools and features that enable network administrators to implement QoS effectively. These tools are designed to help prioritize traffic, manage bandwidth, and ensure the smooth operation of real-time applications.

Cisco IOS QoS Features

Cisco's **IOS (Internetwork Operating System)** provides a rich set of QoS features that can be configured on Cisco routers and switches. Key IOS QoS features include:

- **QoS Policies**: Network administrators can create policies that define how traffic should be treated based on various parameters such as application type, source/destination IP addresses, and DSCP markings.
- **Congestion Management**: Cisco devices support multiple queuing techniques, including **WFQ (Weighted Fair Queuing)** and **CBWFQ**, to ensure fair distribution of bandwidth during congestion.
- **Traffic Policing and Shaping**: Cisco IOS allows network admins to set traffic limits for different applications and users, ensuring fair bandwidth allocation and reducing congestion. Policies can be defined to **police** traffic based on rate limits or **shape** traffic to smooth bursts.
- **Network-Based Application Recognition (NBAR)**: NBAR is a feature that identifies and classifies network traffic at a deep level, allowing QoS policies to be applied more accurately to specific applications (e.g., video, VoIP, or file sharing).

Cisco Catalyst Switches and QoS

Cisco's **Catalyst** switches, particularly those designed for enterprise campuses, are equipped with robust QoS capabilities. These switches support advanced **queue scheduling**, **traffic shaping**, and **marking** features that help optimize traffic flow within local area networks (LANs).

- **Layer 2 and Layer 3 QoS**: Cisco Catalyst switches support both Layer 2 (Ethernet) and Layer 3 (IP) QoS mechanisms, allowing administrators to apply different QoS policies depending on the traffic type and network layer.
- **Multicast QoS**: Cisco supports advanced QoS for multicast traffic, ensuring that video or other multicast-based services are delivered without unnecessary delays or jitter.

Cisco SD-WAN and QoS

Cisco's **SD-WAN (Software-Defined Wide Area Network)** solution also includes advanced QoS capabilities that allow administrators to prioritize and optimize application traffic over WAN links. By using **application-aware routing**, SD-WAN automatically identifies and routes traffic based on its performance requirements. This dynamic approach enables better performance for critical applications, while balancing load across available WAN paths.

- **Dynamic Path Control**: SD-WAN can automatically select the optimal path for traffic, ensuring that latency-sensitive traffic (such as VoIP or video conferencing) uses the best available link, whether it's MPLS, broadband, or LTE.
- **End-to-End QoS**: Through SD-WAN, Cisco enables consistent QoS policies across both **branch offices** and **data centers**, ensuring that mission-critical applications receive the required level of performance no matter where the user is located.

4. Best Practices for Implementing QoS

When implementing QoS in a Cisco network, several best practices can ensure effective prioritization and traffic management:

- **Define Clear Traffic Classes**: Before configuring QoS, define which types of traffic are most critical to your organization (e.g., VoIP, video conferencing, cloud applications) and assign them appropriate priority levels.
- **Start Simple, Then Scale**: Begin with basic QoS policies and expand them as the network grows. For example, start by prioritizing voice traffic and then extend QoS policies to include other critical applications like video and real-time data.
- **Monitor Network Traffic**: Continuously monitor network performance to ensure that QoS policies are being applied effectively and that there are no unexpected bottlenecks or delays.
- **Ensure Consistency Across the Network**: Apply consistent QoS

policies across all network devices to ensure seamless traffic management from end to end. This includes routers, switches, firewalls, and SD-WAN devices.
- **Test and Validate QoS Configuration**: After implementing QoS, run tests to validate that high-priority applications are receiving the necessary bandwidth and low-latency paths, and that low-priority traffic is appropriately delayed or dropped when needed.

In an era where real-time applications and cloud-based services are integral to business operations, **Quality of Service (QoS)** is essential for maintaining high network performance. By prioritizing critical traffic and efficiently managing network resources, organizations can ensure that applications like VoIP, video conferencing, and cloud services perform optimally, even under heavy load. Cisco's advanced QoS tools and technologies, such as **IOS QoS features**, **Catalyst switches**, and **SD-WAN**, provide comprehensive solutions to optimize traffic flow, reduce latency, and enhance overall network efficiency. By implementing QoS best practices, businesses can ensure that their networks remain responsive, reliable, and ready to meet the demands of the modern enterprise.

VLANs for Logical Network Segmentation

In modern networking, **Virtual Local Area Networks (VLANs)** have become a cornerstone for effective network management and security. VLANs allow for the logical segmentation of a physical network, enabling the creation of distinct broadcast domains within a single switched network. This segmentation enhances performance, security, and traffic management by isolating different types of traffic and grouping users or devices according to organizational needs, rather than physical location.

In this section, we'll explore the concept of VLANs in-depth, discuss their key benefits, and explain how they can be leveraged in Cisco environments for efficient network segmentation. We'll also examine practical use cases, best practices, and how Cisco devices and technologies can simplify the configuration and management of VLANs.

1. What is a VLAN?

A **Virtual Local Area Network (VLAN)** is a logical grouping of network devices, regardless of their physical location, that allows them to communicate as if they were on the same physical LAN. Essentially, VLANs break a large broadcast domain into smaller, more manageable ones, allowing administrators to control how traffic flows between different parts of the network.

VLANs are created by assigning a unique **VLAN ID (identifier)** to each logical network segment. This ID is used to tag network frames to ensure they belong to a specific VLAN. When a device sends a data frame, the VLAN ID is embedded in the frame header. Switches that support VLANs can use this information to forward the frame only to devices that are part of the same VLAN.

Key Features of VLANs:

- **Logical Network Segmentation**: VLANs segment a physical network into multiple logical networks, providing better control over traffic and reducing the impact of broadcast traffic.
- **Broadcast Control**: VLANs contain broadcast traffic within their own boundaries, meaning devices in one VLAN do not receive broadcast traffic from other VLANs.
- **Improved Security**: By isolating sensitive devices or data streams into their own VLANs, organizations can enforce security policies that limit access between VLANs.
- **Simplified Network Management**: VLANs make it easier to manage network traffic and ensure that resources are used efficiently, especially in large and complex network environments.

2. Benefits of VLANs in Network Design

VLANs offer a variety of benefits, especially when designing large-scale networks or managing diverse traffic types. Below are the primary advantages of VLAN implementation:

Traffic Segmentation and Isolation

VLANs provide logical separation of network traffic, ensuring that broadcast traffic from one VLAN does not propagate into another. This segmentation helps:

- Reduce unnecessary **broadcast traffic** that could otherwise consume bandwidth.
- Ensure that traffic from one department or group (e.g., HR or Finance) is not seen by other departments, thus **enhancing security**.
- Isolate certain types of traffic, such as **voice**, **video**, or **IoT**, to ensure they do not interfere with general data traffic, thus improving **network performance**.

Improved Security

By using VLANs to separate sensitive devices, systems, or applications from the general network, you can **limit access** to these critical systems. For example, placing critical systems like finance servers or databases on their own VLAN ensures that only authorized users or systems can communicate with them.

- VLANs help enforce security policies that control access between different parts of the network.
- By segmenting a network, it becomes harder for malicious users to penetrate entire networks, since compromising one VLAN doesn't automatically give attackers access to others.

Simplified Network Management

VLANs help reduce the complexity of managing large networks by organizing users into logical groups based on roles, departments, or types of devices. This approach offers better network flexibility and simplifies the task of:

- Assigning IP address schemes and subnets.
- Implementing **Quality of Service (QoS)** policies for specific applications or devices.
- **Troubleshooting and monitoring** network traffic and performance.

Additionally, VLANs allow administrators to make changes to network segmentation without physically moving devices, which is particularly useful in large office spaces or when employees move to different floors or buildings.

Optimized Performance and Scalability

Network performance can be significantly improved through the use of VLANs by limiting the size of broadcast domains. Broadcast traffic is confined to the VLAN in which it originated, preventing unnecessary traffic from spreading across the network.

Moreover, VLANs make networks **more scalable**. As the organization grows, administrators can simply add new VLANs for additional departments or functions, without needing to reconfigure the physical network.

3. Types of VLANs and Their Uses

Cisco supports several types of VLANs, each suited for different purposes within a network. Understanding the different VLAN types will help network administrators design the most effective network for their needs.

Data VLAN

The **Data VLAN**, often referred to as the **default VLAN**, is the most common type of VLAN used in enterprise networks. It is used for general data traffic and typically carries user traffic from applications like web browsing, file sharing, and email.

- **User access ports** on switches are typically assigned to the data VLAN.
- This VLAN is responsible for carrying the bulk of data traffic within the network.

Voice VLAN

A **Voice VLAN** is used to carry **Voice over IP (VoIP)** traffic. Since VoIP applications require consistent bandwidth and low latency, voice VLANs ensure that voice traffic is separated from general data traffic and given higher priority (through **QoS**).

- **Cisco IP phones** typically have ports configured for voice VLANs, allowing voice traffic to bypass congestion and improve call quality.
- Voice VLANs also allow network administrators to apply specific QoS settings to prioritize voice traffic over less-sensitive data traffic.

Management VLAN

The **Management VLAN** is used for managing network devices such as switches, routers, and wireless access points. All management traffic (e.g., configuration, monitoring, and troubleshooting) is carried over this VLAN, and it is usually **isolated** from user data traffic to enhance security.

- Administrators access the management VLAN remotely to configure network devices.
- It is important to secure the management VLAN by limiting access to trusted network devices.

Native VLAN

The **Native VLAN** is a special VLAN used in **802.1Q trunking**. In a trunk link, where multiple VLANs are carried over a single physical link, the native VLAN is the VLAN that carries untagged traffic. If a device sends traffic without a VLAN tag, the switch assigns that traffic to the native VLAN.

- **By default**, VLAN 1 is often assigned as the native VLAN.
- Security best practices suggest changing the native VLAN to another number to prevent potential attacks.

Private VLAN (PVLAN)

A **Private VLAN (PVLAN)** is a more advanced VLAN feature used to enhance security within a VLAN. PVLANs allow the isolation of devices within the same VLAN so that they cannot communicate directly with each other, but still can communicate with a **gateway** or external device.

- This is useful in scenarios where multiple devices in the same VLAN need access to a shared resource, such as a server, but should not be able to communicate directly with each other.

4. VLAN Trunking and Inter-VLAN Routing

To facilitate communication between VLANs, **VLAN trunking** and **Inter-VLAN routing** are necessary concepts to understand.

VLAN Trunking

VLAN trunking refers to the method of carrying multiple VLANs across a single physical link between switches or other network devices. The trunk link tags the traffic with VLAN information, allowing it to be forwarded to the correct VLAN. The most common trunking protocol is **IEEE 802.1Q**, which adds a tag to each Ethernet frame to identify the VLAN to which it belongs.

- **Trunk Ports**: These are the switch ports used to connect switches or network devices that need to carry traffic for multiple VLANs. Trunk ports are configured to pass traffic from multiple VLANs, as opposed to **access ports**, which belong to a single VLAN.

Inter-VLAN Routing

While VLANs allow devices within the same VLAN to communicate, devices in different VLANs require a routing device (router or Layer 3 switch) to facilitate communication between them. This is known as **Inter-VLAN routing**.

- **Router-on-a-Stick**: A common method where a router is connected to a switch via a single trunk link. The router uses sub-interfaces to route traffic between VLANs.
- **Layer 3 Switches**: Modern switches, such as the **Cisco Catalyst** series, can perform Layer 3 routing, allowing them to route traffic between VLANs without the need for a separate router.

5. Configuring VLANs in Cisco Networks

Configuring VLANs on Cisco devices, such as **Catalyst switches**, is a relatively straightforward process, but it requires a clear understanding of the network's requirements. Here are the basic steps for setting up VLANs on a Cisco switch:

Create VLANs: Use the vlan command in global configuration mode to define a new VLAN.

```bash
Switch(config)# vlan 10
Switch(config-vlan)# name HR
```

Assign VLANs to Switch Ports: Assign VLANs to specific ports on the switch, either as access or trunk ports.

```bash
Switch(config)# interface range fa0/1 - 24
Switch(config-if)# switchport mode access
```

```
Switch(config-if)# switchport access vlan 10
```

Configure Trunk Links: For links between switches that need to carry traffic for multiple VLANs, configure trunking.

```bash
Switch(config)# interface gig0/1
Switch(config-if)# switchport mode trunk
```

Virtual Local Area Networks (VLANs) are a powerful tool in network design, providing logical segmentation, enhanced security, and improved traffic management. By separating broadcast domains, VLANs help optimize network performance, reduce congestion, and improve security by isolating traffic based on organizational needs. Cisco offers a robust set of tools to configure and manage VLANs, allowing businesses to build scalable and secure networks that can grow with the demands of modern applications and services. Whether it's creating voice VLANs for high-priority traffic, using private VLANs for security, or leveraging inter-VLAN routing to enable communication across segments, VLANs are essential for efficient network design.

Traffic Shaping and Policing for Bandwidth Management

Effective bandwidth management is critical for maintaining network performance, especially as modern networks become increasingly complex and traffic-heavy. **Traffic shaping** and **traffic policing** are two fundamental techniques used to manage network bandwidth, control traffic flow, and ensure that high-priority applications receive the resources they need without causing congestion or disrupting lower-priority traffic.

In this section, we will explore the concepts of **traffic shaping** and **traffic policing**, how they differ, and how to use them in Cisco environments for optimal network performance. We will also discuss their practical applications, configurations, and best practices for managing network resources efficiently.

1. Understanding Traffic Shaping

Traffic shaping is a technique used to control the amount of traffic sent onto a network in a given period, typically by **smoothing out traffic bursts**. Rather than allowing traffic to be sent as quickly as possible, which could overwhelm network resources or cause congestion, traffic shaping adjusts the flow of traffic to ensure that it stays within acceptable limits and does not cause unnecessary network strain.

Traffic shaping is often applied to applications or traffic flows that exhibit **bursty** behavior, such as video conferencing, VoIP, or file transfers. Without traffic shaping, bursty traffic can cause network congestion, especially during peak times when the network is heavily utilized. Traffic shaping helps **limit the rate** at which traffic enters the network, ensuring that it adheres to an acceptable threshold.

How Traffic Shaping Works

Traffic shaping works by using **buffering** and **rate-limiting** techniques.

The traffic that exceeds the defined limit is queued in a buffer before it is sent out. The rate at which data is sent from the buffer is controlled, ensuring that the traffic is spread out more evenly over time. This helps reduce congestion and allows for more consistent network performance.

In Cisco devices, traffic shaping is typically implemented on **outgoing interfaces**, where the router or switch can buffer traffic before sending it out to the next hop. Cisco offers several tools to implement traffic shaping, including **Committed Access Rate (CAR)** and **Traffic Policing** mechanisms.

Key Components of Traffic Shaping

1. **Committed Information Rate (CIR)**: This is the target rate at which traffic should flow. It is the ideal rate that traffic is shaped to, ensuring that it does not exceed the capacity of the network link.
2. **Burst Rate**: The maximum rate at which traffic can exceed the CIR for short periods, typically in situations where bursts of traffic are unavoidable.
3. **Shaping Buffer**: Traffic that exceeds the CIR is placed in a buffer and delayed before transmission. The buffer size is critical in ensuring that there are no packet drops during peak traffic periods.
4. **Traffic Policing**: While traffic shaping helps smooth traffic, policing can be used to strictly enforce traffic rate limits and drop or remark excessive traffic.

Traffic Shaping in Cisco Devices

In Cisco networks, traffic shaping is typically configured using the **shape** command on **outgoing interfaces**. For example:

```bash
Router(config)# interface gigabitethernet 0/1
Router(config-if)# shape average 500000
```

In this example, traffic shaping is set to an average rate of 500,000 bits per second (500 Kbps), meaning that traffic will be limited to this rate, with any excess traffic queued and transmitted at the controlled rate.

2. Understanding Traffic Policing

Traffic policing is a technique used to enforce traffic rate limits by **monitoring incoming traffic** and either **discarding excess packets** or **remarking** the packets to a lower priority or different QoS level. Unlike traffic shaping, which smooths out traffic flow, traffic policing is more rigid—it is about enforcing a **maximum rate** for traffic, and any excess traffic above that rate is either dropped or marked for lower priority handling.

Traffic policing can be applied to both inbound and outbound traffic, depending on where the policy needs to be enforced. In Cisco devices, traffic policing is typically implemented using the **police** command, and it is often used for limiting traffic that exceeds a predefined rate.

How Traffic Policing Works

When traffic exceeds the defined rate, policing can take one of the following actions:

1. **Dropping Excess Traffic**: If the traffic rate exceeds the policy limit, the excess packets are simply discarded. This is a **hard limit** approach and is useful when excess traffic can be lost without affecting performance or user experience.
2. **Remarking Traffic**: Instead of discarding excess traffic, policing can **remark** the traffic to a lower priority level or different **DSCP** value. This is useful in scenarios where you want to enforce traffic limits but do not want to completely discard packets.
3. **Shaping the Excess Traffic**: In some cases, policing can also initiate traffic shaping for excess traffic, although this is not always the default behavior.

Key Components of Traffic Policing

OPTIMIZING DATA TRAFFIC FLOW

1. **Committed Information Rate (CIR)**: Similar to traffic shaping, CIR is the traffic rate at which the network should operate. This is the rate that the traffic is allowed to exceed without being marked or dropped.
2. **Excess Burst (Be)**: This defines the amount of traffic that can exceed the CIR for a short burst of time.
3. **Conforming Traffic**: Traffic that stays within the defined CIR is allowed through without modification.
4. **Non-Conforming Traffic**: Traffic that exceeds the CIR limit is either dropped or remarked, depending on the configured action.

Traffic Policing in Cisco Devices

To configure traffic policing in Cisco devices, the **police** command is used. For example:

```bash

Router(config)# class-map match-any voice-traffic
Router(config-cmap)# match ip dscp ef
Router(config-cmap)# exit

Router(config)# policy-map police-voice
Router(config-pmap)# class voice-traffic
Router(config-pmap-c)# police 1000000 8000 2000 conform-action transmit exceed-action drop
Router(config-pmap-c)# exit

Router(config)# interface gigabitethernet 0/1
Router(config-if)# service-policy input police-voice
```

In this configuration:

- The class-map identifies the voice traffic.
- The policy-map defines the policing action, setting a CIR of 1,000,000 bps (1 Mbps) and applying actions to conforming and non-conforming traffic.

3. Traffic Shaping vs. Traffic Policing: Key Differences

While both **traffic shaping** and **traffic policing** are used to control the flow of traffic and manage bandwidth, they differ in how they handle excess traffic. Here are the key differences:

Feature	Traffic Shaping	Traffic Policing
Purpose	Smooths traffic flow by buffering and delaying excess traffic	Enforces rate limits by dropping or remarking excess traffic
Impact on Traffic	Delays traffic to ensure it conforms to the rate limit	Drops or remarks traffic that exceeds the rate limit
Configuration Complexity	More complex, as it involves buffering and smoothing	Simpler, but less flexible; typically involves hard limits
Excess Traffic Handling	Excess traffic is buffered and delayed	Excess traffic is dropped or remarked
Use Case	Useful for applications that require burst management (e.g., VoIP, video)	Useful for enforcing strict bandwidth limits (e.g., fair use)

4. Best Practices for Traffic Shaping and Policing

Effective use of traffic shaping and policing ensures that network resources are allocated efficiently and that critical applications maintain optimal performance. Here are some best practices to consider when implementing traffic shaping and policing in a Cisco-based network:

1. Prioritize Mission-Critical Applications

When configuring traffic shaping or policing, ensure that mission-critical applications like VoIP, video conferencing, or cloud services are prioritized. For example, use QoS to assign a higher priority to **voice VLANs** and ensure that they receive the necessary bandwidth even during peak periods. Set appropriate CIR values to make sure these applications have a smooth, uninterrupted experience.

2. Monitor Traffic Regularly

Traffic patterns can change over time as new applications and services are added to the network. Regular monitoring helps identify emerging traffic trends and adjust shaping and policing configurations accordingly.

Cisco's **NetFlow** or **Cisco DNA Center** can be used to gather insights on traffic flow and usage, which can then inform your bandwidth management policies.

3. Avoid Over-Shaping

While traffic shaping helps prevent network congestion, over-shaping can introduce excessive delay, especially for time-sensitive applications like VoIP or video. Be sure to carefully balance the shaping configuration to ensure that delays are minimal and that traffic is not excessively buffered.

4. Consider the Trade-offs Between Shaping and Policing

Decide whether you need to shape traffic or police it based on the type of traffic and the organization's needs. Shaping is more suitable for environments with bursty traffic patterns where smoothing out traffic flow is essential. Policing is better suited for situations where strict traffic limits need to be enforced, and excess traffic should be immediately dropped or remarked.

5. Combine Shaping and Policing

In many cases, a combination of traffic shaping and traffic policing may be necessary to manage traffic flows effectively. For example, you might shape traffic to avoid congestion but also apply policing to enforce a hard limit on specific traffic types. This hybrid approach can offer both flexibility and control over your network resources.

Both **traffic shaping** and **traffic policing** are critical tools in the network administrator's toolkit, helping to manage bandwidth and optimize traffic flow across a network. While **traffic shaping** smooths traffic bursts and ensures consistent delivery, **traffic policing** enforces hard limits on traffic rates, ensuring that excess traffic is either dropped or remarked. When applied effectively, these techniques can improve network performance, enhance user experience, and prevent congestion.

Cisco's robust set of QoS and traffic management features, such as

Traffic Shaping, **Traffic Policing**, and **Cisco's QoS policies**, provide network administrators with the tools they need to control traffic flows and allocate bandwidth efficiently. By understanding and implementing traffic shaping and policing based on specific network requirements, organizations can achieve more predictable, reliable, and optimized network performance.

Load Balancing for Efficient Resource Utilization

In modern network environments, ensuring high availability and optimal performance of applications and services is crucial. One of the most effective strategies for achieving this is **load balancing**. Load balancing is the process of distributing network traffic or computing workloads across multiple resources (such as servers, network links, or processing units) to ensure no single resource is overwhelmed, which in turn optimizes resource utilization, enhances performance, and maintains service reliability.

In this section, we will explore the importance of load balancing in networking, the different types of load balancing methods, and how Cisco solutions can be used to implement load balancing in both traditional and modern network infrastructures. We'll also look at the practical applications, configurations, and best practices for using load balancing to achieve efficient resource utilization and a seamless user experience.

1. What is Load Balancing?

Load balancing refers to the process of distributing incoming network traffic or application requests across multiple servers, devices, or network paths to prevent any single resource from becoming a bottleneck. By ensuring that each resource handles a fair share of the workload, load balancing increases the overall capacity, performance, and resilience of the network infrastructure.

In networking, load balancing is often applied in contexts such as:

- **Web traffic management** (distributing HTTP requests across multiple web servers)
- **Application load balancing** (distributing application traffic to backend servers or clusters)
- **Network link load balancing** (distributing traffic across multiple links for redundancy and higher throughput)
- **Database load balancing** (distributing database queries to different servers or instances)

At its core, load balancing aims to **optimize resource utilization** by ensuring that no single server, link, or network device is underutilized or overburdened, which could result in **slowdowns**, **failures**, or **bottlenecks**.

2. Key Benefits of Load Balancing

Load balancing offers several benefits that contribute to better network performance, improved uptime, and optimized resource allocation. Some of the primary benefits of implementing load balancing include:

1. Improved Performance

By distributing traffic evenly across multiple resources, load balancing ensures that no single resource becomes a performance bottleneck. This results in **faster response times** and better overall performance, particularly in scenarios with high traffic volumes or complex applications.

- Load balancing helps maintain the application or service's responsiveness, even under heavy loads, by spreading traffic among servers that can process requests in parallel.
- With proper load balancing, **latency is reduced**, as traffic is routed to the most available or least congested resource.

2. High Availability and Fault Tolerance

One of the key advantages of load balancing is **high availability**. By distributing traffic across multiple resources, load balancing ensures that if one resource fails, others can take over, minimizing service disruption. This also enables seamless failover capabilities.

- If a server or link becomes unavailable, load balancers automatically reroute traffic to healthy servers or backup paths without disrupting service.
- **Redundancy** is built into the design, as traffic can be directed to alternative resources, ensuring continuous service availability.

3. Scalability

Load balancing enhances the **scalability** of networks by enabling organizations to add more resources (servers, devices, or network links) without worrying about overloading existing infrastructure. As demand grows, new resources can be added, and the load balancer will distribute traffic to utilize the new resources efficiently.

- Scalability is particularly important for cloud-based applications and services, where the demand for resources can fluctuate dynamically.
- Load balancing ensures that performance is maintained even as new servers are added to handle increasing traffic.

4. Optimized Resource Utilization

By balancing traffic effectively across available resources, load balancing ensures that no single server, device, or link is either overburdened or underutilized. This leads to **better resource allocation**, with each resource used to its full potential.

- It maximizes **CPU, memory, and bandwidth utilization** while avoiding bottlenecks that can occur when a single resource becomes overloaded.
- Optimizing resource utilization leads to **cost savings** and greater operational efficiency.

5. Better Security

Load balancing can improve the security of applications and services by enabling **SSL offloading** and distributing incoming traffic across multiple instances of the service. For example:

- **SSL offloading** reduces the computational load on servers by handling encryption and decryption operations at the load balancer level.
- By distributing traffic across multiple servers, the attack surface is increased, and a potential attack targeting one server may not affect the entire system.

3. Types of Load Balancing Methods

There are several methods of load balancing, each suited to different networking environments and use cases. Cisco solutions support various load balancing techniques, allowing administrators to choose the most appropriate method based on the type of traffic, resources, and performance goals.

1. Round Robin Load Balancing

Round Robin is one of the simplest and most common load balancing methods. In a round-robin approach, the load balancer distributes incoming requests to a list of resources (e.g., servers) in a sequential, circular manner. Once the last server in the list receives a request, the load balancer starts over at the first server.

- **Pros**: Simple to configure and efficient for evenly distributed traffic with homogeneous resources.
- **Cons**: Does not take into account the current load or resource utilization of each server, meaning some servers may become overloaded while others remain idle.

2. Least Connections Load Balancing

Least Connections is a more intelligent load balancing method that directs traffic to the server with the least number of active connections. This ensures that the server handling the least amount of traffic is utilized first, preventing overloading of any one server.

- **Pros**: More efficient than round-robin in environments with varying traffic patterns and resource consumption.
- **Cons**: Requires more complex configuration and monitoring, as the load balancer needs to track the number of active connections on each server.

3. Weighted Load Balancing

In **Weighted Load Balancing**, each server or resource is assigned a **weight** based on its processing capability or available resources. The load balancer uses these weights to distribute traffic proportionally, with more powerful servers receiving a greater share of the traffic.

- **Pros**: Effective in heterogeneous environments where servers have different performance capabilities.
- **Cons**: Requires proper weighting configuration to ensure even distribution, particularly when resource utilization varies over time.

4. IP Hash Load Balancing

In **IP Hash** load balancing, a hash function is used to determine which server should handle a request based on the **source IP address** of the incoming traffic. This method ensures that traffic from the same source IP address is always directed to the same server, which can be beneficial for session persistence (also known as **sticky sessions**).

- **Pros**: Ideal for maintaining session persistence, especially in applications that require a user's session to remain on the same server (e.g., e-commerce or online banking).
- **Cons**: May result in uneven distribution of traffic if the hash function

does not produce a uniform distribution.

5. Least Response Time Load Balancing

Least Response Time load balancing directs traffic to the server with the fastest response time, taking into account factors such as server health, load, and network latency. This method ensures that traffic is routed to the server that can respond the quickest, thus improving the overall user experience.

- **Pros**: Ensures optimal performance by prioritizing servers with the lowest response time.
- **Cons**: Can require additional monitoring and dynamic adjustment based on response times.

4. Load Balancing Solutions in Cisco Environments

Cisco provides several solutions for implementing load balancing in network infrastructures, from traditional hardware-based solutions to cloud-driven services. These solutions help organizations distribute traffic efficiently and ensure high availability for applications and services.

1. Cisco Application Control Engine (ACE)

The **Cisco ACE** (Application Control Engine) is a hardware-based load balancer designed for high-performance environments. It supports advanced load balancing methods, such as **SSL offloading, content switching,** and **global server load balancing (GSLB),** making it an ideal solution for enterprise-level applications.

- **SSL Offloading**: The ACE device can offload the SSL encryption and decryption process from web servers, freeing up server resources for application processing.
- **Global Server Load Balancing (GSLB)**: ACE supports GSLB, which allows traffic to be distributed not only within a local network but also across geographically dispersed data centers.

2. Cisco's Integrated Services Routers (ISR)

Cisco's **Integrated Services Routers (ISR)** provide a range of load balancing features for smaller to medium-sized networks. ISRs support both **Layer 4** and **Layer 7** load balancing, as well as basic traffic management features like NAT (Network Address Translation) and firewalling.

- ISRs are ideal for branch offices or remote locations that need a compact, high-performance solution for balancing traffic across multiple paths or servers.

3. Cisco Cloud Load Balancing (Cloud Load Balancer)

As organizations increasingly move to cloud environments, **Cisco Cloud Load Balancer** provides a software-based load balancing solution that works across public and private clouds. It enables seamless distribution of traffic between cloud-based resources, helping organizations scale efficiently and optimize resource utilization in cloud environments.

- **Elastic Load Balancing (ELB)**: The Cisco Cloud Load Balancer supports elastic load balancing, automatically scaling the number of resources available to handle changing traffic demands in cloud environments.

5. Best Practices for Load Balancing

To fully leverage the benefits of load balancing, here are some best practices to follow:

1. Use Session Persistence Where Necessary

If your applications require users to remain connected to the same server for the duration of their session (e.g., for authentication or transaction integrity), ensure that your load balancer supports **session persistence** (sticky sessions). This can be done using methods like **IP Hash** or **cookie-based persistence**.

2. Monitor and Fine-Tune Load Balancing Policies

Regularly monitor traffic patterns, server performance, and response times to ensure that your load balancing configuration is working as expected. Adjust weights, thresholds, or algorithms based on changes in traffic volume or resource utilization.

3. Optimize for High Availability

For critical applications, use load balancing in conjunction with **high availability** configurations like **N+1 redundancy** or **active-passive failover**. This ensures that, in the event of a failure, traffic can still be directed to healthy resources, maintaining service availability.

4. Implement Redundancy

For critical services, ensure that the load balancing infrastructure itself is redundant. This means using multiple load balancers in an active-active or active-passive configuration to eliminate single points of failure.

Load balancing is a powerful and essential tool for modern network management, allowing organizations to efficiently utilize resources, maintain high availability, and ensure optimal application performance. Whether it's used for distributing web traffic, balancing network links, or managing cloud services, load balancing provides the flexibility and scalability needed to handle increasing traffic demands.

By leveraging Cisco's range of load balancing solutions, organizations can implement strategies that ensure both performance and reliability, whether operating in traditional on-premise data centers or cloud environments. With proper configuration and monitoring, load balancing can maximize resource utilization, improve user experience, and safeguard against downtime, all while ensuring that the network is prepared to scale with future demands.

Tools for Traffic Monitoring and Analysis (NetFlow, Prime Infrastructure)

Effective network traffic monitoring and analysis are essential for ensuring optimal performance, security, and reliability within a Cisco-powered network. Understanding traffic patterns, identifying bottlenecks, diagnosing faults, and analyzing usage trends all depend on the right set of tools. Cisco provides powerful solutions like **NetFlow** and **Prime Infrastructure** that enable network administrators to gain deep insights into network activity and performance.

In this section, we will explore two of Cisco's most widely-used tools for traffic monitoring and analysis: **NetFlow** and **Prime Infrastructure**. We will also discuss how these tools can be integrated into a network's daily operations to optimize traffic management and enhance overall network performance.

1. What is NetFlow?

NetFlow is a traffic monitoring protocol developed by Cisco that collects and analyzes flow data across a network. Unlike traditional packet-based monitoring, which examines each individual packet, **NetFlow** captures **flow data** — a summary of communication between two endpoints (e.g., source IP address, destination IP address, ports, and protocols). This aggregated data helps network administrators understand traffic patterns, identify anomalies, and optimize network performance.

NetFlow operates by monitoring IP traffic and reporting metrics based on predefined flow attributes. These attributes can include the number of bytes transferred, the number of packets transmitted, duration, protocol, and the IP addresses involved.

NetFlow data can be collected from network devices such as **routers, switches, and firewalls**, with each device acting as a **NetFlow exporter**. The collected data is then sent to a **NetFlow collector**, which processes the data for analysis, visualization, and reporting.

Key Benefits of NetFlow:

1. **Comprehensive Traffic Analysis**: NetFlow provides detailed visibility into network traffic flows, enabling administrators to identify top talkers (heaviest users), top applications, and most used network paths.
2. **Security Monitoring**: By analyzing traffic flows, NetFlow can help detect abnormal patterns, such as unexpected spikes in traffic, which could indicate security issues like **DDoS attacks**, **data exfiltration**, or **network breaches**.
3. **Performance Optimization**: NetFlow data can be used to track bandwidth usage and pinpoint network congestion, allowing administrators to optimize resource allocation and identify areas where network upgrades are needed.
4. **Troubleshooting**: NetFlow is an invaluable tool for troubleshooting network performance issues. By tracking flow data, administrators can isolate the source of performance degradation, identify network bottlenecks, and optimize the routing of traffic.
5. **Traffic Forecasting and Capacity Planning**: NetFlow data offers insights into long-term trends, helping network managers plan for future capacity needs and avoid future bandwidth constraints by scaling the network proactively.

How NetFlow Works:

1. **Flow Creation**: When a device (e.g., router or switch) receives a packet, it checks whether that packet belongs to an existing flow. A flow is a unidirectional stream of packets that share common properties (e.g., source and destination IP, source and destination port, protocol). If no flow exists, the device creates a new flow.
2. **Flow Exporting**: The device periodically exports flow records (e.g., flow summary information) to a NetFlow collector. This can be done in real-time or on a periodic basis, depending on configuration.

3. **Flow Analysis**: The NetFlow collector aggregates flow data from multiple devices and provides analysis tools for reporting and visualization. This enables administrators to view flow data over specific periods, drill down into specific traffic patterns, and generate traffic reports.
4. **Flow Record Components**: The NetFlow data typically includes the following attributes:

- **Source IP Address**
- **Destination IP Address**
- **Source and Destination Port Numbers**
- **Protocol (TCP, UDP, ICMP, etc.)**
- **Packet and Byte Counts**
- **Input and Output Interfaces**
- **Flow Start and End Times**

NetFlow Versions:

Cisco's NetFlow has evolved over time, with multiple versions offering different features and levels of granularity. The key versions include:

- **NetFlow v5**: One of the most commonly used versions, providing basic flow export with limited support for IPv6.
- **NetFlow v9**: The flexible version of NetFlow that allows for the export of custom flow templates, supporting IPv6 and providing richer flow details.
- **IPFIX (Internet Protocol Flow Information Export)**: Based on NetFlow v9, IPFIX is the IETF standard for flow export, offering even greater flexibility and extensibility for flow data.

Integrating NetFlow for Traffic Analysis:

To implement NetFlow effectively, network administrators should:

- **Enable NetFlow on key network devices**: Routers, switches,

and firewalls should be configured to export flow data to a central NetFlow collector.
- **Use a NetFlow collector**: Collectors receive and process flow data from multiple devices and provide a centralized view of network traffic.
- **Analyze traffic patterns**: Leverage analytics tools to identify key metrics like traffic volume, protocol distribution, and traffic sources. This data helps identify congestion points, optimize routing, and track overall performance.

2. Cisco Prime Infrastructure: A Comprehensive Network Management Solution

Cisco Prime Infrastructure is a comprehensive network management platform designed to simplify and automate the monitoring, configuration, and optimization of Cisco networks. It integrates a wide range of functionalities into a single interface, enabling administrators to manage network devices, troubleshoot performance issues, and analyze traffic effectively.

Cisco Prime Infrastructure provides visibility into every layer of the network, from **core routers** and **distribution switches** to **access points** and **end-user devices**. This centralized management system allows network administrators to ensure the optimal performance of both wired and wireless network infrastructures.

Key Features of Cisco Prime Infrastructure:

1. **Network Visibility and Monitoring**: Cisco Prime Infrastructure provides real-time visibility into network performance. Administrators can track device health, monitor traffic patterns, and detect network bottlenecks or failures quickly.
2. **Automation and Configuration Management**: With **automated provisioning** and **configuration management**, Cisco Prime Infrastructure simplifies device configuration and ensures consistency

across the network. Administrators can deploy configurations to thousands of devices from a centralized platform.
3. **Troubleshooting and Diagnostics**: Prime Infrastructure provides **detailed diagnostics tools**, enabling administrators to quickly identify the root cause of network issues. Features like **cable diagnostics, performance monitoring**, and **event correlation** streamline troubleshooting.
4. **Reporting and Analytics**: Prime Infrastructure generates detailed reports on network performance, traffic usage, and device status. The platform provides historical data, allowing administrators to analyze trends over time and plan for future capacity needs.
5. **Integration with Other Cisco Solutions**: Cisco Prime Infrastructure integrates with other Cisco solutions like **Cisco Identity Services Engine (ISE)** and **Cisco DNA Center**, enabling seamless management of both network access policies and automation workflows.
6. **Security Monitoring**: Prime Infrastructure enhances network security by providing visibility into device compliance, traffic flows, and potential vulnerabilities. By using integration with **Cisco TrustSec**, it enables policy-driven security for network access.

Benefits of Cisco Prime Infrastructure:

1. **Centralized Management**: With Prime Infrastructure, administrators can monitor and manage the entire network from a single, unified console, reducing the complexity of managing distributed devices.
2. **Simplified Network Deployment**: Prime Infrastructure automates network provisioning, reducing manual configuration and the risk of configuration errors. This results in faster deployment times and fewer mistakes during setup.
3. **Enhanced Troubleshooting and Optimization**: The comprehensive monitoring and diagnostic capabilities help identify per-

formance issues early and guide administrators through the troubleshooting process, reducing downtime and optimizing network operations.
4. **Scalability**: Cisco Prime Infrastructure supports scalable network designs, from small branch offices to large enterprise campuses, providing the flexibility to manage a wide range of Cisco network devices and applications.

3. Integrating NetFlow and Prime Infrastructure for Comprehensive Traffic Analysis

While **NetFlow** focuses on gathering and analyzing flow data from network devices, **Cisco Prime Infrastructure** enhances traffic monitoring by providing a comprehensive view of network performance and configuration management. Together, these tools form a powerful combination for traffic analysis and optimization.

- **Centralized Traffic Monitoring**: By integrating NetFlow with Prime Infrastructure, administrators gain a **centralized view of traffic data**, making it easier to correlate flow data with performance metrics and network health.
- **Real-Time Traffic Analysis**: NetFlow's real-time traffic flow data can be processed and visualized through Prime Infrastructure's dashboards, providing administrators with immediate insights into traffic bottlenecks or performance degradation.
- **Proactive Management**: By leveraging NetFlow data in conjunction with Cisco Prime Infrastructure's **automated alerts** and **analytics capabilities**, administrators can proactively manage traffic flow and optimize resource allocation before performance issues arise.
- **Long-Term Trend Analysis**: While NetFlow focuses on real-time data, Cisco Prime Infrastructure's historical reporting capabilities allow for **long-term traffic trend analysis**, helping administrators forecast future bandwidth requirements and plan for network expan-

sion.

The tools for traffic monitoring and analysis — **NetFlow** and **Prime Infrastructure** — are crucial for modern network management. NetFlow provides granular visibility into traffic patterns, helping identify bottlenecks and optimize bandwidth allocation. Cisco Prime Infrastructure, on the other hand, offers a unified platform for network monitoring, configuration management, and diagnostics, helping administrators manage both performance and security.

By using these tools together, network administrators can improve network performance, ensure high availability, and maintain optimal resource utilization. NetFlow's ability to provide deep insights into flow data, combined with Prime Infrastructure's comprehensive network management capabilities, allows for a well-rounded, proactive approach to managing today's complex Cisco-powered networks.

Ensuring Redundancy and High Availability

Designing Redundant Networks to Avoid Single Points of Failure

In modern networking, ensuring **high availability** and **redundancy** is essential to minimize downtime and maintain uninterrupted services. **Single points of failure (SPOF)** are critical vulnerabilities within a network where the failure of a single component, device, or connection can disrupt the entire network or service. The risk of downtime caused by a SPOF is unacceptable in enterprise environments, particularly for mission-critical applications that require constant uptime and performance.

To design a network that ensures high availability, **redundancy** must be a core principle of the architecture. **Redundant network design** involves building in alternative paths, devices, or components that can take over in the event of a failure, thus maintaining the integrity of the system and preventing any service interruptions. This process includes the careful planning and integration of backup components, failover mechanisms, and diverse routing paths to ensure that the network remains resilient in the face of failure.

This section explores the key principles and strategies for designing redundant networks, and how to avoid single points of failure using **Cisco**

technologies and industry best practices.

1. Understanding Single Points of Failure (SPOF)

A **Single Point of Failure (SPOF)** refers to a component or device within a network that, if it fails, will cause the entire system or service to stop functioning. These critical failures can affect network availability, performance, and security, causing downtime, service outages, and potentially significant business disruptions.

Common examples of SPOFs in a network include:

- **Router or Switch Failures**: If a core router or switch goes down and there is no backup path or device in place, network traffic could be completely interrupted.
- **Power Supply**: A failure in a power supply unit (PSU) or a lack of redundant power sources can take down network equipment.
- **Cable or Link Failures**: Single network cables or links can become bottlenecks or points of failure, affecting traffic between critical devices.
- **Single Data Center**: Relying on a single data center for all services or storage is a major SPOF, as its failure can impact the entire organization.
- **DNS or DHCP Servers**: Centralized authentication or directory servers like DNS (Domain Name System) and DHCP (Dynamic Host Configuration Protocol) are often critical to network operations. A failure in these systems can lead to significant disruption.

In a traditional network, identifying and addressing SPOFs involves ensuring that there are alternative paths, devices, or components to handle the load or traffic if one part of the network fails.

ENSURING REDUNDANCY AND HIGH AVAILABILITY

2. Key Strategies for Avoiding Single Points of Failure

Designing a network with redundancy in mind involves a few critical strategies, such as building fault-tolerant topologies, implementing load balancing, and utilizing automated failover systems. Cisco provides a variety of tools and solutions that help address SPOFs effectively.

A. Redundant Network Paths

The most straightforward approach to ensuring network redundancy is to create **multiple, diverse paths** between key network components, including core devices like routers, switches, and firewalls. The goal is to ensure that, in the event of a failure in one path, traffic can still be rerouted through a backup path, preventing downtime.

- **Redundant Routers and Switches**: Implementing two or more routers or switches at key points in the network creates backup devices that can handle traffic if one device fails. By establishing **Hot Standby Router Protocol (HSRP)** or **Virtual Router Redundancy Protocol (VRRP)** on routers, one router becomes the active device while the others stand by in case of failure.
- **Link Aggregation (EtherChannel)**: Combining multiple physical links into a single logical link using **EtherChannel** allows traffic to be balanced across multiple links. If one link fails, the other links continue carrying the traffic, ensuring that there is no single failure point in the network's data transport layer.
- **Multiple Internet Connections**: For critical Internet-facing services, ensuring that there are **multiple ISPs** or internet links can prevent a single link from becoming a SPOF. This can be achieved through **Border Gateway Protocol (BGP)** to enable **dynamic routing** and automatic failover between ISPs.

B. Redundant Power Systems

Power failure is one of the most common causes of network downtime.

Ensuring that every critical network device has redundant power sources is an effective strategy for avoiding this type of SPOF.

- **Dual Power Supplies**: Many Cisco devices, including **routers, switches, and firewalls**, come with **dual power supply units (PSUs)**. If one PSU fails, the second automatically takes over, ensuring continuous power to the device.
- **Uninterruptible Power Supplies (UPS)**: Providing a **UPS** at key network infrastructure points (e.g., data centers, core routers) ensures that devices remain powered during outages, allowing time for failover systems or generator backup systems to take effect.
- **Generator Backup**: For data centers and larger network hubs, implementing backup **generators** for long-term power outages ensures that there is no disruption to network services during extended power failures.

C. Redundant Hardware

The physical hardware used in network infrastructure must also be redundant. If a single device fails, it can lead to network downtime. Building in redundant devices across the network is a proven way to reduce downtime.

- **Clustering and Redundancy Groups**: Network devices can be grouped into **redundant clusters** or configured to work in **high-availability (HA) pairs**. Cisco offers solutions such as **Cisco ASA Firepower** and **Cisco Catalyst** switches, which support clustering for fault tolerance. If one device fails, the second device automatically takes over.
- **Server Redundancy**: In data centers, utilizing server **clustering** or **virtualization** platforms (e.g., VMware HA or Microsoft Failover Clustering) ensures that if one server goes down, the workloads are automatically shifted to other servers without service disruption.

D. Software-Based Redundancy

Redundancy isn't limited to physical components. Software can also play a significant role in ensuring that there is no single failure point in the network.

- **Virtualization and SDN**: By leveraging **Software-Defined Networking (SDN)** and network **virtualization**, networks can be dynamically reconfigured in real-time, ensuring that if a link or device fails, the network can quickly adjust its paths and reroute traffic. Cisco's **DNA Center** and **ACI** solutions offer SDN capabilities that allow network administrators to programmatically manage network redundancy and automatically detect and mitigate failures.
- **Redundant DNS and DHCP Servers**: Implementing multiple **DNS** and **DHCP servers** in a network ensures that these critical services do not become a single point of failure. **DNS load balancing** can be configured to route requests across multiple servers, and DHCP servers can be set up in a **failover pair** to ensure high availability.

3. High Availability Protocols and Technologies

To ensure that redundant devices or links are automatically utilized in the event of a failure, various high-availability protocols are used in network design. These protocols provide automated failover, ensuring that traffic continues to flow even if a device or path fails.

A. HSRP and VRRP

- **HSRP (Hot Standby Router Protocol)** and **VRRP (Virtual Router Redundancy Protocol)** are used to ensure that there is no single point of failure for routers. These protocols allow for two or more routers to work together to appear as a single gateway to the network.
- In case of failure of the primary router, HSRP or VRRP ensures that a backup router takes over the gateway function without disruption,

maintaining the availability of network services.

B. Spanning Tree Protocol (STP)

For **Layer 2 redundancy** (i.e., redundancy within the switching infrastructure), **Spanning Tree Protocol (STP)** is employed to prevent network loops while ensuring that redundant paths are available in case of switch or link failure. STP dynamically blocks one or more links while active and re-enables them in case the primary link fails.

C. Stateful Failover

Stateful failover ensures that a network device, such as a firewall or load balancer, preserves session information during failover. This is critical for applications that require continuous sessions or transactions, such as **VoIP**, **VPNs**, and **database connections**. Cisco's **ASA firewalls** support stateful failover, allowing active traffic to continue seamlessly on backup devices.

D. BGP for Internet Redundancy

For networks that rely on multiple Internet connections, **Border Gateway Protocol (BGP)** allows for dynamic routing decisions based on path availability and policy. In the event of a link failure, BGP can automatically reroute traffic through an alternate path, ensuring that Internet traffic is uninterrupted.

Designing a redundant network is a critical part of ensuring **high availability** and **fault tolerance** in today's enterprise environments. **Single points of failure (SPOF)** can result in costly downtime, service interruptions, and customer dissatisfaction. By carefully considering the key strategies of redundant network paths, hardware, software, and protocols, organizations can ensure that their networks remain resilient and continue to function smoothly, even in the face of failures.

Cisco provides a broad range of tools and technologies that help network engineers design and implement highly available, redundant networks. From **HSRP** and **EtherChannel** to **SDN** and **BGP**, Cisco's solutions allow network architects to implement the redundancy needed to avoid single points of failure and ensure reliable, continuous service.

With a well-designed redundant network, organizations can minimize downtime, enhance service reliability, and maintain the level of performance that is essential for modern business operations.

Cisco High Availability Protocols: HSRP, VRRP, GLBP

High availability (HA) is a critical requirement for modern enterprise networks. In any network, especially those supporting mission-critical applications, minimizing downtime is essential. **High Availability Protocols** play a pivotal role in ensuring that network services remain operational even when individual devices, such as routers or switches, fail. Cisco provides several robust protocols to address this need, including **HSRP (Hot Standby Router Protocol), VRRP (Virtual Router Redundancy Protocol),** and **GLBP (Gateway Load Balancing Protocol)**.

These protocols are designed to provide network redundancy and failover, but each has its own distinct characteristics and use cases. This section provides a comprehensive look at how these protocols function and how they contribute to the high availability of a Cisco network.

1. Hot Standby Router Protocol (HSRP)

HSRP is one of the most commonly used protocols for achieving high availability in networks. It is a Cisco proprietary protocol that ensures there is always a default gateway available for devices in a local area network (LAN). In a typical setup, if the primary router fails, the secondary router (or backup router) can seamlessly take over, ensuring no disruption in network connectivity.

How HSRP Works

HSRP works by creating a **virtual IP (VIP)** address that is shared among a group of routers. The routers in the HSRP group communicate with each other to determine which one will be the **active router** (responsible for forwarding traffic) and which will be the **standby router** (waiting to take over in case of failure). The routers in the group also elect a **virtual MAC address** to be associated with the VIP, so that end devices do not need to change their default gateway in the event of a failure.

- **Active Router**: The router that is currently forwarding traffic for the VIP. It is the one that all hosts in the LAN will use as their default gateway.
- **Standby Router**: The router that is on standby, ready to take over in case the active router fails.
- **Backup Routers**: Additional routers in the HSRP group that can step in if both the active and standby routers fail, although they do not take an active role unless needed.

HSRP routers exchange **hello messages** to track the state of each router in the group. If the active router becomes unreachable, the standby router takes over and starts forwarding traffic.

HSRP Versions

- **HSRP v1**: The original version of HSRP that supports only IPv4 addresses. It is compatible with a limited number of devices (i.e., up to 255 routers in an HSRP group).
- **HSRP v2**: An enhanced version that supports both IPv4 and IPv6 addressing and has expanded functionality, including support for a larger range of routers (up to 1,000 in a group). HSRP v2 also improves security features with more robust authentication mechanisms and enhanced hello time intervals.

HSRP Use Cases

HSRP is typically used in networks where:

- **Single Default Gateway**: Devices in the LAN require a consistent default gateway that is always reachable, even if a router fails.
- **Redundant Gateways**: Networks that require high availability for routing services, typically on enterprise campus networks or edge networks.

HSRP Configuration Example:

```shell
router1(config)# interface g0/1
router1(config-if)# standby 1 ip 192.168.1.1   # Virtual IP
router1(config-if)# standby 1 priority 110    # Higher priority than standby router
router1(config-if)# standby 1 preempt         # Enable preemption, so this router can take over if it has higher priority
router1(config-if)# standby 1 authentication mypassword  # Optional, for secure authentication between routers
```

In this example, **Router 1** is configured to be the **active router** for the HSRP group. If **Router 1** fails, **Router 2**, configured with a lower priority, will take over as the active router.

2. Virtual Router Redundancy Protocol (VRRP)

VRRP is an open-standard protocol that is similar to HSRP in that it provides high availability for default gateways. Unlike HSRP, which is Cisco proprietary, VRRP is supported by a wide range of networking vendors, making it ideal for multi-vendor network environments.

How VRRP Works

Like HSRP, VRRP allows multiple routers to work together to provide a single virtual gateway to clients on the network. In VRRP, the routers in the VRRP group elect a **Master router** that is responsible for forwarding traffic. The other routers in the group act as **Backup routers**.

- **Master Router**: The router currently forwarding traffic for the virtual IP address. Only one router can be the Master at any given time.
- **Backup Routers**: These routers are in standby mode, waiting to take over if the Master router fails.

The **Master router** is chosen based on a priority value configured by the network administrator. If the Master router fails, one of the Backup routers with the next highest priority will take over. In VRRP, the routers communicate through **advertisement messages** sent at regular intervals to inform each other about their status.

VRRP Versions

- **VRRP v2**: This version supports IPv4 addressing and provides the basic redundancy features of VRRP.
- **VRRP v3**: Introduced support for IPv6 addressing and added several enhancements for security and network management, including the ability to assign multiple virtual routers on the same physical interface.

VRRP Use Cases

- **Multi-Vendor Networks**: If an organization uses equipment from multiple vendors, VRRP is a better choice than HSRP because it is not proprietary to Cisco and is supported by other manufacturers.
- **Redundant Gateway Requirement**: When there is a need for a redundant gateway, but the environment includes devices that don't support HSRP.

VRRP Configuration Example:

```shell
router1(config)# interface g0/1
router1(config-if)# vrrp 1 ip 192.168.1.1   # Virtual IP
router1(config-if)# vrrp 1 priority 120    # Higher priority
than backup routers
router1(config-if)# vrrp 1 preempt         # Enable preemption
```

In this case, **Router 1** is configured as the **Master router** with the highest priority.

3. Gateway Load Balancing Protocol (GLBP)

GLBP is another Cisco proprietary protocol designed to provide high availability and load balancing across multiple routers. Unlike HSRP and VRRP, which select a single active router, **GLBP** allows multiple routers in a group to share the traffic load, balancing the traffic based on various algorithms.

How GLBP Works

GLBP assigns a **virtual IP address** to the network, but unlike HSRP and VRRP, **GLBP allows multiple routers to share this virtual gateway address**, with each router taking a portion of the traffic. The routers in a GLBP group work together to provide redundancy and distribute traffic across all routers in the group.

- **Active Virtual Gateway (AVG)**: This router is responsible for assigning virtual MAC addresses to the other routers in the group.
- **Active Virtual Forwarders (AVFs)**: These routers handle the forwarding of traffic destined for the virtual gateway IP. Each AVF is assigned a virtual MAC address by the AVG and distributes traffic to different clients.
- **Load Balancing**: GLBP uses load balancing algorithms such as **round-robin** and **weighted load balancing** to distribute traffic

evenly across the available routers in the group. This can significantly improve network efficiency and optimize resource utilization.

GLBP Use Cases

- **Optimized Traffic Distribution**: GLBP is ideal for networks where load balancing is required in addition to high availability. It is commonly used in large-scale enterprise networks where high availability and efficient traffic distribution are critical.
- **Redundant Internet Gateways**: GLBP can be used to distribute traffic between multiple ISPs or multiple Internet-facing routers in a high-availability design.

GLBP Configuration Example:

```shell
router1(config)# interface g0/1
router1(config-if)# glbp 1 ip 192.168.1.1   # Virtual IP
router1(config-if)# glbp 1 priority 110    # Higher priority to become AVG
router1(config-if)# glbp 1 load-balancing round-robin  # Choose load balancing method
```

In this example, **Router 1** is configured as the **Active Virtual Gateway (AVG)** and will assign virtual MAC addresses to the other routers for traffic forwarding.

Cisco's **HSRP**, **VRRP**, and **GLBP** are all vital protocols for ensuring high availability and redundancy in a network. They serve different purposes but share the goal of preventing single points of failure and maintaining uninterrupted service.

- **HSRP** is typically used in Cisco-specific networks, providing a simple way to ensure that a single gateway IP remains available.
- **VRRP**, being an open standard, is ideal for multi-vendor environments and offers similar functionality to HSRP.
- **GLBP** stands out by adding load balancing to the mix, allowing multiple routers to share the traffic load while still providing high availability.

Each protocol can be configured to fit the specific needs of an organization's network, depending on factors like network size, equipment, and traffic patterns. By implementing these protocols, network administrators can ensure that their infrastructure is resilient, balanced, and prepared for failures, minimizing downtime and maintaining optimal performance.

Redundancy in the Core and Distribution Layers

In a well-designed enterprise network, redundancy is a critical component to ensure high availability, fault tolerance, and continuous service delivery. While redundancy can be applied throughout the entire network, particular emphasis must be placed on the **Core** and **Distribution layers**. These layers are the backbone of the network, responsible for the rapid forwarding of data between devices, segments, and subnets. Failure in either of these layers can disrupt the entire network's performance and service availability, which is why redundancy in these layers is paramount.

This section will cover the key concepts and best practices for ensuring redundancy in the **Core** and **Distribution** layers using Cisco's technologies. We'll explore the importance of these layers, the strategies for implementing redundancy, and the tools available to network architects to achieve this redundancy in modern enterprise environments.

1. The Core Layer: Backbone of the Network

The **Core layer** of a network is responsible for the high-speed and high-capacity forwarding of data between different segments of the network. It acts as the **central hub** for interconnecting the **Access** and **Distribution layers** and provides the necessary paths for communication between different parts of the network, including the Internet, data centers, and remote offices. The Core layer is typically designed with high-performance equipment capable of handling large volumes of traffic at high speeds.

Importance of Redundancy in the Core Layer

Given the Core layer's pivotal role in maintaining the network's stability and performance, **redundancy** is necessary to avoid **single points of failure (SPOF)**. A failure at the Core layer can cause significant disruptions across the entire network, affecting multiple access points, services, and even entire geographic regions. Redundancy ensures that if one device or path fails, traffic is automatically rerouted through an alternate path without interrupting the flow of data.

To implement redundancy effectively in the Core layer, network architects should consider:

- **Redundant Core Routers and Switches**: The Core layer should have at least two redundant Core routers or switches, designed to handle different traffic loads and to provide seamless failover if one device fails.
- **Multiple Physical Paths**: Traffic should be able to flow across multiple physical paths between the Core and Distribution layers. This ensures that the failure of one link or cable does not cause a service disruption.
- **High-Speed Links**: Redundant Core routers should be interconnected using high-bandwidth links to maintain performance and prevent bottlenecks.
- **Spanning Tree Protocol (STP)**: In the event of a link failure, **STP**

helps to prevent network loops while ensuring that traffic is rerouted over alternate paths without network disruption.

Best Practices for Redundancy in the Core Layer

- **Dual Core Routers or Switches**: Implement at least two core devices, each connected to all other layers (Access and Distribution). Use **HSRP**, **VRRP**, or **GLBP** to ensure that one router can fail over to another without dropping traffic.
- **Link Aggregation**: Use **EtherChannel** to combine multiple physical links into a single logical link between Core and Distribution layers. This not only increases bandwidth but also provides redundancy in case one physical link fails.
- **Redundant Power Supplies**: Ensure Core devices have **dual power supplies** and are connected to separate power sources to prevent a single power failure from affecting the Core layer.
- **Routing Protocols**: Use dynamic **routing protocols** such as **OSPF** or **BGP** to quickly adapt to changes in network topology and reroute traffic in case of a failure. BGP is particularly useful in large, multi-site networks where external and internal routing can be affected by link or router failure.

2. The Distribution Layer: Ensuring Reliable Connectivity

The **Distribution layer** is the intermediary layer that connects the Access layer (end-user devices, workstations, etc.) with the Core layer. It performs functions such as routing, quality of service (QoS) control, and access control, and is responsible for enforcing policies related to network traffic management and security. The Distribution layer ensures that traffic from different parts of the network is routed appropriately toward the Core layer for further forwarding.

Importance of Redundancy in the Distribution Layer

Just like the Core layer, the **Distribution layer** is critical to the network's ability to deliver reliable services. A failure in this layer can lead to loss of connectivity between access switches and core routers, disrupting communication across the entire network. Redundancy is particularly important in this layer to ensure:

- **Service Continuity**: If one distribution switch or router fails, another can automatically take over, ensuring uninterrupted connectivity between the Access and Core layers.
- **Load Balancing**: Redundant Distribution devices can help in load balancing, ensuring that traffic is evenly distributed across multiple paths to prevent bottlenecks.
- **Fault Isolation**: By providing redundant devices and paths, failures can be isolated to a small segment of the network without affecting the broader infrastructure.

Best Practices for Redundancy in the Distribution Layer

- **Dual Distribution Routers or Switches**: Like the Core layer, it's crucial to deploy **two or more Distribution layer routers** or switches. These devices should be connected to each other and also to both the **Access** and **Core** layers to provide maximum redundancy.
- **HSRP or VRRP for Redundancy**: Just as in the Core layer, **HSRP**, **VRRP**, or **GLBP** can be implemented in the Distribution layer to ensure that if one device fails, traffic can be seamlessly forwarded to the backup device.
- **Link Aggregation**: Use **EtherChannel** or **Port Channels** between Distribution and Access switches to increase bandwidth and provide link redundancy. Link aggregation helps in creating fault tolerance by allowing multiple physical links to behave as a single logical link.
- **Spanning Tree Protocol (STP)**: To prevent loops in the network and ensure that redundant paths are functional, **STP** should be used in the Distribution layer. **Rapid PVST+** or **MSTP** (Multiple Spanning Tree Protocol) can improve convergence time and stability in case of

failures.

3. Key Technologies for Redundancy in the Core and Distribution Layers

Several Cisco-specific technologies and protocols can be used to enhance redundancy in the Core and Distribution layers, helping to ensure the network remains operational even if individual devices, paths, or links fail.

A. HSRP (Hot Standby Router Protocol)

As discussed earlier, **HSRP** can be used to provide redundancy for **routers in the Distribution layer**. This ensures that in the event of a router failure, traffic can be automatically rerouted through the standby router without disruption. In the Core layer, HSRP ensures that there is always a **primary default gateway** for traffic to be forwarded to, even if the active router goes down.

B. VRRP (Virtual Router Redundancy Protocol)

For multi-vendor environments or where flexibility is needed, **VRRP** is a suitable alternative to HSRP for redundancy. VRRP allows for redundant gateways with failover capabilities and is used in both the **Core and Distribution layers** to provide high availability.

C. GLBP (Gateway Load Balancing Protocol)

For networks that require load balancing in addition to redundancy, **GLBP** can be deployed in the Core and Distribution layers. GLBP ensures that multiple routers share the load of forwarding traffic while also providing backup routes in case one of the routers fails. This makes it particularly useful for **high-traffic networks** that need both **redundancy and load distribution**.

D. EtherChannel and Port Aggregation

Using **EtherChannel** or **port aggregation** between Core and Distribution switches allows network traffic to be distributed across multiple physical links, increasing available bandwidth and providing a failover mechanism in case one link fails. This technology is essential for **high-availability designs** where large volumes of traffic are expected to pass between layers.

Redundancy in the **Core** and **Distribution layers** is essential for maintaining high network availability, ensuring business continuity, and preventing service disruptions. By implementing redundant **Core routers, switches, and links**, organizations can ensure that if one device or path fails, traffic can be rerouted seamlessly, minimizing the impact of a failure.

Cisco's technologies, including **HSRP, VRRP, GLBP**, and **EtherChannel**, provide the necessary tools to design a redundant network with high availability, load balancing, and fault tolerance. Whether it's using **dynamic routing protocols** for fast failover or implementing **power redundancy** for critical devices, network architects must prioritize redundancy in these foundational layers to keep the network resilient against failures.

A well-architected, redundant Core and Distribution layer ensures that the network remains highly available, performing at peak efficiency and with minimal downtime. This is critical for enterprises that depend on their networks to support critical applications and services, whether on-premises or in the cloud.

Cisco's Techniques for Load Balancing Across Data Centers

In today's enterprise networks, businesses are increasingly relying on **multi-data center architectures** to achieve greater scalability, performance, and disaster recovery capabilities. The ability to efficiently distribute network traffic across multiple data centers is essential for ensuring **optimal resource utilization**, **high availability**, and **improved performance** in modern cloud-enabled and hybrid environments. Cisco, with its suite of advanced technologies and solutions, provides a range of techniques for **load balancing** across data centers, ensuring that applications and services can scale horizontally while remaining highly available.

This section will delve into the key **Cisco techniques** and solutions used to **load balance** traffic across data centers, including the use of **Cisco's Application Delivery Controllers (ADCs)**, **Global Server Load Balancing (GSLB)**, **Cisco ACI (Application Centric Infrastructure)**, and **Intelligent Traffic Management**. These technologies help distribute traffic intelligently, optimize resource usage, and maintain high availability in complex, geographically distributed data center environments.

1. Introduction to Load Balancing Across Data Centers

Load balancing refers to the process of distributing network traffic evenly across multiple servers, resources, or locations to avoid overloading a single resource and to ensure that traffic is efficiently handled. In a **data center environment**, load balancing is critical for several reasons:

- **Scalability**: As application demands grow, load balancing ensures that no single server or data center becomes overwhelmed by traffic.
- **High Availability**: By distributing traffic across multiple data centers, load balancing ensures that if one data center experiences

downtime or failure, traffic can be redirected to healthy data centers without service disruption.
- **Geographic Distribution**: For global organizations with a presence in multiple regions, load balancing can direct traffic to the data center closest to the user, improving latency and application response times.

Cisco has developed several solutions to address the unique challenges of balancing traffic across multiple, often geographically dispersed, data centers. These solutions ensure that both **user requests** and **data flows** are efficiently managed across the network.

2. Cisco's Application Delivery Controllers (ADCs)

An **Application Delivery Controller (ADC)** is a device or solution that optimizes the delivery of applications and services across a network by managing traffic and balancing load. Cisco's **Application Control Engine (ACE)** and newer solutions like **Cisco Cloud Services Router (CSR)** or **Cisco Nexus 9000** series switches with integrated load balancing functions serve as powerful ADCs, enabling **high-performance load balancing** in data center environments.

How ADCs Enhance Load Balancing

- **Traffic Distribution**: Cisco ADCs use advanced algorithms (e.g., **round-robin, least-connections, weighted round-robin**) to distribute incoming application traffic to multiple servers or resources within a data center or across multiple data centers. This ensures that no single resource is overwhelmed.
- **Health Monitoring**: Cisco ADCs continuously monitor the health of servers and resources, redirecting traffic away from servers that are down or underperforming to healthy resources. This is critical in a dynamic, highly available environment.
- **SSL Offloading**: ADCs can handle **SSL termination** by decrypting secure connections, offloading the work from application servers,

and improving server performance. This is particularly important when managing encrypted traffic across multiple data centers.
- **Global Load Balancing**: Cisco's ADCs extend their capabilities by integrating with global load balancing technologies, allowing organizations to direct traffic across **multiple data centers** spread across different geographic regions based on factors like proximity, health, or load.

Use Cases for ADCs in Multi-Data Center Load Balancing

- **Application Delivery Optimization**: By deploying Cisco's ADCs, enterprises can optimize traffic distribution not only across the local data center but also across multiple global locations, ensuring efficient and fast delivery of applications to end-users.
- **Disaster Recovery**: In case of a failure in one data center, ADCs can automatically reroute traffic to another operational data center, ensuring continuity of services.
- **Performance Management**: Cisco ADCs enable fine-tuned load balancing strategies that can account for server performance, geographical factors, and user load, ensuring that no data center becomes a bottleneck.

3. Global Server Load Balancing (GSLB)

Global Server Load Balancing (GSLB) is a technique that enables load balancing across **multiple data centers** located in different geographical regions. Cisco's GSLB solution ensures that user traffic is directed to the closest available data center, based on factors such as proximity, load, and availability.

How GSLB Works

GSLB operates at the **DNS level**, where it determines the appropriate data center to which user requests should be routed. The decision is based on a combination of metrics, including:

- **Geographic Location**: GSLB can direct users to the data center nearest to them, reducing latency and improving response times.
- **Server Health**: GSLB continuously monitors the health of data centers and servers, ensuring that if one data center or server is down, traffic is automatically redirected to another healthy data center.
- **Load Metrics**: GSLB can consider the current load and capacity of data centers, distributing traffic to the less congested centers.
- **Performance Optimization**: By dynamically adjusting routing decisions based on real-time conditions, GSLB ensures that users always receive the best possible application performance.

Cisco GSLB Solutions

Cisco provides several GSLB solutions, typically integrated with its **Application Delivery Controllers (ADCs)**. Cisco's **Global Site Selector (GSS)** and **Cisco Cloud ACI** are examples of solutions that enable efficient global load balancing.

- **Cisco GSS (Global Site Selector)**: The Cisco GSS is designed for high-availability environments and provides **intelligent traffic distribution** across geographically dispersed data centers. It uses DNS queries and monitors network health to determine the best data center for user requests.
- **Cisco ACI**: Cisco's **Application Centric Infrastructure (ACI)** integrates seamlessly with GSLB and ADCs to provide end-to-end traffic management and load balancing across multi-site data centers, further optimizing application delivery.

Use Cases for GSLB

- **Global Application Distribution**: GSLB ensures that enterprise applications with a global user base are efficiently distributed across multiple regional data centers, minimizing latency and improving the user experience.

- **Disaster Recovery and Failover**: GSLB helps manage the failover process, ensuring that in case of data center failure, traffic is directed to the next available site without disruption to services.
- **Traffic Optimization**: GSLB allows enterprises to optimize the flow of traffic, sending users to the data center that can handle their requests with the least amount of delay and the best performance.

4. Cisco Application Centric Infrastructure (ACI) for Multi-Site Load Balancing

Cisco ACI (Application Centric Infrastructure) is a software-defined networking (SDN) solution that provides a unified architecture for managing application traffic across multiple data centers. It offers **end-to-end automation**, centralized policy management, and **intelligent traffic distribution**.

How ACI Enhances Load Balancing

ACI integrates load balancing and traffic management directly into the **network fabric**. It enables:

- **Policy-Based Load Balancing**: ACI allows administrators to define policies that automatically adjust traffic distribution based on application needs, traffic load, or resource availability. For example, a policy might prioritize routing traffic to a data center that has sufficient compute resources to handle a sudden spike in traffic.
- **Multi-Site Management**: ACI's **multi-site** capabilities allow it to manage the load balancing of traffic across geographically dispersed data centers, ensuring seamless application delivery and optimal resource utilization.
- **Automated Traffic Flow**: ACI's automation features allow load balancing policies to be applied consistently across all sites, reducing the complexity of manually configuring load balancing across multiple environments.
- **Visibility and Control**: ACI provides deep visibility into traffic

flows, helping administrators understand traffic patterns and make informed decisions about load balancing and optimization strategies.

Use Cases for Cisco ACI in Multi-Site Load Balancing

- **Hybrid Cloud Integration**: Cisco ACI can be used to integrate on-premises data centers with public cloud environments, enabling **load balancing** between different cloud providers and internal data centers.
- **Disaster Recovery**: With ACI's multi-site capabilities, enterprises can implement disaster recovery strategies by directing traffic to a secondary data center in the event of a primary data center failure.
- **Dynamic Load Distribution**: ACI can automatically distribute traffic to the most capable data center, adjusting in real-time to changes in resource availability or traffic load.

Efficient load balancing across multiple data centers is essential for maintaining high availability, optimizing resource usage, and improving application performance. Cisco provides a robust set of tools and techniques for load balancing, including **Application Delivery Controllers (ADCs), Global Server Load Balancing (GSLB)**, and **Cisco ACI**. These technologies ensure that enterprises can distribute traffic intelligently, maintain continuous service even in the face of data center failures, and optimize the user experience across global deployments.

By leveraging Cisco's solutions for load balancing, businesses can ensure that their multi-site or multi-cloud data center architectures are not only **highly available** but also **scalable** and **performance-optimized**. Whether it's **geo-proximity routing, intelligent traffic management**, or **disaster recovery**, Cisco's load balancing strategies provide the flexibility and reliability needed for the modern, distributed network architecture.

ENSURING REDUNDANCY AND HIGH AVAILABILITY

Disaster Recovery Planning and Best Practices

Disaster recovery (DR) is an essential aspect of network design and architecture, especially for modern enterprises that rely on **high-availability systems** and **business-critical applications**. In an increasingly connected world, organizations cannot afford significant downtime, whether due to **natural disasters**, **hardware failures**, **cyberattacks**, or **human error**. For businesses operating in multiple regions or in cloud environments, disaster recovery strategies are crucial to ensuring that data and services remain accessible, regardless of the disaster scenario.

Effective **disaster recovery planning** involves creating a comprehensive strategy to minimize the impact of unexpected events on the business, maintaining operations through recovery processes, and returning to full functionality as quickly as possible. This section covers the essential principles, best practices, and Cisco solutions for designing and implementing a robust disaster recovery plan that ensures **data protection**, **service continuity**, and **rapid recovery** in the event of a disaster.

1. Defining Disaster Recovery in Network Architecture

Disaster recovery refers to the processes and technologies used to **recover IT infrastructure**—including **networks, servers, storage, applications**, and **data**—after an event that causes a disruption in normal operations. In the context of network architecture, disaster recovery focuses on restoring **network connectivity**, **communication systems**, and **critical business applications** that support an organization's operations.

A strong DR plan not only addresses how to recover lost data but also defines how to **maintain business continuity** by restoring network services and infrastructure in a timely manner. Key components of a disaster recovery strategy include:

- **Backup and Replication**: Ensuring that critical data and network

configurations are backed up regularly and stored in multiple locations (e.g., on-premises and in the cloud).
- **Failover Systems**: Establishing redundant systems, devices, and paths to allow uninterrupted service if the primary system or service fails.
- **Recovery Time Objective (RTO)** and **Recovery Point Objective (RPO)**: Defining the maximum acceptable downtime (RTO) and the acceptable amount of data loss (RPO) during a disaster.

2. Key Principles of Disaster Recovery Planning

A comprehensive disaster recovery plan for **network infrastructure** must be built around a set of guiding principles that ensure resilience and rapid recovery. The following principles are fundamental in creating a disaster recovery strategy:

A. Redundancy and High Availability

Redundancy is the foundation of disaster recovery in network architecture. By deploying redundant devices, circuits, and systems at every layer of the network (e.g., **Core**, **Distribution**, **Access**, and **Data Center**), organizations can ensure that if a component fails, there is always an alternative path or device to continue operations.

- **Core Layer Redundancy**: Implement redundant core routers and switches, using **HSRP**, **VRRP**, or **GLBP** to prevent a single point of failure (SPOF) at the network backbone.
- **Data Center Redundancy**: Employ **multi-site** strategies with **load balancing** across geographically dispersed data centers to ensure that if one data center becomes unavailable, traffic can automatically be routed to another active site.

B. Data Replication and Backup

Effective **data replication** and **backup** strategies are vital for disaster recovery. Businesses should replicate critical data between **on-premises** and **cloud environments** or between **multiple data centers**. This ensures that, in the event of a disaster, the most recent data can be quickly restored with minimal disruption.

- **Continuous Data Protection (CDP)**: Implement technologies that provide real-time replication of critical business data to remote locations.
- **Snapshot and Backup Management**: Periodically back up network configurations, application settings, and operating system states to allow recovery to a known working state in the event of a failure.

C. Network Segmentation for Disaster Isolation

Network segmentation is an effective technique for isolating disaster impacts to specific areas of the network. For example, if one segment of the network is affected by a disaster (e.g., a network breach, or power failure), the rest of the network can remain functional. **Virtual LANs (VLANs)** and **subnetting** are commonly used to segment networks and isolate traffic, improving security and resilience.

- **Logical Isolation**: Use **VLANs** and **subnets** to logically isolate critical systems and services from general network traffic. This makes it easier to control which systems should be affected in case of a failure.
- **Failover Pathways**: Redundant pathways across **Core** and **Distribution layers** should ensure that if one path fails, traffic will reroute through alternate paths without significant delays.

D. Geo-Redundancy for Global Coverage

For **global organizations**, a disaster recovery plan should include **geo-redundancy**—deploying data and services in multiple geographic regions to ensure **global business continuity**. Cisco's **Global Server Load Balancing (GSLB)** and **Cisco ACI** enable businesses to balance traffic across geographically distributed sites and ensure that users are always directed to the closest operational data center.

3. Best Practices for Disaster Recovery in Network Architecture

To build a highly resilient network that can withstand and recover from disasters, network architects should follow several best practices that integrate **redundancy**, **automation**, and **monitoring**. These practices help minimize downtime, accelerate recovery times, and ensure data integrity during a disaster.

A. Design for Failure, Not for Perfection

The best disaster recovery plans assume that failure is inevitable and plan accordingly. Rather than designing a network that never fails (which is impractical), focus on building a network that can **fail gracefully** and recover quickly. This includes:

- Designing with **redundant** components (routers, switches, servers).
- Implementing **automated failover** mechanisms to detect failures and reroute traffic without manual intervention.
- Ensuring **backup power** systems (UPS, generators) are in place to support operations during power outages.

B. Prioritize Mission-Critical Services

While disaster recovery is important for all network services, it is crucial to identify **mission-critical applications** and prioritize them in the recovery process. This ensures that business operations can continue even if non-essential services are temporarily offline.

- **High-priority applications** such as email servers, cloud applications, and collaboration tools should be restored first in the event of a disaster.
- **Less-critical applications**, such as development environments or test servers, can be brought back online after essential services are fully restored.

C. Implement Disaster Recovery Testing and Drills

Regular testing of disaster recovery procedures is vital to ensure that the recovery process will work smoothly when needed. Disaster recovery drills simulate various disaster scenarios (e.g., power failure, network breach, data corruption) to ensure the network can recover within predefined recovery objectives.

- **Tabletop exercises**: These exercises simulate disaster scenarios in a controlled environment and evaluate the response of the recovery team and technology.
- **Full-scale failover tests**: Simulating a complete failure of a data center or critical network service to test how quickly the network can switch to backup systems or locations.

D. Automate Failover and Recovery Processes

Automation is key to reducing recovery times and minimizing human error during disaster recovery. Automated systems can detect failures and trigger failover processes without requiring manual intervention, ensuring a faster and more reliable recovery.

- **Automated backup systems**: Set up automated backups that are taken at regular intervals to ensure data consistency.
- **Automated failover**: Using **Cisco's ACI** or **SD-WAN solutions**, automate traffic rerouting and the activation of backup systems to ensure minimal disruption to end-users.

E. Cloud Integration for Backup and Failover

Integrating cloud-based services into your disaster recovery plan ensures that data and applications are available even in the event of on-premises failures. Cloud providers offer robust disaster recovery options, such as **disaster recovery as a service (DRaaS)**, which ensures rapid recovery in cloud environments.

- **Hybrid cloud solutions**: Combine private and public cloud infrastructure to back up critical systems and provide failover locations for data and applications.
- **Cloud-based load balancing**: Use **Cisco Meraki** or **Cisco Cloud ACI** to manage and distribute traffic across both on-premises and cloud-based infrastructure to ensure high availability.

4. Cisco Solutions for Disaster Recovery

Cisco offers several solutions that can be integrated into a disaster recovery plan to ensure the resilience of the network and business continuity.

A. Cisco's SD-WAN (Software-Defined Wide Area Network)

Cisco's **SD-WAN** technology enables organizations to quickly establish redundant, secure connections between remote locations, data centers, and cloud environments. In the event of a disaster, SD-WAN can automatically reroute traffic over the most optimal path, ensuring service continuity.

- **Automatic path selection**: SD-WAN can monitor the health of network links and automatically reroute traffic to the most reliable link available.
- **Centralized management**: SD-WAN allows administrators to centrally manage traffic routing policies, backup options, and failover procedures from a single dashboard.

B. Cisco ACI (Application Centric Infrastructure)

Cisco ACI is particularly useful for managing disaster recovery in multi-site environments. With its **policy-driven automation** and **intelligent traffic distribution**, ACI enables seamless failover between data centers in different geographic locations, maintaining service availability even in the event of a disaster.

- **Multi-site redundancy**: ACI ensures that data and applications are consistently available across multiple data centers, automatically distributing traffic to operational sites in case of a failure.
- **Disaster recovery automation**: ACI provides policy-based automation for rapid failover and recovery processes, minimizing recovery time.

C. Cisco Cloud Services

Cisco's cloud-based solutions, including **

Meraki** and **Cisco Umbrella**, offer disaster recovery capabilities by providing cloud management, secure remote access, and backup solutions that can be accessed from anywhere. These solutions ensure that, even if a disaster affects the on-premises network, business operations can continue seamlessly via cloud services.

A comprehensive disaster recovery plan is essential for any network architecture, especially in multi-site, cloud-based, or globally distributed environments. By following best practices like **redundancy**, **data replication**, **network segmentation**, and **cloud integration**, and leveraging **Cisco's advanced technologies** such as **SD-WAN, ACI**, and **cloud solutions**, enterprises can ensure that their networks are resilient, highly available, and able to recover quickly in the event of a disaster.

Disaster recovery is not just about protecting against data loss; it's about ensuring **continuous business operations** and minimizing disruption to end-users. With Cisco's suite of tools and solutions, organizations can build networks that are not only optimized for performance but also for long-term resilience and disaster recovery.

Software-Defined Networking (SDN) with Cisco

What is SDN and Why is It Important?

Software-Defined Networking (SDN) represents a **paradigm shift** in how enterprise networks are designed, deployed, and managed. Unlike traditional networking models, which rely heavily on hardware-based solutions, SDN abstracts the **control plane** from the **data plane**, centralizing network control and providing a more flexible, programmable, and automated approach to managing network traffic. This shift allows organizations to respond to network demands with **greater agility**, **reduced complexity**, and **improved efficiency**.

As businesses face increasing pressure to support growing numbers of devices, applications, and users, the need for dynamic and scalable networking solutions has never been greater. SDN offers a solution that adapts to the demands of modern enterprises by enabling **automated provisioning**, **real-time traffic management**, and **simplified network operations**. With Cisco's SDN solutions, including **Cisco ACI** and **Cisco SD-WAN**, organizations can gain a competitive edge by optimizing their network for performance, reliability, and security.

In this section, we will explore **what SDN is**, **why it's important**, and how it fundamentally changes the way networks are designed and managed. Additionally, we'll highlight **Cisco's role** in the SDN landscape and how their solutions empower enterprises to **modernize their networks**, achieve **operational efficiency**, and scale effectively.

1. Defining Software-Defined Networking (SDN)

Software-Defined Networking (SDN) is an innovative approach to **network architecture** that decouples the network's **control plane** from the **data plane**. In traditional networks, both the control plane (responsible for routing and traffic management) and the data plane (responsible for forwarding packets) reside within the same hardware device. This architecture limits the flexibility and scalability of the network, as changes to the network configuration require manual intervention and are typically tied to specific hardware devices.

In contrast, SDN separates these two planes, allowing for **centralized control** and **programmability**. The control plane is managed by a **centralized SDN controller**, which communicates with the data plane (the network switches and routers) to determine how packets should be forwarded based on policies and real-time network conditions. This decoupling provides greater flexibility and automation, as network administrators can dynamically change network configurations via software rather than manual hardware reconfiguration.

Key components of SDN include:

SDN Controller: This is the brain of the SDN architecture. It makes centralized decisions about how traffic should flow through the network. It communicates with network devices (like switches and routers) to program them with forwarding rules and configurations.

Southbound APIs (e.g., OpenFlow): These APIs allow communication between the SDN controller and network devices. They provide a standardized interface for managing the data plane.

Northbound APIs: These APIs allow network applications (such as security systems, load balancers, and traffic management tools) to interact with the SDN controller. They enable network administrators to define policies, applications, and services through software.

Network Devices: These are the physical or virtual switches and routers that forward network traffic based on instructions from the SDN controller.

The core advantage of SDN is its ability to **centralize control** and **automate** many aspects of network management, including provisioning, security, load balancing, and traffic optimization. This centralized management approach allows network administrators to create **policy-driven configurations** and **dynamic provisioning** without having to manually configure individual network devices.

2. Why is SDN Important for Modern Networks?

The importance of SDN cannot be overstated, particularly in the context of modern enterprises and data centers, where traditional networking models no longer meet the demands of scalability, agility, and real-time performance. Let's examine the key reasons why SDN is vital for modern network infrastructures:

A. Agility and Flexibility

As businesses grow and adapt, so do their networking needs. Traditional networks, with their reliance on hardware-centric configurations, can be slow to respond to changing demands. **SDN**, however, offers unparalleled **flexibility** by allowing administrators to configure, manage, and optimize the network dynamically through software.

Real-time provisioning: SDN enables on-the-fly configuration changes. For instance, network resources can be allocated or deallocated as needed, and new virtual networks can be spun up without physical reconfiguration.

Dynamic resource allocation: SDN supports dynamic traffic routing and load balancing across various network segments based on demand, ensuring optimal performance and availability at all times.

B. Cost Efficiency

Traditional network management often requires extensive manual configuration and investment in specialized hardware. In contrast, SDN reduces operational costs by simplifying network management and increasing automation.

Reduced hardware dependency: SDN decouples the control plane from the data plane, which means network management does not need to be tied to proprietary hardware. Software-driven solutions can run on commodity hardware or virtualized environments, lowering infrastructure costs.

Automated provisioning and configuration: By automating routine network tasks (e.g., adding new devices, setting up new network segments), SDN minimizes the need for manual intervention, reducing labor costs and the likelihood of configuration errors.

C. Enhanced Network Visibility and Monitoring

SDN allows administrators to gain **greater visibility** into their network's performance and behavior in real-time. This visibility enables proactive management, faster issue resolution, and better capacity planning.

Centralized monitoring: The SDN controller offers a centralized view of the entire network, providing real-time traffic analysis, performance metrics, and health monitoring.

Advanced analytics: SDN controllers can collect vast amounts of data on network usage and traffic patterns, which can be used for predictive analysis, capacity planning, and optimizing network performance.

D. Simplified Network Management

In traditional networks, managing configurations, policies, and security across a distributed set of devices can be cumbersome and error-prone. SDN simplifies network management by centralizing control and providing a **single interface** for administrators to manage policies and configurations across the entire network.

Policy-driven management: Network administrators can define high-level policies (e.g., QoS, security, access control) in the SDN controller, and the controller will automatically enforce these policies across all network devices.

Automated updates: SDN enables administrators to push network updates, configuration changes, and security patches to the entire network from a single, centralized location.

E. Enhanced Security

SDN offers improved security by enabling **granular control** over traffic flows and network access. Security policies can be enforced consistently across the entire network, reducing vulnerabilities and improving network defenses.

Centralized security management: Security policies can be centrally defined and automatically pushed to all network devices, ensuring uniform enforcement across the network.

Dynamic threat response: SDN allows for real-time threat detection and response by enabling automated adjustments to network configurations in response to security events (e.g., blocking suspicious traffic or isolating compromised devices).

Micro-segmentation: SDN can help implement micro-segmentation, which divides the network into isolated segments, limiting the spread of security breaches and making it easier to control and monitor traffic.

F. Scalability

As networks grow, managing and scaling traditional networks becomes increasingly complex. SDN addresses these challenges by providing a scalable, software-based approach to network architecture.

Virtualization: SDN enables network virtualization, allowing enterprises to create multiple virtual networks over a single physical infrastructure. This makes it easy to scale networks to meet growing demands without additional hardware investment.

Elastic scaling: SDN allows for elastic network scaling, meaning the network can automatically scale up or down based on traffic loads, optimizing resource utilization without manual intervention.

3. Cisco's Role in Software-Defined Networking

Cisco has been a leader in driving the adoption of SDN, offering a suite of **SDN solutions** that enable enterprises to implement **software-defined networks** with ease. Cisco's SDN portfolio is designed to help organizations build flexible, automated, and scalable networks that are aligned with business needs.

A. Cisco ACI (Application Centric Infrastructure)

Cisco ACI is a **policy-driven SDN solution** designed for **data center environments**. ACI uses an integrated **architecture** that provides centralized management, dynamic traffic optimization, and security enforcement for modern data center networks.

Automated provisioning and management: ACI automates the network configuration and management, enabling rapid deployment of new applications and services while ensuring security and compliance.

Policy-based automation: ACI uses a policy-driven approach to network management, where administrators can define business requirements (such as application performance, security policies, and availability) and the system will automatically enforce them across the network.

B. Cisco SD-WAN

Cisco SD-WAN is an SDN solution that enables **software-defined management of wide-area networks (WANs)**. With SD-WAN, organizations can manage their network traffic across multiple locations and cloud environments with centralized control, ensuring efficient use of resources and reducing costs.

Application-aware routing: Cisco SD-WAN provides real-time traffic management based on application types, user demands, and network performance, ensuring optimal performance for critical business applications.

- **Cloud integration**: Cisco SD-WAN integrates seamlessly with cloud services, enabling organizations to manage traffic between on-premises and cloud environments, ensuring secure and efficient cloud connectivity.

Cisco's SDN Solutions: ACI and DNA

Cisco has long been a pioneer in network technologies, and its Software-Defined Networking (SDN) solutions—**Application Centric Infrastructure (ACI)** and **Digital Network Architecture (DNA)**—are at the forefront of transforming how businesses design, deploy, and manage their networks. These solutions leverage SDN's core principles of centralized control, programmability, and automation to streamline network management, optimize performance, and enhance security.

In this section, we will explore Cisco's two key SDN solutions—**ACI** and **DNA**—in detail. We will examine how each solution contributes to building a more agile, scalable, and efficient network infrastructure, providing real-world benefits to businesses looking to modernize their networks.

1. Cisco ACI (Application Centric Infrastructure)

Cisco's **Application Centric Infrastructure (ACI)** is a comprehensive SDN solution designed specifically for data center environments. ACI aims to simplify network management by providing **centralized policy-driven automation** and **intelligent traffic management**. It focuses on ensuring that the network is optimized for the **applications** that run on it, hence the name "Application Centric."

Key Features of Cisco ACI

- **Centralized Policy Management**: ACI enables centralized management of network policies via the **APIC (Application Policy Infrastructure Controller)**. The APIC acts as the brain of the ACI fabric, allowing administrators to define policies for **application per-**

formance, **security**, and **network segmentation**. These policies are then automatically pushed to network devices across the fabric.
- **Application-Aware Networking**: ACI enables deep integration with application workloads. This means that ACI can dynamically adjust network resources based on the specific needs of applications, ensuring optimal performance and reliability. For example, if a high-priority application experiences increased traffic, ACI can allocate additional resources to meet demand, ensuring uninterrupted service delivery.
- **Integrated Security**: ACI integrates security policies directly into the network fabric. Security features include **micro-segmentation**, where applications and workloads are isolated from each other, reducing the attack surface. ACI also supports **multi-tenancy**, allowing multiple tenants to securely share the same physical infrastructure while maintaining strict isolation.
- **Simplified Automation and Orchestration**: With ACI, network provisioning and configuration are automated. This reduces the need for manual intervention and the likelihood of errors. ACI integrates with various orchestration tools like **VMware vCenter** and **OpenStack**, making it easier to deploy and manage virtualized environments.
- **End-to-End Visibility**: The ACI solution provides detailed visibility into the health and performance of applications and the underlying network infrastructure. The APIC controller offers insights into traffic patterns, application dependencies, and security posture, enabling network administrators to quickly diagnose issues and make informed decisions.

Benefits of Cisco ACI

- **Enhanced Agility**: ACI provides the agility required for modern applications that are often distributed across hybrid and multi-cloud environments. The ability to **automate** provisioning and

dynamically scale network resources allows enterprises to meet the demands of their most critical applications with ease.
- **Optimized Performance**: By aligning the network infrastructure with application requirements, ACI ensures that network resources are used efficiently. Applications receive the resources they need to perform optimally, whether they are hosted on-premises or in the cloud.
- **Reduced Complexity**: ACI reduces the complexity associated with managing traditional network infrastructures by centralizing policy management and automation. Network administrators can define policies once and have them automatically applied across the entire network, which saves time and reduces the risk of human error.
- **Improved Security**: The integration of security policies into the network fabric ensures that applications and data are protected at every level. **Micro-segmentation** ensures that even if one part of the network is compromised, the rest of the infrastructure remains secure.

2. Cisco DNA (Digital Network Architecture)

Cisco **Digital Network Architecture (DNA)** is another flagship SDN solution from Cisco that provides enterprises with the tools they need to automate and optimize their network infrastructure. Cisco DNA leverages **intent-based networking** to help organizations align their networks with business goals. It integrates advanced technologies like **AI**, **machine learning**, and **automation** to simplify network operations and improve efficiency.

Key Features of Cisco DNA

- **Intent-Based Networking**: At the heart of Cisco DNA is **intent-based networking**, which allows network administrators to define high-level business intents and goals, and the system automatically translates those intents into network configurations. This approach

reduces manual configuration and ensures that network policies are aligned with the organization's objectives.
- **Automation and Orchestration**: Cisco DNA enables **full automation** of network provisioning, configuration, and management. It uses tools like **Cisco DNA Center**, a centralized platform that provides an intuitive interface for network configuration, policy enforcement, and monitoring. With Cisco DNA, organizations can automate the **deployment** and **management** of network devices, reducing the time and effort needed to provision and maintain a network.
- **AI and Machine Learning**: Cisco DNA uses artificial intelligence (AI) and machine learning (ML) to continuously optimize the network based on real-time data and historical trends. These technologies help predict network issues, identify anomalies, and proactively resolve problems before they affect users or applications. This intelligent approach helps maintain a high level of **network performance** and **reliability**.
- **Advanced Security**: Cisco DNA includes robust security features such as **identity-based segmentation, encryption**, and **access control**. Cisco's security solutions, including **Cisco Umbrella** and **Cisco Stealthwatch**, are integrated with DNA to provide end-to-end protection for both on-premises and cloud-based applications.
- **End-to-End Visibility**: Cisco DNA provides comprehensive visibility into the entire network, from the core to the edge. It helps administrators monitor network traffic, identify performance bottlenecks, and optimize resources in real-time. With detailed analytics and reporting, Cisco DNA helps organizations make data-driven decisions to improve network performance.
- **Integration with the Cloud**: Cisco DNA supports cloud-native applications and hybrid environments, providing seamless integration with public and private clouds. It helps enterprises build a **cloud-first strategy**, enabling them to extend their networks into the cloud and manage them through a single, unified interface.

Benefits of Cisco DNA

- **Operational Simplicity**: Cisco DNA simplifies network operations by automating routine tasks, enabling zero-touch provisioning, and reducing human error. This not only speeds up deployment but also improves network reliability and performance.
- **Increased Agility**: With Cisco DNA, businesses can rapidly deploy new applications, add new network devices, or adjust network policies to meet changing demands. This flexibility ensures that organizations can respond to business needs with speed and efficiency.
- **Improved User Experience**: Cisco DNA optimizes network performance to ensure a seamless user experience, whether users are accessing resources on-premises or in the cloud. By continuously monitoring and analyzing network traffic, Cisco DNA helps minimize delays, congestion, and other issues that could negatively impact user experience.
- **Enhanced Security**: Cisco DNA's advanced security features provide proactive threat detection and mitigation. The integration of **Cisco Identity Services Engine (ISE)**, **Cisco Umbrella**, and **Cisco Stealthwatch** ensures that the network is secure, no matter where users or devices are located.
- **Cost Efficiency**: By automating network management tasks and reducing the complexity of network operations, Cisco DNA helps businesses reduce operational costs. It also helps ensure that network resources are used efficiently, minimizing the need for costly hardware upgrades.

3. Comparison: ACI vs. DNA

While both **Cisco ACI** and **Cisco DNA** are powerful SDN solutions, they serve different purposes and are suited to different use cases.

- **Cisco ACI** is primarily focused on **data center environments**, offer-

ing centralized policy management, application-centric networking, and seamless integration with virtualized environments. ACI is ideal for organizations looking to optimize their data center operations, improve application performance, and ensure high availability and security.
- **Cisco DNA**, on the other hand, is more suitable for **enterprise-wide network management**, particularly in hybrid or multi-cloud environments. DNA provides automation, AI-driven optimization, and integrated security across both campus and wide-area networks (WANs). Cisco DNA is a good fit for organizations that need to manage large-scale, complex networks with a focus on operational efficiency and user experience.

Cisco's SDN solutions, **ACI** and **DNA**, provide organizations with the tools they need to transform their network infrastructures and support modern business needs. Whether optimizing data center operations with ACI or automating network management across an enterprise with DNA, Cisco's SDN solutions offer the **flexibility**, **scalability**, and **intelligence** required for today's demanding network environments.

By leveraging the power of **automation**, **AI**, and **centralized control**, Cisco's SDN solutions help businesses build networks that are not only more efficient and secure but also more aligned with their long-term strategic goals. As businesses continue to embrace digital transformation, Cisco's ACI and DNA offer the foundational technologies needed to create agile, future-proof networks.

Understanding Cisco ACI's Application-Centric Approach

Cisco's **Application Centric Infrastructure (ACI)** represents a transformative shift in how enterprise networks are designed, operated, and managed. Traditional networking models, which focus primarily on hardware devices such as routers, switches, and firewalls, are gradually giving way to more **application-centric** architectures. ACI is Cisco's answer to the growing demands of modern data centers and cloud environments, where the needs of applications should drive network design and behavior.

Unlike conventional approaches where network infrastructure is designed around devices and their configurations, ACI focuses on applications as the central point of reference. This application-centric model ensures that the network is not just a static, passive platform for transporting data but an intelligent, dynamic system that understands and adapts to the needs of applications running on it.

In this section, we'll dive into the core principles of Cisco ACI's **application-centric approach**, explaining how it aligns network operations with application requirements, provides end-to-end visibility, and enhances overall network agility.

The Core Concept of Application-Centric Networking

At its core, **Application Centric Networking** means that the network infrastructure is driven by the **needs of the applications** it supports, rather than the other way around. This approach allows organizations to design and manage their networks based on the **intent** of applications and the specific network performance, security, and availability requirements these applications demand.

In a traditional network design, administrators define network policies based on **devices** (routers, switches, firewalls, etc.), creating a rigid framework for how data flows across the network. This model is effective for static networks but becomes increasingly inefficient as networks scale and become more dynamic with the rise of virtualized applications, cloud services, and multi-cloud environments.

Cisco ACI flips this paradigm by allowing administrators to define **application policies** rather than focusing on device configurations. These policies are then automatically implemented and enforced across the network, ensuring that resources are allocated and traffic flows in a way that meets the needs of applications in real-time.

How ACI Works: The Key Components

Cisco ACI introduces a new architecture that combines **hardware** and **software** to deliver a comprehensive solution for application-centric networking. It is powered by **APIC (Application Policy Infrastructure Controller)**, which serves as the central management and policy engine for ACI. Below are the key components and how they work together to implement an application-centric approach:

1. Application Policy Infrastructure Controller (APIC)

The APIC is the heart of Cisco ACI. It is a **centralized controller** that manages and orchestrates the ACI fabric, allowing administrators to define **application policies** that govern how traffic should flow throughout the network. These policies are automatically pushed to the network devices, ensuring that the physical and virtual infrastructure work together in a way that aligns with application requirements.

- **Centralized Control**: APIC provides a centralized point for defining and managing policies, making it easier to maintain consistency across the network. This is particularly important in dynamic environments where applications and network demands can change rapidly.
- **Policy-Driven Automation**: Policies in ACI are defined based on the **business intent** of applications. For instance, an application that

requires low-latency performance would have its own set of policies governing how it should interact with the network, ensuring that data flows in a way that minimizes latency. The APIC ensures that these policies are automatically applied across the network without the need for manual configuration of each individual device.

2. ACI Fabric

The ACI Fabric refers to the underlying **network infrastructure** that supports the ACI solution. It consists of both physical hardware (such as **Leaf** and **Spine** switches) and logical components that work together to deliver high-performance connectivity for applications.

- **Leaf Switches**: These are the access switches that connect directly to endpoints, such as servers or virtual machines (VMs), within the data center. Leaf switches handle ingress and egress traffic, forwarding data between endpoints.
- **Spine Switches**: These are the core switches in the ACI fabric, responsible for routing traffic between Leaf switches. Spine switches are high-performance, high-capacity devices that interconnect all Leaf switches in the network, ensuring optimal data flow.
- **End-to-End Connectivity**: The ACI fabric provides **highly available, low-latency connectivity** between all devices in the network, whether they are physical servers, virtual machines, or containers. This is crucial for applications that rely on fast and reliable data transfers, such as real-time analytics or multimedia applications.

3. Application Profiles and Endpoint Groups (EPGs)

In ACI, **application profiles** and **Endpoint Groups (EPGs)** are key abstractions that allow network policies to be aligned with application needs.

- **Application Profiles**: An application profile is a logical entity that defines the specific requirements for an application within the

network. This includes policies for **traffic flow**, **security**, and **performance**. Application profiles ensure that each application gets the right network behavior to function optimally.
- **Endpoint Groups (EPGs)**: EPGs are collections of endpoints (such as virtual machines or servers) that share similar characteristics or require the same network behavior. EPGs are used to group endpoints according to specific **application requirements**, making it easier to apply policies across multiple devices that belong to the same application or service.

4. Contracts and Policies

In Cisco ACI, **contracts** and **policies** are used to define how different EPGs (or application components) interact with one another.

- **Contracts**: Contracts define the rules for communication between different EPGs. For example, if one EPG is responsible for a web application and another for a database, a contract will specify how these two EPGs can interact. The contract includes security, traffic-flow policies, and Quality of Service (QoS) parameters that ensure the communication meets application requirements.
- **Policies**: Policies are the mechanisms used to enforce the rules defined in contracts. For instance, a policy may dictate that traffic between two EPGs should be encrypted or that certain traffic types are given priority. Policies are automatically applied by the APIC across the ACI fabric.

Benefits of Cisco ACI's Application-Centric Approach

The application-centric approach of Cisco ACI offers several key benefits to organizations looking to optimize their network infrastructure for modern applications and workloads.

1. Agility and Flexibility

One of the primary benefits of an application-centric approach is the **agility** it provides. By aligning network behavior with application requirements, ACI enables rapid deployment and modification of network resources based on changing application needs. This flexibility is especially important in today's fast-moving business environments, where applications may be frequently updated or migrated to the cloud.

- **Automated Network Configuration**: As application requirements change, ACI's automated network provisioning ensures that the underlying infrastructure adapts to meet these new needs, eliminating the need for manual intervention and reducing deployment time.

2. Improved Application Performance

With ACI, network performance is optimized for the specific needs of each application. Whether an application requires high bandwidth, low latency, or secure communication, ACI ensures that the network is configured to deliver these attributes.

- **Dynamic Resource Allocation**: ACI's ability to dynamically allocate resources based on real-time application demands ensures that performance is consistently high, even as network traffic patterns change.

3. Simplified Network Management

By abstracting the network infrastructure and focusing on application policies, ACI simplifies network management. Network administrators no longer need to manually configure each device or worry about low-level network details. Instead, they can define high-level policies that the network automatically implements.

- **Centralized Management**: The APIC controller provides a centralized interface for managing policies across the entire network, reducing the complexity of traditional network management and improving operational efficiency.

4. Enhanced Security and Compliance

With ACI, security is embedded directly into the network fabric. Application policies define not only performance requirements but also security parameters, such as **micro-segmentation** and **access control**. This ensures that sensitive data is protected and that applications are isolated from one another as needed.

- **Micro-Segmentation**: ACI allows for the segmentation of network traffic based on application requirements, preventing lateral movement of threats within the network. This fine-grained control enhances security and ensures compliance with regulatory requirements.

Cisco ACI's **application-centric approach** marks a significant shift in how modern networks are designed and operated. By focusing on the needs of applications rather than just the network infrastructure, ACI provides a **dynamic**, **scalable**, and **automated** framework that allows organizations to optimize their networks for the workloads that matter most. Through centralized policy management, intelligent automation, and deep application integration, ACI enables businesses to meet the demands of today's complex, hybrid IT environments while ensuring high performance, enhanced security, and operational efficiency.

As organizations increasingly rely on cloud services, data center virtualization, and application-driven environments, Cisco ACI's application-centric approach will continue to be a critical enabler of digital transformation.

Automation and Orchestration with Cisco DNA Center

In the world of modern networking, automation and orchestration are essential for managing the complexity and scale of enterprise networks. Cisco's **Digital Network Architecture (DNA)** offers an integrated platform that brings together automation, analytics, and security to help organizations build and manage more agile, secure, and efficient networks. At the core of Cisco DNA is **Cisco DNA Center**, a powerful management and automation platform that enables businesses to automate network operations, optimize traffic flow, ensure consistent policy enforcement, and manage network configurations with ease.

In this section, we will explore how **Cisco DNA Center** streamlines network operations through automation and orchestration, enabling IT teams to reduce manual interventions, minimize human errors, and speed up service delivery.

What is Cisco DNA Center?

Cisco DNA Center is a centralized **network management** and **automation** platform that provides end-to-end lifecycle management for Cisco-powered enterprise networks. It is built around Cisco's **intent-based networking** (IBN) paradigm, where administrators can define the business intent for the network, and the platform automatically configures, optimizes, and maintains the network to meet these requirements.

Cisco DNA Center serves as the single interface for automating tasks such as network provisioning, configuration management, policy enforcement, monitoring, and troubleshooting. By abstracting away the complexity of the underlying network infrastructure, it empowers IT teams to manage large-scale networks more efficiently and effectively.

Key Capabilities of Cisco DNA Center

1. Network Automation

Network automation is one of the primary benefits of using Cisco DNA Center. Through the use of **templates, policies**, and **intent-based networking**, the platform can automatically configure network devices (routers, switches, access points) to meet predefined application and security requirements.

- **Configuration Automation**: Cisco DNA Center automates the configuration of devices based on the network intent, which eliminates manual configuration tasks and reduces the likelihood of configuration errors. Using pre-defined templates and policy-driven automation, administrators can ensure that new devices are automatically configured with the correct settings as soon as they are added to the network.
- **Provisioning**: Cisco DNA Center facilitates rapid network provisioning through automation. Whether deploying a new branch office, extending the network into a new data center, or provisioning new users and devices, DNA Center can automatically configure network devices according to the desired state, ensuring consistency and reducing setup times.
- **Zero-Touch Deployment (ZTD)**: One of the key benefits of Cisco DNA Center is its **zero-touch deployment** capabilities. New devices can be added to the network with minimal intervention. When a device is connected to the network, DNA Center can automatically push the appropriate configurations, making deployment quick and seamless.

2. Intent-Based Networking (IBN)

At the heart of Cisco DNA Center is **intent-based networking**. With IBN, administrators define the "**intent**" of the network, such as ensuring certain applications get high priority, maintaining secure access for remote users, or managing bandwidth for specific departments. Once the intent is defined, DNA Center automatically configures and adjusts the network to meet these requirements.

- **Declarative Network Policies**: Instead of manually configuring devices to meet specific needs, network engineers define **declarative policies**. For example, an administrator might specify that critical applications should always receive priority in network traffic, or that certain users should be restricted from accessing specific resources. DNA Center interprets these high-level policies and translates them into actionable configurations.
- **Real-Time Adjustments**: Cisco DNA Center continuously monitors the network and adjusts configurations dynamically to meet the business intent. If network conditions change—such as increased demand for certain services or the failure of a network component—the platform can automatically adapt, ensuring that the network continues to meet the defined goals without manual intervention.

3. Orchestration and Service Delivery

Orchestration in Cisco DNA Center refers to the automation of multi-device workflows and the coordination of network services across multiple layers of the network. It enables the **end-to-end management** of services such as application deployment, network segmentation, and security policies.

- **Simplified Workflow Automation**: Cisco DNA Center orchestrates workflows across various devices, including routers, switches, wireless access points, and firewalls. This end-to-end orchestration ensures that the network infrastructure is deployed and operated in alignment with business goals.
- **Service Delivery**: DNA Center enables faster service delivery by automating processes like software updates, configuration changes, and security policy enforcement. Whether deploying a new service,

managing network security, or extending the network to a new region, Cisco DNA Center orchestrates all the steps required for seamless service delivery.

4. Network Assurance and Monitoring

Automation is not limited to network deployment; it extends to **ongoing monitoring** and **assurance** as well. Cisco DNA Center provides real-time network monitoring, ensuring that the network continuously meets the desired performance, security, and availability goals.

- **Real-Time Analytics and Monitoring**: Cisco DNA Center provides continuous insights into network performance, identifying bottlenecks, anomalies, or security threats. This visibility is crucial for ensuring that the network is operating optimally and that issues are detected and addressed before they impact end-users.
- **Proactive Troubleshooting**: By leveraging Cisco's **network assurance** capabilities, DNA Center enables network teams to perform proactive troubleshooting. The platform continuously analyzes network health and predicts potential failures, allowing IT teams to take action before an issue escalates.
- **Application and User Experience Monitoring**: Cisco DNA Center doesn't just monitor the network infrastructure; it also focuses on application performance and user experience. By analyzing traffic patterns and performance metrics, it helps network engineers understand how applications are performing across the network and which areas might need optimization.

5. Security Automation

Security is a critical consideration in today's complex network environments, and Cisco DNA Center includes robust security automation features to ensure the network remains safe and compliant.

- **Automated Security Policies**: With Cisco DNA Center, security policies are automatically applied across the network, ensuring that devices are consistently configured according to the security standards. For example, security segmentation policies for different user groups (e.g., employees, guests, IoT devices) can be automatically enforced to prevent unauthorized access.
- **Threat Detection and Mitigation**: DNA Center integrates with **Cisco Identity Services Engine (ISE)** and **Cisco Stealthwatch** to enhance security monitoring and threat detection. If a security breach is detected, DNA Center can automatically apply mitigation actions, such as blocking malicious traffic or isolating affected devices.
- **Compliance**: Cisco DNA Center helps ensure compliance with regulatory standards by automating the application of security and access control policies, enabling real-time reporting and auditing of network activity.

The Benefits of Cisco DNA Center's Automation and Orchestration

By automating and orchestrating network operations, Cisco DNA Center offers several significant benefits:

1. Increased Operational Efficiency

The automation of routine network tasks, such as configuration, provisioning, and troubleshooting, significantly reduces the time and effort required to manage the network. This allows IT teams to focus on strategic initiatives, such as business innovation and network optimization, rather than spending time on manual tasks.

- **Reduced Manual Interventions**: With automated network configurations and policies, the need for manual configuration changes is minimized, reducing the potential for human error and ensuring consistent performance across the network.
- **Faster Service Delivery**: The ability to rapidly deploy and configure

new network devices and services means that businesses can respond more quickly to changing requirements and market demands.

2. Enhanced Network Agility

Cisco DNA Center enables organizations to be more agile in responding to new business needs or changing IT environments. The ability to automatically adjust network configurations in real-time based on application and security requirements means that the network can rapidly adapt to evolving demands.

- **Scalable Automation**: As businesses grow and their network requirements evolve, Cisco DNA Center scales to support larger, more complex networks without requiring proportional increases in manual effort.
- **Business Alignment**: By automating network provisioning and adjustments based on **business intent**, Cisco DNA Center ensures that the network aligns with business objectives, optimizing resources and performance.

3. Improved Network Security

Automation and orchestration in Cisco DNA Center are not only about performance and efficiency—they also play a key role in enhancing network security. Automated security policies, real-time threat detection, and proactive risk mitigation ensure that the network is continuously protected.

- **Consistency in Security Policies**: Automated policy enforcement ensures that security configurations are consistently applied across the network, eliminating gaps in security that could arise from manual misconfigurations.
- **Proactive Threat Mitigation**: By automatically detecting and responding to security threats, Cisco DNA Center helps reduce the potential impact of attacks on the network.

4. Reduced Network Complexity

Cisco DNA Center simplifies network management by consolidating configuration, monitoring, and troubleshooting tasks into a single interface. This centralized approach reduces the complexity of managing large, multi-site networks and helps IT teams maintain control over complex infrastructure.

Cisco DNA Center is a powerful tool that brings together the concepts of **automation** and **orchestration** to streamline network management, enhance security, and improve overall operational efficiency. By automating routine network tasks, orchestrating complex workflows, and aligning network behavior with business needs, it empowers organizations to build more agile, scalable, and secure networks.

As businesses continue to embrace digital transformation, the role of automation and orchestration in managing network complexity will only grow in importance. Cisco DNA Center provides the tools necessary to meet the demands of today's fast-paced, dynamic IT environments, ensuring that organizations can stay ahead of the curve in delivering consistent, high-performance, and secure network services.

Leveraging APIs for Network Automation and Control

In today's dynamic and rapidly evolving network environments, network automation and orchestration are no longer just conveniences—they are essential for maintaining agility, reducing operational overhead, and ensuring consistency in the face of increasing complexity. Central to achieving these objectives is the use of **APIs (Application Programming Interfaces)**, which enable seamless interaction and integration between Cisco's networking solutions, management tools, and external systems. Through APIs, organizations can automate network management tasks, integrate third-party applications, and customize network behaviors to meet specific business requirements.

Cisco's **APIs** empower network administrators to take control of their network infrastructure with greater flexibility, scalability, and efficiency. By integrating APIs into network automation workflows, businesses can create tailored solutions that streamline network operations, enhance data exchange, and improve overall network performance.

This section will delve into the role of APIs in **network automation and control**, highlighting their importance in the context of **Cisco networking** solutions, the benefits they offer, and best practices for leveraging APIs to automate and optimize network management.

What are APIs and Why are They Important in Network Automation?

An **API** is a set of protocols, tools, and definitions that allow one software application to communicate with another. In networking, APIs allow devices, applications, and network management systems to exchange information and control network functions programmatically, without requiring manual intervention.

In the context of **network automation**, APIs provide a way for network administrators to interact with networking devices and platforms such as **Cisco DNA Center**, **Cisco ACI**, and **Cisco Meraki**. APIs allow these systems to be **programmatically controlled**, enabling automation of repetitive tasks, integration with external systems, and customization to suit specific business needs.

The core benefits of using APIs in network automation and control include:

- **Flexibility and Customization**: APIs enable the network to be tailored to specific requirements, allowing organizations to implement custom workflows, integrate with third-party applications, and build automation scripts to address unique needs.

- **Efficiency and Speed**: APIs accelerate network management by eliminating manual tasks and allowing for faster configuration, monitoring, and troubleshooting. Automated workflows can be triggered via API calls, significantly improving response times to network events.
- **Scalability**: As networks grow in size and complexity, APIs provide a scalable method for managing infrastructure. APIs facilitate large-scale automation across distributed networks, enabling seamless configuration, monitoring, and troubleshooting of thousands of devices.
- **Consistency**: APIs ensure that network operations are executed consistently across devices, reducing human error and maintaining uniformity across the network.

Cisco's API Ecosystem

Cisco offers a rich ecosystem of **APIs** that extend across its networking portfolio, from core networking devices to advanced software-defined solutions. Some of the most notable Cisco products that support API integration include:

- **Cisco DNA Center**: Cisco DNA Center provides a RESTful API that enables users to interact programmatically with network devices and services. Through this API, network administrators can automate device provisioning, configure network policies, retrieve performance metrics, and manage network security without manual intervention.
- **Cisco ACI (Application Centric Infrastructure)**: Cisco ACI offers extensive API support for automating data center operations, including application profile creation, tenant management, and policy enforcement. The ACI API allows network administrators to interact with Cisco's **APIC (Application Policy Infrastructure Controller)** and programmatically manage the network fabric.
- **Cisco Meraki**: Cisco Meraki's cloud-managed platform offers

REST APIs for controlling wireless access points, switches, security appliances, and cameras. With Meraki APIs, network administrators can automate device provisioning, manage security policies, and retrieve detailed network analytics.
- **Cisco NX-OS**: For data center and enterprise network environments, **NX-OS** provides APIs for automating the management and configuration of Cisco Nexus switches, offering programmatic control over routing, switching, and security features.

These APIs can be integrated with other Cisco tools, third-party systems, and custom applications, providing a flexible and robust framework for managing network operations.

How APIs Enable Network Automation

1. Device Provisioning and Configuration

One of the most time-consuming and error-prone tasks in traditional network management is **device provisioning** and **configuration**. Cisco's APIs significantly reduce the time and effort required to bring new devices online and configure them to meet network requirements.

- **Automated Provisioning**: Through API calls, new devices can be automatically added to the network, assigned the correct configurations, and made operational without the need for manual intervention. For instance, when a new switch is deployed in a branch office, the DNA Center API can push the relevant configurations—such as VLAN assignments, routing protocols, and access policies—directly to the device.
- **Bulk Configuration**: APIs also enable the bulk configuration of network devices, making it easier to deploy standardized settings across multiple devices at once. This can be especially useful for large-scale networks where hundreds or thousands of devices need to be configured consistently.

2. Network Policy Enforcement

APIs also play a key role in **policy enforcement**. With Cisco DNA Center's API, network administrators can programmatically apply security, QoS, and access control policies across the network. These policies ensure that devices comply with organizational standards, improving security and performance.

- **Security Policy Enforcement**: Through APIs, network security policies can be automatically applied to devices as they are added to the network. This reduces the risk of misconfigurations and ensures that security policies, such as **firewall rules, access control lists (ACLs)**, and **segmentation policies**, are consistently enforced.
- **Quality of Service (QoS)**: APIs can also automate the application of QoS policies to prioritize traffic based on business needs. For instance, voice and video traffic can be prioritized over other types of traffic using API-driven QoS settings, ensuring high-quality communication experiences for end-users.

3. Real-Time Monitoring and Analytics

APIs are invaluable for real-time **network monitoring** and **analytics**. By using Cisco's APIs, administrators can collect data from various network devices, analyze network health, and generate reports for performance optimization.

- **Performance Metrics Collection**: APIs allow for the collection of network performance metrics, such as bandwidth usage, latency, packet loss, and device health. This data can be used to identify performance bottlenecks and optimize resource utilization.
- **Integration with Analytics Tools**: Network analytics platforms, such as **Cisco Prime Infrastructure**, can leverage APIs to pull in real-time data from the network for analysis. The insights provided by these analytics tools can be used to fine-tune configurations, identify emerging network issues, and predict future performance trends.

4. Troubleshooting and Fault Management

API-based automation extends to network **troubleshooting** and **fault management** as well. With APIs, network administrators can automate diagnostic tasks, identify issues, and initiate remediation actions.

- **Automated Diagnostics**: When a network issue occurs, APIs can be used to collect diagnostic information from devices, such as log files, interface statistics, and routing table entries. This data can be fed into troubleshooting workflows that automate the identification of issues.
- **Automated Remediation**: In case of a failure, APIs can trigger automated remediation steps, such as reconfiguring devices, rerouting traffic, or isolating problematic segments of the network. For example, if a critical link goes down, APIs can initiate an automatic failover to a backup link, ensuring that service disruption is minimized.

Best Practices for Leveraging APIs in Network Automation

To successfully leverage APIs for network automation and control, network administrators should follow best practices that ensure reliability, scalability, and security:

1. Standardize API Usage

Standardizing how APIs are used across the organization ensures consistency and simplifies integration. This includes defining a consistent approach to authentication, error handling, and data formats. By using standard protocols (such as RESTful APIs) and adhering to best practices, organizations can ensure that APIs are easily maintained and updated over time.

2. Secure API Access

APIs provide powerful programmatic control over network devices, so securing API access is paramount. Administrators should use secure authentication mechanisms, such as **OAuth 2.0** or **API keys**, to ensure that only authorized systems and users can interact with the network.

- **Role-Based Access Control (RBAC)**: Use RBAC to restrict access to sensitive API functions. Ensure that only authorized administrators or automated systems have access to make configuration changes or view sensitive data.
- **Encryption**: Always use encryption (HTTPS) for API communication to protect sensitive data in transit.

3. Monitor API Usage and Activity

Monitoring API usage is essential for detecting misuse or unauthorized access. Implement logging and monitoring tools to track API requests, analyze usage patterns, and identify potential security incidents.

- **Audit Logs**: Regularly review API access logs to identify any unusual activity, such as unauthorized configuration changes or unexpected traffic patterns.

4. Documentation and Version Control

Good documentation is crucial for effective API management. Ensure that API endpoints, methods, and usage guidelines are well-documented, so developers and administrators can easily integrate and utilize the APIs.

- **Version Control**: As APIs evolve, it's important to maintain version control. Ensure backward compatibility when updating APIs, and provide clear communication about deprecations and new features.

APIs are a game-changer in the world of network automation and control. Cisco's extensive API ecosystem enables network administrators to programmatically interact with network devices, automate configuration tasks, enforce policies, monitor performance, and troubleshoot issues—

all without manual intervention. By leveraging APIs, organizations can build more efficient, scalable, and secure networks that meet the dynamic demands of modern business environments.

With Cisco's APIs, businesses can embrace automation, integrate with third-party tools, and deliver superior network performance while reducing complexity. As network environments continue to grow and evolve, the role of APIs in managing and optimizing these networks will only become more central to achieving operational excellence and agility.

Real-World Application of SDN in Cisco Networks

Software-Defined Networking (SDN) has fundamentally transformed how networks are designed, implemented, and managed. By decoupling the network control plane from the data plane, SDN introduces a level of flexibility, programmability, and automation that was previously unattainable with traditional networking models. Cisco, as one of the leading innovators in the networking space, has embraced SDN and integrated it into a range of solutions designed to provide greater agility, scalability, and efficiency in modern networks.

This section delves into real-world applications of **SDN** in Cisco networks, exploring how businesses and organizations are leveraging SDN to meet the demands of their evolving IT infrastructure. We'll discuss practical use cases, the benefits they bring, and how Cisco's SDN solutions, including **Cisco ACI** (Application Centric Infrastructure), **Cisco DNA**, and **Meraki**, help to drive these transformations.

SDN in Data Center Networks: Cisco ACI

One of the most significant applications of SDN in Cisco networks is in the **data center**. Cisco's **ACI** (Application Centric Infrastructure) represents a paradigm shift in how data centers are managed and optimized. ACI is an SDN solution that provides a policy-driven, automated network fabric that can adapt to changing application needs, offering unprecedented flexibility and operational efficiency.

Case Study: Optimizing Data Center Operations with Cisco ACI

Imagine a large enterprise with multiple data centers spread across the globe. These data centers are home to hundreds of applications with varying traffic profiles, security needs, and performance demands. Managing the network infrastructure of these data centers using traditional methods—where each device is configured and managed manually—is a complex, error-prone, and time-consuming process.

With **Cisco ACI**, the entire data center network can be managed as a unified system, where policies are centrally defined and automatically applied to all network devices. The **ACI policy model** abstracts the physical infrastructure, allowing the network to be managed in terms of applications, rather than individual devices.

For example, an organization might have a mission-critical application that requires high availability, low latency, and strong security. With Cisco ACI, the network administrator can define policies that automatically configure the network to prioritize traffic from that application, ensure redundancy, and enforce security rules. These policies can be dynamically adjusted as the application's needs evolve, without requiring manual intervention.

Key benefits of applying SDN in data center networks with Cisco ACI include:

- **Simplified Management**: ACI's policy-based management abstracts the complexity of configuring individual switches, routers, and firewalls. Administrators define high-level policies for application requirements, and ACI automatically configures the underlying network infrastructure to meet those needs.
- **Faster Provisioning**: With ACI, the process of deploying a new application or service is vastly accelerated. Network provisioning tasks that would traditionally take days or weeks can now be completed in minutes, reducing time-to-market for new services.

- **Operational Efficiency**: SDN with ACI enables **automation** of routine network tasks, such as security policy enforcement, traffic routing, and network segmentation. This reduces the need for manual intervention, minimizes human error, and ensures that network configurations are consistent across the data center.

SDN in Enterprise Campus Networks: Cisco DNA Center

While data centers benefit greatly from SDN, **enterprise campus networks** also see considerable advantages. **Cisco DNA Center** is Cisco's SDN solution for enterprise campus networks, providing centralized management and automation for network configuration, monitoring, and optimization. Cisco DNA Center offers a comprehensive suite of tools to streamline network operations and support the growing demands of modern businesses, including the Internet of Things (IoT), mobile devices, and cloud applications.

Case Study: Managing an Enterprise Campus with Cisco DNA Center

Consider a global organization with thousands of employees working across multiple branches, each of which relies heavily on wireless connectivity, cloud applications, and video conferencing tools. Managing the network infrastructure across these campuses—ensuring that devices are securely connected, traffic is prioritized, and performance is optimized—can quickly become an overwhelming task.

Cisco DNA Center simplifies this process by offering a centralized platform to **design, provision, monitor, and optimize** the network. With **Cisco DNA**, network administrators can define policies for application performance, security, and device access, and the system automatically enforces those policies across all network devices, including **routers**, **switches**, and **access points**.

For instance, when a new device, such as a laptop or mobile phone, connects to the network, Cisco DNA Center can automatically apply the correct access policy based on the device's identity, user role, and location.

If a device belongs to a particular user group (e.g., the finance team), it will be granted access to specific applications and resources while being restricted from accessing sensitive data or systems.

The key benefits of Cisco DNA in enterprise campus networks are:

- **Automated Network Configuration**: Through DNA Center, network administrators can create and apply configurations automatically across the network, reducing the time and complexity involved in manual configuration.
- **Optimized Network Performance**: Cisco DNA's **intent-based networking** allows network administrators to define business intentions (such as prioritizing voice or video traffic) and automatically configure the network to meet those needs. This helps maintain consistent application performance across the network.
- **Enhanced Security**: By leveraging Cisco DNA's **security policies**, network administrators can automatically apply security measures, such as network segmentation, identity-based access control, and threat detection, to ensure that only authorized devices and users can access the network.

SDN in Branch Networks: Cisco Meraki

For branch networks, **Cisco Meraki** offers a cloud-managed SDN solution that simplifies the management of remote networks while ensuring security, scalability, and performance. Meraki's cloud-managed architecture removes the complexity of traditional on-site management by providing an intuitive interface to configure, monitor, and troubleshoot networks from a centralized location.

Case Study: Simplifying Remote Network Management with Meraki

Consider an organization with dozens of remote offices or branches spread across the country. These offices need to be connected to the corporate network securely, with high-performance internet access, and be able to communicate with the data center and cloud-based applications.

With Cisco Meraki, the network administrator can configure and manage all branch offices from a single cloud-based dashboard. As new Meraki devices (such as **MX security appliances**, **MS switches**, and **MR wireless access points**) are deployed at each location, they can be automatically configured via the cloud.

Meraki's SDN capabilities enable the following:

- **Centralized Management**: All Meraki devices across branches can be configured and monitored from a single interface, regardless of physical location. This provides a unified view of the network, making it easier to troubleshoot, perform firmware updates, and apply changes to multiple locations simultaneously.
- **Simplified VPN Setup**: For branch offices, Meraki's SD-WAN solution automatically configures secure **site-to-site VPNs**, ensuring that traffic between branch offices and the data center is encrypted and optimized for performance.
- **Real-Time Monitoring and Alerts**: Meraki's cloud dashboard provides real-time insights into network performance, security incidents, and device health. Administrators can set up automated alerts to notify them of network issues, such as a malfunctioning device or a security breach.
- **Scalable Deployment**: With Meraki, adding new branch offices is a simple process. New devices are shipped with pre-configured settings, and once powered on, they automatically connect to the cloud, receive their configurations, and become operational.

Benefits of SDN in Cisco Networks

Across all use cases—whether in **data centers**, **enterprise campuses**, or **branch networks**—SDN brings a range of **benefits** that enhance operational efficiency, network performance, and flexibility. The key advantages of SDN in Cisco networks include:

1. **Agility and Flexibility**: SDN enables rapid provisioning and adjustment of network configurations, allowing organizations to quickly respond to changing business requirements or unexpected events.
2. **Cost Savings**: By reducing the complexity of network management and automating routine tasks, SDN helps organizations lower operational costs, minimize human error, and reduce the time spent on network provisioning and troubleshooting.
3. **Improved Network Visibility**: SDN solutions, such as Cisco DNA and Meraki, provide comprehensive monitoring and analytics tools that give network administrators greater visibility into network health, performance, and security, enabling proactive management.
4. **Enhanced Security**: SDN solutions like Cisco ACI and Meraki provide robust security features, such as automated policy enforcement, micro-segmentation, and threat detection, ensuring that network traffic remains secure from end to end.
5. **Simplified Network Management**: Centralized management through tools like Cisco DNA Center and Meraki simplifies the network management process, making it easier to configure, monitor, and troubleshoot large-scale networks.

The real-world applications of **SDN** in **Cisco networks** demonstrate how transformative this technology is for businesses across various industries. Whether you're optimizing your data center with **Cisco ACI**, automating your campus network with **Cisco DNA**, or simplifying remote network management with **Cisco Meraki**, SDN provides the tools and frameworks needed to build efficient, scalable, and secure networks that can adapt to the demands of modern IT environments.

Cisco's SDN solutions empower organizations to embrace network automation, improve network performance, and ensure better security—all while reducing operational costs and enhancing agility. As networks continue to evolve and grow more complex, the adoption of SDN will only increase, making it an essential component of future-proof network designs.

Cisco SD-WAN: The Future of Wide Area Networking

What is SD-WAN and How Does it Work?

In today's rapidly evolving digital landscape, organizations are becoming increasingly dependent on cloud applications, mobile workforces, and data-intensive operations. As a result, traditional Wide Area Networks (WANs), which were designed to connect branch offices to data centers over private leased lines or MPLS (Multiprotocol Label Switching), have struggled to keep pace with the modern demands of flexibility, scalability, and performance.

Enter **SD-WAN** (Software-Defined Wide Area Networking)—a revolutionary approach to networking that fundamentally changes how WANs are designed, deployed, and managed. **Cisco SD-WAN** is one of the leading solutions in this space, offering organizations a way to efficiently connect remote locations, cloud services, and data centers with greater speed, security, and agility.

In this section, we'll explore what **SD-WAN** is, how it works, and why it is quickly becoming the go-to solution for businesses seeking to enhance their WAN infrastructure.

CISCO SD-WAN: THE FUTURE OF WIDE AREA NETWORKING

Understanding SD-WAN: A New Era of Networking

At its core, **SD-WAN** is a **virtualized network architecture** that enables businesses to leverage the internet and other low-cost connections, such as broadband, LTE, or 5G, to securely connect branch offices and remote sites to a central network or the cloud. By decoupling the control plane from the underlying hardware, SD-WAN allows businesses to centrally manage network traffic, apply policies, and automatically route data through the most efficient paths, based on real-time conditions.

In essence, SD-WAN takes the traditional, rigid, and often expensive approach to WAN connectivity and transforms it into a **flexible, software-driven model** that optimizes application performance, reduces costs, and enhances security. SD-WAN enables organizations to use multiple types of WAN connections (including private MPLS, broadband internet, and cellular connections) while offering a **centralized, policy-based management** framework.

How Does SD-WAN Work?

1. Centralized Control Plane

One of the key aspects of SD-WAN is its **centralized control plane**, which is responsible for managing the overall behavior of the network. This central management system allows administrators to configure network policies, define application priorities, and monitor network performance across all connected locations, all from a single, easy-to-use dashboard.

In Cisco SD-WAN, the **Viptela platform** (acquired by Cisco) provides a robust control plane that can be accessed via Cisco's SD-WAN Controller. This controller communicates with **SD-WAN Edge devices** (appliances or virtual devices) at remote locations to configure, monitor, and optimize the network. With this centralized model, organizations gain real-time visibility into their entire WAN infrastructure and can quickly respond to changing network conditions.

2. Path Selection and Traffic Routing

One of the most powerful features of SD-WAN is its ability to dynamically select the best path for network traffic. Traditional WANs often rely on static routing, which means data traffic follows predefined, fixed paths regardless of network performance or congestion. With SD-WAN, traffic is intelligently routed based on real-time network conditions, such as link performance, latency, and jitter.

Cisco SD-WAN continuously monitors the available connections and selects the optimal path for each type of application traffic. For instance:

- **Business-Critical Applications**: Traffic for mission-critical applications, such as VoIP or video conferencing, may be routed over a more stable, low-latency connection (like MPLS or LTE) to ensure high performance.
- **Less Time-Sensitive Traffic**: Non-critical traffic, such as bulk data transfers or software updates, may be sent over more cost-effective connections like broadband internet.

The ability to dynamically steer traffic ensures that the most important applications receive the necessary resources while optimizing the use of available WAN links. Cisco's SD-WAN solution uses **Application-Aware Routing** to prioritize and optimize traffic flows, maintaining performance even during periods of high traffic or network congestion.

3. Secure Connectivity

Security is a cornerstone of SD-WAN architecture, and Cisco SD-WAN takes a **zero-trust security model** to protect data traffic across the WAN. Unlike traditional WANs, which often rely on perimeter security, SD-WAN ensures end-to-end encryption and secure connectivity regardless of the type of transport being used. With SD-WAN, each location (branch, remote site, or cloud) is treated as a trusted entity, and communication is encrypted between all sites.

Key security features of SD-WAN include:

- **Encryption**: SD-WAN ensures that data traveling over the public internet is encrypted, protecting sensitive information from interception or tampering.
- **Secure Direct Internet Access (DIA)**: With SD-WAN, branch offices can securely access cloud-based applications directly, without having to route traffic through a central data center. This reduces latency and improves performance, all while maintaining strong security controls.
- **Advanced Threat Protection**: Cisco's SD-WAN integrates with advanced security solutions like **Cisco Umbrella**, **Cisco Stealthwatch**, and **Cisco Secure Firewall**, offering built-in **intrusion detection**, **firewalling**, and **advanced malware protection**.

By implementing security at the edge of the network, SD-WAN ensures that users and applications are protected from threats, regardless of where they are located.

4. WAN Optimization

WAN optimization is another core benefit of SD-WAN. By using intelligent traffic management, SD-WAN can optimize bandwidth usage, reduce latency, and improve the performance of applications running across the WAN. Cisco SD-WAN includes features like **data deduplication**, **compression**, and **caching**, which can dramatically improve the user experience, especially for remote and branch-office workers accessing cloud-based applications.

For example, when a branch office accesses the same application repeatedly, SD-WAN can cache frequently used data locally, reducing the need to send repetitive requests over the network. This reduces the overall bandwidth consumption and improves application response times. Similarly, data compression techniques minimize the amount of data that needs to be transmitted, further optimizing the available bandwidth.

Benefits of SD-WAN

1. Cost Savings

One of the primary reasons organizations adopt SD-WAN is its potential for **cost savings**. Traditional MPLS-based WANs can be expensive, especially when connecting remote sites and branch offices. By allowing organizations to use cheaper broadband internet or LTE connections alongside MPLS, SD-WAN provides a more cost-effective way to manage WAN traffic.

Cisco SD-WAN enables businesses to lower their WAN costs by leveraging **hybrid WAN** models, where MPLS is used for critical traffic, and broadband or internet-based connections are used for less-critical applications. By reducing reliance on expensive MPLS circuits and making better use of available bandwidth, companies can achieve significant savings.

2. Improved Application Performance

With SD-WAN's intelligent path selection and traffic routing capabilities, **application performance** is greatly enhanced. By dynamically routing traffic over the best available path, SD-WAN ensures that users experience high performance when using cloud applications, VoIP, video conferencing, and other latency-sensitive services.

SD-WAN also optimizes bandwidth usage, so even when network congestion occurs, performance remains stable, particularly for mission-critical applications. Cisco's **Application-Aware Routing** ensures that traffic for specific applications is sent over the best path based on real-time performance metrics like latency and jitter.

3. Simplified WAN Management

Traditional WANs require manual configuration and constant monitoring of network devices, making it difficult to manage large-scale networks. SD-WAN simplifies this by providing a **centralized management dashboard** that allows network administrators to configure, monitor, and troubleshoot the entire network from a single location. This **cloud-based management** allows for rapid deployment of new locations, policies, and configurations without the need for extensive on-site intervention.

Cisco SD-WAN offers a **zero-touch provisioning** feature, meaning that new branch locations can be connected to the network with minimal manual configuration. The SD-WAN devices automatically connect to the centralized controller and receive the correct configuration, making it easier and faster to scale network operations.

4. Flexibility and Agility

With SD-WAN, businesses can quickly adapt to changes in their network needs. Whether it's connecting new offices, expanding cloud application usage, or handling increases in mobile workforce demand, SD-WAN enables fast, flexible, and scalable deployment. Cisco SD-WAN's support for multiple transport types—MPLS, broadband, LTE, and 5G—gives organizations the flexibility to choose the most suitable connection for each location and application.

SD-WAN is rapidly becoming the preferred solution for organizations seeking to modernize their WAN infrastructure. By enabling businesses to **optimize performance**, **reduce costs**, and **enhance security**, SD-WAN offers a range of benefits that traditional WAN solutions simply cannot match. Cisco's SD-WAN platform, powered by **Viptela**, provides a robust, scalable, and secure foundation for organizations to support their evolving networking needs, from cloud applications to remote offices.

As businesses continue to embrace cloud computing, mobile workforces, and digital transformation, the role of SD-WAN in providing agile, cost-effective, and high-performance networking will only increase. Cisco's SD-WAN solutions empower businesses to stay ahead of the curve, delivering fast, reliable, and secure connectivity across their global networks.

Cisco Viptela SD-WAN: Key Features and Benefits

As organizations increasingly adopt cloud services, mobile solutions, and a distributed workforce, the need for a robust, flexible, and secure network architecture becomes paramount. Cisco's **Viptela SD-WAN** is one of the leading solutions in the software-defined wide-area networking (SD-WAN) space, designed to help enterprises achieve seamless connectivity, optimize performance, and ensure security across their entire network infrastructure.

Viptela SD-WAN, now part of Cisco's portfolio after the company's acquisition of Viptela in 2017, brings a cloud-first approach to WAN architecture. It empowers businesses to manage complex networks with greater simplicity, agility, and security, while delivering a superior user experience. In this section, we will explore the **key features and benefits** of Cisco Viptela SD-WAN and how it stands out in the competitive SD-WAN market.

Key Features of Cisco Viptela SD-WAN

1. Centralized Cloud-Based Control

One of the defining features of Cisco Viptela SD-WAN is its **centralized control plane**. This cloud-based management system provides a unified platform for configuring, monitoring, and managing the entire SD-WAN infrastructure, regardless of how large or geographically dispersed the network may be.

The **Viptela vManage** platform serves as the core of the SD-WAN control plane. It enables network administrators to define policies, deploy configurations, and monitor network health from a single console. Because vManage is cloud-based, administrators can access the platform from anywhere, allowing for faster troubleshooting, easier management of remote sites, and simplified software updates and patching.

Key aspects of the centralized control plane include:

- **Automated provisioning**: New branch offices or remote sites can be added to the network quickly using **zero-touch provisioning**. Once the hardware is physically installed, it automatically connects to vManage, receives its configuration, and becomes operational.
- **Policy-driven management**: Policies for routing, security, and quality of service (QoS) can be defined at a high level and automatically applied to all sites across the network. This ensures consistency and reduces configuration errors.

2. Intelligent Path Selection and Dynamic Traffic Routing

Cisco Viptela SD-WAN provides **intelligent path selection** that dynamically determines the best available route for each type of application traffic. This is a major departure from traditional WANs, which rely on static routing and often result in inefficient use of available bandwidth.

Through the **vSmart** control plane, Viptela SD-WAN continuously monitors the state of all available WAN links—whether they are MPLS, broadband, LTE, or 5G—and makes real-time decisions on the optimal path for each application's traffic. For example:

- **Latency-sensitive applications**, such as VoIP and video conferencing, might be routed over a dedicated MPLS or LTE connection for guaranteed performance.
- **Non-time-sensitive traffic**, such as software updates or data backups, can be sent over more cost-effective broadband internet links.

By constantly evaluating link performance, SD-WAN ensures that mission-critical applications are prioritized while maintaining optimal network performance for all traffic. This real-time traffic steering is essential for improving the end-user experience, especially in distributed environments where connectivity can fluctuate.

3. Advanced Security Features

Security is a top priority in the design of Cisco Viptela SD-WAN.

Traditional WANs often rely on perimeter-based security, such as firewalls and VPNs, to protect the network. However, SD-WAN goes beyond perimeter security by embedding **security features directly into the network architecture**.

Key security capabilities in Cisco Viptela SD-WAN include:

- **End-to-end encryption**: Viptela SD-WAN encrypts data traffic between all locations, ensuring that sensitive information remains protected even when it traverses the public internet or other untrusted networks.
- **Secure direct internet access (DIA)**: With SD-WAN, branch offices can access cloud-based applications directly, bypassing the data center and reducing latency. Even in these cases, the connection is secured with encryption and application-level security policies.
- **Zero-trust security**: The Viptela SD-WAN uses a **zero-trust security model**, where every device and user is treated as untrusted until proven otherwise. This approach minimizes the attack surface by ensuring that all traffic is authenticated and authorized, regardless of its origin.

Additionally, Cisco Viptela SD-WAN integrates with Cisco's **Umbrella** security platform, offering **cloud-delivered security** that protects against malware, phishing, and other online threats. The integration of these advanced security features makes Cisco Viptela SD-WAN a highly secure solution for organizations of all sizes.

4. Application-Aware Routing

Cisco Viptela SD-WAN leverages **application-aware routing**, which intelligently steers traffic based on the specific needs of each application. By analyzing real-time network conditions such as latency, jitter, packet loss, and bandwidth availability, Viptela can dynamically adjust the routing of application traffic to ensure optimal performance.

The system can automatically prioritize **mission-critical applications** (e.g., voice, video, or real-time collaboration tools) over **lower-priority traffic** (e.g., email or file transfers). This ensures that end-users have the best experience possible when using time-sensitive applications, even when network congestion or link failures occur.

The application-aware routing also allows businesses to **set policies** for specific applications, enabling them to guarantee performance levels for key business applications while ensuring more efficient use of available bandwidth.

5. Scalable and Flexible Architecture

As businesses grow and evolve, their networking needs change. Cisco Viptela SD-WAN is designed with **scalability** and **flexibility** in mind, making it easy to expand the network without the need for major overhauls or complex upgrades. Whether an organization is adding new branches, connecting remote workers, or expanding its cloud presence, Viptela SD-WAN can seamlessly scale to meet those demands.

The solution supports a **wide range of deployment options**, including physical appliances, virtual devices, and cloud-based solutions. This flexibility allows organizations to tailor their SD-WAN architecture to their specific needs, while still benefiting from the central management and optimization features that make SD-WAN so effective.

6. Integrated WAN Optimization

Cisco Viptela SD-WAN also includes **WAN optimization** features that help improve application performance, reduce bandwidth consumption, and enhance the overall user experience. Through techniques like **data compression**, **deduplication**, and **caching**, Viptela SD-WAN can optimize traffic across the WAN, ensuring faster application response times, especially for remote or branch office locations.

By integrating WAN optimization into the SD-WAN architecture, businesses can achieve **higher throughput** and **lower latency** for applications that rely on large file transfers or real-time data access. This reduces the strain on network bandwidth and improves application performance, particularly in remote or low-bandwidth environments.

Benefits of Cisco Viptela SD-WAN

1. Cost Efficiency

One of the primary advantages of Cisco Viptela SD-WAN is its ability to reduce network costs. Traditional WAN solutions, such as MPLS, can be expensive, especially for large or globally distributed enterprises. Viptela SD-WAN enables organizations to leverage **cost-effective internet links** (e.g., broadband or LTE) for a significant portion of their traffic, while still maintaining high performance and security.

By adopting a hybrid WAN model, businesses can achieve cost savings by reducing their dependence on expensive MPLS circuits and instead use more affordable broadband connections for less critical traffic. This flexibility allows businesses to optimize network spending without sacrificing performance or reliability.

2. Increased Network Agility and Flexibility

Cisco Viptela SD-WAN provides organizations with the agility to rapidly scale and adapt their network infrastructure as needed. With the ability to quickly deploy new branch offices, remote locations, or cloud applications, businesses can respond to changing business needs without the delays and complexities of traditional WAN deployments.

The centralized cloud-based management of Viptela SD-WAN also allows administrators to make policy changes and network configurations in real-time, ensuring that the network can quickly adapt to new requirements or unforeseen disruptions.

3. Enhanced Security and Compliance

With integrated security features like **encryption**, **secure internet access**, and **zero-trust security**, Cisco Viptela SD-WAN enhances the overall security posture of the network. These features help businesses protect sensitive data, meet compliance requirements, and ensure that branch offices and remote workers are securely connected to corporate applications and resources.

The ability to enforce **application-level security policies** and **filter malicious traffic** makes Cisco Viptela SD-WAN particularly valuable for organizations in highly regulated industries, such as healthcare, finance, and government, where data security and compliance are critical.

4. Simplified Network Management

Cisco Viptela SD-WAN simplifies the complex task of managing large, distributed WANs. With its **centralized management** via vManage, network administrators can gain full visibility into the health and performance of the entire network. The **zero-touch provisioning** of new sites and the ability to **automate software updates** and configuration changes reduce manual intervention and the risk of configuration errors, leading to smoother network operations.

Additionally, Cisco Viptela SD-WAN integrates with **advanced analytics** and monitoring tools, providing valuable insights into network performance, application behavior, and traffic patterns, enabling proactive management and troubleshooting.

Cisco Viptela SD-WAN represents a transformative approach to WAN design and management, offering organizations a powerful, flexible, and secure solution for connecting remote sites, branch offices, and cloud applications. With its **centralized control**, **intelligent traffic routing**, **robust security**, and **cost-efficiency**, Viptela SD-WAN is well-suited to meet the demands of modern enterprises. Whether you're looking to enhance application performance, reduce networking costs, or increase operational agility, Cisco Viptela SD-WAN provides a comprehensive, scalable solution that supports business growth and innovation.

Optimizing Data Traffic Over WAN Links

In the context of modern enterprise networking, optimizing data traffic over WAN (Wide Area Network) links is a critical task that directly impacts the performance, reliability, and cost-effectiveness of a network. With an increasing reliance on cloud-based applications, remote work, and geographically dispersed offices, ensuring efficient data flow across WAN links is paramount. Optimizing data traffic ensures that resources are used effectively, applications perform as expected, and users experience minimal latency.

This section will delve into the various techniques and strategies employed by Cisco and other networking solutions to optimize data traffic over WAN links, with a focus on **traffic engineering**, **bandwidth management**, **latency reduction**, **error correction**, and **cost efficiency**. By implementing these strategies, organizations can enhance overall network performance, support critical business applications, and reduce operational costs.

Understanding WAN Traffic Optimization

WAN optimization is a set of technologies and techniques used to enhance the performance and efficiency of wide-area networks by improving data transfer rates, reducing latency, minimizing packet loss, and optimizing bandwidth usage. As enterprises transition from legacy networking models to more modern, cloud-centric architectures, WAN optimization becomes essential for ensuring that performance remains optimal as network traffic grows.

Optimizing traffic over WAN links involves:

- **Reducing latency**: Minimizing the time it takes for data to travel across the network, particularly for mission-critical, real-time applications like voice or video conferencing.
- **Minimizing packet loss**: Ensuring that data packets reach their

destination without loss, especially for applications sensitive to data loss, such as VoIP or video streaming.
- **Maximizing available bandwidth**: Ensuring that the full bandwidth capacity of WAN links is utilized effectively, without unnecessary congestion or bottlenecks.

For businesses that rely heavily on remote offices or cloud-based services, these optimizations can greatly improve the end-user experience, reduce service interruptions, and increase network uptime.

Cisco's Traffic Optimization Solutions

Cisco provides a suite of tools and technologies to optimize traffic over WAN links, ensuring that networks remain responsive, reliable, and cost-effective.

1. Cisco WAN Optimization (WAAS)

Cisco's **Wide Area Application Services (WAAS)** is a key component in WAN optimization. WAAS enhances application performance over WANs by leveraging several techniques to reduce the amount of data transmitted, optimize application delivery, and ensure that bandwidth is used efficiently.

Key features of Cisco WAAS include:

- **Data Deduplication**: This technology eliminates redundant data across the WAN, reducing the amount of information transmitted. By storing a single copy of repeated data, only unique data needs to be sent across the network, saving bandwidth.
- **Compression**: WAAS uses various compression techniques to shrink the size of data packets, further reducing the amount of traffic sent over the WAN.
- **Protocol Optimization**: WAAS accelerates and optimizes protocols like HTTP, CIFS (Common Internet File System), and SMB (Server Message Block) that are typically used in file sharing and application

access, which can be inefficient over WAN links.
- **Caching**: Frequently accessed data is cached locally at remote locations or branch offices, ensuring that only new or updated data needs to be fetched across the WAN. This reduces latency and accelerates response times for users.

By improving throughput, reducing latency, and ensuring efficient bandwidth utilization, Cisco WAAS significantly enhances user experience and increases the overall efficiency of WAN traffic.

2. Cisco SD-WAN and Traffic Engineering

Cisco's **SD-WAN solution** offers advanced traffic optimization capabilities by leveraging **intelligent path selection** and **application-aware routing** to ensure data traffic is routed in the most efficient way possible.

- **Application-Aware Routing**: Cisco SD-WAN can intelligently direct traffic based on the type of application, the required quality of service (QoS), and the performance of available links. For example, voice and video traffic can be given priority and routed over high-performance, low-latency links, while non-time-sensitive traffic like backups or file transfers can be directed over lower-cost broadband links.
- **Dynamic Path Selection**: Cisco SD-WAN continuously monitors the performance of all available WAN links (MPLS, broadband, LTE, etc.) in real-time. If a primary link becomes congested or suffers from latency or packet loss, the system dynamically reroutes traffic to a better-performing link, ensuring continuous application performance.
- **WAN Path Optimization**: Cisco SD-WAN uses real-time performance metrics (e.g., latency, jitter, and packet loss) to make data routing decisions on a per-application basis. This feature ensures that critical applications experience minimal disruption, even if the WAN link quality fluctuates.

By optimizing traffic paths based on real-time network conditions, Cisco SD-WAN ensures that data is always sent via the best possible route, thereby improving performance and reducing costs.

3. Cisco vManage for Network Traffic Insights

Cisco's **vManage** platform, part of its SD-WAN solution, provides a centralized interface for configuring, managing, and optimizing network traffic. vManage allows administrators to gain real-time visibility into network performance and apply traffic management policies across the entire network.

- **Policy-Driven Traffic Management**: Through vManage, administrators can define traffic policies that control how applications are routed across the network. For example, a policy might prioritize VoIP traffic over video or direct cloud traffic over MPLS links.
- **Traffic Analytics and Visibility**: vManage offers detailed analytics, allowing administrators to understand traffic flows, identify potential bottlenecks, and optimize network performance proactively.

With these features, organizations can ensure that their network traffic is optimized according to business priorities and network performance criteria.

Bandwidth Management Techniques

Effective bandwidth management is a cornerstone of WAN traffic optimization. By ensuring that bandwidth is allocated appropriately, organizations can avoid congestion and maintain optimal application performance.

1. Traffic Shaping

Traffic shaping is a technique used to control the flow of data within a network to ensure that bandwidth is used efficiently. It involves the deliberate delaying or buffering of traffic to smooth out bursts and ensure a consistent flow.

For example, Cisco SD-WAN can shape traffic by slowing down non-critical traffic (such as file transfers or large backups) to ensure that latency-sensitive applications (like voice or video) have priority access to available bandwidth. This prevents bandwidth from becoming overloaded and reduces the chances of congestion or packet loss.

Traffic shaping is particularly useful in networks where bandwidth is limited, such as branch offices with lower-speed connections or remote sites with unreliable internet access. It helps prevent network slowdowns and ensures that mission-critical applications perform optimally.

2. Traffic Policing

Traffic policing is a technique used to enforce bandwidth limits for different types of traffic. It involves monitoring and controlling the rate at which data is transmitted across a network. Policing works by **marking** or **dropping** packets that exceed the predefined traffic limits.

For example, Cisco SD-WAN solutions can apply traffic policing rules to restrict the bandwidth usage of non-critical traffic or lower-priority applications. This ensures that essential traffic, such as real-time communications or cloud-based applications, always has the resources it needs to function properly.

By enforcing traffic policies and ensuring that users do not exceed their allocated bandwidth, traffic policing helps maintain the stability and predictability of network performance.

Latency Reduction Techniques

Reducing **latency** is particularly important for real-time applications such as VoIP, video conferencing, and interactive collaboration tools, where even small delays can have a significant impact on the user experience. Cisco provides several techniques to minimize latency across WAN links.

1. WAN Path Optimization with Cisco SD-WAN

Cisco SD-WAN employs **path optimization** techniques to reduce latency by dynamically selecting the best available path for traffic. By continuously monitoring network conditions, such as packet loss, latency, and jitter, SD-WAN can switch to the most optimal path in real time. This ensures that traffic experiences minimal delay, even if the network conditions fluctuate.

2. Application Acceleration with WAN Optimization

Cisco's **WAAS** solution and SD-WAN platforms incorporate technologies that accelerate application performance, thereby reducing latency. Techniques such as **data compression**, **deduplication**, and **protocol optimization** can significantly reduce the time it takes for data to travel across the WAN, especially for bandwidth-intensive applications like file transfers, CRM systems, and ERP systems.

Error Correction and Network Resilience

In addition to optimizing bandwidth usage and reducing latency, maintaining a **high level of data integrity** is crucial. WAN links are subject to errors, including packet loss, jitter, and network congestion, all of which can negatively impact application performance.

Forward Error Correction (FEC)

Forward Error Correction (FEC) is a technique used to correct errors in transmitted data by adding redundancy. If a packet is lost or corrupted during transmission, FEC allows the receiver to reconstruct the lost data using the redundant information sent with the packet. This reduces the need for retransmissions, helping to minimize delays and improve the overall efficiency of the network.

Cisco SD-WAN and other WAN optimization solutions integrate FEC to improve the resiliency of WAN traffic, particularly for real-time and high-priority applications.

Optimizing data traffic over WAN links is a critical component of modern enterprise networking. By leveraging technologies such as Cisco SD-WAN, WAN optimization, traffic shaping, and intelligent routing, organizations can ensure that their networks deliver superior performance, reduce operational costs, and support mission-critical applications across geographically distributed locations. As businesses continue to adopt cloud-first strategies and expand their global reach, WAN optimization will play an increasingly important role in driving network efficiency and enhancing the user experience.

Security Considerations in SD-WAN Deployments

As enterprises continue to embrace **Software-Defined Wide Area Networks (SD-WAN)** for their flexibility, scalability, and cost-effectiveness, ensuring the security of the network becomes a paramount concern. SD-WAN solutions, such as Cisco's Viptela and Meraki platforms, enable businesses to securely connect their branch offices, remote locations, and data centers over any type of underlying transport network—whether MPLS, broadband, or LTE. However, while SD-WAN offers significant advantages in terms of performance and network agility, it also introduces new security challenges that must be addressed to prevent cyber threats, data breaches, and unauthorized access.

This section delves into the key security considerations that organizations should take into account when deploying SD-WAN solutions. We will explore how SD-WAN affects network security, the potential risks, and the best practices for mitigating these risks to ensure the integrity, confidentiality, and availability of network resources.

1. The Security Implications of SD-WAN

One of the main advantages of SD-WAN is its ability to enable secure, direct-to-cloud connectivity for branch offices and remote users. Traditional WAN architectures often rely on backhauling traffic through a central data center, which can introduce latency and increase complexity. With SD-WAN, traffic can be routed securely across multiple public and private links, including the internet, without having to go through a central hub.

However, this increased flexibility introduces several new security considerations:

- **Traffic Encryption**: Since SD-WAN solutions use the internet as part of the underlying transport, ensuring that traffic is securely encrypted is critical. Without proper encryption, data is exposed to interception and tampering, especially in transit across untrusted networks such as the public internet.
- **Endpoint Security**: SD-WAN deployments often connect remote offices, branch locations, and even mobile users to the corporate network. This makes the network edge more vulnerable to threats. Proper endpoint security measures must be implemented to ensure that devices connecting to the network do not introduce vulnerabilities.
- **Segmentation and Isolation**: With SD-WAN, organizations can segment traffic based on application types or user roles. While this improves network performance and flexibility, it also introduces the potential risk of misconfigured policies that could lead to unauthorized access or data leakage.

2. Cisco's SD-WAN Security Features

Cisco has built a suite of security features directly into its SD-WAN solutions to mitigate the security risks associated with SD-WAN deployments. These include:

a. End-to-End Encryption

Cisco SD-WAN offers **end-to-end encryption** for all data in transit across the WAN. By default, SD-WAN traffic is encrypted using IPsec (Internet Protocol Security), which ensures that even if the data is intercepted during transmission, it cannot be read by unauthorized parties. This encryption extends across all SD-WAN tunnels, including both public and private transport networks.

- **IPsec Encryption**: Cisco SD-WAN automatically encrypts data packets using strong cryptographic protocols, protecting data from interception.
- **AES-256 Encryption**: The encryption standard used is AES (Advanced Encryption Standard) with 256-bit keys, which is highly secure and resistant to brute-force attacks.

b. Secure Internet Access

SD-WAN solutions often enable branch offices to connect directly to the internet, bypassing traditional centralized data centers. However, this introduces the risk of exposing the network to internet-borne threats, such as malware, DDoS (Distributed Denial of Service) attacks, and unauthorized access.

To mitigate these risks, Cisco SD-WAN integrates with **Cloud Security Gateways** (CSG) and **Secure Web Gateways** (SWG), providing security filtering and inspection for all internet-bound traffic. These solutions help to detect and block malicious traffic before it reaches the network or endpoints.

- **Web Filtering**: Cisco's integration with SWGs ensures that traffic to

known malicious websites or services is blocked in real time.
- **Malware Detection**: By using Cisco's Threat Defense technologies, SD-WAN solutions can inspect encrypted traffic for malicious payloads and detect threats without compromising performance.

c. Zero Trust Security Model

One of the most important security models for SD-WAN deployments is **Zero Trust**. In a Zero Trust architecture, trust is never implicitly granted, regardless of the network's origin. Each request for access is authenticated and authorized based on identity, context, and security posture, rather than the physical location of the device or user.

Cisco SD-WAN integrates Zero Trust security principles by:

- **Identity-Based Policies**: Access control is based on user identity, device health, and application type, rather than relying on perimeter-based defenses.
- **Granular Segmentation**: SD-WAN allows for highly granular segmentation of traffic, meaning that even if an attacker gains access to one part of the network, they cannot easily move laterally to other parts of the network.

d. Secure Direct Internet Access (DIA)

As businesses increasingly rely on cloud-based applications, enabling **Direct Internet Access (DIA)** for remote sites or branch offices becomes essential. Cisco SD-WAN provides secure DIA by encrypting traffic and using intelligent routing to ensure that branch offices can directly access cloud services without sending traffic back through a centralized data center, reducing latency.

- **SSL Inspection**: Cisco SD-WAN solutions can inspect **SSL-encrypted traffic** for threats, including malware and phishing attempts, that might otherwise evade traditional firewalls.
- **Cloud Security Integration**: Integration with Cisco Umbrella (a

cloud-delivered security service) provides threat intelligence and security filtering to protect branch offices from internet-based attacks while ensuring that cloud application performance is not hindered.

3. Network Segmentation and Micro-Segmentation

Effective **network segmentation** is critical for minimizing attack surfaces and preventing lateral movement by attackers once they gain initial access to the network. Cisco's SD-WAN solution allows organizations to create **virtualized network segments** for different types of traffic, applications, or users.

- **Traffic Segmentation**: Cisco SD-WAN allows for the creation of virtual networks, each with its own policies and security controls. For example, voice traffic can be isolated from corporate data traffic to ensure optimal performance and security.
- **Micro-Segmentation**: By applying more granular security policies to individual devices and users, organizations can isolate potential threats and prevent them from spreading across the network. This is particularly useful in preventing malware from propagating within the organization.

a. Secure Application Segmentation

SD-WAN can enforce different levels of security policies for various types of applications. For example, critical applications such as voice or financial systems can be assigned higher security policies and isolated from less critical traffic, reducing the likelihood of a security breach affecting these systems.

b. Dynamic Segmentation for Cloud Environments

As enterprises move to hybrid and multi-cloud environments, managing security at the cloud edge is vital. Cisco SD-WAN allows for dynamic segmentation of cloud applications based on their sensitivity or importance to the business, ensuring that traffic is appropriately routed and secured.

4. Threat Intelligence Integration

With the rapid increase in cyber threats, having real-time access to up-to-date threat intelligence is essential for identifying and mitigating risks as they emerge. Cisco's SD-WAN solutions integrate seamlessly with Cisco's **Threat Intelligence Director** and **Cisco Talos**, a globally recognized threat intelligence group.

- **Automatic Threat Detection**: Cisco Talos continuously analyzes network traffic for patterns of known threats and vulnerabilities. Any new or emerging threats can be automatically flagged and mitigated.
- **Real-Time Security Updates**: Cisco SD-WAN automatically incorporates the latest threat intelligence to adjust security policies and defenses dynamically.

By leveraging Cisco's integrated threat intelligence, SD-WAN deployments can stay ahead of evolving threats, offering organizations a proactive approach to securing their networks.

5. Security Monitoring and Logging

Continuous **security monitoring** is essential for detecting anomalies, potential breaches, or unauthorized access in real time. Cisco SD-WAN provides robust monitoring and logging features that integrate with **Cisco Stealthwatch** and other network security monitoring solutions.

- **Real-Time Visibility**: Cisco SD-WAN provides centralized visibility into network traffic, enabling administrators to monitor traffic patterns, detect malicious behavior, and apply security measures promptly.
- **Security Event Logging**: Detailed logs of security events are maintained, providing the necessary data for audits, troubleshooting, and compliance reporting.

6. Multi-Cloud and Hybrid Cloud Security

In today's enterprise landscape, many organizations operate in **hybrid cloud environments** where applications and data are spread across both on-premises data centers and public/private clouds. Cisco SD-WAN facilitates secure multi-cloud connectivity and ensures that data and applications are protected across the entire hybrid environment.

- **Encrypted Cloud Connectivity**: SD-WAN ensures that all traffic between branch offices and cloud providers is encrypted, protecting data in transit.
- **Cloud Security Policies**: Cisco SD-WAN integrates with leading cloud security solutions to enforce security policies across cloud environments, ensuring that security is consistently maintained regardless of the location of the applications or data.

While SD-WAN solutions like Cisco's offer tremendous benefits in terms of agility, performance, and cost efficiency, they also introduce new security challenges. As businesses adopt SD-WAN to support the growing demand for cloud applications, direct internet access, and remote work, ensuring robust security becomes a top priority.

By implementing a comprehensive security strategy that includes encryption, threat intelligence, Zero Trust principles, and endpoint security, organizations can confidently deploy SD-WAN while protecting their networks from evolving cyber threats. With Cisco's suite of security features, including end-to-end encryption, secure internet access, application segmentation, and real-time threat detection, businesses can enjoy the benefits of SD-WAN while maintaining a secure, resilient, and trusted network environment.

Integrating Cisco SD-WAN with Cloud Applications

As businesses increasingly move their workloads and applications to the cloud, the traditional methods of routing traffic through on-premises data centers have become inefficient and costly. Traditional WAN architectures, which often require backhauling traffic through a centralized location, introduce latency, complexity, and additional bandwidth consumption. In contrast, **Software-Defined WAN (SD-WAN)** solutions, such as Cisco SD-WAN, offer a more agile and scalable way to connect branch offices, remote locations, and cloud environments with direct, secure connectivity.

The ability to integrate SD-WAN with cloud applications is one of the key reasons organizations are adopting SD-WAN technologies. With Cisco SD-WAN, enterprises can ensure **optimized performance** for their cloud applications while maintaining **security**, **visibility**, and **control** over their network traffic. This section explores how Cisco SD-WAN integrates with cloud applications, the benefits of this integration, and the best practices for deploying SD-WAN in a cloud-first environment.

1. The Shift to Cloud-First Networks

In the past, enterprises relied on **MPLS-based WAN** architectures that routed all traffic through centralized data centers. However, with the shift to cloud computing, businesses are increasingly leveraging SaaS (Software as a Service) platforms, cloud-native applications, and hybrid cloud environments, making the need for traditional WAN architectures less relevant.

Cloud applications, such as **Office 365**, **Salesforce**, **Amazon Web Services (AWS)**, **Microsoft Azure**, and **Google Cloud Platform (GCP)**, are accessed directly from branch offices and remote locations. Backhauling traffic to a central data center introduces unnecessary latency and reduces performance for cloud-hosted applications, which ultimately degrades the user experience.

Cisco SD-WAN solves this problem by allowing organizations to bypass the data center and establish **direct-to-cloud** connections. This approach reduces the complexity and latency associated with traditional WAN architectures while enabling businesses to harness the full benefits of the cloud.

2. Cisco SD-WAN and Cloud-Optimized Routing

Cisco SD-WAN optimizes the delivery of cloud applications by intelligently routing traffic across multiple transport networks—such as MPLS, broadband, LTE, or 5G—based on real-time application needs. Cisco's SD-WAN solution incorporates **intelligent path control**, which dynamically chooses the best available path for each application. This feature is particularly critical for **cloud-based applications**, where performance, availability, and latency are paramount.

Key Features of Cisco SD-WAN for Cloud Applications:

- **Dynamic Path Selection**: Cisco SD-WAN continuously monitors the quality and performance of network paths and selects the best route based on factors like latency, jitter, packet loss, and bandwidth. For cloud applications, this ensures that traffic is routed over the most optimal link, minimizing delays and maintaining application performance.
- **Direct-to-Cloud Connectivity**: With Cisco SD-WAN, branch offices and remote users can connect directly to cloud applications without backhauling traffic through centralized data centers. This direct connection reduces latency and improves overall application performance.
- **Performance-Based Application Routing**: Cisco SD-WAN enables **application-aware routing**, where network paths are chosen based on specific application requirements, such as low-latency or high-bandwidth applications. For cloud-hosted apps, this ensures optimal

performance for critical workloads.
- **Cloud Integration with Public and Hybrid Clouds**: Cisco SD-WAN can seamlessly integrate with cloud services from providers like AWS, Azure, and GCP. It supports **multi-cloud** environments, ensuring that traffic between branch offices and the cloud is both secure and optimized.

3. Benefits of Integrating Cisco SD-WAN with Cloud Applications

Integrating Cisco SD-WAN with cloud applications delivers several key benefits to enterprises, from performance optimization to improved security. These benefits include:

a. Improved Performance for Cloud Applications

One of the most significant benefits of SD-WAN integration with cloud applications is the **improved application performance**. Traditional WAN architectures, which rely on backhauling traffic to a centralized data center, introduce latency and performance degradation. With Cisco SD-WAN, traffic can be routed directly to cloud services, minimizing delays and improving the responsiveness of cloud applications.

By using **direct-to-cloud access** and **dynamic path selection**, Cisco SD-WAN ensures that cloud applications are always delivered with the best possible performance, regardless of network conditions. This is particularly important for business-critical applications like **voice over IP (VoIP)**, **video conferencing**, and **cloud-based enterprise resource planning (ERP)** systems.

b. Enhanced Security for Cloud-Based Traffic

Although cloud applications offer a wide range of benefits, they also introduce security challenges. Traffic between branch offices and cloud services must be encrypted and protected from unauthorized access. Cisco SD-WAN provides **end-to-end encryption**, ensuring that data in transit is secure as it moves across public networks.

- **Secure Cloud Connectivity**: With Cisco SD-WAN, cloud traffic is encrypted using strong security protocols such as **IPsec**, which ensures that cloud-based data is protected from potential eavesdropping or tampering.
- **Cloud Security Integration**: Cisco SD-WAN integrates with cloud security services like **Cisco Umbrella** and **Cisco CloudLock** to provide an additional layer of security. These services offer real-time threat intelligence and protection against malware, phishing, and other cyberattacks targeting cloud applications.
- **Micro-Segmentation for Cloud Resources**: Cisco SD-WAN can be used to enforce **micro-segmentation** policies for cloud applications. By segmenting traffic based on application type or user role, organizations can limit exposure and contain potential threats to specific cloud workloads.

c. Simplified Management and Visibility

Managing cloud applications and networks can be challenging, especially when there are multiple cloud providers and remote sites to manage. Cisco SD-WAN offers a **centralized management platform**, which simplifies the monitoring and control of cloud application traffic.

- **Cisco SD-WAN vManage**: Cisco's vManage platform provides a centralized, cloud-based interface to configure, monitor, and troubleshoot SD-WAN deployments. This interface offers full visibility into application performance, traffic patterns, and security events across both cloud and on-premises networks.
- **Application Analytics**: With Cisco SD-WAN, network administrators can monitor the performance of cloud applications in real time, identifying issues like network congestion, latency spikes, or application slowdowns. This visibility helps IT teams quickly address issues before they impact users.
- **Zero Touch Provisioning (ZTP)**: Cisco SD-WAN allows for **Zero Touch Provisioning**, which simplifies the deployment and con-

figuration of SD-WAN devices. This is especially beneficial for organizations with remote branch offices that need secure, cloud-enabled connectivity with minimal manual configuration.

d. Cost Savings and Operational Efficiency

Traditional WAN architectures that rely on MPLS for cloud connectivity are expensive and inefficient. By using SD-WAN, organizations can replace costly MPLS circuits with more affordable broadband internet connections without sacrificing performance or security.

- **Reduced WAN Costs**: With Cisco SD-WAN, businesses can utilize cost-effective broadband internet or LTE connections to establish cloud connectivity, significantly reducing their reliance on expensive MPLS.
- **Optimized Bandwidth Usage**: Cisco SD-WAN allows for efficient **bandwidth utilization** by dynamically directing traffic over the best available link. This helps organizations optimize their cloud application usage while controlling costs.

4. Best Practices for Integrating Cisco SD-WAN with Cloud Applications

To ensure a successful integration of Cisco SD-WAN with cloud applications, organizations should follow a set of best practices. These practices will help maximize the performance, security, and scalability of the solution while ensuring that cloud applications run efficiently across the network.

a. Assess Your Cloud Traffic Needs

Before deploying Cisco SD-WAN for cloud applications, organizations should assess their cloud application traffic and determine their specific needs. This includes understanding the types of applications used (e.g., SaaS, IaaS, PaaS), their bandwidth requirements, and the criticality of application performance. By gaining insights into traffic patterns, IT teams can design SD-WAN policies that optimize cloud traffic and ensure that critical applications receive the necessary resources.

b. Implement End-to-End Security for Cloud Traffic

As cloud traffic is often routed over the public internet, securing it is essential. Cisco SD-WAN's **end-to-end encryption, secure internet access**, and integration with cloud security services should be leveraged to ensure the confidentiality and integrity of cloud-based data.

c. Plan for Scalability

Cloud environments are dynamic and constantly evolving. When designing your SD-WAN architecture, it is essential to plan for scalability to accommodate future growth in cloud usage. Cisco SD-WAN offers **multi-cloud integration** and the ability to scale as your organization expands its use of cloud applications.

d. Leverage Automation and Orchestration

Automation is key to maintaining agility and operational efficiency in SD-WAN deployments. Cisco SD-WAN's **automation and orchestration features** help streamline network management tasks, such as traffic routing, policy enforcement, and configuration changes. By using Cisco's **DNA Center** or **vManage**, organizations can automate routine tasks, reducing the risk of human error and improving overall operational efficiency.

The integration of Cisco SD-WAN with cloud applications represents a powerful solution for modern enterprises seeking to optimize their network infrastructure. By offering direct, secure, and optimized connectivity to cloud services, Cisco SD-WAN improves performance, enhances security, simplifies management, and reduces costs.

Organizations that adopt Cisco SD-WAN can unlock the full potential of their cloud applications, ensuring that they run efficiently, securely, and at scale. By following best practices for deployment and leveraging Cisco's advanced features, enterprises can confidently move toward a cloud-first networking approach, positioning themselves for long-term success in an increasingly digital world.

Case Study: Implementing Cisco SD-WAN in a Multi-Branch Environment

As organizations grow and expand, maintaining efficient, secure, and cost-effective network connectivity across multiple branch locations becomes increasingly complex. Traditional WAN architectures—relying on private MPLS lines and backhauling traffic through a central data center—are often expensive and do not scale well in today's cloud-first world. To address these challenges, many enterprises are turning to **Software-Defined WAN (SD-WAN)** solutions, which offer significant advantages in terms of flexibility, performance, and cost.

This case study explores how a **global enterprise** with numerous branch offices deployed **Cisco SD-WAN** to optimize their network performance, reduce costs, and simplify management across their multi-branch environment.

1. The Organization: A Global Retail Enterprise

Company Overview: Our case study focuses on a large multinational retail company with a **global footprint**, operating in more than 20 countries. The company has more than **100 branch offices** and retail locations across North America, Europe, Asia, and South America. Their network needs to support a wide range of services, including **point-of-sale (POS) systems**, **customer relationship management (CRM)** tools, **cloud-based inventory management**, and **video conferencing** for collaboration among geographically dispersed teams.

The Challenge

The company's traditional WAN infrastructure—based on a mix of **MPLS connections** and private leased lines—was becoming increasingly difficult to manage and scale. Specific challenges included:

- **High WAN Costs**: MPLS lines were expensive, especially as the company continued to expand. The cost per branch location for dedicated MPLS circuits became prohibitive.
- **Latency and Performance Issues**: Traffic destined for cloud-based applications like **Salesforce**, **Office 365**, and **Amazon Web Services (AWS)** had to be routed through centralized data centers, causing unnecessary latency and performance bottlenecks.
- **Complex Network Management**: Managing a traditional WAN across 100+ branch offices with multiple service providers and varying bandwidth capabilities proved challenging. Network performance monitoring and troubleshooting were time-consuming and inefficient.
- **Scalability Concerns**: As the company continued to open new locations, scaling their network to meet increasing demands became more complex and resource-intensive. New branches required lengthy installation times for MPLS circuits and network configurations.

The company realized that a modern solution was needed to address these challenges and support their growing reliance on cloud applications and the digital transformation of their retail operations.

2. Solution: Cisco SD-WAN Deployment

The company decided to deploy **Cisco SD-WAN**, recognizing the solution's ability to optimize WAN performance, provide direct access to cloud applications, and reduce network costs. Cisco's SD-WAN platform would address their three primary goals: **improving network performance**, **reducing costs**, and **simplifying management** across their multi-branch environment.

Deployment Strategy

The deployment was carried out in a phased approach, with the following key steps:

Assessment and Planning: Before the deployment, the IT team conducted a thorough network assessment to understand the traffic patterns, application requirements, and current WAN performance. They identified the specific branch locations that would benefit most from SD-WAN and developed a deployment plan based on the following objectives:

- **Direct-to-Cloud Access**: Bypassing centralized data centers to improve performance for cloud applications.
- **Dynamic Path Selection**: Ensuring that traffic would always be routed over the most optimal path based on real-time conditions (e.g., latency, jitter, packet loss).
- **Security and Encryption**: Maintaining secure, encrypted connections between branch offices and cloud services.
- **Centralized Management**: Enabling simplified network configuration, monitoring, and troubleshooting through a single dashboard.

Pilot Program: The company selected **five branch offices** for a pilot deployment. These branches represented a cross-section of the company's network requirements, including remote locations, high-traffic retail stores, and regional offices that relied heavily on cloud applications. The pilot deployment included the installation of **Cisco vEdge routers**, which would form the foundation of the SD-WAN solution.

SD-WAN Deployment: The SD-WAN deployment involved configuring the Cisco SD-WAN appliances (vEdge routers) at each branch and connecting them to the central management platform, **Cisco vManage**. The SD-WAN solution was integrated with the company's existing **MPLS** links and broadband connections, allowing for a hybrid WAN environment. The SD-WAN solution automatically detected and classified network traffic, prioritized it according to the company's needs, and selected the optimal path for each application.

Migration to Full SD-WAN: After successfully completing the pilot program, the company began expanding the SD-WAN solution to all other branch locations. The phased rollout allowed the company to minimize disruptions to day-to-day operations and ensure that each branch was optimized for cloud application performance.

3. Benefits Realized from the Cisco SD-WAN Deployment

After implementing Cisco SD-WAN, the company realized a range of benefits that significantly improved their network performance, reduced costs, and simplified their IT operations. Some of the key benefits included:

a. Improved Network Performance

Cisco SD-WAN allowed the company to **optimize cloud application performance** by enabling **direct-to-cloud access**. Previously, all traffic to cloud services like **Salesforce** and **Office 365** was routed through a central data center, causing delays and poor performance. With Cisco SD-WAN, traffic from remote branches was directed straight to the cloud, bypassing the data center and reducing latency.

Additionally, **dynamic path selection** allowed Cisco SD-WAN to automatically choose the best network path based on real-time conditions. For instance, when an MPLS link experienced high latency or packet loss, SD-WAN seamlessly switched traffic to an available broadband or LTE link without impacting application performance.

b. Cost Savings

One of the most immediate benefits of Cisco SD-WAN was **cost reduction**. The company was able to replace **expensive MPLS circuits** with more affordable broadband internet connections for many of its branch offices. With the ability to combine different types of transport (MPLS, broadband, LTE) into a hybrid network, the company was able to maintain high performance while dramatically lowering their network expenses.

Furthermore, **zero-touch provisioning (ZTP)** enabled faster and more efficient branch office deployments, further reducing the operational costs associated with network installation and management.

c. Simplified Network Management

The company was able to reduce the complexity of managing a multi-branch WAN through **centralized network management** using Cisco vManage. This single-pane-of-glass interface allowed the IT team to monitor traffic performance, configure policies, and troubleshoot issues across all locations without having to manually log into individual devices. The automation of routine network tasks further reduced the administrative burden.

Additionally, the **real-time visibility** provided by Cisco vManage enabled the IT team to proactively identify and resolve issues before they impacted end-users, improving overall network reliability.

d. Enhanced Security and Compliance

With **end-to-end encryption** and **secure direct cloud access**, Cisco SD-WAN helped the company improve the security of its cloud-based applications. By encrypting all traffic between branches and the cloud, the company was able to protect sensitive customer data and ensure that the network was secure from unauthorized access.

Cisco SD-WAN also integrated with the company's existing **cloud security solutions**, including **Cisco Umbrella** and **Cisco Threat Grid**, to provide an additional layer of protection. This integration allowed the company to apply consistent security policies across all locations, ensuring that cloud applications were protected from cyber threats.

e. Greater Agility and Scalability

Cisco SD-WAN allowed the company to quickly **scale their network** as they opened new branches and expanded their global presence. The **Zero-Touch Provisioning (ZTP)** feature allowed new branches to be brought online with minimal effort, making it faster and easier to scale the network without extensive manual intervention. Additionally, Cisco SD-WAN's ability to integrate with multiple transport technologies—MPLS, broadband, and LTE—enabled the company to adapt quickly to changing business needs.

The deployment of Cisco SD-WAN provided the global retail enterprise with the **performance**, **cost-efficiency**, and **scalability** it needed to support its growing cloud-based applications and multi-branch operations. By implementing SD-WAN, the company was able to improve network performance, reduce costs, simplify network management, and enhance security—all while supporting its digital transformation.

As more enterprises move to a cloud-first model, SD-WAN will continue to be a cornerstone of modern networking. Cisco's SD-WAN solution offers a future-proof approach to managing network traffic, providing businesses with the flexibility, agility, and performance they need to stay competitive in an increasingly digital world. This case study demonstrates how Cisco SD-WAN can transform a traditional WAN into a high-performance, secure, and cost-effective cloud-ready network.

Cisco Meraki: Simplified Network Management

Introduction to Cisco Meraki

In today's fast-paced business environment, organizations require reliable, scalable, and easy-to-manage networking solutions. Network infrastructure must be able to handle increasing demands for bandwidth, security, and performance, all while ensuring seamless connectivity across distributed sites, mobile users, and cloud-based applications. **Cisco Meraki**, a cloud-managed networking solution, has emerged as a leader in addressing these challenges by offering a simplified, highly automated approach to network management.

Cisco Meraki, which was acquired by Cisco in 2012, provides a wide range of network solutions including **routers**, **switches**, **wireless access points**, **security appliances**, and **surveillance cameras**, all integrated and managed via the **cloud**. The promise of Meraki lies in its ability to streamline network operations, reduce the complexity of day-to-day management, and improve visibility across distributed networks without the need for specialized IT expertise.

In this section, we will provide a detailed overview of Cisco Meraki, its features, benefits, and how it simplifies network management for enterprises of all sizes. Whether for a small business or a global corporation, Meraki offers a powerful solution to improve operational efficiency, performance, and scalability across the network.

1. What is Cisco Meraki?

Cisco Meraki is a cloud-based, centrally managed networking solution that enables businesses to deploy, monitor, and manage their entire network infrastructure remotely. Using the Meraki cloud dashboard, IT teams can configure and troubleshoot network devices from any location, without the need for on-site intervention or complex configurations. This approach eliminates the need for specialized network expertise, making Meraki an attractive choice for organizations with limited IT resources.

Meraki offers a **holistic suite of networking products**, including:

- **Wireless LAN (Wi-Fi)**: Access points that provide fast, secure, and scalable wireless networks.
- **Switches**: Managed Ethernet switches designed for high-performance, reliable connectivity.
- **Security Appliances**: Enterprise-grade firewalls and security solutions that protect against external threats.
- **Mobile Device Management (MDM)**: A unified platform to manage and secure mobile devices and applications within the organization.
- **Security Cameras**: Integrated video surveillance solutions that provide real-time monitoring and analytics.
- **Sensors**: A range of devices for monitoring environmental conditions, such as air quality and temperature.

The key differentiator of Meraki is its **cloud management**. The entire Meraki ecosystem is managed from a centralized web-based dashboard, accessible from any device with an internet connection. This cloud-driven architecture allows for real-time monitoring, policy enforcement, troubleshooting, and updates—no matter where the devices are located. By centralizing control, Meraki eliminates the need for complex on-site configurations, manual updates, and hardware-based management systems.

2. The Cloud Management Model

Cisco Meraki is powered by a **cloud-based architecture**, which means that all network management tasks—including configuration, monitoring, troubleshooting, and firmware updates—are handled remotely through the Meraki dashboard. This eliminates the need for time-consuming manual interventions and significantly reduces the complexity of managing large-scale networks.

Key Features of the Cloud Management Model:

- **Web-Based Dashboard**: The Meraki dashboard is the central management interface. Accessible via any web browser, the dashboard allows administrators to configure, monitor, and troubleshoot network devices from anywhere in the world. The intuitive interface is designed for users at all levels of technical expertise, allowing easy configuration of complex network policies and settings.
- **Zero-Touch Provisioning**: Meraki devices come with a plug-and-play setup process, meaning devices can be deployed to any location without requiring an on-site IT expert. Devices automatically connect to the Meraki cloud and download their configuration settings, making deployment faster and less error-prone.
- **Automated Updates**: One of the major advantages of the cloud-managed Meraki platform is the ability to deliver **automated firmware updates**. Meraki automatically pushes updates to devices, ensuring that the network is always running the latest, most secure software without manual intervention.
- **Real-Time Monitoring**: Meraki's cloud-based management platform provides real-time monitoring and analytics of network performance, security, and health. Administrators can view detailed reports, including traffic statistics, device health, and event logs, helping them proactively address issues before they affect users or applications.

- **Scalability**: Because Meraki is cloud-based, expanding or modifying the network is quick and efficient. New devices can be added to the network, and configurations can be pushed to them remotely, without the need for manual intervention. This makes Meraki an ideal solution for organizations that need to scale quickly across multiple locations, such as retail chains, franchises, or remote offices.

3. Key Features of Cisco Meraki

Cisco Meraki provides an integrated suite of solutions that span across various aspects of network infrastructure, security, and management. Below are the key features of Cisco Meraki that make it a compelling solution for modern enterprises:

a. Simplified Network Configuration and Deployment

Meraki devices are designed to be easily deployed and configured using a cloud-based dashboard. Once devices are connected to the internet, they automatically reach out to the Meraki cloud to download their configurations. This **zero-touch provisioning** allows businesses to deploy new devices without the need for local IT intervention or specialized networking knowledge.

- **Automated Device Setup**: Devices automatically pull down configuration settings from the cloud when powered on. This eliminates the need for IT teams to manually configure each device on-site.
- **Centralized Configuration**: All network settings are configured through a single interface, allowing administrators to define policies for Wi-Fi access, VLANs, security rules, and traffic shaping across the network.

b. Real-Time Monitoring and Analytics

Meraki provides detailed visibility into network performance with real-time monitoring tools. The **Meraki dashboard** offers comprehensive analytics for all network traffic, device health, and security events.

CISCO MERAKI: SIMPLIFIED NETWORK MANAGEMENT

- **Traffic Analytics**: Administrators can track the types of applications being used across the network, identify bandwidth hogs, and determine the source of performance issues.
- **Device Health Monitoring**: The dashboard provides status indicators for all devices in the network, including access points, switches, and security appliances. IT teams can quickly identify and resolve any issues, reducing downtime.
- **Event Logs**: Meraki provides a rich set of logs and reports to assist with troubleshooting, security monitoring, and compliance audits.

c. Security and Compliance

Security is a top priority for any network, and Cisco Meraki offers several advanced security features that help protect against unauthorized access and cyber threats.

- **Integrated Security Appliances**: Meraki's security appliances (MX series) include enterprise-grade firewalls, VPN support, content filtering, intrusion detection, and protection (IDS/IPS), and malware protection.
- **Cloud-Based Security**: Since Meraki is cloud-managed, security updates are automatically pushed to the devices, ensuring the latest patches are always applied.
- **VPN Support**: Meraki's **site-to-site** and **client VPN** capabilities ensure secure remote access to the network. Additionally, Meraki's VPN client can be used to connect branch offices, mobile workers, and remote sites securely.

d. Wireless and Wired Network Management

Meraki provides both wireless and wired network solutions that are fully integrated into the cloud management platform.

- **Wi-Fi Management**: Meraki access points are designed for easy deployment and management. They offer enterprise-level security,

including WPA3 encryption, advanced guest networking features, and seamless roaming across large areas.
- **Switching Solutions**: Meraki switches integrate seamlessly into the Meraki cloud platform, allowing for easy management of wired Ethernet networks. Meraki's switches offer features such as **PoE** (Power over Ethernet), **layer 2 and layer 3 switching**, and **port-level configuration**.

e. Scalability and Flexibility

Cisco Meraki's cloud-managed solution is designed to scale from small office networks to large global networks. The scalability of Meraki is one of its most powerful features, allowing businesses to deploy devices across multiple locations and remotely manage them from anywhere.

- **Global Scalability**: With Meraki, organizations can deploy devices across the globe without worrying about local configuration or expertise. The centralized cloud management allows for uniform network policies across all locations.
- **Multi-Device Management**: Meraki supports the management of not just networking devices, but also mobile devices and security cameras, offering a comprehensive solution for businesses of all sizes.

4. Benefits of Cisco Meraki

Cisco Meraki offers several advantages to organizations looking for a simplified and efficient networking solution:

- **Reduced IT Complexity**: The cloud-managed nature of Meraki reduces the need for specialized IT staff to maintain and configure network devices. IT teams can focus on more strategic initiatives, as day-to-day network management tasks are streamlined.
- **Cost Efficiency**: Meraki eliminates the need for on-premises hardware controllers and management systems, which can be costly

to maintain and upgrade. With Meraki's subscription-based pricing, businesses can reduce capital expenditures and operate on a more predictable cost structure.
- **Improved Agility**: Meraki's zero-touch provisioning and cloud-based management make it easier to deploy new devices and scale the network as business needs evolve.
- **Security and Compliance**: Meraki ensures that all devices are kept up to date with the latest security patches, reducing the risk of security breaches. The platform also simplifies compliance with industry standards by providing easy access to logs and reports.
- **Better Visibility and Control**: Meraki provides real-time visibility into network performance, device status, and security events, allowing for proactive troubleshooting and optimization.

Cisco Meraki is revolutionizing the way organizations manage their networks. With its cloud-based management, zero-touch provisioning, and integrated security features, Meraki provides a comprehensive, scalable, and cost-effective solution for businesses of all sizes. Whether you are deploying a network for a small office or managing a global enterprise, Meraki simplifies network operations, increases security, and ensures that your network infrastructure can keep pace with the demands of modern business.

By leveraging Meraki's intuitive dashboard, centralized management capabilities, and advanced network performance features, businesses can achieve better control over their networks, reduce operational overhead, and improve overall network performance. As the world becomes increasingly connected and reliant on cloud applications, Cisco Meraki stands at the forefront of a new era of network management—one that offers simplicity, flexibility, and security.

Benefits of Cloud-Managed Networking

Cloud-managed networking has emerged as a revolutionary approach to network design and management, especially as businesses continue to scale and embrace digital transformation. The traditional on-premise networking model, while still common in many legacy systems, has limitations in flexibility, scalability, and ease of management. In contrast, **cloud-managed networking** offers an array of benefits that can significantly enhance network performance, reduce operational complexity, and improve overall business efficiency.

Cisco Meraki, one of the leading cloud-managed networking platforms, exemplifies these benefits, but cloud-managed solutions in general are transforming the networking landscape. Below, we explore the key advantages of adopting cloud-managed networking, highlighting why this model is so attractive to businesses of all sizes.

1. Simplified Network Management

One of the most significant advantages of cloud-managed networking is the **simplification of network management**. Traditionally, managing a network required on-site infrastructure, often involving complex setups for each device, along with continuous manual updates and configurations. With cloud-managed networks, administrators can manage the entire network remotely from a centralized cloud platform, drastically reducing the amount of time and effort needed for day-to-day network management.

- **Centralized Management Interface**: Cloud-managed networking solutions, such as Meraki's dashboard, provide a single, intuitive interface for administrators to configure, monitor, and troubleshoot network devices across multiple locations. This reduces the need for multiple management tools and physical intervention, enabling IT teams to quickly resolve issues and deploy new devices.

- **Zero-Touch Deployment**: Cloud-managed devices can be configured automatically once they are connected to the internet. This "zero-touch provisioning" model allows devices to automatically retrieve their configurations from the cloud, eliminating the need for manual on-site configuration and reducing the risk of human error.
- **Automatic Software Updates**: Cloud-managed solutions provide continuous updates to devices, meaning network devices are always running the latest software. This feature ensures that devices are equipped with the latest security patches, performance improvements, and feature enhancements without the need for manual intervention.

2. Scalability and Flexibility

Cloud-managed networking provides unparalleled scalability and flexibility, two critical factors for modern businesses that are expanding and evolving rapidly. Whether an organization is adding new branch offices, deploying new devices, or adjusting network policies, cloud-managed solutions make it easy to scale and adapt.

- **Easy Expansion**: Cloud-based platforms like Meraki allow businesses to scale their networks without the complexity typically associated with traditional, hardware-based solutions. New devices can be added to the network simply by connecting them to the cloud, where configurations are automatically applied.
- **Seamless Integration**: As businesses grow and new devices are added, cloud-managed networks can seamlessly integrate new technologies without disrupting the overall architecture. This flexibility allows organizations to adapt their network infrastructures to new needs or business demands without having to rebuild their network from the ground up.
- **Global Deployment**: Cloud-managed solutions enable businesses to deploy networks across multiple geographic locations. Whether it's a single device in a small office or a large-scale network spanning

several countries, network administrators can manage all devices from a single dashboard.

3. Improved Security

Security is a critical concern for any modern network, and cloud-managed solutions offer several advantages when it comes to protecting data and devices. Cloud-based networks can implement consistent security protocols across all devices and locations, ensuring a **higher level of protection** and reducing the risk of vulnerabilities.

- **Centralized Security Management**: Cloud-managed solutions enable businesses to apply uniform security policies across the entire network, including firewalls, access control, and threat detection. Administrators can enforce strict security measures from the cloud, reducing the likelihood of human error or inconsistencies between different parts of the network.
- **Real-Time Security Updates**: Cloud-managed networks provide continuous, automatic updates for security patches and new threat signatures, ensuring that devices are always protected against the latest threats. In contrast, traditional on-premise networks often require manual intervention to deploy critical updates.
- **Secure Remote Access**: Many cloud-managed networking platforms provide **secure remote access** solutions, including VPNs and secure tunneling protocols. This is especially important for businesses with a mobile or remote workforce, as it allows employees to access the corporate network securely from anywhere in the world.
- **Advanced Threat Detection**: Cloud-managed solutions can include sophisticated threat detection features powered by machine learning and artificial intelligence. These tools can automatically identify unusual patterns of behavior or potential attacks and take corrective action, often before human administrators are aware of the threat.

CISCO MERAKI: SIMPLIFIED NETWORK MANAGEMENT

4. Cost Efficiency

Cloud-managed networks offer a **cost-effective** alternative to traditional networking models, which can be expensive to deploy and maintain. By eliminating the need for on-site controllers, expensive hardware, and specialized IT resources, businesses can significantly reduce both capital and operational expenses.

- **Lower Upfront Costs**: Traditional network infrastructures often require significant upfront investment in hardware such as routers, switches, and controllers. With cloud-managed networking, these costs are minimized, as the management and control functions are handled in the cloud, reducing the need for costly on-premise equipment.
- **Reduced Operational Costs**: Cloud-managed solutions can cut operational costs by reducing the amount of time and resources spent on routine network maintenance, updates, and troubleshooting. With automated updates and remote management, businesses can reduce the number of on-site IT staff needed, freeing up resources for more strategic initiatives.
- **Predictable Subscription Pricing**: Many cloud-managed networking providers, including Cisco Meraki, offer a subscription-based pricing model. This model allows businesses to pay a consistent, predictable fee for network management services, avoiding the large, unpredictable costs associated with traditional networking.

5. Real-Time Monitoring and Troubleshooting

Cloud-managed networking solutions offer **real-time visibility** into the performance of the entire network. This centralized monitoring capability allows administrators to quickly detect and address issues, ensuring that network downtime is minimized and business operations are not impacted.

- **Instant Alerts and Notifications**: Cloud-managed networks can send automated alerts if any device or application is experiencing issues, such as low bandwidth, device failure, or security breaches. Administrators can then take immediate action to address the problem, often without needing to be on-site.
- **Detailed Analytics and Reporting**: With real-time monitoring, network administrators can access detailed performance metrics and analytics. This includes data on traffic flow, bandwidth usage, device health, and more. Such insights help IT teams identify performance bottlenecks, optimize resource usage, and improve network efficiency.
- **Remote Troubleshooting**: Because cloud-managed networking platforms are accessible from anywhere, administrators can troubleshoot and resolve issues without needing to be physically present at the device location. This capability can be particularly valuable for businesses with distributed networks or remote offices.

6. Enhanced Collaboration and Productivity

With cloud-managed networking, employees can stay connected and productive, even if they are working remotely or in different office locations. A cloud-driven network ensures that data and applications are always accessible, regardless of the user's location.

- **Consistent User Experience**: Cloud-managed networks can provide a **consistent user experience** across all locations and devices. Whether employees are working from headquarters or a remote branch, they have access to the same services, applications, and network resources.
- **Seamless Collaboration**: Cloud-based networks support various collaboration tools, such as video conferencing, file sharing, and real-time messaging platforms, all of which require a reliable and high-performance network. With cloud-managed networking, businesses

can ensure these tools work seamlessly, even with a large, distributed workforce.
- **Optimized Performance for Cloud Applications**: As businesses increasingly rely on cloud-based applications (e.g., SaaS platforms), cloud-managed networks can optimize traffic flow to ensure fast and reliable access to these services. This includes prioritizing bandwidth for business-critical applications and ensuring that users are not experiencing slowdowns or outages.

7. Sustainability and Environmental Benefits

Cloud-managed networking can also contribute to a company's **sustainability efforts** by reducing its environmental footprint. Traditional network setups require large data centers, on-site hardware, and continuous power consumption. In contrast, cloud-managed solutions offer several environmental benefits:

- **Energy Efficiency**: By offloading the heavy lifting of network management to the cloud, businesses can reduce the amount of on-site hardware required. This can lead to lower energy consumption and a smaller carbon footprint, particularly in data centers.
- **Less Hardware Waste**: Cloud-managed networks can extend the life of existing hardware and reduce the need for frequent hardware upgrades. Devices are often more energy-efficient, and the cloud management model allows for more centralized, efficient resource allocation.

Cloud-managed networking represents a fundamental shift in how organizations design, deploy, and manage their networks. By providing centralized control, automation, real-time monitoring, and enhanced security, cloud-managed solutions like Cisco Meraki are empowering businesses to create efficient, scalable, and cost-effective networks. The benefits of cloud-managed networking are clear: simplified management, improved security, scalability, cost savings, and a better user experience.

As businesses continue to grow, expand, and adapt to the digital age, cloud-managed networks will remain a critical enabler of these transformations. The shift to the cloud has already begun, and organizations that embrace cloud-managed solutions will be well-positioned to thrive in an increasingly connected world.

Setting Up and Managing Meraki Networks

Cisco Meraki's cloud-managed networking platform is designed to simplify the setup, configuration, and ongoing management of enterprise-grade networks. Whether you're setting up a single office network or a multi-branch organization, Meraki's intuitive interface and powerful automation tools make it possible to deploy and manage networks quickly and efficiently.

In this section, we will explore the process of setting up a Meraki network from scratch and discuss key management features that make Meraki a preferred choice for businesses looking to streamline network operations. We will also touch on some best practices to ensure smooth ongoing management and optimal network performance.

1. Getting Started with Cisco Meraki

The first step in setting up a Meraki network is to ensure you have the appropriate hardware. Meraki offers a range of devices to suit various network requirements, including **Meraki access points (APs)** for wireless connectivity, **Meraki switches** for wired network connections, **Meraki firewalls** for security, and **Meraki routers** for wide-area networking (WAN).

Step 1: Choosing the Right Meraki Devices

Before you begin configuring your Meraki network, it's important to choose the right Meraki devices based on your business needs. Cisco Meraki offers the following:

- **Meraki Access Points**: These devices deliver high-performance Wi-Fi and are perfect for offices, schools, hospitals, or any space requiring reliable wireless connectivity. They come in various models designed for different deployment environments, including indoor and outdoor use, with advanced features like **band steering**, **client load balancing**, and **seamless roaming**.
- **Meraki Switches**: Meraki's cloud-managed switches allow businesses to build a wired network with powerful features such as **automated configuration**, **VLAN support**, **port security**, and **traffic prioritization**. These switches come in various models, supporting different speeds (1G, 10G) and offering PoE (Power over Ethernet) options for devices like phones, cameras, and APs.
- **Meraki Security Appliances (MX Series)**: These appliances offer enterprise-grade security features, such as advanced **firewall protection**, **VPN support**, **content filtering**, **intrusion detection**, and **malware protection**. They are crucial for ensuring that the network is safe from external threats.
- **Meraki Routers**: For organizations that need high-performance WAN capabilities, Meraki routers provide seamless routing, load balancing, and failover capabilities across multiple sites.

Once you've identified the required devices, you can order them directly from Cisco or an authorized reseller.

Step 2: Creating a Meraki Dashboard Account

The next step is to create a **Meraki Dashboard** account. The Meraki Dashboard is the cloud-based management interface that allows you to configure and manage all Meraki devices from a single pane of glass. It's the heart of the Meraki ecosystem and makes network management intuitive.

1. **Sign up**: Go to the Meraki Dashboard website and sign up for an account if you don't have one.
2. **Claim Your Devices**: After logging in, you'll need to claim your Meraki devices (APs, switches, routers, etc.). This is done by entering the unique serial numbers that come with each device. Once devices are claimed, they will appear in the Meraki Dashboard, ready for configuration.

Step 3: Initial Device Setup

With the devices claimed and the account set up, you can begin configuring your network.

1. **Physical Device Setup**: Unbox your Meraki devices and physically install them according to your network requirements. This might involve connecting access points, switches, or security appliances to the network infrastructure and ensuring that they are powered up and connected to the internet.
2. **Connecting Devices to the Dashboard**: Once the devices are powered on, they will automatically reach out to the Meraki cloud to sync with the Meraki Dashboard. This process is simple and doesn't require manual configuration of each device.
3. **Configuration Wizard**: Meraki provides an easy-to-follow **setup wizard** to configure network basics. This might include assigning IP addresses, creating wireless SSIDs, setting VLANs, and configuring security policies. Meraki devices automatically download the latest firmware during this process, ensuring you're using the most up-to-date software with the latest features and security patches.

Step 4: Defining Network Architecture

After the initial setup, the next step is to define the network architecture in the Meraki Dashboard. This will include:

- **Network Design**: Whether you're creating a single local area network (LAN) or a multi-site wide-area network (WAN), you can segment and configure different types of networks in the dashboard. You can create VLANs (Virtual Local Area Networks), assign IP address ranges, and define policies based on the needs of your organization.
- **Wireless Configuration**: For wireless networks, you'll configure SSIDs (Service Set Identifiers), enable encryption, set up guest access, configure bandwidth limits, and enable features like **band steering** to optimize the use of different frequency bands (2.4 GHz and 5 GHz). You can also configure **Roaming** to ensure that mobile devices stay connected when moving between access points.
- **Security Configuration**: Meraki's security appliance can be configured for VPN (Virtual Private Network), firewall policies, and content filtering. You'll set rules for inbound and outbound traffic, define VPN tunnels for remote access, and block unwanted websites or content categories.

Step 5: Finalizing the Setup and Testing

Once the configuration is complete, it's important to test the network and ensure everything is functioning as expected. Check for:

- **Network Performance**: Test connectivity, latency, and bandwidth to ensure that the network is providing adequate performance. Tools like **speed tests** and **client health monitoring** in the Meraki Dashboard can help identify performance bottlenecks.
- **Security Tests**: Ensure that firewall and security policies are working correctly. You can simulate external attacks or unauthorized access attempts to verify that security measures are functioning as intended.
- **User Experience**: Conduct tests to ensure that users can seamlessly connect to the wireless network, experience stable connections, and access the necessary applications.

2. Ongoing Management and Monitoring

Once the Meraki network is up and running, the next step is to use the Meraki Dashboard to continually monitor and manage network health. Cisco Meraki provides several tools and features to help IT teams manage networks at scale and respond quickly to issues.

Real-Time Monitoring

- **Network Health Dashboard**: Meraki's intuitive dashboard provides an overview of the health of all network devices, including APs, switches, and security appliances. You can see which devices are online, any devices that are offline, and their current performance status.
- **Client Monitoring**: The dashboard also allows you to view the status of individual devices connected to your network, including usage data, client health, and connection quality. This helps identify potential issues with individual users or devices.
- **Alerts and Notifications**: You can configure automatic email or SMS alerts to notify you of any significant events in the network, such as device failures, performance issues, or security alerts. These real-time notifications help you take action before minor issues become major disruptions.

Network Insights and Analytics

- **Traffic Analysis**: Meraki provides detailed traffic analysis, allowing you to see which applications, devices, or websites are using the most bandwidth. This is valuable for identifying and addressing performance issues, optimizing bandwidth usage, and prioritizing critical applications.
- **User Insights**: Gain insights into user activity across the network, such as application usage, data consumption, and device health. This can help you identify any patterns or potential issues that could affect

network performance or security.

Firmware and Software Updates

Meraki devices are automatically updated with the latest firmware, but it's essential to periodically check for firmware updates in the Meraki Dashboard. Keeping your devices up to date ensures that you benefit from the latest security patches, performance enhancements, and feature additions.

- **Scheduled Updates**: You can schedule automatic or manual firmware updates for all devices to ensure minimal disruption to network operations. The Meraki Dashboard makes it easy to apply updates across all network devices simultaneously, saving time and effort.

Troubleshooting and Support

- **Diagnostic Tools**: The Meraki Dashboard provides built-in diagnostic tools to help troubleshoot network issues. For example, you can run ping tests, trace routes, and check connectivity between devices or sites to diagnose any problems.
- **Support and Resources**: If needed, Meraki provides 24/7 technical support. You can open a support ticket directly from the Meraki Dashboard and get assistance with any issues you're encountering. Additionally, Meraki offers a wealth of online resources, including documentation, community forums, and knowledge base articles.

3. Best Practices for Managing Meraki Networks

- **Network Segmentation**: To optimize performance and enhance security, segment your network using VLANs and ensure that sensitive data is isolated from less critical network traffic. Meraki's easy-to-use VLAN management makes this process seamless.

- **Regularly Review Security Policies**: Keep security policies up to date by periodically reviewing and adjusting access control lists (ACLs), firewall rules, and VPN settings. This ensures that your network remains secure as new threats emerge.
- **Monitor Device Health**: Continuously monitor device health in the Meraki Dashboard. This includes checking for outdated firmware, devices that are nearing end-of-life, and any devices with abnormal behavior or performance issues.
- **User Experience Optimization**: Regularly test user experience across the network to identify any performance issues. Use Meraki's client monitoring tools to proactively resolve issues before they affect end users.
- **Backup Configurations**: Periodically back up network configurations to avoid data loss in case of a failure or unexpected event. Meraki provides cloud-based configuration backups, making it easy to restore settings if needed.

Setting up and managing a Meraki network offers a simplified and efficient approach to handling complex network operations. With the cloud-based Meraki Dashboard, businesses can easily deploy, monitor, and manage network devices at scale. By leveraging Meraki's powerful features—such as centralized control, real-time monitoring, automated updates, and robust security tools—organizations can optimize network performance, reduce administrative overhead, and ensure a seamless user experience. Whether you're managing a small office or a large, distributed network, Meraki's solution provides the tools needed for effective network management with minimal effort.

Security Features in Meraki Networks

Cisco Meraki is well-known for providing comprehensive, cloud-managed networking solutions, and one of the standout features of Meraki's ecosystem is its robust security capabilities. As organizations increasingly rely on their networks for critical operations, ensuring that the network is secure from internal and external threats is essential. Meraki's security features combine ease of use, automated policy enforcement, and real-time threat detection, giving businesses confidence that their networks are safeguarded against cyber threats.

In this section, we will explore the various security features that Meraki provides, how they work, and how they can be leveraged to create a secure and resilient network.

1. Integrated Security in Meraki Devices

Meraki's devices—whether switches, routers, access points, or security appliances—are built with security in mind, providing a unified solution that integrates security measures directly into the network architecture. Here are some of the key security features provided by Meraki devices:

Next-Generation Firewall (NGFW)

Meraki's security appliances, particularly the **Meraki MX series**, include next-generation firewall features that provide granular control over network traffic. These firewalls are capable of inspecting and filtering traffic based on specific criteria, such as application type, user identity, and destination IP addresses. This helps prevent unauthorized access and ensures that only legitimate, trusted traffic flows through the network.

Some key capabilities of Meraki's next-gen firewall include:

- **Layer 7 Application Firewall**: This feature allows you to block or restrict specific applications (e.g., Facebook, YouTube, etc.) or application categories (e.g., streaming media, social media, etc.). This

ensures that bandwidth is used effectively and prevents network congestion caused by non-business-related applications.
- **Intrusion Prevention System (IPS)**: The IPS feature detects and blocks suspicious activity in real-time by examining packets for known attack patterns. This helps protect your network from common threats, including DDoS attacks, malware, and exploits.
- **Content Filtering**: Meraki security appliances come with built-in content filtering capabilities that help block access to inappropriate or malicious websites. This can be based on predefined categories (e.g., gambling, adult content, or social media) or customized to block specific URLs.
- **Advanced Threat Protection**: Meraki devices use threat intelligence feeds to help identify and mitigate advanced threats in real time. These include zero-day threats and emerging attack vectors that may not yet be recognized by traditional signature-based security systems.

Virtual Private Network (VPN)

Meraki's VPN capabilities provide secure remote access for users and sites. Whether you need to connect remote employees to the corporate network or create secure communication channels between multiple branch offices, Meraki's VPN solutions can meet the need without the complexity of traditional VPN setups.

- **Site-to-Site VPN**: Meraki's **AutoVPN** feature allows for secure, automatic VPN tunnels between Meraki devices at different locations. It simplifies the process of securely connecting multiple branch offices, data centers, or cloud-based infrastructure without requiring manual configuration.
- **Client VPN**: The **Client VPN** feature provides remote workers with a secure and encrypted connection to the company's network. It supports several protocols, including **L2TP** and **IPSec**, and can be configured to allow or restrict access based on user credentials and device status.

Both types of VPN ensure that sensitive data is encrypted during transit and that remote workers can securely access resources as if they were on the corporate LAN.

Secure Network Access Control (NAC)

Meraki's **Network Access Control** (NAC) features help ensure that only authorized devices can connect to the network. This helps reduce the risk of rogue devices or unauthorized users gaining access to critical network resources.

- **Identity-Based Access Control**: Meraki integrates seamlessly with **Active Directory** or **Radius** servers to authenticate users and devices. Access control policies can be set based on user groups or roles, allowing for a more granular level of control over which users or devices are allowed to access specific network resources.
- **Device Health and Compliance**: Meraki devices can be configured to check the health of devices trying to join the network. For example, only devices that are running the latest antivirus software or that are up to date with security patches can be allowed access.
- **Per-User and Per-Device Policies**: Meraki's cloud-managed approach enables you to configure security policies on a per-user or per-device basis. This makes it easier to ensure that specific users or groups are restricted from accessing sensitive data, while other users can access the resources they need.

Secure Wi-Fi with Meraki Access Points

Meraki's wireless access points are designed to provide secure, high-performance Wi-Fi across the enterprise, and their security features include:

- **WPA3 Encryption**: Meraki APs support **WPA3**, the latest Wi-Fi security protocol, which provides stronger encryption and better protection against brute-force attacks. WPA3 also offers enhanced protection for open networks and public Wi-Fi deployments, improv-

ing security in high-traffic environments.
- **Rogue AP Detection**: Meraki access points can detect unauthorized access points (rogue APs) that may be attempting to connect to the network. If a rogue AP is identified, Meraki will alert the network administrator, allowing them to take corrective action.
- **Captive Portal**: For guest Wi-Fi networks, Meraki provides a customizable **captive portal** that can authenticate guests and enforce specific usage policies (e.g., bandwidth limits, access restrictions). You can also integrate social media logins or integrate with external authentication systems.

Meraki's Cloud-Based Security Dashboard

Meraki's cloud-based Dashboard is at the core of its security management. From the Dashboard, network administrators can manage security settings, monitor network activity, and respond to security incidents in real time.

- **Real-Time Security Alerts**: The Meraki Dashboard provides real-time notifications of security incidents, such as attempted intrusions or abnormal traffic patterns. Administrators can set up customized alerts to notify them about specific threats or events that require immediate attention.
- **Comprehensive Security Logs**: The Dashboard stores detailed logs of network activity, including user access, device connections, and firewall events. These logs can be used for forensic analysis, auditing, and troubleshooting security issues.
- **Cloud Security Updates**: Meraki devices are automatically updated with the latest security patches and firmware, ensuring that they stay protected against known vulnerabilities without the need for manual intervention.

2. Meraki's Advanced Threat Detection and Mitigation

Meraki's advanced security features go beyond simple packet filtering and access control to detect and mitigate more sophisticated threats.

Threat Intelligence and Malware Protection

Meraki leverages cloud-based threat intelligence to identify and block emerging threats. These include **botnets**, **advanced persistent threats (APT)**, and **zero-day attacks**. Meraki devices use machine learning algorithms and threat data from Cisco Talos, a leading cybersecurity intelligence organization, to provide real-time protection.

- **Cisco Talos Threat Intelligence**: Talos provides threat feeds that are integrated directly into the Meraki Dashboard. These feeds continuously update Meraki's security appliances with information about emerging threats, malware, and suspicious activity patterns.
- **Malware Blocking**: Meraki security appliances can block known malware sites and automatically quarantine infected devices from the network. This helps contain security breaches and prevents malware from spreading throughout the network.

Intrusion Detection and Prevention Systems (IDS/IPS)

Meraki's **IDS/IPS** capabilities provide real-time detection and prevention of attacks. By examining incoming and outgoing network traffic for patterns associated with malicious activity, Meraki's security appliances can stop attacks before they cause damage. This is especially useful in defending against threats like:

- **DDoS attacks**: Meraki can identify and mitigate Distributed Denial of Service (DDoS) attacks that might overload network resources or disrupt services.
- **SQL injection** and other common web-based attacks.
- **Port scanning** and reconnaissance activities.

DNS Security (DNSSEC)

Meraki devices also support **DNS Security Extensions (DNSSEC)**, a protocol that adds an additional layer of security to DNS by ensuring that DNS responses come from trusted sources. This prevents DNS spoofing, a common attack vector used by cybercriminals to redirect traffic to malicious websites.

3. Meraki's Cloud-Based Security Updates and Reporting

One of the key benefits of Cisco Meraki is the automatic cloud-based updates and continuous security improvements that come with the platform. Because Meraki is cloud-managed, all security features are kept up to date automatically, reducing the administrative burden of maintaining security.

- **Cloud Security Updates**: Meraki's devices automatically download security updates and patches directly from the cloud. This ensures that devices are always running the latest software, which reduces the risk of exposure to known vulnerabilities.
- **Reporting and Auditing**: Meraki provides detailed security reports that can be accessed at any time. These reports include data on firewall activity, intrusion detection, VPN usage, and network health. The cloud-based nature of these reports ensures that they are always up to date and accessible from anywhere.

Meraki offers a comprehensive suite of security features that integrate seamlessly into the network infrastructure, making it easy for businesses to secure their networks without the complexity of traditional security solutions. By providing features such as next-generation firewalls, VPN support, device and user access control, and real-time threat detection, Meraki ensures that both internal and external threats are mitigated. Furthermore, its cloud-managed platform simplifies security management, making it easier to monitor, update, and protect the network from anywhere in the world.

The combination of advanced security features, ease of use, and seamless integration across Meraki's cloud-managed ecosystem makes it a powerful choice for organizations seeking a secure, scalable, and efficient networking solution. Whether protecting local area networks, securing remote access, or safeguarding wireless networks, Meraki provides the tools businesses need

Meraki for Wireless, SD-WAN, and Security Management

Cisco Meraki is renowned for its holistic, cloud-managed network solutions, which integrate seamlessly to provide a unified approach to networking. A key advantage of Meraki is how it simplifies the management of complex network environments while delivering high performance, security, and scalability. Three core areas in which Meraki excels are **Wireless Networking**, **SD-WAN** (Software-Defined Wide Area Networking), and **Security Management**. By combining these technologies in one unified platform, Meraki helps organizations streamline their network operations and ensure that their systems are secure, efficient, and resilient.

In this section, we will explore how Meraki brings together these technologies to enhance network performance, simplify management, and secure enterprise environments.

1. Meraki for Wireless Networking

Wireless networking has become the backbone of modern organizations, especially with the increasing reliance on mobile devices, cloud-based applications, and IoT (Internet of Things) devices. Meraki provides an enterprise-grade wireless solution that is easy to deploy, manage, and scale, all while offering robust security and high performance.

Meraki Access Points: Simplifying Wireless Management

Meraki's **access points (APs)** are designed to provide seamless wireless connectivity, ensuring that users and devices have consistent, high-speed access to the network. Key features of Meraki's wireless solutions include:

- **Cloud-Managed Wi-Fi**: Meraki's APs are fully managed via the cloud-based **Meraki Dashboard**, making it easy to deploy and configure wireless networks across multiple locations. Through the Dashboard, network administrators can monitor Wi-Fi performance, set up security policies, and make configuration changes in real-time, all from a single interface.
- **Advanced Radio Frequency (RF) Management**: Meraki APs feature advanced RF management that automatically optimizes the wireless signal, ensuring the best possible coverage and minimizing interference. This includes automatic adjustment of transmit power and channel selection, which helps mitigate congestion and improves the overall network performance.
- **Seamless Roaming**: Meraki's wireless network enables users to roam seamlessly across different access points without experiencing drops in connection. This is particularly important for mobile workers, as it ensures they can stay connected as they move throughout the building or campus without interruptions.
- **High-Density Environments**: Meraki's APs are specifically designed to perform well in high-density environments, such as conference rooms, auditoriums, or large public spaces. Through features like **band steering**, **load balancing**, and **airtime fairness**, Meraki ensures that high-traffic areas can handle large numbers of devices without degradation in performance.

Wi-Fi Security and Authentication

Meraki's wireless security features are built to protect the network from unauthorized access and attacks. These features include:

- **WPA3 Encryption**: Meraki supports the latest **WPA3** encryption standard, which offers stronger security than its predecessors (WPA2), especially when protecting open networks in public spaces. WPA3 prevents common attacks, such as brute-force password cracking, and protects data confidentiality.
- **Guest Networking with Captive Portal**: Meraki offers a customizable **captive portal** for guest networks, allowing administrators to control access and define usage policies for visitors. The portal can include authentication options like **social media logins**, **email-based access**, or even **SMS-based access codes**. This helps ensure that guest users only have access to certain parts of the network, preventing unauthorized access to sensitive internal resources.
- **Rogue AP Detection**: Meraki's APs continuously scan the environment for rogue access points that could be trying to impersonate legitimate APs in order to perform man-in-the-middle attacks or gain unauthorized access to the network. If a rogue AP is detected, the system can alert the network administrator in real-time, allowing them to take immediate action.

2. Meraki SD-WAN: Optimizing Wide Area Networks

Software-Defined WAN (SD-WAN) is an emerging technology that revolutionizes how businesses manage and optimize wide-area network (WAN) traffic. Meraki's SD-WAN solution simplifies WAN management by offering centralized control and visibility, improved network performance, and enhanced security.

The Power of Meraki SD-WAN

Meraki's SD-WAN solution is built into the **Meraki MX** series security appliances and leverages the cloud to dynamically optimize traffic across WAN links, including broadband, MPLS (Multiprotocol Label Switching), and LTE connections. The solution provides:

- **Dynamic Path Selection**: Meraki SD-WAN automatically chooses

the best path for each data packet based on real-time network conditions, such as link quality, latency, and bandwidth utilization. This ensures that critical applications (e.g., VoIP, video conferencing, or ERP systems) receive the best performance while less critical traffic uses alternative links.
- **Centralized Management**: Meraki's SD-WAN is managed through the Meraki Dashboard, giving network administrators full visibility into WAN performance across all branches or locations. The dashboard allows administrators to set up and enforce policies, monitor network health, and troubleshoot issues without having to manually configure each individual device.
- **Bandwidth Aggregation**: With Meraki SD-WAN, businesses can aggregate bandwidth from multiple internet links (e.g., MPLS, broadband, LTE) to increase throughput and ensure high availability. If one link fails, traffic is automatically rerouted to an available link without interruption, providing seamless continuity of service.
- **Simplified Configuration**: Meraki SD-WAN eliminates the need for complex, manual configuration by providing automatic VPN setup between Meraki devices at remote locations. This simplifies the deployment of SD-WAN, making it accessible to organizations without requiring advanced networking expertise.

Enhanced Security with Meraki SD-WAN

In addition to performance optimization, Meraki SD-WAN offers built-in security features to protect data as it travels across the WAN:

- **Auto VPN**: Meraki's **AutoVPN** technology simplifies the process of establishing secure VPN tunnels between remote sites and the main office. The automatic configuration of VPN tunnels reduces human error and ensures that data is securely encrypted during transit.
- **Integrated Security**: Meraki SD-WAN integrates with the Meraki MX security appliance's **next-generation firewall** and **intrusion prevention system (IPS)**, providing end-to-end security across the

WAN. This integration ensures that traffic is not only optimized for performance but also protected from cyber threats.
- **Cloud Security**: Traffic going through Meraki SD-WAN can be routed to Meraki's cloud-based security infrastructure, which inspects the traffic for threats before allowing it to reach the internal network. This is particularly beneficial for organizations using cloud-based applications and services.

3. Meraki for Network Security Management

Network security is paramount in today's interconnected world, and Meraki's security features are designed to protect the network from both internal and external threats. With Meraki's cloud-managed approach to security, organizations can deploy, monitor, and manage security policies with minimal effort, all while maintaining a high level of protection.

Next-Generation Firewall (NGFW) and Threat Protection

The **Meraki MX series** security appliances serve as the foundation for Meraki's network security offerings, integrating multiple security features into a single device:

- **Next-Generation Firewall (NGFW)**: The Meraki MX series appliances include a powerful, application-aware firewall that allows administrators to enforce granular security policies. The firewall inspects traffic up to Layer 7 (Application Layer) and allows administrators to block or prioritize specific applications, ensuring that the network remains secure while also managing bandwidth efficiently.
- **Intrusion Prevention System (IPS)**: Meraki's integrated IPS helps detect and prevent malicious activity within the network. The system is continuously updated with threat intelligence from Cisco Talos to block known exploits, viruses, and vulnerabilities in real-time.
- **Content Filtering**: Meraki provides content filtering capabilities, allowing organizations to block access to inappropriate websites or malicious online content. Content filtering can be based on

predefined categories (e.g., adult content, gambling) or custom settings tailored to an organization's needs.

Advanced Security Services

Meraki also offers several advanced security services to enhance the protection of the network:

- **Malware Protection**: Meraki devices offer malware protection through integration with **Cisco Talos** threat intelligence. This provides real-time detection of malware and known attack signatures, helping block threats before they can cause damage.
- **Cloud-Based Security Updates**: As a cloud-managed solution, Meraki automatically pushes the latest security updates and patches to all connected devices, ensuring that networks are always protected from known vulnerabilities.
- **End-to-End Encryption**: Meraki supports **end-to-end encryption** for traffic between Meraki devices and remote users, ensuring that sensitive data is always protected during transmission.

Meraki Security at Scale

For larger organizations or those with distributed networks, Meraki's cloud-based architecture ensures that security policies are consistent across all locations, regardless of their geographic spread. This centralized management approach eliminates the need for manual configuration at each site, reducing the risk of misconfigurations and enabling faster response times to emerging threats.

The scalability of Meraki's security solutions also allows organizations to grow their networks while maintaining strong security posture, with the ability to scale from small branch offices to large global enterprises.

Meraki offers a comprehensive solution for wireless networking, SD-WAN, and security management, all integrated into a single cloud-managed platform. By providing easy-to-deploy, high-performance access points, optimized SD-WAN for better WAN link management, and robust security features like next-gen firewalls, intrusion prevention systems, and malware protection, Meraki makes network management simple and secure. These features make Meraki particularly attractive to organizations looking for scalable, secure, and easy-to-manage networking solutions that can adapt to the evolving demands of modern enterprises. Whether you're deploying a wireless network, optimizing your WAN, or ensuring enterprise-grade security, Meraki delivers the tools needed for success.

Best Practices for Scaling Meraki Deployments

As organizations grow, so do their networking needs. Whether expanding to multiple locations, adding new users, or adopting more cloud-based services, scaling a network efficiently becomes crucial. Cisco Meraki offers an intuitive, cloud-managed solution that simplifies network scaling, making it an excellent choice for organizations of all sizes. However, to ensure smooth scaling and avoid potential issues, it is important to follow best practices when deploying Meraki networks.

In this section, we will explore the best practices for scaling Meraki deployments, including considerations for network architecture, security, monitoring, and management. These guidelines will help organizations build resilient, high-performing networks that grow with their needs while maintaining security and reliability.

1. Plan for Network Segmentation

One of the foundational principles of scaling a network is to effectively segment it to ensure that different types of traffic are isolated, monitored, and managed independently. Meraki simplifies network segmentation through **VLANs** (Virtual LANs), which allow network administrators to create logical subnets within a physical network. This is especially important as the network grows and more users, devices, and applications are added.

Key Considerations for VLANs in Meraki Deployments:

- **Use VLANs to Isolate Traffic**: As the network expands, different types of traffic (e.g., corporate, guest, IoT devices, and voice) should be logically separated. Meraki allows administrators to set up multiple VLANs, ensuring that critical applications or sensitive data are isolated from non-essential traffic.
- **Simplify Network Management**: By using VLANs, network traffic is better organized, making it easier to manage and troubleshoot. VLANs help reduce network congestion by limiting the scope of broadcast traffic to each VLAN.
- **Ensure Scalability with Hierarchical VLAN Design**: As the network grows, creating a hierarchy of VLANs can help organize traffic more efficiently. For example, you might separate IoT devices into their own VLAN while grouping administrative devices on a separate VLAN.
- **Implement Inter-VLAN Routing**: Meraki devices like the MX security appliances support inter-VLAN routing, enabling communication between VLANs while ensuring traffic is routed efficiently.

2. Leverage Meraki's Cloud Management Platform

One of the main advantages of Meraki is its **cloud-based management** platform, the **Meraki Dashboard**, which allows for centralized monitoring, configuration, and troubleshooting. This cloud-based approach significantly simplifies scaling, as new devices can be added remotely and managed from a single interface, regardless of location.

Best Practices for Cloud Management:

- **Utilize Configuration Templates**: As you scale your network, using Meraki's configuration templates can save time and ensure consistency across multiple sites. Templates allow you to apply the same configuration settings to multiple devices or sites without manually configuring each one. This is particularly useful for setting up network-wide policies, SSID configurations, or security settings.
- **Automate Device Provisioning**: Meraki's cloud management simplifies the process of adding new devices to the network. By registering devices in the cloud, they are automatically configured based on pre-set templates and policies. This process reduces the time it takes to deploy new hardware and ensures all devices are aligned with the organization's standards.
- **Monitor Performance Across Multiple Locations**: With the Meraki Dashboard, administrators can monitor the health of their entire network from a single pane of glass. This includes tracking bandwidth usage, detecting bottlenecks, checking device status, and identifying potential security threats. As you scale, this centralized visibility becomes crucial in maintaining network performance and uptime.

3. Optimize Wireless Coverage for Scalability

As your network grows, so too will the need for reliable and seamless wireless coverage. Meraki's **wireless access points (APs)** are designed to deliver high-performance, enterprise-grade Wi-Fi coverage in a variety of environments, from small offices to large campus networks.

Best Practices for Scaling Wireless Networks:

- **Plan for Coverage with RF Design**: Before deploying Meraki APs, take time to design the radio frequency (RF) layout to ensure proper coverage and avoid interference. Tools like **Meraki's RF spectrum analyzer** can help map out the optimal placement for APs, ensuring that wireless signals are strong and reliable across your network.
- **Deploy Multiple APs for Redundancy**: To prevent coverage gaps and improve overall network reliability, consider deploying multiple APs in high-traffic or mission-critical areas. Meraki's cloud-managed APs support **seamless roaming** for users, ensuring they experience uninterrupted connectivity as they move between access points.
- **Use Meraki's Auto RF Feature**: Meraki APs come equipped with automatic radio frequency (RF) management features, which automatically adjust the transmission power and channel selection based on the current environment. This helps to mitigate interference and optimize wireless performance without requiring manual adjustments.
- **Plan for High-Density Areas**: For areas with a large number of users (e.g., conference rooms or large campuses), Meraki's APs support features like **band steering** and **load balancing** to ensure that each device receives a fair share of available bandwidth and that wireless congestion is minimized.

4. Maintain Redundancy and High Availability

As networks scale, the risk of single points of failure increases, making it critical to build redundancy into your design. Meraki provides several tools and features to ensure high availability, which is essential for mission-critical applications.

Best Practices for Redundancy in Meraki Deployments:

- **Deploy Redundant Meraki MX Appliances**: The **Meraki MX security appliances** offer high availability (HA) configurations that allow you to deploy a pair of devices for failover. This means that if one appliance fails, the other can take over seamlessly, ensuring that the network remains up and running. Use **HSRP** (Hot Standby Router Protocol) or **VRRP** (Virtual Router Redundancy Protocol) to ensure that routing remains intact during failover.
- **Ensure WAN Redundancy with SD-WAN**: Meraki's SD-WAN feature allows multiple WAN links (e.g., broadband, MPLS, or LTE) to be aggregated for better reliability. By configuring multiple internet links, Meraki can automatically reroute traffic in the event of a failure, ensuring that the network stays connected.
- **Use Dual ISP Connections for Internet Redundancy**: To prevent internet outages from impacting business operations, consider using multiple internet service providers (ISPs) to provide redundancy. Meraki's SD-WAN automatically manages traffic across multiple ISPs, ensuring continuous access even if one connection goes down.

5. Manage Security as You Scale

Security is a top priority when scaling a network, especially as more devices and locations are added. Meraki's cloud-managed security features are designed to protect the network without adding complexity, even as it grows.

Best Practices for Scalable Network Security:

- **Use Meraki's Integrated Security Features**: Meraki's **next-gen firewall** (NGFW), **intrusion prevention system** (IPS), and **malware protection** can be applied consistently across the entire network, whether you're deploying to a single branch or multiple locations. These security features automatically receive updates via the cloud, ensuring your network is always protected from the latest threats.
- **Leverage Role-Based Access Control (RBAC)**: As you scale the network, it's important to define who has access to what resources. Meraki allows you to set up **role-based access control (RBAC)**, ensuring that only authorized users can access specific configurations, devices, or data. RBAC helps prevent unauthorized access and maintains the security of your growing network.
- **Enable Cloud-Based Security Policies**: Meraki's cloud management platform allows you to define security policies once and apply them consistently across all devices and locations. This includes **content filtering**, **VPN policies**, **malware protection**, and **guest network security**.
- **Monitor Network Security Continuously**: As the network grows, it becomes even more important to continuously monitor and analyze traffic for potential threats. Meraki's cloud-based management allows administrators to access real-time reports and insights, which can be used to detect anomalies and take corrective actions before issues escalate.

6. Plan for Future Growth and Flexibility

A key aspect of scaling a Meraki deployment is to plan for future expansion, ensuring that the network can grow without requiring a complete overhaul. Meraki's solutions are inherently flexible, allowing organizations to scale with ease as their needs evolve.

Best Practices for Future-Proofing Meraki Deployments:

- **Adopt a Modular Approach**: Meraki's devices and cloud management platform are designed with modularity in mind. This means that you can add new devices, expand coverage, and increase capacity as needed without disrupting existing operations.
- **Regularly Review Network Performance**: As the network grows, performance needs may change. Meraki's **monitoring tools** provide insights into bandwidth utilization, device status, and application performance, which can help you identify areas that need expansion or optimization.
- **Stay Updated with New Features**: Cisco regularly adds new features and improvements to the Meraki platform. Keeping your devices up to date with the latest firmware ensures that you benefit from the newest technologies, security features, and optimizations, which is particularly important as you scale.

Scaling a network with Meraki is made easier by the platform's cloud-managed architecture, automated provisioning, and built-in scalability features. By following best practices for network segmentation, redundancy, security, and monitoring, organizations can ensure that their Meraki deployments grow seamlessly and remain efficient, secure, and reliable as their network demands increase. With Meraki, enterprises can easily expand their network infrastructure while maintaining high performance and reducing operational complexity, ensuring a future-proof solution for their networking needs.

Implementing Zero Trust Architecture with Cisco

The Zero Trust Security Model: Principles and Benefits

The Zero Trust (ZT) security model represents a fundamental shift in how organizations approach cybersecurity. Unlike traditional security models that operate on the assumption that users or devices inside the network can be trusted by default, Zero Trust assumes that every device, user, and system—whether inside or outside the network—poses a potential threat. Therefore, it requires strict verification before granting access to any resource, enforcing a "never trust, always verify" policy.

The Zero Trust model has gained significant traction in recent years as organizations face increasingly sophisticated threats, such as insider attacks, ransomware, and data breaches. In this section, we will explore the core principles of Zero Trust, its key components, and the benefits it offers for modern enterprises. We will also delve into how Cisco's solutions align with the Zero Trust framework and can help organizations implement this robust security posture.

1. Principles of Zero Trust Security

Zero Trust is built upon several guiding principles designed to minimize risk by enforcing continuous validation of every user, device, and connection. These principles are essential for creating a security model that adapts to modern challenges, especially in a world where remote work, cloud applications, and BYOD (Bring Your Own Device) policies are the norm.

1.1 "Never Trust, Always Verify"

The core principle of Zero Trust is the idea that no user or device should be implicitly trusted, regardless of their location within the network. Trust is not granted by default, even to internal users or systems that have previously been verified. Every access request is considered suspicious until verified.

Key aspects:

- **User and Device Authentication**: Zero Trust requires that each user and device be authenticated before gaining access to any resource. This includes implementing strong multi-factor authentication (MFA), device posture checks, and continuous monitoring of access requests.
- **Contextual Access Control**: Access decisions are based on factors such as the user's identity, device health, location, and the sensitivity of the requested resource. Even if a user is on the corporate network, their access will be contingent on their security status.

1.2 Least-Privilege Access

The principle of least privilege dictates that users and devices should only have access to the minimum level of resources necessary to perform their job functions. This limits the potential damage that can occur if an account is compromised.

Key aspects:

- **Role-Based Access Control (RBAC)**: Zero Trust networks use RBAC to enforce least-privilege access. By assigning roles to users based on their job responsibilities, organizations can limit access to critical systems and data.
- **Micro-Segmentation**: Network segmentation into smaller, isolated zones (often referred to as micro-segmentation) is crucial in a Zero Trust model. This allows access to be granted only to the specific areas of the network that a user or device needs to access, making lateral movement by attackers more difficult.

1.3 Continuous Monitoring and Authentication

Zero Trust emphasizes continuous verification of user and device behavior, monitoring their activities and posture in real time to detect anomalous behavior that may indicate a breach.

Key aspects:

- **Behavioral Analytics**: Continuous monitoring of network traffic, user behavior, and device health is essential in identifying suspicious activities. This can include detecting unusual login times, abnormal data transfers, or requests from unfamiliar devices or locations.
- **Adaptive Authentication**: Based on real-time risk assessments, Zero Trust frameworks may adapt authentication requirements dynamically. For instance, if a user attempts to access sensitive data from an unknown device or geographic location, the system may prompt additional authentication steps or deny access altogether.

1.4 Trust Zones and Granular Access Control

Zero Trust incorporates the idea of dividing the network into distinct zones, each with its own security policies. This granular approach ensures that even if an attacker gains access to one part of the network, they cannot easily move across the entire infrastructure.

Key aspects:

- **Micro-Segmentation**: By isolating different parts of the network into micro-segments, the attack surface is reduced. For example, sensitive financial data, human resources, or intellectual property could reside in highly controlled zones that are separate from other departments or systems.
- **Application-Level Security**: Zero Trust also extends to the application layer, ensuring that only authorized users or devices can access specific applications or services, even if they are on the same network.

1.5 Strong Encryption for Data at Rest and in Transit

In a Zero Trust model, encryption plays a critical role in ensuring data integrity and confidentiality. All communications, whether internal or external, should be encrypted to protect sensitive information from interception or tampering.

Key aspects:

- **End-to-End Encryption**: Zero Trust mandates that all communication channels be encrypted, whether data is moving across the internet, between devices, or within internal networks.
- **Encryption of Data at Rest**: Data stored within an organization's infrastructure should also be encrypted, ensuring that even if a device or system is compromised, the attacker cannot access or misuse the data.

2. Key Benefits of Zero Trust Security

Adopting the Zero Trust security model offers several significant advantages for organizations, especially in today's increasingly complex and dynamic threat landscape.

2.1 Enhanced Security Posture

By continuously verifying users and devices, enforcing least-privilege access, and segmenting the network, Zero Trust minimizes the attack surface and reduces the risk of breaches. Traditional perimeter defenses, such as firewalls and VPNs, are increasingly ineffective at protecting against sophisticated threats like insider attacks or advanced persistent threats (APTs).

Benefits:

- **Reduction of Insider Threats**: Zero Trust limits the damage that can be done by internal threats, as users only have access to the specific resources they need.
- **Minimization of Lateral Movement**: Micro-segmentation and granular access controls make it more difficult for attackers to move laterally through the network, even if they gain initial access.

2.2 Better Compliance and Regulatory Adherence

Zero Trust is particularly beneficial for organizations that need to comply with stringent regulatory standards, such as GDPR, HIPAA, or PCI-DSS. By ensuring continuous authentication, encryption, and data segmentation, Zero Trust models can help organizations demonstrate compliance and mitigate the risk of non-compliance penalties.

Benefits:

- **Data Privacy**: Zero Trust's focus on encryption and controlled access ensures that sensitive data is protected, helping organizations comply with privacy regulations.
- **Auditing and Reporting**: Zero Trust solutions typically include detailed logs and reporting capabilities, making it easier for organizations to track access patterns and maintain an audit trail for compliance purposes.

2.3 Agility and Flexibility for Modern Workforces

The traditional network perimeter is increasingly irrelevant in the era of cloud computing, mobile devices, and remote work. Zero Trust is inherently designed to support modern, distributed workforces. By enabling secure access to applications and data from anywhere, organizations can

embrace the flexibility of remote work without compromising security.
Benefits:

- **Remote and Hybrid Work Support**: Zero Trust ensures that remote workers or branch offices are subject to the same stringent access controls and authentication checks as on-premises employees.
- **Cloud-Ready Security**: As organizations move to the cloud, Zero Trust provides a robust framework for securing cloud applications and services, regardless of whether they are hosted on public or private clouds.

2.4 Simplified Management and Cost Efficiency

Although implementing Zero Trust may initially seem complex, many organizations find that it streamlines network management and reduces costs in the long run. By centralizing policy enforcement and automating many security processes, Zero Trust reduces the need for extensive manual intervention and monitoring.
Benefits:

- **Centralized Control**: Zero Trust allows for centralized management of security policies, making it easier to enforce consistent security standards across the entire organization.
- **Reduced Complexity**: By eliminating the need for multiple disparate security tools, Zero Trust can simplify network architecture, reducing the number of systems that need to be maintained and patched.

2.5 Risk Mitigation in Cloud and Hybrid Environments

As organizations increasingly adopt cloud-based services, they must secure access to both on-premises and cloud resources. Zero Trust offers an ideal security model for hybrid environments, ensuring that all applications, whether on-premises or in the cloud, are protected with consistent security policies.

Benefits:

- **Cloud Security**: Zero Trust frameworks can extend to cloud services, ensuring that only authenticated and authorized users can access cloud applications and data.
- **Seamless Integration with Cloud Providers**: Zero Trust can be integrated with popular cloud providers like AWS, Azure, and Google Cloud, providing a unified security approach across all environments.

3. Cisco's Zero Trust Solutions

Cisco has developed a range of products and technologies designed to support the implementation of the Zero Trust security model. Cisco's solutions offer comprehensive protection across users, devices, applications, and data. Some of the key Cisco solutions aligned with Zero Trust include:

- **Cisco Identity Services Engine (ISE)**: Provides identity-based network access control, enforcing authentication and policy enforcement across users and devices.
- **Cisco Duo Security**: A robust multi-factor authentication (MFA) solution that ensures only authorized users can access critical resources, both on-premises and in the cloud.
- **Cisco Umbrella**: A cloud security platform that offers protection against threats and malware, providing secure access to cloud applications and preventing malicious activity.
- **Cisco Secure Network Analytics**: Helps monitor network traffic and detect anomalies in real-time, supporting the continuous verification of users and devices.

The Zero Trust security model offers a comprehensive and modern approach to cybersecurity, addressing the challenges posed by today's complex, distributed networks. By eliminating the implicit trust granted to users and devices, Zero Trust minimizes the attack surface and ensures that every access request is continuously verified. Cisco's portfolio of Zero Trust solutions provides organizations with the tools needed to implement this robust security framework across their infrastructure. Whether securing on-premises data centers, remote workers, or cloud environments, Zero Trust offers a scalable and effective model for modern cybersecurity.

Cisco Identity Services Engine (ISE)

Cisco Identity Services Engine (ISE) is a comprehensive network security policy platform that enables organizations to implement effective identity-based access control across their networks. ISE provides centralized management of network access policies for both wired and wireless networks, and is a critical component in securing modern enterprise environments. It supports the Zero Trust security model by ensuring that only authorized users and devices can access network resources, and it integrates seamlessly with other Cisco security products to create a robust, multi-layered security posture.

In this section, we'll dive deep into the key features, functionalities, and benefits of Cisco ISE, as well as its role in supporting Zero Trust architecture and enhancing overall network security.

1. What is Cisco Identity Services Engine (ISE)?

Cisco ISE is a network access control (NAC) solution that provides centralized policy management, identity-based access control, and guest networking capabilities. It enables organizations to define and enforce security policies based on user identity, device type, location, and other contextual information. ISE's role is to authenticate, authorize, and account for users and devices attempting to access network resources, ensuring that access is granted based on predefined policies that align with security requirements.

Key Features of Cisco ISE:

- **Identity-Based Access Control**: ISE allows organizations to enforce network access policies based on the identity of users, devices, and applications. By integrating with enterprise directories like Microsoft Active Directory or LDAP, ISE can authenticate and authorize users based on their roles within the organization.
- **Multi-Factor Authentication (MFA)**: To ensure stronger security, ISE supports multi-factor authentication (MFA) to validate users' identities through something they know (password), something they have (smart card, token), or something they are (biometrics). This is crucial for preventing unauthorized access.
- **Guest Access Management**: ISE offers a flexible guest access management system that enables organizations to provide controlled access to visitors or temporary users. Guest users can be given limited access to network resources based on policies, and their activities can be monitored for compliance.
- **Device Profiling**: Cisco ISE is capable of automatically detecting and profiling devices connecting to the network. It can distinguish between different types of devices—such as laptops, smartphones, printers, and IoT devices—and apply different policies based on device types, operating systems, and security posture.
- **Policy Enforcement**: ISE integrates with a variety of Cisco network devices, including switches, wireless controllers, and firewalls, to enforce access policies. This ensures that only compliant devices and authenticated users can access the network, and it can dynamically assign VLANs, QoS settings, and firewall rules based on the policy associated with the user or device.

- **Contextual Awareness**: Cisco ISE uses contextual information—such as device location, time of day, and network behavior—to make access decisions. This level of granularity helps to enhance security by limiting access to critical resources based on real-time factors.
- **Reporting and Logging**: ISE offers extensive logging, reporting, and audit capabilities that allow organizations to monitor access activities and ensure compliance with security and regulatory policies. This also provides insights into network behavior, which can be helpful for detecting suspicious activities or trends.

2. Cisco ISE in Zero Trust Security Architecture

As organizations increasingly adopt the Zero Trust security model, Cisco ISE plays a pivotal role in ensuring that access control is robust, adaptive, and contextually aware. Zero Trust operates on the principle that no one, whether inside or outside the network, should be trusted by default, and every access request should be verified.

Zero Trust with Cisco ISE:

- **Continuous Authentication and Authorization**: In a Zero Trust environment, users and devices are continuously validated. Cisco ISE's ability to continuously assess user and device health ensures that access is granted based on real-time authentication and authorization, in line with the Zero Trust "never trust, always verify" model.
- **Micro-Segmentation**: Cisco ISE supports micro-segmentation by allowing policies to be defined for specific network segments or individual devices. For instance, a user with access to the HR department's network might not have access to financial systems or other sensitive areas of the organization, even if they are both on the same network. This prevents lateral movement and minimizes potential damage in case of a breach.
- **Contextual Policy Enforcement**: ISE's integration with contextual information—such as user identity, device type, location, and time of

access—ensures that access decisions are not static but adapt to real-time conditions. This supports the Zero Trust approach by limiting access based on a dynamic risk assessment.
- **Guest Access and Isolation**: Cisco ISE can enforce strict policies for guest access, ensuring that temporary users (such as contractors or visitors) only have access to the necessary resources and are isolated from critical network areas. This is especially important in Zero Trust environments where even external users must undergo strict authentication and authorization checks.

How Cisco ISE Supports Zero Trust Goals:

- **Identity and Device Authentication**: ISE verifies that only authenticated and authorized users and devices can connect to the network. It supports multi-factor authentication (MFA), which provides an additional layer of security. In the Zero Trust model, this helps prevent unauthorized access, even if an attacker has obtained login credentials.
- **Access Control Based on Policy**: ISE ensures that access to sensitive resources is tightly controlled and only granted to users and devices that meet specific policy requirements. This principle aligns with Zero Trust's least-privilege access philosophy, where users can only access what they need to perform their roles.
- **Continuous Monitoring and Response**: Cisco ISE integrates with Cisco's Security Information and Event Management (SIEM) systems, allowing for real-time monitoring of network access activity. If an anomaly is detected—such as unusual access attempts or behavior—the system can immediately enforce stricter access policies or revoke access altogether, aligning with the Zero Trust principle of continuous validation.

3. Benefits of Cisco ISE

Cisco ISE brings several key benefits to enterprises looking to implement robust access control and enhance network security. These benefits are amplified when ISE is deployed as part of a Zero Trust security model.

3.1 Improved Security Posture

By enforcing stringent authentication and authorization policies, Cisco ISE helps mitigate risks associated with unauthorized access and insider threats. The ability to continuously verify users, devices, and their security posture ensures that only authorized individuals can access critical resources.

- **Reduction of Insider Threats**: Since Cisco ISE continuously verifies the identity and health of devices, it significantly reduces the risk of insider threats.
- **Dynamic Risk-Based Access Control**: By considering the security posture and context of users and devices, Cisco ISE can apply policies dynamically to reduce the attack surface and improve security.

3.2 Simplified Network Access Management

Cisco ISE provides centralized policy management, allowing administrators to define and enforce consistent access policies across the entire network. It supports a wide range of authentication methods (such as 802.1X, MAB, and web authentication) and integrates with network devices, making it easier to manage access across both wired and wireless infrastructures.

- **Simplified Policy Enforcement**: ISE's policy enforcement capabilities ensure that network access is always aligned with organizational security policies.
- **Automated Access Decisions**: Based on user and device context, ISE automatically assigns appropriate network resources, reducing manual intervention and streamlining the management process.

3.3 Streamlined Compliance and Reporting

Cisco ISE offers detailed reporting and auditing capabilities that simplify compliance with industry regulations, such as PCI-DSS, HIPAA, and GDPR. It enables organizations to track access and monitor network activity, ensuring that policies are being followed and that any violations are quickly identified.

- **Comprehensive Logging and Auditing**: Cisco ISE maintains detailed logs of authentication and authorization activities, providing an audit trail that can be used for compliance reporting and forensic investigations.
- **Real-Time Reporting**: Administrators can quickly generate reports to demonstrate compliance with regulatory standards and track user access patterns.

3.4 Scalability and Flexibility

Cisco ISE is highly scalable, making it ideal for organizations of all sizes, from small enterprises to large global networks. Its flexibility allows it to adapt to changing network topologies and business needs, ensuring that security policies can grow with the organization.

- **Scalable Architecture**: ISE can be deployed in a distributed or centralized architecture, depending on the size and complexity of the network.
- **Cloud Integration**: Cisco ISE integrates seamlessly with cloud services, enabling secure access for cloud-based applications and remote users.

4. Cisco ISE and Zero Trust: A Perfect Match

Cisco ISE's identity-based access control, policy enforcement, and continuous authentication features make it a natural fit for implementing Zero Trust in enterprise networks. By ensuring that all users, devices, and applications are continuously authenticated, verified, and monitored, ISE helps organizations achieve the core goals of Zero Trust security: minimizing risk, preventing unauthorized access, and improving overall network security.

As enterprises face evolving cybersecurity challenges, adopting Zero Trust principles with Cisco ISE can strengthen defenses against a wide range of threats and protect critical assets in an increasingly complex digital landscape.

Cisco Identity Services Engine (ISE) is a powerful solution for managing network access and security in modern enterprise environments. By leveraging its capabilities in authentication, policy enforcement, and monitoring, organizations can enforce strict security measures and implement a Zero Trust architecture. With the growing need for robust network security, Cisco ISE provides the necessary tools for ensuring that only authenticated, authorized, and compliant users and devices can access critical resources, mitigating risks and enhancing overall network protection.

Network Segmentation and TrustSec for Zero Trust

Network segmentation and Cisco TrustSec are two foundational elements that support the Zero Trust security model by providing more granular control over who can access what resources, when, and under what conditions. While Zero Trust emphasizes "never trust, always verify" at the perimeter and throughout the network, network segmentation and TrustSec provide the critical mechanisms to enforce these principles at a more granular, contextual level. Together, they limit the blast radius of potential attacks, enhance security posture, and minimize risk.

In this section, we'll explore how network segmentation and Cisco TrustSec play a pivotal role in implementing Zero Trust and how they can be used to strengthen security across enterprise environments.

1. What is Network Segmentation?

Network segmentation is the practice of dividing a network into smaller, isolated subnetworks or segments. Each segment has its own set of access policies, helping to limit the movement of unauthorized users or devices within the network. In a segmented network, even if an attacker compromises one segment, they are unable to freely access other areas without first bypassing additional security controls.

Key Benefits of Network Segmentation:

- **Reduced Attack Surface**: By dividing the network into smaller, isolated segments, you reduce the attack surface. For instance, sensitive data and critical infrastructure can be placed in their own segments, making it much harder for attackers to gain access to them.
- **Limited Lateral Movement**: In the event of a breach, segmentation prevents attackers from easily moving laterally within the network. If an attacker compromises a segment (e.g., an IoT network), they cannot automatically access more critical systems, like the finance or HR networks, unless specifically allowed by policy.
- **Improved Performance**: By isolating traffic into specific segments, network performance can be improved, as data traffic is limited to necessary routes rather than being broadcast across the entire network.
- **Easier Compliance**: Network segmentation helps meet various regulatory compliance requirements by isolating sensitive data and ensuring that only authorized users and devices can access it.

How Network Segmentation Supports Zero Trust:

In the Zero Trust model, trust is never assumed, and every access request must be verified. Network segmentation plays a key role in implementing Zero Trust because it allows organizations to:

- **Enforce Least Privilege Access**: With segmentation, only users and

devices that are explicitly authorized are allowed to access specific network segments. For example, a user working in the finance department can be given access to financial applications but not to engineering resources. This aligns with Zero Trust's least privilege access principle.
- **Contain Threats**: By isolating resources in segmented parts of the network, even if an attacker compromises one part, their access is confined to that segment, limiting the damage they can do.
- **Control Access Based on Context**: Network segmentation enables more granular control of access to specific applications or data based on contextual factors like user role, device health, or the time of day. This contextual access control is a fundamental principle of Zero Trust, which focuses on continuous evaluation.

2. Cisco TrustSec: Secure Network Segmentation and Policy Enforcement

Cisco TrustSec is an integrated security solution that simplifies network segmentation and enhances security by dynamically enforcing access policies across the network. It is a software-defined solution that enables organizations to implement segmentation without the need for complex, hardware-based VLAN configurations. TrustSec uses Security Group Tags (SGTs) to define roles and policies for users and devices, providing a more flexible and scalable approach to segmentation.

TrustSec supports the Zero Trust model by ensuring that access control is tightly enforced across all devices, applications, and users, based on predefined security policies. This solution integrates with other Cisco security products, providing a unified security approach across both physical and virtual network infrastructures.

How Cisco TrustSec Works:

- **Security Group Tags (SGTs)**: TrustSec uses SGTs to assign users, devices, and applications to security groups. These tags are then used to enforce policies, ensuring that users can only access resources associated with their security group, regardless of the network segment they are in. For example, an employee in the HR department might have an SGT of "HR," which restricts their access to HR-related resources.

- **Policy-Based Access Control**: TrustSec enables the creation of access control policies based on the SGTs assigned to users and devices. These policies can be enforced dynamically across the network, ensuring that access is always aligned with security requirements. This eliminates the need for manually configuring network segmentation based on IP address or VLAN.
- **End-to-End Segmentation**: Cisco TrustSec allows segmentation across the entire network—whether the user or device is connected to a wired, wireless, or VPN network. This ensures consistent, end-to-end segmentation, regardless of where the user or device is physically located within the network.
- **Integration with Cisco ISE**: TrustSec works seamlessly with Cisco Identity Services Engine (ISE), which handles the authentication and authorization of users and devices. ISE dynamically assigns SGTs to users and devices based on their identity, role, and security posture, ensuring that policies are consistently applied.

Benefits of Cisco TrustSec for Zero Trust:

- **Simplified Segmentation**: By abstracting network segmentation through SGTs rather than relying on complex VLAN configurations, TrustSec makes segmentation more flexible and easier to manage.
- **Dynamic Access Control**: Access to network resources is granted based on the user's security group, identity, and device posture, ensuring that access is always based on contextual factors. This supports the Zero Trust philosophy of "never trust, always verify."
- **Scalability**: TrustSec enables scalable segmentation across large, complex networks. As organizations grow, TrustSec can be deployed

to extend segmentation and enforce consistent security policies across the entire infrastructure.
- **Integration with Existing Infrastructure**: TrustSec can be deployed on top of existing Cisco infrastructure, meaning that organizations don't need to replace their hardware to gain the benefits of this segmentation solution.

3. TrustSec and Network Segmentation in Zero Trust Architecture

When implementing a Zero Trust security model, network segmentation and TrustSec complement each other by providing the necessary tools to isolate critical resources and enforce policies that ensure only authorized entities can access sensitive information. In Zero Trust, network segmentation does not mean creating a simple network perimeter but involves segmenting the network in a way that dynamically adapts to user and device behavior.

3.1 Granular Access Control:

In a Zero Trust model, access to sensitive systems and data must be continuously validated and limited to only the necessary resources. TrustSec allows organizations to apply policies that ensure granular control over network traffic, where access is determined by the user's identity, role, device health, and security posture.

For example, even if a user has access to a segment of the network, TrustSec ensures that their ability to access specific applications, services, or data is further restricted based on their role. This ensures that users are only given the minimum level of access they need to perform their job, thus minimizing the risk of unauthorized access.

3.2 Isolation of Critical Resources:

With network segmentation and TrustSec, organizations can isolate critical resources and ensure that access to these resources is restricted to authorized users or devices. For example, administrative access to servers, databases, or management interfaces can be confined to trusted administrators and applications, reducing the risk of unauthorized access from compromised endpoints or insiders.

By isolating sensitive data and critical infrastructure, network segmentation prevents lateral movement within the network. Even if an attacker gains access to one part of the network, TrustSec ensures that they cannot easily access more critical systems or applications.

3.3 Continuous Verification of Security Posture:

One of the core principles of Zero Trust is that trust is never implicit. Network segmentation and TrustSec support this principle by continuously verifying the security posture of devices and users before granting access to resources. If a device's security posture changes (e.g., if it is found to be compromised or out of compliance), TrustSec can automatically deny access or limit the device's access to certain network segments, ensuring that threats are contained before they can escalate.

4. Best Practices for Network Segmentation and TrustSec Implementation

To effectively implement network segmentation and TrustSec for Zero Trust, organizations should follow these best practices:

- **Define Security Groups Based on Roles**: Start by defining Security Group Tags (SGTs) based on user roles, device types, or application requirements. This helps ensure that access policies are aligned with the organization's security needs and simplifies segmentation.
- **Enforce Least Privilege Access**: With TrustSec, ensure that users and devices are given only the minimum access they need. Avoid over-provisioning access and apply strict controls for sensitive resources.
- **Monitor and Review Segmentation Policies**: Continuously monitor network traffic and review segmentation policies to ensure that they are aligned with business requirements and security standards. Regularly update policies to reflect changing business needs or security threats.
- **Integrate with Existing Identity Management Systems**: Cisco

TrustSec works best when integrated with identity management solutions like Cisco Identity Services Engine (ISE). This enables dynamic assignment of SGTs based on user and device context, streamlining policy enforcement.
- **Use Contextual Data for Dynamic Access Control**: Incorporate contextual data, such as device health, user behavior, and location, when defining segmentation policies. This ensures that access decisions are made based on the full context of the user and device.

Network segmentation and Cisco TrustSec play a critical role in supporting the Zero Trust security model by providing the granular control and flexibility needed to secure modern enterprise networks. By segmenting the network and using TrustSec's dynamic policy enforcement, organizations can better manage access, reduce the risk of lateral movement, and ensure that critical resources are protected. Together, network segmentation and TrustSec help organizations adopt Zero Trust principles and maintain a robust security posture, even as networks continue to grow and evolve.

Policy Enforcement with Cisco TrustSec and ISE

In modern network security, policy enforcement is central to ensuring that only authorized users and devices can access the network and its resources. Cisco TrustSec, when integrated with Cisco Identity Services Engine (ISE), offers a powerful, flexible, and dynamic approach to policy enforcement that can greatly enhance an organization's security posture. By combining TrustSec's network segmentation capabilities with ISE's identity and access management features, organizations can ensure that access decisions are based on real-time, context-driven information, thus enabling a Zero Trust model across the network.

In this section, we will delve into how Cisco TrustSec and ISE work together to enforce network policies, provide access control, and protect sensitive resources within an enterprise environment.

1. The Role of Cisco Identity Services Engine (ISE) in Policy Enforcement

Cisco ISE is a comprehensive identity and access management (IAM) solution that provides centralized policy control for authentication, authorization, and accounting (AAA) within a network. ISE integrates with various network devices, including routers, switches, firewalls, and wireless controllers, to ensure that users and devices are authenticated and authorized to access network resources.

ISE is pivotal in enabling dynamic and granular policy enforcement by evaluating the identity of users and devices, their security posture, and the context in which they are requesting access. When combined with TrustSec, ISE allows for a policy-driven, scalable, and flexible security model.

Key Functions of Cisco ISE in Policy Enforcement:

- **Authentication**: ISE authenticates users and devices by verifying their credentials, such as username and password, certificates, or biometric data. This ensures that only legitimate entities are allowed to access the network.
- **Authorization**: Based on the authentication process, ISE determines the appropriate level of access to network resources. Policies are applied to ensure users and devices can only access resources they are authorized to use.
- **Accounting and Auditing**: ISE provides detailed logging and reporting on user and device activity, enabling network administrators to monitor and audit access, track security events, and respond to potential security incidents.
- **Contextual Awareness**: ISE incorporates contextual information such as the user's role, device type, and security posture to make more

informed access control decisions. This is essential for implementing dynamic access control policies in a Zero Trust model.
- **Integration with External Systems**: ISE integrates with external identity providers (e.g., Active Directory, LDAP) and security systems (e.g., Cisco AMP, Firepower) to enhance authentication, authorization, and security posture assessment.

2. Cisco TrustSec and ISE: How They Work Together

Cisco TrustSec and ISE are complementary solutions that together enforce consistent, dynamic, and context-driven policies across the network. TrustSec provides the network segmentation and access control enforcement, while ISE provides the identity-based authentication and policy decision engine. Together, they enable secure, granular access across a diverse range of users, devices, and applications.

TrustSec's Role in Policy Enforcement:

- **Dynamic Access Control**: With TrustSec, access to specific network resources is dynamically assigned based on Security Group Tags (SGTs) instead of relying on static IP addresses or VLAN configurations. TrustSec ensures that users, devices, and applications are assigned to specific security groups, each with its own set of policies. This dynamic segmentation aligns with Zero Trust principles, ensuring that even if a user is authenticated, their access is restricted based on their role, device health, and other contextual factors.
- **Enforcing Security Group-Based Access**: TrustSec assigns each user or device to a specific security group. The group's access rights to network resources are defined by policies in ISE. TrustSec tags packets with Security Group Tags (SGTs) that correspond to the access rights assigned by ISE. This ensures that all access control decisions are enforced consistently across the network, whether the user is connected to a wired, wireless, or VPN network.

- **Granular Network Segmentation**: TrustSec's use of SGTs allows for highly granular control over network access. For example, an employee in the HR department may be tagged with an HR SGT and allowed access to sensitive HR resources but will be denied access to engineering or finance systems. By limiting access based on security group membership, TrustSec effectively prevents unauthorized access and reduces lateral movement within the network.

ISE's Role in Policy Enforcement:

- **User and Device Authentication**: ISE authenticates users and devices based on various factors, such as credentials (username/password), device certificates, or multi-factor authentication (MFA). Once authenticated, ISE evaluates the user or device's security posture to determine their level of access. ISE works with TrustSec to assign the appropriate SGT based on the user's identity and role, ensuring that only authorized individuals can access sensitive data or systems.
- **Authorization Policies**: ISE defines authorization policies that determine which resources a user or device is allowed to access based on their identity, security posture, and other contextual data. These policies can be very granular, taking into account factors such as device type (laptop, mobile device, IoT device), device health, user role, time of day, and location.
- **Context-Aware Access Control**: With ISE, administrators can implement policies that are based on the context in which the user or device is accessing the network. For example, ISE can check whether the user is accessing the network from a trusted device or from an unfamiliar location, and dynamically adjust their access rights accordingly.
- **Integration with Threat Intelligence**: ISE integrates with Cisco's threat intelligence systems, such as Cisco Advanced Malware Protection (AMP) and Cisco Firepower, to ensure that devices attempting to access the network are not compromised. If a device is deemed

untrusted or if it is in an unhealthy state (e.g., outdated security patches, known malware), ISE can deny access or place the device in a quarantine VLAN until it complies with security policies.

3. How TrustSec and ISE Enforce Zero Trust Policies

In a Zero Trust architecture, the guiding principle is that no device, user, or application should be implicitly trusted. Every access request is verified continuously, and access is granted based on strict policies. TrustSec and ISE work together to enforce Zero Trust principles by providing identity-based access control, segmentation, and dynamic policy enforcement.

3.1 Continuous Authentication and Authorization:

Unlike traditional security models, where once a user is authenticated, they have broad access to network resources, Zero Trust relies on continuous authentication and authorization. Cisco ISE plays a crucial role here by continuously verifying the identity and security posture of users and devices.

For example, a user who has authenticated to the network may still have their access rights re-evaluated during the session based on changes in their context. If the user's device becomes non-compliant or if they move to a different network segment, ISE can dynamically revoke access or adjust the user's security group, which TrustSec enforces through SGTs.

3.2 Least Privilege Access Control:

TrustSec and ISE enable the implementation of least privilege access control by restricting users and devices to only the resources they need for their role. For instance, a contractor working on a temporary project may be granted access only to the necessary applications and data for the duration of their contract. Once their role changes, their access rights can be automatically updated by ISE and enforced by TrustSec.

This enforcement of least privilege access is an essential component of Zero Trust, as it reduces the potential attack surface and limits the scope of potential breaches.

3.3 Segmentation to Contain Threats:

Network segmentation, a critical component of Zero Trust, ensures that even if an attacker manages to compromise one part of the network, they are unable to move laterally or escalate their privileges. TrustSec's dynamic segmentation allows administrators to quickly isolate a compromised device or user from other critical network resources, preventing the spread of a potential attack.

For example, if an endpoint is found to be infected with malware, ISE can immediately detect the threat and enforce a policy that quarantines the infected device in a separate network segment. TrustSec enforces this segmentation by applying appropriate SGTs to isolate the device from the rest of the network.

3.4 Real-Time Enforcement and Logging:

Both TrustSec and ISE provide real-time policy enforcement and logging, ensuring that access decisions are continuously monitored and recorded. This enables network administrators to quickly respond to potential security incidents, audit user activity, and maintain compliance with regulatory requirements.

In the case of a security event, such as a breach attempt or unauthorized access, TrustSec ensures that network traffic is immediately blocked, while ISE provides detailed logs and alerts that help security teams investigate the incident and take appropriate action.

4. Best Practices for Policy Enforcement with Cisco TrustSec and ISE

To effectively enforce policies with Cisco TrustSec and ISE, organizations should follow best practices that help maximize security, flexibility, and scalability:

- **Define Clear Roles and Access Policies**: Create clear and distinct security roles for users, devices, and applications. This will help to define which resources each group should have access to, ensuring that least privilege access is enforced at all times.

- **Leverage Dynamic Access Control**: Use contextual information, such as device health, user location, and the time of access, to dynamically adjust access rights and ensure that only authorized and compliant devices are allowed to connect.
- **Regularly Update and Review Policies**: Continuously monitor the network and update policies based on emerging threats, compliance requirements, and business needs. Regular reviews ensure that security policies remain effective and aligned with the organization's evolving needs.
- **Integrate ISE with Other Security Systems**: ISE works best when integrated with other Cisco security solutions, such as Cisco AMP, Firepower, and Stealthwatch. These integrations provide a comprehensive security approach that enhances the detection and mitigation of security threats.
- **Monitor and Audit Access**: Regularly audit network access logs to ensure that policies are being enforced correctly and that no unauthorized access has occurred. This will help in identifying gaps in security policies and quickly responding to security incidents.

By following these best practices, organizations can ensure that Cisco TrustSec and ISE provide robust, scalable, and dynamic policy enforcement, forming a critical component of a Zero Trust security architecture.

The combination of Cisco TrustSec and Cisco Identity Services Engine (ISE) offers a powerful, flexible, and scalable solution for policy enforcement within a Zero Trust architecture. By integrating network segmentation with identity-based access control, these solutions ensure that only authorized users and devices can access sensitive resources, while minimizing the risk of lateral movement and security breaches. The integration of TrustSec and ISE helps organizations enforce policies dynamically, based on real-time context, security posture, and user identity, making them an essential part of a modern, secure network infrastructure.

Real-World Example: Implementing Zero Trust in an Enterprise Network

As organizations face increasing cyber threats, the traditional approach of securing a network perimeter is no longer sufficient. A growing number of companies are adopting a **Zero Trust** model, which assumes that no entity—whether inside or outside the network—should be trusted by default. This includes devices, users, and applications. Instead, everything must be verified, continuously monitored, and granted access only based on explicit trust policies.

In this section, we'll walk through a **real-world example** of how a global enterprise might implement Zero Trust using **Cisco TrustSec** and **Identity Services Engine (ISE)** to protect critical resources and manage access dynamically. The example will cover the steps, benefits, and lessons learned during the implementation of a Zero Trust security model in a large-scale network environment.

1. Overview of the Organization and Network Setup

Consider a large multinational organization with a distributed workforce, spanning multiple regions across the globe. The company handles sensitive data, including intellectual property, financial records, and personal information of customers and employees. The organization has a traditional **hub-and-spoke** network design, where remote offices connect to a central data center, and employees use a mix of corporate laptops, mobile devices, and IoT devices to access company resources.

The company's network setup includes:

- **Corporate Headquarters (HQ)**: The main data center, hosting the company's critical systems, databases, and applications.

- **Regional Offices**: Smaller offices scattered across different countries, each with its own local infrastructure but relying on HQ for centralized services.
- **Remote Workers**: Employees working from home or traveling, accessing company resources via VPN or cloud-based applications.

The company is looking to modernize its security approach due to the growing concerns over increasing cyberattacks, particularly from ransomware, phishing, and insider threats. The existing security perimeter model is no longer sufficient to protect sensitive data, especially given the widespread use of cloud services and mobile devices.

2. Adopting a Zero Trust Security Model

In response to these challenges, the organization decides to implement a **Zero Trust Architecture (ZTA)** to better safeguard its network, applications, and data. The company chooses to leverage Cisco's **TrustSec** and **Identity Services Engine (ISE)** to build a Zero Trust model across its network infrastructure.

Key Principles of the Implementation:

1. **Assume Breach**: The company operates under the assumption that there may already be attackers inside the network or that attackers could infiltrate at any time. As such, the network is built to minimize trust, authenticate all entities, and limit lateral movement.
2. **Least Privilege Access**: Access is granted based on the specific needs of users, devices, and applications, ensuring that they can only access the resources necessary for their role. By implementing **Security Group Tags (SGTs)** through Cisco TrustSec, the company ensures users and devices are segmented into groups with strict access controls.
3. **Continuous Verification**: Cisco ISE provides real-time authentication and authorization checks to ensure that users and devices

remain compliant throughout their session. This includes checking device health and user context and adjusting access privileges dynamically.

3. Step-by-Step Implementation Process

Step 1: Identifying Critical Assets and Defining Access Policies

The first step is to **identify critical assets**—data, applications, and systems that need to be protected—and define the **access policies** that govern who can access them. The company needs to determine:

- **Who** should be allowed to access specific assets (e.g., which users, devices, and applications).
- **When** access should be granted (e.g., during business hours or only when connected to a secure network).
- **Where** access can occur from (e.g., specific IP addresses, regions, or trusted networks).
- **How** access should be controlled (e.g., through multi-factor authentication, device posture checks, etc.).

The company works with Cisco ISE to define and categorize access policies based on **user roles**, **device types**, and **location**. For instance, **HR employees** are allowed to access sensitive personnel data, but they must connect from an approved corporate laptop with endpoint security software installed and up-to-date.

Step 2: Implementing Identity-Based Access Control with ISE

Cisco **ISE** is deployed to centralize user authentication, device posture assessment, and authorization. The company integrates ISE with its existing **Active Directory (AD)** to authenticate users based on their roles, departments, and privileges.

Key actions include:

- **User Authentication**: All users (including remote employees) are

required to authenticate using **multi-factor authentication (MFA)** before accessing any corporate resources, such as email, file shares, and applications.
- **Device Posture Checks**: Cisco ISE evaluates the security posture of devices trying to connect to the network. Devices must meet specific criteria (e.g., up-to-date antivirus software, operating system patches, encryption) to be granted access. If a device is non-compliant, it may be quarantined or denied access to certain resources.
- **Dynamic VLAN Assignment**: Based on the authentication process, ISE dynamically assigns users and devices to specific **VLANs** and **Security Group Tags (SGTs)** based on their roles, device type, and security posture. For instance, a user working from a corporate laptop will be assigned to a secure VLAN, while an IoT device (e.g., a printer) will be segmented into a separate VLAN with more restricted access.

Step 3: Enforcing Network Segmentation with TrustSec

To ensure that even if a device or user is compromised, they cannot easily move laterally across the network, the company uses **Cisco TrustSec** to enforce **network segmentation**.

Key actions include:

- **Segmentation**: TrustSec uses **Security Group Tags (SGTs)** to dynamically segment the network based on the role and trust level of the user or device. For instance, employees in the Finance department might be tagged with an **SGT** that allows access only to financial data, while employees in the Sales department are tagged with an SGT that limits access to customer relationship management (CRM) data.
- **Access Control**: TrustSec tags all network traffic with **SGTs** and enforces access control policies at every switch and router in the network. These policies are based on the SGTs, ensuring that users and devices can only communicate with resources that they are authorized to access.

By leveraging TrustSec, the company ensures that access to critical assets is strictly controlled and segmented, limiting the potential impact of a breach.

Step 4: Continuous Monitoring and Real-Time Policy Enforcement with ISE

Once the system is in place, the organization uses **Cisco ISE** for continuous monitoring and real-time enforcement of policies. ISE integrates with **Cisco Stealthwatch** and **Cisco AMP (Advanced Malware Protection)** to detect any anomalies or threats.

Key actions include:

- **Real-Time Monitoring**: ISE continuously monitors the network, auditing user and device activity. Any attempt by a user or device to access unauthorized resources triggers an immediate alert, allowing network administrators to respond quickly.
- **Dynamic Policy Adjustments**: ISE automatically adjusts the security policies based on real-time context. For instance, if a user connects from an unfamiliar location, ISE can enforce additional security checks or reduce access rights until the user's identity is fully verified.
- **Threat Detection and Response**: If a device shows signs of compromise (e.g., malware detection), ISE can isolate the device from the network, and TrustSec ensures that the compromised device is blocked from accessing other critical network resources.

Step 5: Periodic Audits and Updates

After the Zero Trust architecture is fully implemented, the company conducts periodic audits to ensure that security policies remain up-to-date and effective. This includes reviewing **access logs**, validating **user roles**, and ensuring **device compliance**.

Additionally, as the organization grows, it uses **Cisco ISE** to scale the Zero Trust model by adding new user groups, devices, and applications, and adjusting policies as necessary.

4. Lessons Learned and Benefits

The implementation of Zero Trust in this enterprise network, powered by **Cisco TrustSec** and **ISE**, provides several key benefits:

- **Reduced Attack Surface**: By enforcing strict segmentation and least privilege access, the company significantly reduces the risk of lateral movement by attackers.
- **Enhanced Threat Detection and Response**: The real-time monitoring and dynamic policy enforcement help detect suspicious behavior early, minimizing the damage from potential breaches.
- **Improved Compliance**: With more granular control over user and device access, the company is better able to meet compliance requirements for data protection and privacy regulations.
- **Scalable Security**: As the organization expands, the Zero Trust model scales seamlessly, allowing the company to integrate new users, devices, and cloud services while maintaining a high level of security.

Adopting Cisco TrustSec and ISE for implementing a Zero Trust architecture allows organizations to safeguard their critical resources, reduce risk, and gain better control over network access. Through dynamic, identity-driven policies, continuous monitoring, and network segmentation, this approach ensures that security is consistently enforced across the network, regardless of location, device, or user.

Firewalls and Intrusion Prevention with Cisco

Cisco ASA and Firepower Firewalls

In today's complex and constantly evolving threat landscape, securing the network perimeter is a critical aspect of any organization's cybersecurity strategy. **Firewalls** play a fundamental role in protecting the network by monitoring and controlling incoming and outgoing traffic based on pre-determined security rules. Cisco, a leader in network security solutions, offers two primary firewall products—**Cisco ASA (Adaptive Security Appliance)** and **Cisco Firepower**—that deliver robust protections while providing advanced security capabilities for enterprise networks.

This section provides a comprehensive overview of **Cisco ASA** and **Firepower Firewalls**, highlighting their features, capabilities, and differences. We will also discuss how these solutions integrate with other Cisco security tools to create a holistic, multi-layered defense strategy for network protection.

1. Overview of Cisco ASA (Adaptive Security Appliance)

The **Cisco ASA** is a well-established firewall solution that has been widely used in enterprises for securing their network perimeters. Originally developed as a traditional **stateful firewall**, Cisco ASA has evolved into a comprehensive security appliance offering a combination of advanced features such as VPN support, intrusion prevention, and content filtering.

Key Features of Cisco ASA:

- **Stateful Inspection**: Cisco ASA performs stateful inspection of network traffic, meaning it keeps track of the state of active connections and only allows traffic that matches a known, established connection to pass through. This ensures that only valid traffic is permitted, making it difficult for attackers to bypass the firewall.
- **VPN Support**: ASA offers robust **VPN** capabilities, supporting **site-to-site** and **remote access VPNs**. These VPN types provide secure connections for users working remotely or across branch offices, ensuring encrypted and protected communications.
- **Network Address Translation (NAT)**: ASA includes **NAT** capabilities that allow private IP addresses to be mapped to public ones for outbound internet access. This provides both security and scalability, as it helps to conceal the internal network from external entities.
- **Intrusion Prevention System (IPS)**: Cisco ASA includes basic **intrusion prevention** features, allowing it to monitor traffic for signs of malicious activity. It can detect and block various types of network-based attacks, including denial-of-service (DoS) and buffer overflow attacks.
- **High Availability and Scalability**: ASA supports **High Availability (HA)** configurations, allowing organizations to deploy multiple firewalls for redundancy and load balancing. This ensures that the firewall infrastructure remains operational even if one device fails.
- **Advanced Threat Protection**: With **Cisco Advanced Malware Protection (AMP)** and **Cisco URL Filtering** features, ASA can identify and block malicious files and URLs, providing an added layer of defense against evolving threats.

Deployment Scenarios for Cisco ASA:

- **Perimeter Defense**: Cisco ASA is commonly deployed at the **network perimeter** to defend against external threats. It acts as a first line of defense for protecting internal resources from unauthorized access and malicious traffic.
- **Remote Access**: ASA's VPN capabilities make it a popular choice for providing **secure remote access** to users, allowing employees to connect to corporate resources safely from any location.
- **Branch Office Connectivity**: ASA's site-to-site VPN support allows **branch offices** to securely connect to the central corporate network, enabling seamless communication between geographically dispersed locations.

2. Cisco Firepower Firewalls: Advanced Threat Defense and Unified Security

While Cisco ASA is widely used for perimeter defense, **Cisco Firepower** represents the next evolution in firewall technology. Cisco Firepower combines traditional firewall features with advanced **intrusion prevention, threat intelligence**, and **application visibility** to provide a more comprehensive and integrated approach to network security. Cisco Firepower is built on a **next-generation firewall (NGFW)** architecture that offers deeper insights and more granular control over network traffic.

Key Features of Cisco Firepower:

- **Next-Generation Firewall (NGFW)**: Unlike traditional firewalls, Firepower operates as an NGFW, which integrates additional layers of security such as application-layer filtering, **intrusion prevention**, and **advanced threat intelligence**.
- **Application Visibility and Control (AVC)**: Firepower provides detailed visibility into **applications** running on the network. It can identify and control specific applications, even when they are hidden under common ports (such as HTTP/HTTPS). This capability enables security teams to enforce **application-level policies** and

block unwanted apps, reducing the attack surface.
- **Advanced Threat Protection**: Firepower integrates with **Cisco Threat Grid** to provide advanced malware analysis and **sandboxing**. This allows the firewall to detect, analyze, and block sophisticated threats such as zero-day attacks and ransomware before they reach critical resources.
- **Intrusion Prevention System (IPS)**: Cisco Firepower includes a robust **IPS** that scans all inbound and outbound traffic for known attack signatures, as well as behavioral anomalies. Firepower's IPS can block attacks in real-time based on predefined rules or automatically adjusted security policies.
- **URL Filtering and Anti-Malware**: Cisco Firepower provides **URL filtering** to block access to malicious or inappropriate websites and **anti-malware** capabilities to detect and stop threats such as viruses, worms, and Trojans.
- **Integrated Threat Intelligence**: Cisco Firepower integrates with Cisco's **Threat Intelligence** platform, allowing it to stay updated with the latest threat intelligence feeds. This integration helps to quickly identify and mitigate new and emerging threats, ensuring the network is always protected.
- **High Availability and Scalability**: Like ASA, Firepower supports **HA** configurations and can be deployed in clustered environments to ensure redundancy and scalability.

Deployment Scenarios for Cisco Firepower:

- **Enterprise Perimeter Defense**: Cisco Firepower is often deployed at the network perimeter to defend against a wide variety of external threats, including **DDoS attacks**, **malware**, and **phishing** attempts.
- **Data Center Security**: Firepower's deep visibility and advanced filtering make it an ideal solution for securing **data centers**, where applications and sensitive data need to be protected against advanced persistent threats (APTs).

- **Cloud Security**: As organizations migrate to the cloud, Firepower can extend its protective capabilities to **hybrid cloud environments** by integrating with **Cisco Umbrella** and **Cisco CloudLock**. This ensures that cloud-based workloads remain secure, regardless of location.
- **Remote Site Protection**: Firepower can be deployed in remote sites to provide **unified security** across the entire organization, enabling consistent threat defense even for branch offices or remote workers.

3. Cisco ASA vs. Cisco Firepower: Key Differences

While both **Cisco ASA** and **Cisco Firepower** offer robust security capabilities, there are significant differences between the two. Understanding these differences is crucial for choosing the right solution for your organization's needs.

Comparison of Features:

Feature	Cisco ASA	Cisco Firepower
Firewall Type	Stateful Firewall	Next-Generation Firewall (NGFW)
Intrusion Prevention	Basic IPS	Advanced IPS with Threat Intelligence
Application Control	Limited Application Awareness	Full Application Visibility and Control
Advanced Threat Protection	Limited (AMP available)	Full advanced threat protection (Advanced Malware Protection, Sandbox)
VPN Support	Site-to-Site, Remote Access	Site-to-Site, Remote Access
URL Filtering	Available	Advanced URL Filtering and Anti-Malware
Scalability	Moderate scalability	Highly scalable, suited for large enterprises
Cloud Integration	Limited	Seamless integration with cloud services
Deployment Options	Physical, Virtual	Physical, Virtual, Cloud

When to Choose Cisco ASA:

- **Small to Medium-Sized Networks**: Cisco ASA remains an excellent choice for smaller or less complex network environments that need reliable firewall protection, VPN access, and basic intrusion prevention.

- **Existing Cisco ASA Installations**: Organizations that already have Cisco ASA in place may choose to stick with it, as it integrates well into Cisco's broader security ecosystem and offers a more familiar user interface.
- **Cost-Effective Security**: If budget is a concern, ASA can provide strong perimeter defense and VPN capabilities without the higher cost of next-generation firewall features.

When to Choose Cisco Firepower:

- **Advanced Threat Protection**: Firepower is the ideal choice for organizations that need advanced **threat intelligence**, application-level security, and deep packet inspection.
- **Highly Regulated Environments**: For industries like healthcare, finance, and government, where compliance with strict security standards is critical, Firepower's advanced IPS, malware analysis, and sandboxing capabilities provide an added layer of security.
- **Cloud and Hybrid Network Environments**: Firepower offers better integration with cloud environments, making it a strong candidate for organizations that are migrating to or already utilizing hybrid cloud infrastructures.

Both **Cisco ASA** and **Cisco Firepower** are powerful solutions for protecting your organization's network perimeter, each offering a unique set of features and benefits. Cisco ASA is an established, reliable choice for basic firewall and VPN capabilities, while Cisco Firepower provides advanced, next-generation firewall features that offer greater visibility, control, and threat detection.

By evaluating the specific needs of your organization—including your threat landscape, compliance requirements, and network architecture—you can choose the most appropriate Cisco firewall solution to ensure robust protection against today's increasingly sophisticated cyber threats. Integrating these firewalls into a broader Cisco security architecture can provide a comprehensive defense strategy that addresses both known and emerging risks, ensuring the resilience and security of your enterprise network.

Configuring Next-Generation Firewalls (NGFW)

Next-generation firewalls (NGFWs) like **Cisco Firepower** go beyond traditional stateful firewalls by providing advanced capabilities such as **deep packet inspection, application awareness, intrusion prevention**, and **advanced malware protection**. These firewalls are critical for defending against modern threats that target vulnerabilities at multiple layers of the network, from the application layer down to the network layer.

Configuring an NGFW such as **Cisco Firepower** requires a solid understanding of network security principles, as well as the specific configuration tasks involved in deploying and managing an NGFW within an enterprise network. This section covers the key concepts, configuration steps, and best practices for implementing and optimizing **Cisco Firepower NGFWs**.

1. Basic Configuration of Cisco Firepower NGFW

To effectively configure a Cisco Firepower NGFW, you must understand the basic setup and management of the device, including connecting the hardware, configuring network interfaces, setting up firewall rules, and applying security policies.

Initial Setup and Installation

1. **Hardware Deployment**: Before configuring the Cisco Firepower NGFW, ensure that the device is physically deployed in the appropriate location within the network, typically at the perimeter or between critical segments of your network.

2. **Accessing the Device**: You can access and configure Cisco Firepower via:

- **Direct Console Access**: Connect to the console port using a terminal emulator (e.g., PuTTY or Tera Term) through a serial cable.
- **Firepower Management Center (FMC)**: The **FMC** is used to centrally manage and configure Firepower devices. Ensure the Firepower appliance is properly connected to FMC for management.

The initial configuration typically includes setting up management IP addresses, the administrator credentials, and configuring basic system settings such as hostname and domain name.

Basic Device Configuration Steps:
Assigning Management IP Addresses:

- Configure the Firepower device's **management interface** IP address, which will be used to connect to the device for further configuration.
- If you're using a **Firepower Management Center (FMC)**, ensure that the device is registered with the FMC.

Network Interface Configuration:

- The Firepower device requires configuration of **network interfaces** to connect to various parts of the network (e.g., internal network, external internet connection, DMZ).
- For each interface, assign an appropriate **IP address**, **subnet mask**, and specify the interface type (e.g., inside, outside, or DMZ).

Defining Security Zones:

- In Firepower, **security zones** are used to group interfaces that share a similar security posture.
- Create zones for **inside**, **outside**, and **DMZ** (or any custom zones

based on your network design).

Configuring Basic Firewall Rules:
Creating Access Control Policies:

- **Access Control Policies (ACP)** define what traffic is allowed or denied between security zones.
- Create ACPs to filter traffic based on **IP addresses**, **ports**, **protocols**, and **applications**.
- Use **application control** features to define granular traffic filtering policies based on application types rather than just IP or port numbers.

Defining NAT (Network Address Translation) Policies:

- Cisco Firepower allows configuration of NAT policies to manage address translation between internal and external networks.
- **Source NAT (SNAT)** and **Destination NAT (DNAT)** are often used to manage outbound and inbound traffic, respectively.

Security Policies:

- Configure **intrusion prevention system (IPS)** policies to monitor and block traffic patterns associated with known attack signatures.
- Apply **URL filtering** and **anti-malware** policies to block access to malicious websites and detect and block harmful files.

2. Advanced Configuration of Cisco Firepower NGFW

Beyond the basic setup, configuring advanced features of Cisco Firepower NGFWs involves setting up **application-layer filtering, advanced malware protection (AMP), intrusion prevention**, and **network traffic monitoring**. These features provide the deep visibility and threat protection needed for modern enterprise networks.

Intrusion Prevention System (IPS) Configuration:
Enabling IPS:

- Cisco Firepower's IPS feature uses a signature-based system to detect and block network-based attacks, such as buffer overflows, DoS (Denial of Service) attacks, and more.
- To enable IPS, navigate to the **Policies** section in the Firepower Management Center (FMC) and select **Intrusion Policy**.

Configuring IPS Rules:

- Cisco Firepower provides a comprehensive set of predefined IPS **signature rules** that can be applied directly or customized for your specific needs.
- You can fine-tune the IPS policies based on traffic behavior, attack severity, and the importance of the assets being protected. IPS policies are highly customizable, allowing the creation of **exclusion rules** and **exceptions** based on organizational requirements.

Application Visibility and Control (AVC):
Enabling Application Control:

- Cisco Firepower's **Application Visibility and Control (AVC)** feature identifies and controls over 4,000 applications that run on your network.
- From the **Access Control Policy** in the FMC, select **Application Control** and configure it to block or allow specific applications based on your security posture.

Creating Application Rules:

- Define policies that block unwanted applications (e.g., social media,

peer-to-peer file sharing) or allow business-critical applications (e.g., VoIP, CRM tools).
- Use **App ID** for fine-grained application classification. This feature allows the firewall to identify and control applications regardless of port or protocol used.

Advanced Malware Protection (AMP) Configuration:
Activating AMP:

- Cisco Firepower integrates **AMP for Networks** to provide real-time threat detection and advanced malware protection.
- To enable AMP, navigate to the **Policies** section in FMC and select **Advanced Malware Protection**.

Configuring File Policies:

- AMP enables the monitoring and analysis of files that pass through the firewall. You can configure file policies to inspect files for known threats, block malicious files, and analyze unknown files in a sandbox environment.
- Enable **File Reputation** to leverage Cisco's cloud-based intelligence to identify files with suspicious or malicious behavior.

URL Filtering Configuration:
Defining URL Filtering Policies:

- With **URL Filtering**, you can block access to known malicious websites or restrict access to certain categories of websites (e.g., adult content, social media).
- Set up **URL categories** and assign them to your Access Control Policies to filter traffic accordingly.

Categorizing URLs:

FIREWALLS AND INTRUSION PREVENTION WITH CISCO

- You can apply custom categories or use Cisco's built-in categories to define which URLs are blocked or allowed based on business needs and security requirements.

3. Monitoring and Logging

An essential aspect of managing a Next-Generation Firewall is ensuring that you can **monitor traffic**, **view logs**, and **perform analysis** for potential security events.
Monitoring Traffic:
Traffic Flow Monitoring:

- Cisco Firepower provides tools for monitoring real-time traffic flow and identifying performance bottlenecks or suspicious activity.
- Use **FMC dashboards** and **reports** to gain insights into network traffic, user activity, and overall security posture.

Event Monitoring:

- Enable **Event Logging** to keep track of key security events, such as traffic that matches access control policies, IPS alerts, or malware detections.
- **Correlation Policies** allow you to aggregate events from multiple sources and detect more complex threats.

Log Analysis:
Setting Up Logging:

- Configure the firewall to send logs to an external syslog server, SIEM (Security Information and Event Management) system, or the Firepower Management Center for detailed analysis.
- **Log Retention** and **Archiving**: Set policies for log retention based on your organization's compliance requirements.

Analyzing Security Events:

- Review logs for **intrusion prevention** alerts, malware detections, and **application control** events to identify potential threats.
- Regularly analyze the logs to stay proactive in preventing breaches and adjusting security policies accordingly.

4. Best Practices for Cisco Firepower NGFW Configuration

To ensure your Cisco Firepower NGFW is optimized for performance, security, and scalability, follow these best practices:

1. **Use a Defense-in-Depth Strategy**: Leverage multiple layers of security, such as IPS, URL filtering, application control, and AMP, to provide comprehensive protection.
2. **Regularly Update Signatures and Threat Intelligence**: Ensure that your firewall is running the latest IPS signature database and threat intelligence feeds. Regular updates improve the detection and prevention of emerging threats.
3. **Review and Fine-Tune Security Policies**: Continuously review your access control policies to ensure they align with your evolving business needs. Customize policies based on traffic patterns and risk assessments.
4. **Monitor Network Traffic**: Regularly monitor network traffic and use logging tools to identify unusual behavior, unauthorized access attempts, or other suspicious activities.
5. **Plan for High Availability**: Ensure that your Cisco Firepower devices are deployed in **HA** configurations to provide fault tolerance and minimize downtime in the event of a device failure.

Configuring and managing **Cisco Firepower** NGFWs requires careful planning and a thorough understanding of your network's security needs. With its advanced features such as IPS, application control, malware protection, and URL filtering, Firepower is an essential component of a modern, multi-layered security architecture. By following best practices for configuration, monitoring, and maintenance, you can ensure your Firepower device provides robust, proactive protection against a wide range of network-based threats, ensuring your organization's security posture is resilient to evolving risks.

Intrusion Prevention Systems (IPS) with Cisco

Intrusion Prevention Systems (IPS) are a critical component of network security, designed to detect and respond to malicious activities that attempt to breach a network. Cisco's IPS solutions provide a comprehensive approach to threat detection, prevention, and response, offering deep visibility into network traffic, advanced analysis of potential threats, and automated countermeasures to neutralize malicious activities before they can cause significant damage.

In this section, we will explore the fundamentals of **Cisco's IPS solutions**, how they work, their key features, configuration best practices, and real-world applications in enterprise networks.

1. Introduction to Intrusion Prevention Systems (IPS)

An **Intrusion Prevention System (IPS)** is a network security technology that continuously monitors network traffic for signs of malicious behavior and can automatically take action to block or mitigate these threats. Unlike Intrusion Detection Systems (IDS), which only detect potential intrusions and alert administrators, an IPS actively prevents attacks in real time by blocking malicious traffic.

Cisco's IPS technology is integrated into several of its security solutions, including the **Cisco Firepower NGFW** and **Cisco ASA** devices. It uses various techniques such as **signature-based detection**, **anomaly detection**, and **behavioral analysis** to identify and stop attacks like viruses, worms, denial-of-service (DoS) attacks, and unauthorized access attempts.

Key Functions of IPS:

- **Traffic Inspection**: IPS inspects inbound and outbound network traffic for known attack signatures, anomalous traffic patterns, and behavioral anomalies.
- **Real-Time Protection**: When an attack is detected, the IPS can take immediate actions, such as blocking traffic, issuing alerts, or blocking connections.
- **Proactive Defense**: By identifying and stopping threats early, an IPS provides a proactive defense layer that enhances overall network security.

2. Cisco IPS Solutions Overview

Cisco offers a range of solutions for intrusion prevention, integrated within its security appliances such as **Cisco Firepower** and **Cisco ASA with FirePOWER Services**. These solutions offer a comprehensive suite of tools for detecting, blocking, and responding to threats in real time.

Cisco Firepower IPS

Cisco Firepower IPS is part of the **Cisco Firepower NGFW**, a unified platform that combines advanced firewall functionality with intrusion prevention, malware detection, and more. It provides robust IPS capabilities to protect against a wide range of cyber threats. Firepower IPS is powered by Cisco's **Next-Generation IPS (NGIPS)** technology and is capable of identifying attacks across multiple layers of the network stack, from the network layer all the way to the application layer.

Key Features of Cisco Firepower IPS:

- **Signature-Based Detection**: Cisco Firepower IPS uses a continually updated signature database to detect known threats, including viruses, worms, and malware. Signatures are maintained by Cisco's **Talos Security Intelligence** team, which is one of the largest commercial threat intelligence teams.
- **Behavioral Analysis**: In addition to signature-based detection, Cisco Firepower IPS also uses advanced behavioral analysis to identify abnormal traffic patterns, helping to detect new or unknown threats that do not have a signature.
- **Application Layer Protection**: Cisco Firepower IPS can examine traffic at the application layer to identify threats that are often missed by traditional network-layer firewalls.
- **Context-Aware Detection**: The system is designed to understand the context of network traffic, including which devices are involved and the applications in use, allowing it to better detect sophisticated attacks that might evade traditional detection methods.
- **Centralized Management**: Firepower IPS can be centrally managed through the **Firepower Management Center (FMC)**, allowing administrators to configure policies, analyze threats, and view real-time traffic data from a single interface.

Cisco ASA with FirePOWER Services IPS

The **Cisco ASA** with **FirePOWER Services** integrates IPS functionality with the **Cisco ASA 5500-X Series Firewalls**. This solution combines the ASA's robust stateful firewall capabilities with the advanced threat protection of FirePOWER, providing a comprehensive defense against a wide range of cyberattacks.

Key Features of Cisco ASA with FirePOWER Services IPS:

- **Integrated Threat Defense**: The ASA with FirePOWER integrates IPS with other security services such as advanced malware protection (AMP), URL filtering, and application visibility, providing multi-layer protection in one solution.

- **Advanced Threat Intelligence**: Powered by **Cisco Talos**, the ASA with FirePOWER can leverage global threat intelligence to quickly identify and block emerging threats.
- **Customizable IPS Policies**: Administrators can create custom policies based on organizational needs, defining which types of traffic should be inspected and which should be allowed or blocked.
- **Inline Protection**: When IPS is enabled in an inline configuration, it actively blocks traffic that matches attack signatures or anomalous behavior, preventing attacks before they reach the network.

3. IPS Detection Methods

Cisco IPS uses several advanced detection methods to identify malicious traffic patterns. These detection methods work together to provide comprehensive protection against both known and unknown attacks.

Signature-Based Detection

Signature-based detection is the most common form of intrusion prevention. It relies on a database of attack signatures—predefined patterns of malicious traffic that are known to be associated with specific exploits or vulnerabilities. When a packet matches a signature, the IPS triggers an alert and can take action to block or mitigate the threat.

- **Advantages**: Effective for known threats and exploits that have established patterns.
- **Limitations**: Not effective against zero-day attacks or novel threats that don't have a known signature.

Anomaly-Based Detection

Anomaly-based detection identifies deviations from normal network behavior. By establishing a baseline of "normal" traffic patterns, the IPS can flag traffic that significantly deviates from this baseline as suspicious.

- **Advantages**: Can detect new, previously unknown threats or attacks

that lack specific signatures.
- **Limitations**: May produce more false positives compared to signature-based detection.

Behavioral Analysis

Behavioral analysis is a more sophisticated method that looks at traffic patterns over time, helping to detect sophisticated attacks that may evade both signature-based and anomaly-based detection. Cisco Firepower IPS uses machine learning and advanced statistical models to analyze the behavior of network traffic and detect potential threats.

- **Advantages**: Capable of detecting new, previously unseen attacks by analyzing traffic behavior.
- **Limitations**: Requires significant processing power and may introduce delays in detection.

4. Configuring Cisco IPS

Configuring Cisco IPS involves several key steps, including setting up the sensor, creating policies, tuning alerts, and fine-tuning detection signatures. Here is a brief guide to configuring Cisco IPS:

1. Initial Setup

- **Install the Firepower device** or **Firepower Services** on the Cisco ASA.
- **Connect the device to the network** and configure basic network settings, such as IP addresses for management interfaces.
- Register the device with the **Firepower Management Center (FMC)** if using Cisco Firepower or with the ASA if using FirePOWER Services.

2. Policy Configuration

- **Access Control Policies**: Create policies that specify which types of traffic should be inspected and which should be allowed or blocked. These policies can be customized based on network segments or specific types of applications.
- **Intrusion Policies**: Define **intrusion detection and prevention policies** based on your network's risk profile. Specify the type of detection (signature, anomaly, or behavior-based) and configure appropriate actions to take when an attack is detected (e.g., blocking, alerting, or logging).

3. Signature Configuration

- **Enable or disable IPS signatures** based on your organization's needs. Cisco's **signature update service** provides frequent updates to ensure that new threats are recognized and mitigated.
- You can also customize the IPS signatures, adding or removing signatures based on traffic analysis or organizational security policies.

4. Alerts and Logging

- **Configure logging** and alerting to track potential intrusions. Cisco IPS systems allow administrators to set thresholds for logging severity and determine whether alerts should be sent via email or integrated with an external **SIEM (Security Information and Event Management)** system.

5. Fine-Tuning the IPS

- **Tuning** involves adjusting signature sensitivities, creating exceptions for trusted traffic, and filtering out false positives. Fine-tuning is critical for ensuring the IPS system provides accurate and efficient protection without overwhelming administrators with unnecessary alerts.

5. Best Practices for Cisco IPS Configuration

To optimize the performance of Cisco IPS and enhance network security, organizations should follow best practices:

1. **Regular Signature Updates**: Ensure that IPS signatures are regularly updated to protect against the latest known threats.
2. **Use a Defense-in-Depth Approach**: Combine IPS with other security technologies, such as firewalls, anti-malware software, and access control, to create multiple layers of protection.
3. **Tune IPS Policies Regularly**: Regularly review and adjust IPS policies to reflect changing network traffic patterns and emerging threats.
4. **Monitor Logs and Alerts**: Continuously monitor alerts and logs to identify trends in network traffic and potential threats. Use SIEM systems for better correlation of security events.
5. **Ensure High Availability**: Deploy IPS in a high-availability configuration to ensure continuous protection and minimize downtime.

6. Real-World Use Cases of Cisco IPS

Cisco IPS solutions have been widely adopted across various industries to protect sensitive data, prevent network breaches, and secure critical infrastructure. Here are some practical use cases where IPS can provide significant protection:

1. **Preventing Data Breaches**: An IPS can detect and block suspicious activities such as SQL injection attacks, cross-site scripting (XSS), and other vulnerabilities that may be exploited by attackers to steal sensitive data.
2. **Blocking Malware and Ransomware**: IPS can prevent malware and ransomware from entering the network by inspecting files and identifying suspicious patterns associated with malicious payloads.

3. **Stopping DDoS Attacks**: IPS can identify and block Distributed Denial-of-Service (DDoS) attacks by monitoring traffic volumes and blocking malicious IP addresses or abnormal traffic spikes.
4. **Protecting Cloud Environments**: With the increasing adoption of cloud-based applications, Cisco IPS can help protect data stored in the cloud from unauthorized access, malware, and other threats.

Cisco's Intrusion Prevention Systems offer advanced protection against a wide range of network-based threats, providing real-time detection and prevention of cyberattacks. By leveraging signature-based detection, anomaly detection, and behavioral analysis, Cisco's IPS solutions enable businesses to defend their networks against known and emerging threats. Effective configuration, fine-tuning, and regular updates are essential for maximizing the performance of IPS and ensuring robust security in today's dynamic threat landscape.

Integrating Cisco Firewalls into a Multi-Layer Security Architecture

In the modern network security landscape, defending against advanced threats requires more than just a single perimeter defense. A comprehensive security strategy involves multiple layers of protection, each designed to address different types of threats and attack vectors. Cisco firewalls, including the **Cisco ASA** (Adaptive Security Appliance) and **Cisco Firepower** series, play a critical role in these multi-layer security architectures. By integrating these firewalls with other security solutions, organizations can achieve a **defense-in-depth** strategy that maximizes their ability to detect, block, and mitigate threats before they can cause significant damage.

This section will explore how to integrate Cisco firewalls into a multi-layer security architecture, the benefits of doing so, and best practices for deployment. We will also discuss how these firewalls work alongside other technologies like **Intrusion Prevention Systems (IPS)**, **Security Information and Event Management (SIEM)** systems, **Endpoint Detection and Response (EDR)** tools, and **cloud security platforms** to create a resilient, scalable, and adaptive security environment.

1. Understanding Multi-Layer Security Architecture

A multi-layer security architecture is designed to provide **multiple lines of defense** to protect against a broad range of cyber threats. Each layer focuses on a specific aspect of network security, ensuring that if one layer is breached, the others still provide protection. The layers typically include:

- **Perimeter Security**: This includes firewalls, VPNs, and network segmentation to protect the boundary between the internal network and the outside world.
- **Internal Security**: This layer focuses on protecting critical assets inside the organization, such as data, servers, and internal applications. This can include segmentation, access controls, and internal firewalls.
- **Application Security**: Application firewalls, web application firewalls (WAF), and security protocols ensure that applications are not vulnerable to attacks like SQL injection or cross-site scripting (XSS).
- **Endpoint Security**: This includes anti-virus software, endpoint detection and response (EDR) tools, and device control to protect individual devices, such as laptops, workstations, and mobile devices.
- **Data Security**: This layer focuses on data encryption, data loss prevention (DLP), and backup and recovery systems to protect sensitive information at rest and in transit.
- **Cloud Security**: For organizations leveraging cloud computing services, cloud security platforms provide protection for workloads, applications, and data hosted in the cloud.

In such a security framework, Cisco firewalls—whether **ASA**, **Firepower**, or other next-generation devices—are central to securing the network perimeter and often extend into internal network zones, thus forming a key part of the multi-layer security architecture.

2. The Role of Cisco Firewalls in Multi-Layer Security

Cisco firewalls provide **stateful packet inspection, intrusion prevention, VPN support, URL filtering**, and **advanced malware protection**—all critical features for a robust multi-layer security strategy. These firewalls help secure traffic between networks, users, and applications, ensuring that only legitimate communication passes through.

Cisco firewalls contribute to multi-layer security in the following ways:

a. Perimeter Defense

The most obvious role of Cisco firewalls in multi-layer security is their placement at the network perimeter. They are often the first line of defense against external threats, such as:

- **Unauthorized access attempts**: Cisco firewalls filter traffic entering or leaving the network, blocking unauthorized access attempts.
- **DDoS attacks**: Cisco firewalls can help mitigate **Distributed Denial of Service (DDoS)** attacks by analyzing traffic for malicious patterns and filtering out invalid packets.
- **Intrusions and malware**: Cisco firewalls with **next-generation capabilities** (such as the **Firepower NGFW**) can detect and block malware, ransomware, and other types of malicious traffic entering the network from the outside.

b. Segmentation and Internal Security

While firewalls are typically positioned at the perimeter, they also play an important role in **internal segmentation**. In a multi-layer security model, the internal network is often divided into **zones** or **subnets** based on the sensitivity of the data or applications they contain. Cisco firewalls can be deployed between these zones to enforce security policies and prevent lateral movement in case of a breach.

For example:

- **DMZ (Demilitarized Zone)**: Cisco firewalls can segregate external-facing services, such as web servers or email servers, from the internal network to reduce the impact of potential breaches.
- **Critical Asset Protection**: Cisco firewalls can be deployed to create secure zones around sensitive assets, such as financial data, intellectual property, and databases, ensuring that only authorized users and systems have access to them.

c. Intrusion Detection and Prevention

Cisco firewalls integrate with intrusion detection and prevention systems (IDPS) to offer an additional layer of threat detection and prevention. The **Cisco Firepower** platform, for instance, includes **Next-Generation Intrusion Prevention (NGIPS)** capabilities, which combine signature-based and behavior-based detection methods to identify known and unknown threats. When a threat is detected, the firewall can block it in real-time, preventing it from entering the network.

d. VPN and Secure Remote Access

In today's distributed and remote work environments, securing remote access to the corporate network is crucial. Cisco firewalls provide **VPN (Virtual Private Network)** functionality, ensuring that remote users can securely access the network without exposing sensitive data to the internet. Cisco's **AnyConnect VPN client** and **IPsec VPNs** enable secure access for mobile workers, branch offices, and remote sites, creating a **secure tunnel** for traffic to pass through.

3. Integrating Cisco Firewalls with Other Security Technologies

While Cisco firewalls provide an essential layer of defense, they must work in concert with other security technologies to provide a comprehensive multi-layered defense. Integrating Cisco firewalls with the following technologies strengthens the overall security posture:

a. Intrusion Prevention Systems (IPS)

Cisco firewalls, particularly the **Firepower NGFW**, include built-in IPS functionality. However, in complex environments, external IPS solutions can complement firewalls by providing additional threat detection. For instance, integrating **Cisco Firepower** IPS sensors with **Cisco ASA** firewalls enhances detection capabilities and provides advanced defense against sophisticated attacks. When combined, these solutions ensure that any threat attempting to bypass the firewall is detected and mitigated at the earliest opportunity.

b. Security Information and Event Management (SIEM)

SIEM systems collect and analyze security data from multiple devices within the network, providing administrators with real-time insights into potential security incidents. By integrating Cisco firewalls with SIEM solutions such as **Splunk**, **IBM QRadar**, or **ArcSight**, administrators can correlate logs and alerts across the entire infrastructure, allowing for faster identification and response to threats. For example, if a firewall detects an intrusion attempt and an IPS detects unusual activity, the SIEM system can consolidate this information and trigger a unified response.

c. Endpoint Detection and Response (EDR)

Cisco firewalls can be integrated with **Endpoint Detection and Response (EDR)** solutions to enhance protection at the endpoint level. EDR tools provide real-time monitoring and incident response capabilities for endpoints, detecting suspicious behavior, and stopping malware before it spreads. By correlating data from firewalls and EDR solutions, organizations can ensure that an endpoint is protected both from external threats (e.g., attackers trying to access the network) and internal threats (e.g., malware on the endpoint).

d. Cloud Security Solutions

As more organizations move to the cloud, **cloud security** solutions become an integral part of the multi-layer security strategy. Cisco firewalls can be integrated with **cloud security platforms**, such as **Cisco Umbrella**, to provide comprehensive protection for both on-premises and cloud-hosted applications. For example, **Cisco ASA with FirePOWER** can protect cloud workloads by inspecting traffic to and from cloud applications, blocking threats, and enforcing security policies.

4. Best Practices for Integrating Cisco Firewalls in Multi-Layer Security

To ensure the maximum effectiveness of Cisco firewalls within a multi-layer security architecture, consider the following best practices:

a. Centralized Management

Using centralized management tools like **Cisco Firepower Management Center (FMC)** or **Cisco Security Manager (CSM)** simplifies the configuration and monitoring of multiple Cisco firewalls across the network. These tools provide a unified interface for policy management, threat analysis, and incident response, improving efficiency and visibility.

b. Policy Alignment

Ensure that security policies across firewalls and other security solutions (such as IPS, SIEM, and EDR) are aligned. Policies should be consistent across the network, ensuring that there are no gaps or overlaps in protection. This consistency helps to minimize security risks and ensures a coordinated response to threats.

c. Regular Updates and Patching

Cisco firewalls should be regularly updated with the latest security patches and threat signatures. Threat landscapes evolve constantly, and Cisco frequently releases updates for its firewall firmware and signature databases to address new vulnerabilities and emerging attack vectors.

d. Performance Monitoring

Regularly monitor the performance of Cisco firewalls, especially when they are deployed in high-traffic environments. Performance issues, such as latency or packet drops, can affect the firewall's ability to inspect and filter traffic effectively. Tools like **Cisco Prime Infrastructure** can help monitor network performance and detect issues before they become serious problems.

Integrating Cisco firewalls into a multi-layer security architecture is a critical step in creating a robust defense against modern cyber threats. Cisco firewalls provide state-of-the-art protection against external and internal threats, malware, DDoS attacks, and more. By working in conjunction with other security technologies like IPS, SIEM, EDR, and cloud security solutions, Cisco firewalls ensure that all attack vectors are covered, providing a comprehensive and resilient security posture.

By following best practices for configuration, management, and integration, organizations can leverage Cisco firewalls to build a flexible, scalable, and secure network environment capable of defending against the ever-evolving threat landscape.

Cloud Security with Cisco Umbrella

As organizations increasingly migrate to the cloud, traditional network security paradigms are evolving to accommodate the dynamic nature of cloud environments. Securing cloud-based resources, applications, and data has become a top priority, especially with the rise in remote work, mobile devices, and cloud-first strategies. **Cisco Umbrella** is a cloud-native security platform that provides comprehensive protection for users and devices, regardless of their location. It combines **secure internet gateway (SIG)** capabilities, **DNS-layer security**, and **cloud-delivered firewall** services to safeguard against a wide range of threats, including malware, phishing attacks, and data exfiltration attempts.

In this section, we'll explore how **Cisco Umbrella** enhances cloud security, its key features and benefits, and how organizations can leverage it to protect their cloud environments and users from evolving cyber threats.

1. What is Cisco Umbrella?

Cisco Umbrella is a **cloud-based security solution** that offers a comprehensive approach to threat prevention and internet security. Traditionally, security solutions like firewalls, VPNs, and DNS filtering operated at the network perimeter, which posed challenges in securing remote workers, branch offices, and cloud-based applications. Cisco Umbrella shifts the security model to the cloud, providing an **always-on, proactive layer of defense** that can be deployed globally without the need for traditional on-premises hardware.

At its core, Cisco Umbrella acts as a **secure internet gateway** (SIG), which combines multiple security functions into a single platform to protect users from threats when accessing the internet. It leverages **DNS-layer security**, **URL filtering**, **cloud-delivered firewall**, **threat intelligence**, and **web traffic inspection** to prevent malicious activities and enforce security policies across all user devices—whether they are on the corporate network, at home, or traveling abroad.

2. Key Features and Benefits of Cisco Umbrella

a. DNS-Layer Security

The foundation of Cisco Umbrella's security architecture is its **DNS-layer security**. DNS (Domain Name System) is essentially the "address book" of the internet, translating human-readable domain names (like **www.example.com**) into IP addresses that computers use to communicate. When a user attempts to access a website, a DNS query is made to resolve the domain name.

Cisco Umbrella provides **DNS filtering** to block access to malicious websites at the DNS resolution level. By leveraging **threat intelligence** and continuously updating its domain blacklist, Umbrella can **prevent access to known malicious domains** even before the user connects to them. This proactive defense blocks threats before they can execute on the endpoint, preventing phishing, malware downloads, and command-and-control traffic from reaching the device.

Key benefits include:

- **Fast, low-latency protection**: Umbrella's DNS filtering is efficient and lightweight, meaning it doesn't introduce delays in user browsing.
- **Block harmful domains**: By blocking access to malicious domains, Umbrella stops threats before they reach the endpoint or network.
- **Advanced threat intelligence**: Cisco's **Talos Intelligence Group** continuously updates Umbrella's threat intelligence to ensure that new threats are identified and blocked quickly.

b. Secure Web Gateway (SWG) and URL Filtering

While DNS-layer security provides a first line of defense, Cisco Umbrella goes further with its **Secure Web Gateway (SWG)** functionality, which provides deeper inspection of web traffic. Umbrella's SWG capability inspects both **HTTP** and **HTTPS** traffic, enabling real-time blocking of malicious content and applications.

- **URL filtering**: Umbrella can block access to specific websites or categories of websites based on pre-defined policies, such as social media, gambling sites, or malicious URLs.
- **Web traffic inspection**: Umbrella inspects encrypted traffic (SSL/TLS) without decrypting it, enabling it to detect threats in encrypted web traffic without compromising privacy.

This feature is especially useful in environments where users access web applications and cloud services, as it ensures that web-based threats are blocked regardless of where users are located.

c. Cloud Firewall

Cisco Umbrella also includes a **cloud-delivered firewall** that provides traditional network security controls, such as port blocking, protocol filtering, and application-level traffic inspection. The firewall enforces security policies based on **user identity, geolocation**, and **application type**, enabling fine-grained control over internet traffic.

The cloud firewall is **highly scalable** and allows administrators to create rules for controlling traffic flowing into and out of their cloud environments. Since the firewall is delivered from the cloud, there is no need for on-premises hardware, which reduces deployment complexity and offers greater flexibility for cloud-first environments.

d. Threat Intelligence and Advanced Malware Protection

Cisco Umbrella leverages the **Talos Intelligence Group**, one of the largest commercial threat intelligence teams in the world, to provide **real-time protection** against known and emerging threats. Umbrella's threat intelligence feeds allow it to quickly detect and block new malware, ransomware, and phishing campaigns by analyzing domain names, IP addresses, and traffic patterns across billions of devices worldwide.

Umbrella's **Advanced Malware Protection (AMP)** can detect malicious payloads and fileless malware that may try to exploit vulnerabilities in the system. It integrates with other Cisco security tools, such as **Cisco AMP for Endpoints** and **Cisco Stealthwatch**, to enhance overall threat detection across the entire network.

e. Cloud Access Security Broker (CASB) Integration

Cisco Umbrella integrates with a **Cloud Access Security Broker (CASB)**, providing **visibility and control** over the use of cloud applications. With the rise of **Shadow IT**, where employees use unsanctioned cloud applications, it's important to monitor and enforce policies around cloud app usage. Cisco Umbrella can identify cloud applications in use across your network, determine which are risky or unsanctioned, and block or restrict access as needed.

This integration helps organizations maintain control over their cloud application environments while preventing risky or non-compliant apps from putting the network at risk.

3. Benefits of Using Cisco Umbrella for Cloud Security

a. Simplified Security Management

One of the biggest challenges in securing modern IT environments is managing and configuring a multitude of point solutions that may have limited visibility into each other. Cisco Umbrella consolidates multiple security layers (DNS filtering, URL filtering, firewall, malware protection) into a single platform, reducing the complexity of security management. Its cloud-based nature means there's no need for on-premises hardware or software, simplifying deployment and management.

Umbrella provides an easy-to-use dashboard that allows administrators to set policies, monitor threats, and generate reports in real-time. This centralized management streamlines security operations and helps ensure that security policies are enforced consistently across the organization.

b. Scalability and Global Protection

Since Cisco Umbrella is **cloud-delivered**, it's highly scalable, making it an ideal solution for businesses of all sizes. Whether you're a small business with a handful of remote employees or a large enterprise with thousands of global offices, Cisco Umbrella can scale to meet your needs. The cloud architecture also provides **global protection**, meaning users can be protected regardless of their geographic location, which is especially important for organizations with remote workers or offices in multiple regions.

c. Reduced Risk of Data Breaches

Data breaches are often the result of initial compromises via malicious websites, phishing emails, or insecure cloud applications. Cisco Umbrella's proactive approach to threat prevention reduces the likelihood of such breaches by blocking access to known threats at the DNS level before they reach the endpoint or network. By preventing malware, phishing, and command-and-control communication, Umbrella minimizes the risk of a successful attack.

Additionally, Umbrella's **integration with Cisco's security stack**, such as **Cisco AMP for Endpoints**, **Cisco Stealthwatch**, and **Cisco**

Firepower NGFW, provides a comprehensive approach to detecting and responding to threats, further enhancing your ability to mitigate risk.

d. Improved User Experience and Performance

Unlike traditional security solutions, which can introduce latency or slow down browsing speeds, Cisco Umbrella's DNS-layer security is designed to operate with **minimal impact on network performance**. It leverages Cisco's global infrastructure to provide fast DNS lookups, ensuring that users experience minimal delays while being protected. By using a cloud-delivered approach, Umbrella also ensures that there are no bottlenecks in traffic inspection, even when dealing with high traffic volumes or large numbers of remote workers.

4. Best Practices for Implementing Cisco Umbrella

To get the most out of Cisco Umbrella and ensure its effective deployment, consider the following best practices:

- **Integrate Umbrella with Existing Security Tools**: For maximum protection, integrate Cisco Umbrella with other Cisco security solutions like **Cisco AMP**, **Cisco Stealthwatch**, and **Cisco Firepower NGFW**. This will provide a comprehensive, unified approach to threat detection and response.
- **Define and Enforce Security Policies**: Configure Umbrella's policies based on user roles, departments, or locations to ensure that the right security measures are in place for different types of users. This includes blocking access to specific categories of websites (e.g., gambling, social media) or applying different levels of malware protection.
- **Monitor and Analyze Threat Intelligence**: Take advantage of Umbrella's detailed reporting and analytics capabilities to gain insights into potential security threats. Review the logs and reports regularly to stay on top of emerging threats and adjust security policies as needed.

- **Educate Users**: While Umbrella provides automated security, it's essential to educate users about best practices for internet security, phishing awareness, and the risks of using unapproved cloud applications (Shadow IT).

Cisco Umbrella offers a comprehensive, cloud-delivered security solution that provides robust protection against the wide range of threats targeting modern, distributed networks. By leveraging DNS-layer security, web traffic inspection, cloud firewalls, and advanced threat intelligence, Umbrella helps organizations safeguard their users, data, and cloud environments with minimal complexity.

As businesses continue to embrace cloud-first strategies, **Cisco Umbrella** ensures that they can extend their security perimeter into the cloud, securing remote workers, branch offices, and mobile users without compromising performance or user experience. By integrating Cisco Umbrella into your network security architecture, you can build a more resilient, scalable, and proactive defense against today's most sophisticated cyber threats.

Case Study: Securing a Network Perimeter with Cisco Firewalls

In this case study, we'll explore how an organization leveraged Cisco Firewalls, specifically **Cisco ASA** (Adaptive Security Appliance) and **Cisco Firepower** Next-Generation Firewalls (NGFW), to secure its network perimeter, protect sensitive data, and enable secure access for remote workers. This real-world example will illustrate how Cisco firewalls integrate into a broader network security architecture, providing a comprehensive, multi-layered defense against evolving threats.

Background: The Need for Robust Network Security

The organization in this case study is a global financial institution with thousands of employees spread across multiple regions. As the organization embraced digital transformation and moved many of its services to the cloud, it faced a growing number of security challenges:

- **Increasing Cyber Threats**: The institution faced an increased threat landscape, including advanced persistent threats (APTs), DDoS (Distributed Denial of Service) attacks, and attempts to exploit vulnerabilities in legacy applications.
- **Remote Work and Cloud Adoption**: The shift to remote work and reliance on cloud applications introduced new entry points for cybercriminals, with users needing secure access to company resources from anywhere in the world.
- **Compliance Requirements**: As a financial organization, the company had stringent regulatory and compliance requirements, including data protection laws such as GDPR, PCI-DSS, and financial industry standards. Failure to meet these standards could result in heavy fines and reputational damage.

The institution recognized the need for a more secure, scalable, and flexible perimeter defense solution—one that would allow them to control traffic, protect sensitive data, and prevent unauthorized access to both on-premises and cloud environments. To meet these demands, the company decided to implement a robust firewall solution, combining **Cisco ASA Firewalls** and **Cisco Firepower NGFW** to create a comprehensive security strategy.

Choosing Cisco Firewalls for Network Security

The organization chose Cisco's firewalls based on several factors that made the Cisco solution a good fit for their requirements:

1. **Comprehensive Threat Detection and Prevention**: Cisco Firepower NGFW offered deep packet inspection, intrusion prevention, advanced malware protection (AMP), and URL filtering to identify and mitigate threats in real-time.
2. **Scalability and Flexibility**: As the organization expanded its global presence and integrated more cloud-based applications, they needed a solution that could scale with the business. Cisco's solutions offered flexibility and scalability to accommodate future growth.
3. **Integration with Existing Cisco Infrastructure**: The organization already had Cisco routers and switches deployed, and using Cisco firewalls ensured seamless integration into the existing network infrastructure, reducing deployment complexity.
4. **Advanced Security Features**: The combination of Cisco ASA and Firepower NGFW provided an advanced level of security, including **VPN (Virtual Private Network)** support for remote access, **site-to-site connectivity**, **deep packet inspection**, and **automated threat intelligence** from Cisco Talos.

Deployment Strategy: Building a Multi-Layered Perimeter Defense

The network security architecture was designed using a **multi-layered defense** approach. The perimeter was secured using Cisco ASA and Cisco Firepower Firewalls, which provided the first line of defense against external threats. The deployment was divided into several key components:

1. Cisco ASA as the Primary Edge Firewall

The Cisco **ASA 5500-X Series Firewalls** were deployed as the **primary**

edge security device at the network perimeter. ASA firewalls acted as the first layer of defense, inspecting traffic entering and leaving the corporate network. The main responsibilities of the ASA firewalls included:

- **Stateful Inspection**: ASA performed **stateful packet inspection** (SPI) to ensure that only legitimate, established connections were allowed through the firewall, while blocking any suspicious or unauthorized traffic.
- **VPN Services**: ASA provided secure remote access for employees through **SSL and IPsec VPN**. This allowed employees to securely access corporate resources from anywhere, even when working remotely or traveling.
- **Access Control**: ASA allowed the institution to define granular **access control policies**, specifying which users or devices could access certain network resources, based on IP address, user identity, or time of access.
- **NAT (Network Address Translation)**: The ASA firewalls also provided **NAT** capabilities to hide internal network addresses, protecting the internal network from direct exposure to the internet.

2. Cisco Firepower NGFW for Advanced Threat Detection and Prevention

The **Cisco Firepower NGFW** was deployed in a dual mode—both at the edge and within internal network segments—to provide enhanced **intrusion prevention**, **malware protection**, and **web filtering**. Cisco Firepower offered:

- **Advanced Threat Protection (ATP)**: Firepower NGFW utilized **AMP (Advanced Malware Protection)** to detect and prevent malware that may attempt to enter the network through web traffic, email attachments, or USB devices.
- **Intrusion Prevention System (IPS)**: Firepower's built-in IPS continuously inspected network traffic for known attack signatures,

vulnerabilities, and anomalous behaviors. This helped detect and block sophisticated attacks such as **zero-day exploits** and **DDoS** attacks.
- **URL Filtering**: Firepower was configured to block access to malicious or non-compliant websites by filtering URLs based on predefined policies. This functionality ensured that users could not access harmful content or sites that could compromise network security.
- **Application Visibility and Control**: Firepower provided **Application Visibility and Control (AVC),** enabling the institution to identify and block specific applications, such as unauthorized cloud services or peer-to-peer protocols, which could pose a risk to network integrity.

3. Integration with Cisco Umbrella for Cloud Security

In addition to on-premises firewalls, the organization integrated **Cisco Umbrella** to provide cloud-delivered security for users accessing the internet from outside the corporate network. Cisco Umbrella worked seamlessly with ASA and Firepower to extend protection to remote users and branch offices, regardless of their location.

Umbrella's **DNS-layer security** blocked access to known malicious domains before any malicious content could even be loaded on a user's device. The organization was able to enforce security policies consistently across their entire global workforce, ensuring that remote workers and branch offices were protected against web-based threats, including phishing and malware.

4. High Availability and Redundancy

To ensure **business continuity** and minimize downtime, the organization implemented **high availability (HA)** configurations for both ASA and Firepower devices. This included:

- **Active/Active HA for Firepower**: Two Firepower devices were configured in an active/active HA setup, allowing traffic to be load-balanced between both devices. This ensured that the network would remain protected even if one of the devices failed.

- **Failover for ASA**: ASA firewalls were configured in a **failover pair** to ensure that if one firewall failed, the other would take over without any interruption in service. This failover capability provided **zero downtime** for VPN users and critical business applications.

Security Monitoring and Incident Response

To monitor and respond to security events in real time, the organization leveraged Cisco's **Security Information and Event Management (SIEM)** solution, **Cisco Stealthwatch**, along with the Firepower Management Center (FMC). These tools provided centralized **logging**, **reporting**, and **incident response** capabilities.

- **Centralized Logging and Analysis**: Cisco's **Firepower Management Center (FMC)** collected logs from all Cisco firewalls and security devices, providing a **single pane of glass** for real-time monitoring and analysis. Security administrators could quickly identify threats, analyze traffic patterns, and investigate suspicious activities.
- **Automated Threat Intelligence**: The integration with **Cisco Talos** provided real-time threat intelligence feeds, enabling the organization to stay ahead of emerging threats. Firepower NGFW and ASA firewalls automatically updated their signature databases to detect new attack vectors and vulnerabilities.
- **Incident Response and Forensics**: In the event of a security breach, Cisco's **AMP** and **Stealthwatch** provided incident response teams with the data needed to analyze the attack's origin, scope, and impact. This helped ensure a rapid and effective response to contain and mitigate the threat.

Results and Outcomes

The deployment of **Cisco ASA** and **Firepower NGFW** firewalls, integrated with **Cisco Umbrella**, significantly enhanced the organization's network security posture. Some of the key results were:

- **Reduced Attack Surface**: The organization experienced a substantial reduction in attacks originating from external threats, as the firewalls effectively blocked a wide range of malware, phishing, and DDoS attacks.
- **Improved Remote Work Security**: Remote employees were able to securely access corporate resources through VPNs, while Cisco Umbrella provided additional protection against web-based threats, even when accessing the internet from home or on the go.
- **Compliance Adherence**: The security enhancements enabled the organization to meet its compliance requirements, including PCI-DSS, GDPR, and industry-specific standards. The comprehensive logging and reporting capabilities ensured that the institution could quickly generate compliance reports.
- **Operational Efficiency**: The integration of Cisco firewalls with the organization's broader security infrastructure (such as Cisco's SIEM, AMP, and Stealthwatch) streamlined security operations and improved threat detection and response times.

By deploying Cisco ASA and Firepower NGFW firewalls, along with cloud security solutions like Cisco Umbrella, the financial institution successfully secured its network perimeter against a wide range of cyber threats. The multi-layered defense architecture, with high availability configurations, enabled the organization to protect both its on-premises infrastructure and remote workers. The integration of advanced threat intelligence and centralized monitoring further enhanced their ability to detect, analyze, and respond to security incidents quickly.

This case study underscores the importance of using a comprehensive, integrated approach to network security—one that incorporates both traditional perimeter defense solutions and cloud-delivered security technologies. By adopting Cisco's firewalls and security solutions, organizations can create a resilient, scalable, and highly secure network environment capable of withstanding the evolving landscape of cyber threats.

Case Studies in Network Architecture

Enterprise Network Design for a Global Corporation

In this case study, we explore how a large, multinational corporation implemented a highly scalable and reliable network architecture to meet the demands of its global operations. The company, a leading player in the pharmaceutical industry, needed to ensure secure, high-performance connectivity for thousands of employees across multiple continents. The solution needed to support everything from business-critical applications to cloud-based services, while maintaining high availability and performance across diverse geographical locations.

Business Requirements and Challenges

The pharmaceutical corporation's network design needed to address several core business requirements:

1. **Global Connectivity**: With offices, research centers, and manufacturing facilities spread across North America, Europe, Asia, and emerging markets, the network had to seamlessly connect these locations with minimal latency, ensuring smooth collaboration across borders.
2. **High Availability and Redundancy**: Given the critical nature of the business, uptime was paramount. Any downtime would not only

affect employee productivity but could also jeopardize regulatory compliance, manufacturing processes, and research data integrity.
3. **Cloud and Data Center Integration**: The company was rapidly migrating its internal applications to the cloud, making it imperative to design a network that integrated seamlessly with both on-premises data centers and cloud platforms, ensuring consistent performance.
4. **Security**: With sensitive intellectual property (IP), patient data, and proprietary research at stake, the network had to implement a robust security architecture that prevented unauthorized access, malware, and data breaches.
5. **Scalability**: As the business expanded into new markets, the network needed to scale quickly to accommodate more users, devices, and increased data traffic, all while ensuring that performance was not compromised.
6. **Compliance**: As a global corporation, the company had to adhere to various regional regulatory requirements, including those related to healthcare and patient data privacy (such as HIPAA in the U.S. and GDPR in Europe).

Network Architecture Design

To address these business requirements, the company adopted a **Cisco-based network architecture**, leveraging Cisco's comprehensive portfolio of networking hardware, software, and security solutions. The design utilized Cisco's **hierarchical network model**, which divides the network into three distinct layers: the core, distribution, and access layers.

1. Core Layer: The Backbone of the Network

At the heart of the network lies the **core layer**, which serves as the high-speed backbone, connecting different parts of the network—whether on-premises data centers or remote offices. The key considerations for this layer were:

- **Redundant, High-Performance Core Switches**: The core layer

used **Cisco Nexus 7000** series switches, providing high bandwidth and support for high-availability configurations. Redundancy was achieved through **multi-chassis link aggregation** (MLAG) and **Virtual PortChannel (vPC)** technology, ensuring that no single failure would disrupt network services.
- **Interconnectivity with Cloud Providers**: Given the company's reliance on cloud services, the core layer had to support high-bandwidth, low-latency connections to major cloud providers like AWS, Microsoft Azure, and private cloud platforms. To accomplish this, the core was integrated with **Cisco Cloud Connect** solutions, ensuring secure and efficient cloud-to-network connectivity.
- **Global Network Routing**: To support global operations, the core layer utilized **Cisco ASR 1000 Series routers** for high-speed routing, incorporating **Border Gateway Protocol (BGP)** for inter-domain routing between offices and data centers. These routers also managed **quality of service (QoS)** policies to prioritize business-critical traffic such as voice and video communications.

2. Distribution Layer: Aggregation and Policy Enforcement

The **distribution layer** acts as an intermediary between the core and access layers, responsible for policy enforcement, traffic routing, and the aggregation of user access. Key components of this layer included:

- **Cisco Catalyst 9000 Series Switches**: These switches provided centralized traffic management and integrated network security features. The distribution layer also housed **firewalls** for internal segmentation and **intrusion prevention systems (IPS)** to detect and prevent unauthorized access.
- **VLAN Segmentation and Access Control**: To ensure compliance with regulatory standards and improve security, the network was divided into several **Virtual LANs (VLANs)**, each dedicated to specific departments or functions (e.g., finance, research and development, HR, etc.). This segmentation reduced the attack surface by limiting

access to sensitive data. The use of **Cisco Identity Services Engine (ISE)** allowed the organization to enforce **network access control policies** and ensure that only authorized devices and users could access specific segments of the network.

- **Redundant WAN Links**: The distribution layer featured multiple **WAN connections**, each backed by different service providers to ensure high availability. **Cisco SD-WAN** technology was used to intelligently route traffic based on real-time conditions, ensuring the most efficient path for data to travel between offices, data centers, and cloud services.

3. Access Layer: End-User Connectivity

The **access layer** connects end-users to the network, typically through wired or wireless devices. This layer had to support thousands of employees in offices and remote locations, providing seamless connectivity, secure access, and reliable performance.

- **Wired Access**: For employees working in corporate offices, the access layer utilized **Cisco Catalyst 9300 Series switches** with **Power over Ethernet (PoE)** capabilities to provide both data and power to IP phones, security cameras, and wireless access points (APs). These switches supported high-speed Ethernet and advanced QoS features to ensure consistent voice and video performance.

- **Wireless Access**: In larger offices and open spaces, the access layer relied on **Cisco Meraki** wireless access points to provide scalable, cloud-managed wireless connectivity. Meraki's **cloud-based dashboard** allowed IT administrators to easily monitor network traffic, configure policies, and troubleshoot issues without needing on-site intervention.

- **Remote and Branch Office Connectivity**: To support employees working remotely or in branch offices, the access layer was extended via **Cisco AnyConnect VPN** for secure remote access. Additionally, **Cisco Meraki MX** security appliances were deployed in branch offices to provide a cloud-managed security solution, including firewall, SD-WAN, and intrusion detection.

Cloud Integration and Hybrid Cloud Architecture

As part of its digital transformation strategy, the company increasingly relied on cloud-based services. A hybrid cloud architecture was implemented to seamlessly integrate on-premises resources with cloud platforms. Key elements of this architecture included:

- **Cloud Direct Access**: Cisco's **Cloud Connectivity** solutions, including **Cisco Cloud Center** and **Cisco InterCloud** services, enabled seamless connections to public and private cloud environments. This ensured that business-critical applications could access cloud-hosted services without introducing latency or security risks.
- **Data Center Interconnect**: The company's data centers in different regions were interconnected using **Cisco's Data Center Interconnect (DCI)** solutions, such as **Cisco ONS 15454** and **Cisco Nexus 9000** series switches. This allowed data and applications to move across data centers and clouds with minimal disruption and high security.
- **Cloud Security**: To ensure a secure and consistent cloud experience, **Cisco Umbrella** was deployed to protect users regardless of their location, blocking access to malicious sites and phishing attempts. **Cisco Cloudlock**, a cloud security solution, was also used to ensure data security and compliance in cloud storage environments, such as AWS and Azure.

Security Architecture and Compliance Considerations

With sensitive data and compliance requirements at the forefront, security was woven throughout the entire network design. The organization adopted a **defense-in-depth** approach, incorporating multiple layers of security, including:

- **Next-Generation Firewalls (NGFW)**: Cisco Firepower NGFWs were deployed at both the **edge** and **data center** to protect against external threats. These firewalls provided **intrusion prevention**, **URL filtering**, and **advanced malware protection (AMP)** to block malicious traffic before it could enter the network.
- **Zero Trust Security Model**: Cisco's **Identity Services Engine (ISE)** was used to enforce a **Zero Trust** security model, where every access request was verified before being allowed, regardless of whether it originated inside or outside the corporate network. This ensured that only authenticated devices and users could access sensitive data and applications.
- **Compliance Auditing and Logging**: The network was configured to log and store all traffic data for auditing purposes, ensuring that compliance requirements (such as GDPR, HIPAA, and PCI-DSS) were met. **Cisco Stealthwatch** provided continuous monitoring of the network to detect any potential security breaches or anomalies.

Performance Optimization and Traffic Management

To optimize network performance across its global operations, the organization implemented **Cisco's QoS** policies across all layers of the network, prioritizing traffic based on application requirements. The network design included:

- **Traffic Shaping and Policing**: At the **distribution** and **core** layers, traffic shaping and policing were implemented to prioritize real-time applications, such as **video conferencing**, **VoIP**, and **collaboration tools**, while limiting bandwidth usage for non-essential services.
- **Load Balancing**: Cisco's **Application Delivery Controllers (ADCs)** were used to implement load balancing for critical applications, ensuring that resources were distributed evenly across

servers and that users experienced minimal downtime.

By leveraging Cisco's advanced network architecture solutions, the pharmaceutical corporation was able to design a highly secure, scalable, and resilient network that met the growing demands of a global, cloud-first business. The network design successfully integrated on-premises and cloud-based resources, ensured high availability across multiple regions, and complied with industry regulations. The combination of Cisco's cutting-edge technologies and strategic planning allowed the company to future-proof its network infrastructure, ensuring it could continue to scale and meet evolving business needs.

This case study highlights the importance of a **holistic, multi-layered approach to network architecture**, with careful consideration of scalability, security, and integration. For enterprises seeking to design a global network, Cisco's solutions offer a robust, flexible, and highly reliable framework for supporting critical business operations and digital transformation.

Small Business Network Design Using Cisco Meraki

Small businesses often face unique challenges when it comes to networking. They need a reliable, secure, and scalable network infrastructure that supports their operations, ensures seamless connectivity, and enables growth—yet they typically operate with limited IT resources and budgets. Cisco Meraki, with its cloud-managed architecture and easy-to-use interfaces, provides an ideal solution for small businesses looking to design and manage a high-performance network without the complexity and cost typically associated with traditional networking solutions.

In this section, we will explore how small businesses can leverage Cisco Meraki's portfolio of networking products to design a robust, scalable, and secure network infrastructure that meets their specific needs.

CASE STUDIES IN NETWORK ARCHITECTURE

Business Requirements and Challenges for Small Businesses

Small businesses have specific requirements and challenges when it comes to network design:

1. **Cost-Effective Solutions**: Small businesses operate under tight budgets and need solutions that provide value for money without sacrificing quality or performance.
2. **Simplicity and Ease of Management**: With limited IT staff or even none at all, small business owners need a network solution that is easy to configure, monitor, and maintain without requiring deep technical expertise.
3. **Scalability**: As small businesses grow, their network needs evolve. The network infrastructure should be scalable enough to support an increasing number of users, devices, and applications.
4. **Reliability and High Availability**: Small businesses rely heavily on their network for day-to-day operations, making uptime a critical requirement. A network that is unreliable or prone to downtime can severely impact productivity and customer satisfaction.
5. **Security**: While small businesses may not face the same scale of cyberattacks as larger enterprises, they are still vulnerable to data breaches, malware, and other security threats. Protecting sensitive customer data and business information is essential.
6. **Remote Connectivity**: As more businesses adopt flexible work environments, remote connectivity for employees, partners, and customers is increasingly important. A secure and efficient remote access solution is required to ensure business continuity.

Cisco Meraki's Portfolio for Small Business Network Design

Cisco Meraki offers a comprehensive range of cloud-managed networking products that can address the unique needs of small businesses. These solutions provide scalability, security, and performance with minimal complexity. The Meraki portfolio includes **wireless access points (APs)**, **switches**, **security appliances**, and **SD-WAN** technology, all managed through a centralized, cloud-based dashboard.

1. Cisco Meraki Wireless Access Points (APs)

Wireless connectivity is the backbone of modern small business networks. Whether employees are working from desks, meeting rooms, or mobile devices, reliable Wi-Fi is critical. Cisco Meraki APs offer:

- **Ease of Setup**: Meraki APs are designed to be simple to deploy, with the configuration done via the Meraki Dashboard, a cloud-based interface. There's no need for complex on-site setup or IT expertise.
- **Performance**: Meraki APs support high-speed Wi-Fi standards (Wi-Fi 5 and Wi-Fi 6), ensuring fast, reliable connections for multiple users and devices simultaneously.
- **Advanced Features**: Features such as **seamless roaming**, **band steering**, and **airtime fairness** ensure that the wireless network remains fast and stable even as the number of users and devices grows.
- **Security**: Meraki's APs come with built-in security features such as **WPA3 encryption, intrusion detection**, and **secure guest access**. The cloud-managed platform also provides automatic updates and patches to ensure the network is always protected from the latest vulnerabilities.

2. Cisco Meraki Switches

As small businesses expand, they need to ensure that their wired network infrastructure can handle increased traffic and provide seamless connectivity across multiple devices and departments. Cisco Meraki switches provide:

- **Port Flexibility**: Meraki offers a wide range of switch models, from compact 8-port to larger 48-port configurations, ensuring that businesses can scale their network as needed.

CASE STUDIES IN NETWORK ARCHITECTURE

- **Cloud Management**: Like Meraki's wireless APs, the switches are managed via the Meraki Dashboard, which makes configuration, monitoring, and troubleshooting simple and intuitive. Network admins can view real-time traffic analytics, configure VLANs, and monitor network health from anywhere.
- **Layer 2 and Layer 3 Switching**: Meraki's switches support both **Layer 2** and **Layer 3** features, including VLAN tagging, routing, and **Quality of Service (QoS)** for prioritizing business-critical traffic.
- **Security and Monitoring**: With features like **port security**, **access control lists (ACLs)**, and **802.1X authentication**, Meraki switches ensure that only authorized devices can access the network. The dashboard provides detailed reporting and alerting to track network performance and security.

3. Cisco Meraki Security Appliances (MX Series)

Small businesses need comprehensive security solutions to protect their network, data, and devices from external threats. Cisco Meraki MX security appliances integrate a wide range of security features into a single, easy-to-deploy device. Features include:

- **Next-Generation Firewall (NGFW)**: The Meraki MX series provides a stateful firewall, filtering traffic based on a variety of parameters (IP addresses, ports, protocols, etc.), protecting against unauthorized access.
- **Intrusion Detection and Prevention (IDS/IPS)**: Built-in IDS/IPS functionality detects and prevents malicious activity on the network in real-time. The MX appliances are powered by Meraki's cloud-based security intelligence, ensuring the network is constantly updated with the latest threat data.
- **VPN Support**: Secure, remote access is enabled with **Site-to-Site VPN** and **Client VPN** capabilities, allowing remote employees and branch offices to securely access the corporate network from anywhere.

- **Advanced Malware Protection**: The Meraki MX provides protection against viruses, spyware, and other forms of malware with deep packet inspection and cloud-powered threat detection.
- **Traffic Shaping and QoS**: The MX security appliances include traffic shaping features that allow small businesses to prioritize critical applications, such as VoIP or video conferencing, over less important traffic.

4. Cisco Meraki SD-WAN for Optimized WAN Connectivity

For small businesses with multiple locations or remote workers, connecting all users securely and efficiently across wide-area networks (WAN) can be challenging. Cisco Meraki's **SD-WAN** solution simplifies WAN management by enabling:

- **Intelligent Traffic Routing**: Meraki SD-WAN dynamically chooses the best WAN connection (MPLS, broadband, LTE, etc.) for each application, optimizing performance and minimizing latency for critical business applications.
- **Automatic Failover**: In the event of a WAN link failure, Meraki's SD-WAN automatically switches traffic to a secondary link, ensuring business continuity with no manual intervention required.
- **Centralized Management**: Meraki's cloud-based dashboard enables network administrators to configure SD-WAN, monitor network performance, and troubleshoot from anywhere, making remote site management easy and efficient.

Designing a Small Business Network with Cisco Meraki

Now that we've outlined the capabilities of Cisco Meraki's products, let's look at how a small business might design a network using Meraki's solutions.

1. Assessing Business Needs

Before designing the network, a small business must assess its needs:

- **Number of Users and Devices**: Consider how many employees, devices, and IoT endpoints will be connected to the network. For example, if the business has 30 employees and expects 50 devices (desktops, laptops, mobile phones, IP phones, etc.), the network design should accommodate this scale, with enough headroom for future growth.
- **Bandwidth Requirements**: Depending on the business operations, bandwidth needs will vary. For example, a business with video conferencing, VoIP, or cloud-based applications will require more bandwidth than one that primarily uses email and web browsing.
- **Security Requirements**: Identify the types of data the business handles. Sensitive customer data (e.g., payment information or health records) requires a higher level of security.

2. Network Design and Equipment Selection

Based on the assessment, the business will select the appropriate Cisco Meraki products. For example, a simple Meraki network might include:

- **Meraki MR Series Access Points** for wireless coverage.
- **Meraki MS Series Switches** to handle wired connections.
- **Meraki MX Security Appliance** for integrated firewall and VPN capabilities.
- **Meraki SD-WAN** to optimize WAN performance for branch offices or remote workers.

3. Configuration and Setup

Once the hardware is chosen, network configuration can begin using the **Meraki Dashboard**. Key tasks include:

- **Setting up Wireless SSIDs**: Configure the Meraki APs to broadcast the appropriate SSIDs (e.g., one for staff, one for guests) and enable security features like WPA3 encryption.
- **VLANs and IP Addressing**: Create and configure VLANs for

different departments or services to ensure proper segmentation and security.
- **Firewall Rules and VPN**: Configure firewall rules to block unwanted traffic and set up VPNs for secure remote access.
- **Traffic Shaping and QoS**: Prioritize voice and video traffic to ensure performance during peak usage times.

4. Monitoring and Maintenance

Once the network is deployed, the **Meraki Dashboard** provides real-time monitoring and performance analytics. This allows businesses to quickly identify issues, monitor bandwidth usage, and optimize network settings as needed. Cloud-based management ensures that the network is always up-to-date with the latest software patches and security updates.

SD-WAN Deployment for a Distributed Organization

In today's business environment, where organizations are increasingly operating across multiple geographic locations and embracing remote work, traditional Wide Area Network (WAN) architectures are often not sufficient to meet the demands of modern enterprises. As a result, Software-Defined WAN (SD-WAN) has emerged as the go-to solution for organizations seeking to optimize their networks for flexibility, performance, and security. This section will explore how SD-WAN can be deployed to effectively support the network needs of a distributed organization, with a focus on Cisco's SD-WAN solutions.

What is SD-WAN?

Software-Defined WAN (SD-WAN) is an intelligent, software-based network solution that uses centralized control and management to optimize the delivery of applications and services across a wide area network. Unlike traditional WANs, which rely on static routing, SD-WAN can dynamically route traffic across multiple connection types (MPLS, broadband, LTE, etc.) based on real-time network conditions, policies, and application requirements. The result is a more agile, cost-effective, and secure network infrastructure.

For a distributed organization, SD-WAN offers several key advantages:

1. **Cost Savings**: By leveraging more affordable broadband and public internet connections, SD-WAN reduces reliance on expensive MPLS circuits.
2. **Improved Performance**: SD-WAN dynamically adjusts traffic routing to avoid congestion and ensure low-latency connections for critical applications.
3. **Enhanced Security**: SD-WAN typically includes built-in security features such as encryption, firewall protection, and secure tunneling, which ensure secure data transfer between branch offices, data centers, and the cloud.
4. **Simplified Management**: Centralized management through a cloud-based dashboard allows for easier configuration, monitoring, and troubleshooting of the WAN.

The Need for SD-WAN in a Distributed Organization

In a distributed organization, where offices, remote locations, and cloud services need to be connected seamlessly, SD-WAN offers a solution that can address several challenges associated with traditional WANs:

1. **Diverse Network Connections**: A distributed organization often relies on multiple types of internet connections, including MPLS, broadband, and 4G/5G connections. SD-WAN enables the integration of these diverse connections into a unified, optimized network, without sacrificing performance or security.
2. **Traffic Prioritization**: As organizations adopt more cloud-based applications and services (such as SaaS), the need for intelligent traffic management becomes paramount. SD-WAN enables organizations to prioritize mission-critical traffic (e.g., voice, video, cloud applications) over less-critical traffic, ensuring consistent performance

across all sites.

3. **Remote and Branch Office Connectivity**: With the rise of remote work, branch offices, and mobile users, traditional VPN solutions often struggle to meet the demands for secure, high-performance connectivity. SD-WAN makes it easy to extend secure and optimized access to remote users and branch offices, regardless of their location.
4. **Real-Time Monitoring and Troubleshooting**: Managing a large-scale WAN with multiple remote sites can be complex. SD-WAN provides real-time monitoring of network performance, enabling IT teams to identify bottlenecks, troubleshoot issues quickly, and ensure optimal network operation at all times.

Cisco SD-WAN Solution for Distributed Organizations

Cisco offers one of the most comprehensive and scalable SD-WAN solutions on the market, designed to address the specific needs of distributed organizations. The Cisco SD-WAN solution leverages the power of Cisco's Viptela platform to provide a unified, secure, and flexible network that spans across branch offices, data centers, and the cloud.

Key components of Cisco SD-WAN include:

- **Cisco Viptela SD-WAN**: Cisco's SD-WAN platform offers a cloud-first approach to WAN management, enabling businesses to easily deploy, scale, and manage their WAN architecture. It offers a centralized control plane for traffic steering, policy enforcement, and network visibility, while the data plane is distributed across branch offices and data centers. Cisco Viptela SD-WAN supports a wide range of connectivity options, including broadband internet, MPLS, and LTE, enabling organizations to optimize cost and performance based on their specific needs.
- **Security Features**: Cisco SD-WAN integrates built-in security features such as end-to-end encryption, secure VPN tunnels, and segmentation capabilities. It also supports the integration of advanced security tools like Cisco Umbrella, which provides cloud security and

threat intelligence.
- **Application-Aware Routing**: Cisco SD-WAN uses application-aware routing to ensure that the right traffic takes the right path based on real-time conditions. For example, voice and video traffic can be prioritized and routed over low-latency links, while less time-sensitive traffic can be routed over less expensive broadband connections. This capability is crucial for ensuring that cloud applications perform optimally, even in distributed environments.
- **Cloud Integration**: As more organizations migrate to cloud-based applications and services, SD-WAN plays a critical role in ensuring seamless connectivity between on-premise data centers and cloud environments like AWS, Microsoft Azure, and Google Cloud. Cisco's SD-WAN solution natively integrates with leading cloud platforms to optimize traffic flow and ensure secure, reliable access to cloud resources.

Best Practices for Deploying SD-WAN in a Distributed Organization

Successfully deploying SD-WAN for a distributed organization requires careful planning and a strategic approach. Here are some best practices for deploying Cisco SD-WAN in a distributed environment:

1. **Assess Network Requirements**: Begin by assessing the specific needs of your organization, including the types of applications used, performance requirements, and the types of connectivity available at each branch or remote location. This will help determine the optimal network topology and traffic management policies.
2. **Leverage Centralized Management**: Take advantage of the centralized management capabilities provided by Cisco SD-WAN. Use the Cisco Viptela dashboard to configure, monitor, and troubleshoot your entire WAN infrastructure from a single, easy-to-use interface.
3. **Implement Security Policies**: SD-WAN offers enhanced security features, but it's crucial to configure security policies that align with your organization's needs. Ensure that encryption, segmentation,

and access control are properly configured to protect sensitive data and ensure secure communication between sites.

4. **Ensure Scalability**: As your organization grows, your SD-WAN solution should be able to scale to accommodate new sites, users, and applications. Cisco SD-WAN supports flexible deployment models and can scale from a small number of sites to hundreds or even thousands of locations, ensuring that your WAN infrastructure remains agile as the business expands.

5. **Optimize Application Performance**: Use application-aware routing and traffic optimization techniques to prioritize critical applications and minimize latency. This ensures that cloud applications, voice/video communications, and business-critical services receive the necessary bandwidth and low-latency connections.

6. **Plan for Business Continuity**: SD-WAN is designed to provide high availability and resilience, but it's important to implement redundancy and failover strategies. Make use of multiple links, automatic path selection, and load balancing to ensure that your SD-WAN network remains operational even in the event of a link failure.

7. **Monitor and Fine-Tune**: Regularly monitor your SD-WAN deployment to ensure that it is performing optimally. Use the reporting and analytics features of Cisco SD-WAN to identify trends, monitor network health, and fine-tune traffic routing policies as needed.

Benefits of SD-WAN for Distributed Organizations

Deploying SD-WAN in a distributed organization can provide several key benefits:

1. **Cost Efficiency**: By enabling the use of broadband internet and other affordable links, SD-WAN reduces the need for expensive MPLS connections, leading to significant cost savings without compromising on network performance or security.

2. **Enhanced Flexibility**: SD-WAN offers the flexibility to connect

remote offices, branch locations, and mobile workers securely and efficiently, regardless of their geographical location.
3. **Improved Application Performance**: With features like application-aware routing and dynamic path selection, SD-WAN ensures that business-critical applications receive the highest levels of performance, minimizing latency and improving user experience.
4. **Increased Security**: Built-in security features such as encryption, secure tunneling, and segmentation help ensure that sensitive data is protected across all sites, preventing unauthorized access and potential data breaches.
5. **Simplified Management**: Centralized control through the Cisco SD-WAN management platform makes it easier to configure, monitor, and troubleshoot the network, saving time and reducing operational complexity for IT teams.
6. **Scalability**: SD-WAN can easily scale as your organization grows, supporting new branch offices, remote locations, and cloud applications without requiring major network overhauls.

Cisco SD-WAN provides a powerful, flexible, and cost-effective solution for distributed organizations looking to optimize their WAN infrastructure. With its ability to integrate multiple types of connections, optimize traffic flow, and ensure secure, high-performance application delivery, SD-WAN is the future of wide-area networking. By implementing Cisco's SD-WAN solutions, distributed organizations can achieve the agility, scalability, and security they need to support their growing business needs and stay ahead in an increasingly competitive digital landscape.

Building High-Performance Data Centers with Cisco ACI

In today's increasingly complex IT landscape, data centers are the backbone of many organizations, housing critical applications, data storage, and network services that drive business operations. However, as businesses scale and adopt cloud-first strategies, traditional data center architectures often fall short in terms of flexibility, performance, scalability, and security. To address these challenges, organizations are turning to Software-Defined Networking (SDN) solutions like **Cisco Application Centric Infrastructure (ACI)** to build modern, high-performance data centers.

Cisco ACI is an integrated SDN solution designed to optimize the management and operation of data center networks. It delivers a highly flexible, scalable, and automated network infrastructure that allows organizations to quickly adapt to changing business needs, improve network performance, and secure critical workloads. This section will delve into the key principles of Cisco ACI, its benefits for data center design, and how it can be leveraged to build high-performance, future-proof data centers.

What is Cisco ACI?

Cisco Application Centric Infrastructure (ACI) is a next-generation network architecture that integrates both hardware and software to optimize data center networking. ACI enables data centers to be more agile, secure, and efficient by automating network provisioning, monitoring, and troubleshooting while providing deep visibility into application performance. At the heart of Cisco ACI is the **Application Policy Infrastructure Controller (APIC)**, which acts as the centralized management and automation platform for the ACI fabric.

Cisco ACI is based on a **leaf-and-spine** architecture, a modern data center design that eliminates bottlenecks associated with traditional network topologies. This architecture, combined with ACI's software-defined policies, allows for efficient network resource allocation, seamless application deployment, and continuous optimization of data flows.

Key Components of Cisco ACI

Application Policy Infrastructure Controller (APIC):

- The APIC is the centralized software controller that governs the ACI fabric. It enables network automation by providing policy-based management, configuration, and monitoring for all devices in the ACI fabric. The APIC allows administrators to define policies based on application requirements, which can be automatically implemented and enforced across the entire data center.

ACI Fabric:

- The ACI fabric consists of a set of leaf switches and spine switches that form the network topology. The leaf switches connect directly to servers, storage, and other endpoints, while the spine switches provide interconnectivity between the leaf nodes. The spine-leaf architecture ensures efficient data traffic flow, reducing latency and avoiding network congestion.

Leaf and Spine Switches:

- **Leaf Switches**: These are the switches at the edge of the network, where end devices like servers, storage arrays, and network appliances are connected. They communicate with spine switches to route traffic through the fabric.
- **Spine Switches**: Spine switches provide high-speed interconnection between leaf switches, creating a non-blocking network fabric. They ensure that traffic flows quickly and efficiently between leaf switches without bottlenecks.

End-Host Networking:

- ACI also integrates end-host connectivity, whether it is physical servers, virtual machines, or cloud-based workloads. This integration allows ACI to manage and optimize both physical and virtual network traffic using the same set of policies and infrastructure.

Key Benefits of Cisco ACI for Data Center Design
Automated Network Provisioning:

- One of the primary benefits of Cisco ACI is its ability to automate network provisioning. Traditionally, setting up a new server or application in a data center requires manual configuration of multiple network devices, such as switches, routers, and firewalls. With ACI, this process is simplified. The APIC automates network provisioning based on the application's requirements, allowing IT teams to focus on higher-value tasks and reducing the time required to deploy new workloads.

Application-Centric Policy Management:

- Cisco ACI's policy-driven approach to network management means that network configurations are aligned with the needs of applications. Unlike traditional networks, where devices and networks are configured separately, ACI allows organizations to define policies based on application needs. These policies are then automatically enforced across the network fabric, ensuring that applications receive the resources they require, without manual intervention.

Improved Scalability:

- Cisco ACI's leaf-and-spine architecture is designed to scale efficiently, enabling businesses to expand their data center infrastructure as needed without introducing bottlenecks. The architecture eliminates the need for complex and expensive upgrades by ensuring that each new leaf switch can be easily added to the fabric without disrupting existing network operations. Whether an organization is adding new servers, storage, or cloud services, Cisco ACI makes it easy to scale the data center to meet growing demands.

Reduced Latency and Enhanced Performance:

- The leaf-and-spine design also ensures that traffic between endpoints is optimized for low latency. Unlike traditional hub-and-spoke network architectures, where traffic between devices must pass through multiple intermediate switches, Cisco ACI's fabric architecture allows for direct communication between leaf switches. This minimizes latency and ensures that applications and services perform optimally, even in high-traffic environments.

End-to-End Visibility and Monitoring:

- Cisco ACI provides deep visibility into the entire data center network, offering administrators real-time insights into network performance and application traffic. This visibility extends from physical hardware to virtual machines and cloud-based workloads, allowing network operators to identify and resolve issues quickly. Furthermore, Cisco ACI integrates with Cisco's network management and monitoring tools, such as **Cisco Network Assurance Engine** (NAE), to automate troubleshooting and proactive network management.

Network Segmentation and Micro-Segmentation:

- Cisco ACI offers advanced network segmentation capabilities that allow organizations to isolate different types of traffic and applications. Using a feature called **micro-segmentation**, businesses can create highly secure zones within the data center, minimizing the risk of lateral movement by attackers and enhancing the overall security posture of the network.

Security Integration:

- Security is a critical concern in modern data centers, and Cisco ACI integrates security features at every level of the infrastructure. In addition to micro-segmentation, ACI supports integration with **Cisco Identity Services Engine (ISE)** for network access control (NAC) and **Cisco Firepower** for advanced threat detection and prevention. These integrations ensure that data centers are protected from both internal and external security threats.

Best Practices for Building High-Performance Data Centers with Cisco ACI

Start with a Strong Foundation:

- The success of a high-performance data center with Cisco ACI begins with solid architecture planning. Begin by defining the applications and workloads that the data center will support, and determine the bandwidth, security, and availability requirements for each. Then, design the ACI fabric to meet these needs, ensuring that the leaf and spine topology can accommodate expected traffic loads without congestion.

Leverage Automation for Efficiency:

- One of the biggest advantages of ACI is automation. Use the APIC to define policies that are tied to application requirements, and let the system automatically configure the network. This minimizes human error, reduces configuration time, and ensures consistency across the data center.

Integrate with Cloud and Hybrid Environments:

- Many modern data centers are hybrid, with workloads spread across on-premises data centers and public or private clouds. Cisco ACI supports hybrid cloud environments, enabling seamless connectivity between on-premises and cloud resources. Use ACI's integration with **Cisco Cloud ACI** and **ACI Multi-Site Orchestrator** to extend policies and management capabilities across multiple data centers and cloud environments.

Optimize for High Availability:

- A high-performance data center needs to be resilient and highly available. Implement redundancy at the spine and leaf levels to ensure that traffic can be rerouted if any switch fails. Use **virtual Port Channels (vPCs)** for link aggregation and to prevent network loops. Additionally, consider incorporating **Cisco ACI's Fault Domain** capabilities to further enhance redundancy and minimize the risk of downtime.

Focus on Security from the Start:

- In an increasingly complex threat landscape, it's essential to integrate security into the design of the data center. Use **micro-segmentation** to isolate sensitive workloads, implement policy-based access controls, and integrate advanced threat prevention tools to safeguard the network.

Monitor and Optimize Continuously:

- The performance of your data center should be continuously monitored using Cisco ACI's real-time analytics. Leverage tools like **Cisco AppDynamics** and **Cisco Network Assurance Engine** to gain insights into application performance and network health. Optimize traffic flow by adjusting policies and configurations as needed to maintain peak performance.

Real-World Applications of Cisco ACI

- **Data Center Consolidation**: A large multinational corporation consolidating multiple regional data centers into a single, centralized infrastructure could leverage Cisco ACI to ensure seamless traffic flow, reduce network complexity, and enhance scalability.
- **Cloud and Hybrid Cloud Integration**: A global financial services provider with a mix of on-premises and cloud-based workloads could use Cisco ACI to manage both environments with consistent policies, improving network visibility, security, and performance across its global infrastructure.

Cisco ACI is a transformative solution for organizations looking to build high-performance, scalable, and secure data centers. With its application-centric, policy-driven approach, ACI enables businesses to automate network provisioning, improve application performance, and scale their infrastructure in a flexible, cost-effective manner. Whether building a new data center or modernizing an existing one, Cisco ACI provides the tools and capabilities needed to meet the demands of today's business environment while laying the foundation for future growth and innovation.

CASE STUDIES IN NETWORK ARCHITECTURE

Real-World Cisco Deployments: Key Lessons Learned

Deploying Cisco's network architecture and solutions can have a transformative effect on an organization's network infrastructure, but like any complex technology, successful implementation requires careful planning, alignment with business goals, and attention to operational details. Across a range of industries and use cases, businesses have adopted Cisco solutions—whether for data center optimization, SD-WAN, or security architecture—to enhance performance, scalability, and security.

In this section, we'll explore key lessons learned from real-world Cisco deployments. These lessons highlight best practices and common pitfalls, offering valuable insights for enterprises planning their own Cisco-based network transformations.

1. The Importance of Alignment Between Business Goals and IT Infrastructure

One of the most critical factors for success in any Cisco deployment is ensuring alignment between the organization's business goals and its IT infrastructure. Cisco's broad portfolio of network solutions is highly flexible, enabling customization for a wide range of business needs, from improving operational efficiency to supporting digital transformation initiatives.

Lesson Learned: Prior to implementation, businesses should invest time in understanding the strategic objectives they aim to achieve with their Cisco infrastructure. For example, a retail chain looking to optimize customer experience through high-performance Wi-Fi should focus on Cisco Meraki for wireless network solutions, while a company aiming to streamline global communication and network security might look toward Cisco SD-WAN and Cisco Firepower for integrated, secure WAN solutions.

- **Example**: A global healthcare organization deployed Cisco ACI in its data centers to enable faster application deployment and provide better service for clinicians and patients. However, the deployment was delayed due to initial confusion between IT departments and business leadership regarding the organization's scalability requirements. A clearer understanding of these goals at the outset could have sped up the process.

2. Prioritize Network Segmentation and Security from the Start

Network segmentation and security should be a priority when deploying Cisco solutions, especially when scaling a network or moving to the cloud. While scalability and performance are important, a network without robust security policies will ultimately be vulnerable to breaches and attacks. Cisco ACI's micro-segmentation capabilities, Cisco Firewalls, and Identity Services Engine (ISE) provide comprehensive solutions to ensure network traffic is isolated and monitored.

Lesson Learned: In large-scale deployments, it's easy to overlook security during the early phases of design. Implementing robust segmentation, security policies, and access controls at the outset of the deployment can save considerable time and effort later on. Many companies have learned the hard way that a network without proper security layers creates vulnerability points that are difficult to mitigate retroactively.

- **Example**: A financial services firm chose Cisco Firepower NGFWs to protect its core applications. However, initial deployments lacked sufficient segmentation between sensitive customer data and operational systems. As the network expanded, this security gap became evident, requiring a costly reconfiguration. Integrating segmentation from the beginning would have been more cost-effective.

3. Plan for Scalability and Redundancy Early in the Design

One of Cisco's core strengths is its ability to provide scalable solutions that grow with the needs of the business. However, businesses often underestimate the importance of planning for scalability and redundancy in the early phases of a deployment. This can lead to performance bottlenecks, network congestion, and even downtime as the network expands.

Lesson Learned: Cisco's leaf-and-spine architecture, available with Cisco ACI, is an excellent example of a scalable and redundant design, but the capacity for expansion needs to be factored in at the outset. It's essential to design the core, distribution, and access layers with scalability in mind. Planning for future traffic loads and redundancy is key to avoiding disruptions in service as the network grows.

- **Example**: A manufacturing company with global operations adopted Cisco ACI to optimize its data center networking. Initially, the design did not account for future growth, and within a year, the company had to upgrade its spine switches to handle increased traffic. By considering future needs in the design phase, they could have avoided this costly upgrade and optimized the network's expansion from the start.

4. Leverage Automation and Orchestration to Streamline Operations

Automation is one of the greatest advantages of Cisco's solutions. The integration of automation into network management helps reduce human error, ensures consistency, and allows for rapid deployment of applications. Cisco DNA Center and Cisco ACI's policy-driven management simplify network provisioning, monitoring, and troubleshooting, which is critical in large, dynamic environments.

Lesson Learned: Organizations that fully embrace automation through Cisco tools like **Cisco DNA Center** and **Cisco ACI** see significant improvements in operational efficiency. Those that delay or resist automation may face higher costs, slower response times, and more frequent manual interventions.

- **Example**: A global retailer that adopted Cisco Meraki for its branch office networks used Meraki's cloud-managed platform for seamless updates and monitoring. The automation features allowed them to deploy hundreds of new locations with minimal manual effort. However, a missed opportunity arose in automating security policy enforcement, leading to gaps in protection across the network. Ensuring that security automation was tightly integrated with network management would have eliminated this oversight.

5. Ensure Seamless Integration Across Multi-Vendor Environments

Many organizations use a mix of technologies and vendor products across their IT infrastructure. A common challenge during Cisco deployments, especially in large and complex environments, is ensuring that Cisco devices integrate seamlessly with existing hardware and software solutions.

Lesson Learned: While Cisco provides a comprehensive range of products, the reality is that many enterprises rely on multi-vendor environments. Successful deployments require ensuring interoperability and compatibility across different vendor solutions. Cisco's **open standards** and APIs are key to making this possible, but careful planning is needed to ensure smooth integration.

- **Example**: A large government agency deployed Cisco ACI to enhance the efficiency of its data centers. However, the initial integration of Cisco's SDN solution with existing legacy systems caused some unexpected issues due to incompatible software and firmware. Ensuring that compatibility testing was performed early in the process would have avoided these integration challenges and ensured a more seamless deployment.

6. Invest in Training and Skill Development

Cisco's advanced networking solutions require specialized knowledge and expertise to operate effectively. One common pitfall during real-world deployments is underestimating the level of training required for

IT staff to manage and operate these sophisticated systems.

Lesson Learned: It's crucial to invest in ongoing training for network engineers and administrators. Cisco offers extensive certification programs, including **CCNP, CCIE**, and other specialized certifications, to ensure that employees have the right skills to manage and troubleshoot Cisco-based infrastructures. Organizations should allocate resources for training early in the deployment process and ensure that staff have access to the latest learning materials.

- **Example**: A telecommunications company that deployed Cisco SD-WAN across its branch offices faced performance issues during the initial deployment. The lack of experienced engineers who understood SD-WAN configuration best practices contributed to suboptimal routing decisions and network instability. Providing the right training upfront helped the company resolve these issues and optimize their SD-WAN deployment for better performance.

7. Focus on End-User Experience

At the core of any network architecture project is the need to deliver a positive end-user experience. For enterprises, this means ensuring that end-users, whether employees or customers, enjoy seamless access to applications, secure connectivity, and fast response times.

Lesson Learned: One key takeaway from successful Cisco deployments is the importance of prioritizing end-user experience. Using **Cisco's Quality of Service (QoS)** features and deploying **Cisco Meraki's cloud-managed solutions** can help ensure that traffic is prioritized based on application needs, and that users enjoy a seamless experience, even during periods of high demand.

- **Example**: A financial services company deployed Cisco's SD-WAN to ensure secure, high-performance access to critical applications for remote employees. During the implementation, the company found that traffic prioritization for VoIP calls and video conferencing was critical for maintaining productivity. By adjusting the QoS settings and monitoring performance, they were able to optimize the network to meet end-users' needs.

Key Takeaways for Future Cisco Deployments

Real-world Cisco deployments provide invaluable insights for organizations looking to build or scale their network infrastructures. Successful Cisco implementations hinge on clear alignment with business goals, a focus on security, scalability, and automation, and careful consideration of integration challenges. By learning from the experiences of others and implementing best practices, businesses can maximize the return on investment from Cisco solutions and build networks that are secure, agile, and future-proof.

The key takeaways for any organization planning a Cisco deployment include:

- Aligning IT infrastructure with business objectives.
- Prioritizing security and network segmentation.
- Planning for scalability and redundancy in the early design phases.
- Embracing automation and orchestration for operational efficiency.
- Ensuring compatibility and integration in multi-vendor environments.
- Investing in training to build internal expertise.
- Focusing on end-user experience to ensure network success.

By following these guidelines, businesses can avoid common pitfalls and unlock the full potential of Cisco's networking solutions, creating robust, high-performance infrastructures that drive business success.

Multi-Vendor Environments and Cisco Integration

Challenges in Multi-Vendor Network Architectures

In today's interconnected world, businesses increasingly rely on diverse networking solutions from multiple vendors to meet the varied demands of their operations. These multi-vendor network architectures are common in both small-scale and enterprise-level environments, driven by the need for flexibility, cost optimization, and specialized capabilities. However, while multi-vendor environments offer significant advantages, they also come with unique challenges that must be addressed to ensure smooth operations, security, and scalability.

In this section, we'll examine the key challenges faced by organizations operating in multi-vendor network environments and explore strategies for overcoming these obstacles. This will provide insights into how Cisco's solutions, when integrated into such environments, can provide powerful tools to address these challenges while ensuring interoperability and maintaining network performance.

1. Interoperability Issues

Challenge: One of the most significant hurdles in multi-vendor network environments is ensuring interoperability between devices and software from different manufacturers. Different vendors use proprietary protocols, standards, and interfaces, which can result in communication failures or degraded network performance. The lack of uniformity in configuration, data formats, and network management protocols can create significant integration and compatibility issues.

In a multi-vendor architecture, devices might support different routing protocols (e.g., OSPF, EIGRP, BGP) or different versions of the same protocol. These differences can create challenges when trying to configure devices to work together, especially in terms of maintaining consistent data flow, ensuring network stability, and avoiding bottlenecks.

Solution: To overcome these interoperability challenges, businesses need to adopt standards-based solutions wherever possible. Cisco, for example, emphasizes open standards and protocols to facilitate interoperability with other vendors' hardware. Cisco devices are designed to support a wide range of industry-standard protocols such as MPLS, OSPF, BGP, and SNMP, which enables seamless integration with devices from other manufacturers.

- **Example:** A global organization using Cisco switches in its core network, paired with third-party routers in branch offices, had to deal with discrepancies in routing protocols. By ensuring that both Cisco and non-Cisco devices supported the same routing protocols (e.g., BGP for inter-domain routing), the company was able to bridge the gap between different vendor solutions and maintain network stability.

2. Complex Network Management

Challenge: Managing a multi-vendor network is inherently more complex than managing a homogeneous network environment. Different vendors have different network management interfaces, tools, and monitoring systems, leading to a fragmented view of the network. This lack of unified visibility can complicate troubleshooting, performance monitoring, and day-to-day network operations.

For example, administrators may need to log into different systems to monitor traffic, performance metrics, and device health for each vendor's equipment. This siloed approach increases operational overhead, introduces the potential for missed alarms or alerts, and creates difficulties in coordinating efforts across different teams managing different devices.

Solution: To address this challenge, businesses should consider using unified network management platforms that can provide a single pane of glass for monitoring and controlling devices from multiple vendors. Cisco's **DNA Center**, **Cisco Prime Infrastructure**, and **Meraki Dashboard** offer centralized network management tools that can integrate with third-party devices, providing visibility and control over all network components, even in multi-vendor environments.

By using such tools, network administrators can gain a holistic view of their infrastructure, identify issues quickly, and take corrective action without needing to manually manage each vendor's tools.

- **Example:** An international company with a mixed vendor environment was facing challenges in monitoring network health and performance. By integrating Cisco Prime Infrastructure, which allowed them to manage both Cisco and non-Cisco devices from a single interface, they significantly reduced the complexity of network management and improved their ability to respond to incidents promptly.

3. Security Risks and Compliance Challenges

Challenge: In multi-vendor environments, ensuring consistent security policies and maintaining compliance with industry standards becomes more difficult. Each vendor may have different security features, configurations, and default settings, which can create gaps in the overall security posture of the network. Additionally, different vendors may have different patch management processes, leading to discrepancies in security updates and vulnerability mitigation across devices.

A major risk in such environments is the difficulty in applying consistent security policies across the entire network. For example, a security policy designed for Cisco devices may not be directly applicable to a third-party vendor's equipment, requiring custom configurations and manual interventions.

Solution: To mitigate these risks, organizations should focus on establishing consistent security policies that can be applied across the entire network, regardless of the vendor. Cisco's **Identity Services Engine (ISE)** and **TrustSec** technologies offer robust capabilities for applying security policies and managing network access across heterogeneous network environments.

Cisco ISE, for instance, can be used to enforce network access control policies and manage user authentication, even for non-Cisco devices. Additionally, organizations should use consistent encryption methods (e.g., IPsec VPNs, SSL/TLS) and ensure that all vendors' devices are compatible with these security protocols.

- **Example:** A healthcare provider that relied on both Cisco and non-Cisco devices for its wide-area network faced challenges in maintaining HIPAA compliance due to inconsistent security configurations. After deploying Cisco ISE for centralized policy enforcement, the organization was able to standardize authentication and encryption policies across all devices, ensuring compliance with regulatory standards.

4. Vendor Lock-in and Lack of Flexibility

Challenge: While multi-vendor environments offer flexibility, businesses may find themselves inadvertently locked into specific vendors for certain technologies, limiting their ability to make the most cost-effective or performance-optimized choices. Vendor lock-in occurs when proprietary technologies, such as software-defined networking (SDN) solutions or hardware interfaces, create dependencies that restrict the organization's ability to switch vendors or integrate new solutions.

Moreover, when a business selects one vendor for a core network function (e.g., routing), it may encounter challenges when trying to incorporate solutions from other vendors for related functions, such as security or WAN optimization.

Solution: To reduce the risk of vendor lock-in, businesses should prioritize solutions that adhere to open standards and offer flexibility in integration. Cisco's approach to network architecture includes a strong emphasis on **interoperability**, **openness**, and **standards-based design**. For example, Cisco ACI (Application-Centric Infrastructure) and **Cisco SD-WAN** are designed to integrate seamlessly with non-Cisco devices, allowing businesses to use the best solution for each part of their network without being tied to a single vendor.

By using open standards and modular design principles, businesses can more easily adopt new technologies and integrate them into their existing network infrastructure.

- **Example:** A financial institution with Cisco ACI for data center management found that integrating new technologies from other vendors (such as VMware for virtualized environments) was more straightforward than expected. Cisco's open standards and APIs enabled them to remain flexible and adaptable without becoming overly dependent on one specific vendor.

5. Performance Optimization and Traffic Flow Management

Challenge: Optimizing network performance in a multi-vendor environment can be difficult due to differences in the way various devices handle traffic and prioritize data flows. For instance, one vendor's device may have more advanced Quality of Service (QoS) features, while another might offer higher throughput but lack deep packet inspection capabilities.

Without uniform performance monitoring tools, it can be challenging to achieve a consistent level of performance across the entire network. Moreover, identifying and mitigating performance bottlenecks can become a time-consuming process, especially when troubleshooting issues that span across devices from different vendors.

Solution: The key to overcoming performance challenges is deploying an effective network monitoring solution that provides end-to-end visibility across the entire infrastructure. Cisco's **NetFlow** and **Prime Infrastructure** solutions, as well as **Cisco Meraki's Dashboard**, can integrate with non-Cisco devices to monitor traffic patterns, prioritize critical applications, and optimize performance.

By using performance monitoring tools and ensuring that QoS policies are uniformly applied across the network, organizations can reduce latency, minimize packet loss, and optimize data flow across their multi-vendor network.

- **Example:** A global supply chain management firm faced performance degradation as its network grew in complexity with the addition of third-party routers and firewalls. By deploying Cisco Prime Infrastructure and utilizing **NetFlow analytics**, they were able to identify bottlenecks at the edge of their network and optimize traffic flow, resulting in a 30% improvement in overall network performance.

Navigating Multi-Vendor Network Challenges with Cisco Integration

Operating a multi-vendor network architecture presents unique challenges, but with the right strategies and tools, businesses can effectively manage these complexities. The key to overcoming these challenges lies in ensuring interoperability, simplifying network management, enforcing consistent security policies, reducing vendor lock-in, and optimizing performance.

Cisco offers a range of solutions and best practices to help businesses address these challenges head-on. By prioritizing open standards, investing in centralized management platforms, and leveraging automation and monitoring tools, organizations can create robust, scalable, and secure multi-vendor network environments that meet their evolving needs.

Ultimately, the ability to integrate Cisco's technologies with those of other vendors, while maintaining a focus on network performance, security, and operational efficiency, will enable businesses to navigate the complexities of multi-vendor environments and build networks that are adaptable, resilient, and future-proof.

Integrating Cisco with Non-Cisco Devices

In many network environments, businesses must rely on a combination of Cisco and non-Cisco devices to meet their diverse needs. Whether it's due to legacy systems, cost considerations, or the specialized capabilities of non-Cisco devices, integrating Cisco's solutions with devices from other vendors is a common challenge. Achieving seamless interoperability between Cisco and non-Cisco devices is critical to maintaining a stable, secure, and high-performance network infrastructure.

In this section, we'll explore the strategies, tools, and best practices for integrating Cisco networking solutions with non-Cisco devices in a multi-vendor environment. We'll also look at the role of standards-based design, Cisco's flexible software and hardware solutions, and real-world examples of integration challenges and solutions.

1. The Need for Integration in Multi-Vendor Environments

As organizations expand their networks, they often find themselves incorporating hardware and software from multiple vendors to take advantage of specialized features, pricing models, or vendor-specific capabilities. While Cisco is a leader in networking solutions, there are several reasons why businesses might choose non-Cisco devices, including:

- **Cost Considerations:** Non-Cisco devices may offer more affordable options for smaller or budget-conscious organizations.
- **Specialization:** Non-Cisco vendors often offer specialized solutions in areas such as security, wireless, and SD-WAN.
- **Legacy Systems:** Many organizations have invested heavily in non-Cisco devices and are reluctant to replace them entirely due to the cost and disruption involved.

However, integrating Cisco with non-Cisco devices can create challenges due to differences in proprietary technologies, protocols, and management interfaces. Ensuring that these devices work together effectively is essential for maintaining a cohesive network.

2. Ensuring Interoperability Between Cisco and Non-Cisco Devices

The primary challenge when integrating Cisco devices with those from other vendors is ensuring **interoperability**—the ability for devices from different manufacturers to communicate and work together as part of a unified network infrastructure. This issue arises because each vendor typically uses proprietary technologies for routing, switching, and management, which can result in conflicts when trying to make different devices work together.

Key Strategies for Achieving Interoperability:

- **Standard Protocols:** One of the most effective ways to ensure interoperability is by using open, standards-based protocols. Cisco devices are designed to support a wide range of industry-standard protocols, such as **BGP**, **OSPF**, **MPLS**, and **SNMP**, which allows them to integrate easily with devices from other vendors that also support these protocols. By prioritizing these protocols, organizations can create a network infrastructure where all devices, regardless of vendor, can exchange information seamlessly.
- **Virtualization and Abstraction Layers:** Cisco's **Software-Defined Networking (SDN)** solutions, such as **Cisco ACI** and **Cisco SD-WAN**, provide an abstraction layer that decouples the control and data planes. This allows for the seamless integration of devices from different vendors into a cohesive network. With SDN, traffic management, policy enforcement, and security features can be applied consistently across the entire network, regardless of whether the devices are Cisco or non-Cisco.
- **Unified Network Management Platforms:** Tools like **Cisco DNA Center** and **Cisco Prime Infrastructure** are designed to centralize network management, enabling administrators to control and monitor devices from multiple vendors. These platforms use open APIs to integrate with third-party devices, providing a single

interface for managing the network infrastructure.

Example: A global financial institution used Cisco's **ACI** solution in its data centers but also needed to integrate older switches from Juniper Networks and legacy routers from HP. By leveraging ACI's open APIs and standard protocols, they were able to create a policy-driven network architecture that supported seamless communication across Cisco and non-Cisco devices, reducing manual configuration errors and improving overall network stability.

3. Cisco's Integration Tools and Solutions for Multi-Vendor Environments

To facilitate smooth integration, Cisco provides several tools and technologies that ensure compatibility and communication between its devices and those from other vendors.

- **Cisco Prime Infrastructure:** Cisco Prime provides a comprehensive solution for managing multi-vendor networks. It offers support for a range of devices, not just Cisco equipment, enabling administrators to manage non-Cisco devices alongside Cisco routers, switches, and firewalls. Cisco Prime uses SNMP (Simple Network Management Protocol) and other standard protocols to collect data from a variety of devices, allowing for centralized monitoring, troubleshooting, and configuration.
- **Cisco Meraki Dashboard:** Cisco's Meraki cloud-managed network solution is designed for simplicity, offering a centralized dashboard for managing network devices such as switches, routers, firewalls, and access points. The Meraki platform integrates with non-Cisco devices through open APIs and standardized interfaces, making it easy to monitor and configure devices from different vendors in a hybrid cloud environment.
- **Cisco Network Assurance Engine (NAE):** Cisco's NAE offers

MULTI-VENDOR ENVIRONMENTS AND CISCO INTEGRATION

intelligent insights and proactive management capabilities for network operations, using automation and analytics to monitor and validate network behavior. When integrating non-Cisco devices, NAE can be used to ensure that configurations, security policies, and network performance remain consistent across all devices, identifying potential issues before they impact network reliability.

- **Cisco Identity Services Engine (ISE):** Cisco ISE is a powerful network access control solution that supports multi-vendor environments. It can enforce authentication, authorization, and accounting (AAA) policies for devices from multiple vendors. ISE uses standards-based protocols like RADIUS and TACACS+ to communicate with non-Cisco devices, enabling consistent access control and security policy enforcement across the network.

4. Network Automation and Orchestration

As networks become more complex, automation and orchestration tools play an increasingly important role in simplifying multi-vendor network integration. Cisco's **DNA Center**, **ACI**, and **SD-WAN** solutions all include automation features that make it easier to integrate and manage networks with devices from various vendors.

- **Cisco DNA Center:** DNA Center is Cisco's enterprise network automation and management platform, designed to simplify the deployment and operation of network infrastructure. It includes automation tools that enable the provisioning, configuration, and monitoring of network devices from multiple vendors using templates and workflows. Through integration with third-party devices, DNA Center allows for consistent policy enforcement, QoS (Quality of Service), and security across a multi-vendor network.
- **Cisco ACI:** Cisco's ACI provides an automation-driven approach to data center networking, enabling simplified deployment, management, and troubleshooting. ACI's policy-driven architecture

can integrate with third-party hardware and software, providing consistent network policy enforcement across both Cisco and non-Cisco devices.
- **Cisco SD-WAN:** Cisco's SD-WAN solution uses automation to optimize WAN performance, simplify deployments, and integrate with cloud-based services. It also supports the integration of non-Cisco WAN devices, allowing businesses to create a hybrid SD-WAN architecture with both Cisco and non-Cisco devices for optimized traffic routing and load balancing.

5. Security Considerations in Multi-Vendor Environments

Security is one of the most critical aspects of integrating Cisco with non-Cisco devices. When devices from different vendors are part of the same network, ensuring consistent security policies and protecting against vulnerabilities becomes a significant challenge. Differences in device configurations, default settings, and security features can create gaps in the security architecture, which may be exploited by attackers.

Best Practices for Securing Multi-Vendor Networks:

- **Unified Security Policies:** A unified security strategy that can be applied consistently across both Cisco and non-Cisco devices is essential. Cisco's **TrustSec** and **ISE** solutions provide centralized security policy management, ensuring that all devices, regardless of vendor, adhere to the same security standards and access control protocols.
- **Segmentation and Isolation:** Network segmentation and isolation can help minimize the attack surface. With Cisco's **TrustSec** technology, businesses can segment their networks logically, enforcing security policies based on user roles, device types, or traffic characteristics, even when devices from multiple vendors are involved.
- **Regular Patching and Updates:** It is crucial to ensure that all devices, both Cisco and non-Cisco, are regularly updated to mitigate

vulnerabilities. Cisco's **Prime Infrastructure** and **DNA Center** can assist in tracking and managing device updates and patches across the network.

Example: A large e-commerce company used a combination of Cisco and third-party firewalls to secure its global network. By implementing **Cisco TrustSec** for network segmentation and using **Cisco ISE** to manage authentication and access control, the company was able to ensure that security policies were applied uniformly across all devices, reducing the risk of security breaches in their multi-vendor environment.

Seamless Integration for Optimized Network Performance

Integrating Cisco with non-Cisco devices is an essential capability for businesses that require flexibility, cost-effectiveness, and the ability to leverage specialized technologies from different vendors. By focusing on **open standards**, using **centralized management platforms**, and leveraging **automation and orchestration**, organizations can successfully integrate devices from multiple vendors into a cohesive, high-performance network infrastructure.

Cisco's emphasis on **interoperability, open APIs**, and **security-first design** makes it possible to create a unified, manageable, and secure network, even in complex, multi-vendor environments. As businesses continue to evolve, the ability to seamlessly integrate diverse technologies will be a key enabler of growth, agility, and innovation in network architecture.

Cisco Interoperability Tools and Features

In today's multi-vendor network environments, achieving seamless interoperability is crucial to ensuring network performance, security, and manageability. Cisco provides a range of tools and features designed specifically to facilitate smooth integration with non-Cisco devices and technologies. These tools not only ensure compatibility but also help streamline network management, enhance security, and optimize performance.

In this section, we will explore the various interoperability tools and features that Cisco offers to help businesses successfully integrate Cisco devices with those from other vendors, ensuring that their networks operate as a cohesive, efficient, and secure entity.

1. Cisco DNA Center: Centralized Management for Multi-Vendor Networks

Cisco **DNA Center** is a comprehensive network management platform that provides centralized control for network automation, policy management, and monitoring. Designed to work with Cisco's networking hardware, DNA Center also includes the ability to integrate non-Cisco devices into the network, providing administrators with a single pane of glass for managing the entire infrastructure.

Key Features for Interoperability:

- **Open APIs and Integration with Third-Party Devices:** DNA Center supports open APIs, which enable integration with third-party devices, allowing businesses to extend their Cisco network management capabilities to non-Cisco equipment. This integration enables network administrators to configure, monitor, and troubleshoot non-Cisco devices alongside Cisco devices, ensuring consistency in policy enforcement and operations.
- **Intent-Based Networking:** DNA Center leverages intent-based networking, which automates network configurations based on business objectives and policies. By integrating non-Cisco devices into this framework, network administrators can apply consistent configurations and policies across all devices, simplifying network management and enhancing operational efficiency.

- **Automation and Assurance:** DNA Center's automation capabilities help streamline network deployment and configuration, while its assurance tools provide continuous monitoring and validation of network behavior. By using DNA Center, businesses can ensure that non-Cisco devices are properly configured, monitored, and optimized in the context of the larger network.

Example: A multinational company using both Cisco and third-party wireless access points (APs) integrated its entire network under Cisco DNA Center. By leveraging DNA Center's open APIs, the company was able to configure, monitor, and troubleshoot both Cisco and non-Cisco APs from a single interface, significantly reducing operational complexity and increasing network uptime.

2. Cisco Prime Infrastructure: Simplified Multi-Vendor Network Management

Cisco Prime Infrastructure provides a powerful platform for managing and monitoring a wide range of network devices from different vendors. It offers comprehensive capabilities for configuration, monitoring, and troubleshooting, and supports a wide array of network devices, including those from non-Cisco vendors.

Key Features for Interoperability:

- **Cross-Vendor Device Support:** Cisco Prime Infrastructure uses **SNMP (Simple Network Management Protocol)** and other industry-standard protocols to manage devices from various vendors. This enables IT teams to monitor and manage network devices, such as switches, routers, firewalls, and APs, from both Cisco and non-Cisco vendors in a single interface.
- **Unified Configuration and Monitoring:** With Prime Infrastructure, administrators can apply configuration changes, firmware updates, and security patches to both Cisco and non-Cisco devices

using the same workflows and policies. This reduces manual intervention and ensures consistency across the network, making the integration of devices from multiple vendors much easier.
- **Policy Management:** Cisco Prime supports role-based access control (RBAC) and policy management for devices from multiple vendors, ensuring that access and configurations are consistent with business requirements and security policies. It helps simplify the management of complex networks and reduces the risk of human error when configuring devices from different vendors.

Example: A large enterprise with a mix of Cisco and third-party switches used Cisco Prime Infrastructure to manage its entire network. The IT team was able to use the same tools to configure, monitor, and optimize both Cisco and non-Cisco switches, ensuring smooth interoperability and reducing operational overhead.

3. Cisco ACI (Application Centric Infrastructure): Simplifying Data Center Integration

Cisco ACI is a software-defined networking (SDN) solution designed to simplify the management and operation of data centers. ACI's policy-driven approach allows businesses to automate and optimize their data center operations, and it also supports integration with non-Cisco devices.

Key Features for Interoperability:

- **Open APIs for Multi-Vendor Integration:** Cisco ACI supports integration with third-party devices through open APIs and industry-standard protocols like **BGP**, **OSPF**, and **VXLAN**. This allows ACI to interoperate with non-Cisco devices such as switches, routers, and firewalls, ensuring that network policies and traffic flows are consistent across the entire network infrastructure.
- **Cross-Vendor Automation:** With ACI's policy-based automation,

businesses can integrate non-Cisco devices into their data center architecture while maintaining consistent network policies. ACI's **policy engine** automatically applies consistent network configurations and security rules across both Cisco and third-party devices, reducing the need for manual configuration and ensuring network stability.
- **End-to-End Visibility:** Cisco ACI provides end-to-end visibility into network traffic, including devices from other vendors. This enables administrators to monitor network performance and troubleshoot issues across the entire network, regardless of the vendor, using a single unified interface.

Example: A global tech company integrated Cisco ACI with its existing third-party servers and switches. The use of open APIs allowed the company to implement a single policy model that applied to both Cisco and non-Cisco devices, simplifying network management and reducing the complexity of maintaining a multi-vendor data center.

4. Cisco TrustSec: Network Segmentation and Security

Cisco TrustSec is a security solution designed to provide network segmentation and access control across Cisco and non-Cisco devices. TrustSec simplifies the enforcement of security policies by using software-defined segmentation to control network traffic based on roles, devices, and applications.

Key Features for Interoperability:

- **Role-Based Access Control (RBAC):** TrustSec uses RBAC to ensure that only authorized devices and users can access specific parts of the network. This capability is critical in a multi-vendor environment where devices from different vendors may have varying levels of access to network resources.
- **Software-Defined Segmentation:** TrustSec enables software-

defined segmentation, which simplifies the creation and enforcement of network segments. This allows businesses to logically segment their network traffic based on policies, rather than relying on traditional VLAN-based segmentation. TrustSec integrates with third-party devices through **IEEE 802.1X** and other open standards, ensuring that non-Cisco devices can be securely integrated into the network.
- **End-to-End Policy Enforcement:** TrustSec ensures consistent security policy enforcement across the network, regardless of the vendor. By integrating Cisco and non-Cisco devices under a single security policy framework, organizations can minimize security risks and enhance network resilience.

Example: A financial services company integrated Cisco TrustSec to enforce security policies across its mixed-vendor network. TrustSec allowed the company to segment sensitive financial data from less critical traffic, ensuring that only authorized devices, whether Cisco or non-Cisco, could access high-value resources.

5. Cisco SD-WAN: Simplifying Wide Area Network Integration

Cisco SD-WAN offers a scalable and flexible solution for managing WAN connectivity across distributed organizations. It supports integration with a wide variety of third-party devices, including routers, firewalls, and WAN optimization solutions.

Key Features for Interoperability:

- **Multi-Vendor WAN Integration:** Cisco SD-WAN is designed to integrate seamlessly with devices from non-Cisco vendors, allowing businesses to leverage existing WAN infrastructure and ensure consistent connectivity across all locations. Cisco's SD-WAN uses industry-standard protocols like **BGP**, **IPsec**, and **GRE** to provide seamless communication between Cisco and non-Cisco devices.

- **Centralized Control and Automation:** Cisco SD-WAN provides centralized control and automation, making it easier to manage WAN policies, security configurations, and traffic routing across Cisco and non-Cisco devices. This reduces the complexity of managing WANs with mixed devices and ensures that policies are consistently applied across the entire network.
- **Optimized Performance and Security:** Cisco SD-WAN integrates with Cisco security solutions such as **Umbrella** and **Firepower**, as well as third-party security appliances, to deliver secure and optimized WAN performance. This ensures that businesses can leverage the best security features from both Cisco and non-Cisco devices.

Example: A retail chain with multiple branches around the country used Cisco SD-WAN to integrate its Cisco and third-party routers. The SD-WAN solution allowed the company to centrally manage its WAN, apply security policies, and optimize traffic routing, regardless of the devices in use at each location.

Achieving Seamless Integration in a Multi-Vendor Environment

Cisco's suite of interoperability tools and features is designed to make it easier for businesses to integrate Cisco devices with those from other vendors, ensuring that their networks operate efficiently, securely, and with minimal disruption. By leveraging **open APIs**, **centralized management platforms**, and **policy-driven automation**, organizations can create a seamless and unified network, even in complex, multi-vendor environments.

Cisco's commitment to standards-based design, flexibility, and security ensures that businesses can take full advantage of the best solutions from both Cisco and non-Cisco vendors, optimizing network performance and simplifying management. With the right tools in place, organizations can enjoy the benefits of an integrated, high-performance network that supports the demands of modern business.

Hybrid Network Models: Cisco and Open-Source Solutions

In today's rapidly evolving network landscape, businesses increasingly seek flexibility, cost-effectiveness, and innovation. The use of **hybrid network models**, combining traditional enterprise solutions like Cisco with open-source alternatives, is becoming a strategic approach to meeting these needs. By integrating the reliability, security, and scalability of Cisco with the flexibility and lower costs offered by open-source solutions, organizations can achieve an optimal balance of performance, cost, and innovation.

In this section, we will explore the concept of hybrid network models, focusing on how businesses can integrate Cisco networking solutions with open-source technologies. We'll examine the benefits, challenges, and practical considerations for leveraging both proprietary Cisco solutions and open-source tools to build efficient, scalable, and resilient networks.

1. The Rise of Hybrid Network Models

A **hybrid network model** refers to the integration of proprietary (often vendor-specific) networking solutions with open-source technologies and tools. Cisco, as a leader in the networking space, offers enterprise-grade products that are highly reliable, secure, and scalable. However, the growing adoption of open-source solutions in networking is pushing organizations to explore hybrid architectures. These models allow businesses to leverage the best of both worlds: robust, feature-rich Cisco solutions alongside customizable and cost-effective open-source tools.

Key Drivers of Hybrid Network Adoption:

- **Cost Efficiency:** Open-source solutions often offer reduced upfront and licensing costs compared to proprietary systems, making them an attractive alternative for businesses seeking to reduce expenses without compromising functionality.
- **Flexibility and Customization:** Open-source technologies offer greater flexibility in terms of configuration and customization. Businesses can modify open-source tools to meet specific requirements, something that is often more challenging with proprietary solutions.
- **Innovation and Community Support:** Open-source tools often benefit from continuous innovation driven by large developer communities. These communities can provide quick fixes, updates, and innovations that proprietary vendors may not be able to match at the same speed.

By combining the enterprise-grade reliability and support of Cisco's solutions with the customizable nature of open-source technologies, organizations can create networks that are more adaptable, efficient, and cost-effective.

2. Cisco and Open-Source Solutions: Areas of Integration

Hybrid network models often focus on integrating **Cisco's networking hardware and software solutions** with open-source networking protocols, software, and management tools. Below, we'll explore some of the key areas where Cisco's enterprise solutions can integrate with open-source alternatives.

Router and Switch Configuration: Cisco Routers and Open-Source Routing Protocols

One area where Cisco products can seamlessly integrate with open-source solutions is in **routing and switching**. Cisco routers and switches are known for their high reliability and advanced features, including **routing protocols** like **EIGRP**, **OSPF**, and **BGP**. However, in hybrid models, businesses may choose to integrate these Cisco devices with open-source routing software such as **Quagga** or **FRRouting** (FRR), which provide an open-source alternative to traditional routing protocols.

- **Integration with FRR:** FRR is an open-source routing suite that supports a wide range of protocols including OSPF, BGP, and IS-IS. It can be installed on Linux-based servers and configured to work alongside Cisco routers in a hybrid environment. By using FRR in combination with Cisco hardware, businesses can leverage advanced open-source features while benefiting from Cisco's robust hardware for high-throughput routing.
- **Integration Benefits:** This hybrid approach allows businesses to maintain flexibility, reduce costs, and leverage community-driven innovations while ensuring the reliability and performance of Cisco hardware for mission-critical applications.

Network Management: Cisco DNA Center and Open-Source Monitoring Tools

Another area of integration is **network management and monitoring**. Cisco's **DNA Center** provides centralized control for automating, managing, and optimizing Cisco networks. However, some businesses may wish to integrate open-source tools like **Zabbix**, **Nagios**, or **Prometheus** to monitor not only Cisco devices but also third-party or open-source network components.

- **Zabbix for Multi-Vendor Monitoring:** Zabbix is a highly scalable open-source monitoring tool that can be used to monitor a wide range of network devices, including Cisco hardware. Businesses can integrate Zabbix with Cisco's DNA Center to extend their monitoring capabilities, enabling them to track performance across all network devices—whether they're from Cisco, other vendors, or open-source components.
- **Open-Source Network Automation with Ansible:** While DNA Center provides automation and orchestration, open-source tools

MULTI-VENDOR ENVIRONMENTS AND CISCO INTEGRATION

like **Ansible** can be integrated to automate configurations across both Cisco and non-Cisco devices. Ansible can be used to configure network devices, deploy updates, and monitor configurations in a multi-vendor environment, providing automation flexibility that complements Cisco's enterprise-grade solutions.

Firewalls and Security: Cisco Firepower and Open-Source Security Tools

When it comes to **network security**, Cisco's **Firepower** firewalls offer advanced features like intrusion prevention, application visibility, and URL filtering. However, businesses can complement Cisco's firewalls with open-source security tools such as **Suricata**, **pfSense**, or **IPFire** to extend their security posture.

- **Suricata for Threat Detection:** Suricata is an open-source network IDS/IPS engine that can be deployed alongside Cisco Firepower firewalls to provide additional layers of threat detection and prevention. Suricata integrates well with other open-source tools and can be customized to suit specific security needs.
- **pfSense for VPN and Router Capabilities:** pfSense is an open-source firewall and router software distribution based on FreeBSD. Many businesses use Cisco Firepower for enterprise firewall needs, but they may also deploy pfSense in remote locations for VPN connectivity or as an additional security layer. The two systems can work in parallel to protect the network at both the core and edge.

Wireless Networking: Cisco Meraki and Open-Source WLAN Solutions

Cisco's **Meraki** is a cloud-managed wireless solution that simplifies the deployment and management of wireless networks. However, some organizations may also want to integrate open-source wireless solutions like **OpenWrt** or **DD-WRT**, which provide customizable firmware for routers and wireless access points.

- **OpenWrt for Wireless Customization:** OpenWrt is an open-source firmware project that allows users to customize the software running on wireless routers and access points. Businesses can deploy Cisco Meraki for enterprise-grade wireless management and performance while using OpenWrt on lower-cost or custom hardware to extend wireless capabilities or create more flexible network configurations.

3. Challenges in Implementing Hybrid Network Models

While hybrid network models offer significant benefits, they also come with challenges that businesses must address to ensure smooth integration and optimal performance. Some of the key challenges include:

Complexity of Integration

Integrating proprietary Cisco solutions with open-source tools can be complex, especially when the open-source solutions are not natively compatible with Cisco's ecosystem. For example, configuring open-source routing protocols to work with Cisco hardware requires a solid understanding of both the Cisco and open-source technologies, as well as their interaction. This complexity can lead to extended deployment times and additional costs for training and troubleshooting.

Support and Maintenance

Cisco products come with enterprise-level support and service contracts, ensuring that any issues with Cisco devices are resolved quickly. However, with open-source tools, support is typically community-driven, and troubleshooting can be more challenging. Additionally, open-source software may not have the same level of tested, pre-configured solutions as Cisco products, which can increase the risk of deployment errors.

Security Concerns

While open-source tools are often secure, they do not always meet the same security standards as Cisco's proprietary solutions. Integrating open-source security tools with Cisco's advanced firewalls and intrusion prevention systems requires careful consideration to ensure there are no gaps in protection. Moreover, maintaining consistent security policies across both Cisco and non-Cisco devices can be difficult in complex environments.

4. Best Practices for Hybrid Network Integration

To maximize the benefits of hybrid network models and address integration challenges, businesses should follow several best practices:

- **Use Open Standards:** Leveraging open standards, such as **SNMP**, **REST APIs**, and **BGP**, ensures that Cisco and open-source devices can communicate and interoperate effectively. Open standards simplify integration and minimize compatibility issues, making it easier to deploy and manage hybrid networks.
- **Test and Validate Compatibility:** Before fully integrating open-source solutions with Cisco hardware, businesses should test and validate compatibility to ensure that the devices work as expected in the hybrid environment. This will help prevent network disruptions and reduce troubleshooting time.
- **Centralized Management Platforms:** Using centralized management platforms like **Cisco DNA Center** or **Cisco Prime Infrastructure** can help streamline the management of both Cisco and non-Cisco devices. These tools provide visibility and control over the entire network, enabling businesses to maintain consistent configurations, policies, and security measures across the network.
- **Plan for Security and Compliance:** Security should be a top priority when integrating Cisco solutions with open-source technologies. Businesses should implement multi-layer security models that incorporate Cisco's advanced security features alongside open-source tools. Additionally, businesses must ensure that they comply with industry standards and regulations when deploying hybrid network models.

The Future of Hybrid Network Models

Hybrid network models that combine **Cisco solutions** with **open-source tools** offer organizations greater flexibility, cost-efficiency, and innovation. These models allow businesses to harness the power of Cisco's enterprise-grade hardware and software while benefiting from the customization and cost savings of open-source technologies.

By carefully selecting the right open-source tools and integrating them effectively with Cisco's networking solutions, organizations can build more agile, scalable, and cost-effective networks that meet the demands of modern business. However, successful implementation requires careful planning, testing, and an understanding of the complexities of both proprietary and open-source technologies. The benefits, however, far outweigh the challenges, providing a powerful approach to building next-generation networks.

Best Practices for Multi-Vendor Network Design

As organizations move towards a **multi-vendor network architecture**, they must adopt best practices to ensure that the integration of different network devices, software, and protocols from various vendors, including Cisco, works seamlessly and efficiently. Multi-vendor environments offer significant advantages, such as flexibility, cost savings, and access to specialized features from different providers, but they also present unique challenges related to interoperability, management complexity, and support.

In this section, we will outline the best practices for designing and managing multi-vendor networks, focusing on ensuring compatibility, optimizing performance, and simplifying network management. By adhering to these principles, businesses can build robust, scalable, and secure networks that leverage the strengths of multiple vendors.

1. Ensure Interoperability and Compatibility

One of the primary challenges of a multi-vendor network is ensuring **interoperability** between different hardware, software, and network protocols. Each vendor has its own set of configurations, management interfaces, and proprietary technologies. To avoid compatibility issues and ensure that all devices communicate effectively, follow these best practices:

Use Open Standards and Protocols

Open standards ensure that devices from different vendors can communicate and exchange data without vendor lock-in. Common open standards and protocols to consider include:

- **IP (Internet Protocol)** for addressing and routing
- **SNMP (Simple Network Management Protocol)** for network monitoring and management
- **BGP (Border Gateway Protocol)** and **OSPF (Open Shortest Path First)** for routing
- **IEEE 802.1Q** for VLAN tagging
- **NETCONF** and **REST APIs** for network automation and configuration

When possible, prioritize the use of open standards to ensure that equipment from different vendors can interoperate effectively, even if the underlying technology varies. This will reduce the risk of configuration errors and improve network stability.

Check Vendor Compatibility and Integration Tools

Before purchasing multi-vendor devices, research the specific **interoperability tools and features** each vendor provides. Cisco, for example, has several integration tools designed to work with third-party devices. Additionally, many vendors offer management platforms or APIs that enable the configuration and monitoring of devices from different manufacturers in a centralized manner. These tools can simplify network management and reduce integration complexity.

Test Compatibility in a Lab Environment

To ensure seamless operation in a multi-vendor environment, organizations should create a **lab environment** to test new devices and configurations before deploying them to production. This testing phase allows network engineers to identify any compatibility issues, performance bottlenecks, or security vulnerabilities before affecting the live network. Testing also provides an opportunity to assess the effectiveness of integration tools, automation systems, and management interfaces in a controlled setting.

2. Simplify Network Management with Centralized Platforms

Managing a multi-vendor network can quickly become complex without the right tools. To maintain efficiency and streamline day-to-day operations, it's important to deploy centralized network management platforms that allow administrators to monitor and configure devices from multiple vendors from a single interface.

Leverage Cisco DNA Center for Multi-Vendor Management

While **Cisco DNA Center** is designed to manage Cisco devices, it also supports a variety of third-party devices through integrations. DNA Center's **network automation, monitoring, and policy enforcement** features can extend to non-Cisco equipment, enabling centralized management across the entire network. For instance, **multi-vendor network visibility** can be integrated via SNMP or third-party device plugins, allowing network engineers to view and manage configurations, performance metrics, and security policies for both Cisco and non-Cisco devices from a single console.

Use Multi-Vendor Network Automation Platforms

Many modern network management platforms support multi-vendor environments, offering robust network automation, configuration, and monitoring capabilities for devices from different vendors. **Ansible, Puppet**, and **SaltStack** are examples of **open-source network automa-**

MULTI-VENDOR ENVIRONMENTS AND CISCO INTEGRATION

tion tools that can be configured to support a wide range of vendor devices, including Cisco, Juniper, Arista, and others. These platforms enable network engineers to automate routine tasks such as firmware upgrades, configuration changes, and policy enforcement across different vendors, saving time and reducing human error.

Ensure Consistent Network Monitoring and Logging

With multiple vendors in the network, it's critical to have a **consistent monitoring and logging strategy** in place. Tools like **Prometheus**, **Grafana**, or **SolarWinds** can integrate with both Cisco and non-Cisco devices to provide real-time visibility into network performance. Centralized logging tools, such as **Splunk** or **ELK (Elasticsearch, Logstash, Kibana)**, can aggregate log data from various vendors' devices to provide insights into the network's health and security status.

3. Design for Scalability and Flexibility

When designing a multi-vendor network, scalability and flexibility must be prioritized to ensure the network can grow and adapt over time. A network designed to be scalable can easily accommodate new vendors, technologies, and services without major redesigns.

Use Modular and Layered Network Designs

A **modular network design** is ideal for multi-vendor environments, as it allows for easy upgrades and the introduction of new technologies. For example, using the **three-layer hierarchical model** (core, distribution, and access layers) provides the flexibility to add or replace devices from different vendors at each layer of the network without disrupting other parts of the network. Additionally, adopting a **spine-leaf topology** for data centers enables businesses to scale by simply adding more spine switches or leaf switches as demand increases, regardless of the vendor.

Adopt Virtualization and SDN for Flexibility

Network virtualization and **Software-Defined Networking (SDN)** can greatly improve the flexibility of a multi-vendor network. **SDN controllers** abstract the physical network hardware and provide a centralized control plane that allows administrators to manage the network programmatically, regardless of the underlying devices. This approach simplifies the integration of new vendors and technologies, as the SDN controller can handle the configuration and traffic management of devices from multiple vendors without requiring manual intervention.

Build Redundant and Resilient Designs

In a multi-vendor environment, redundancy is crucial for ensuring high availability. Design the network with redundant **links**, **devices**, and **power supplies** from multiple vendors to prevent single points of failure. For instance, you might deploy Cisco switches alongside devices from another vendor, ensuring that if one vendor's equipment fails, the other can take over without disrupting network operations. Additionally, use **link aggregation** and **multi-path routing** to ensure that the network remains available even if one path fails.

4. Security and Compliance in Multi-Vendor Environments

Multi-vendor network environments often present unique security challenges. Security policies, access controls, and monitoring tools must be configured in a way that applies consistently across the entire network, regardless of the device's manufacturer.

Implement Consistent Security Policies Across Vendors

To maintain a consistent security posture, organizations should implement **network-wide security policies** that are vendor-agnostic. Tools like **Cisco Identity Services Engine (ISE)** can integrate with devices from different vendors to enforce security policies such as access control, authentication, and device compliance. Similarly, using **802.1X** for port-based network access control ensures that only authorized devices can connect to the network, regardless of the device's manufacturer.

Secure Multi-Vendor Network Segments with VLANs

VLANs (Virtual Local Area Networks) allow network administrators to logically segment the network into isolated parts, improving security and reducing the risk of unauthorized access. In a multi-vendor environment,

VLAN configurations should be consistent across all devices to ensure secure and efficient traffic flow between different segments. For example, segmenting guest, internal, and administrative traffic into separate VLANs helps contain potential security breaches.

Monitor Security Threats Across Multi-Vendor Devices

A centralized **Security Information and Event Management (SIEM)** system can aggregate logs and events from all devices in the network, regardless of vendor. By integrating tools like **Cisco Umbrella** (for cloud security) or third-party SIEM solutions like **Splunk** or **LogRhythm**, businesses can monitor security events across their entire network and quickly detect and respond to threats.

5. Ongoing Maintenance and Support

Support and maintenance in a multi-vendor network can be more challenging than in a single-vendor environment, as troubleshooting and resolving issues may involve multiple vendors. To manage ongoing maintenance effectively:

- **Establish Clear Support Channels**: Ensure that support agreements with each vendor are clearly defined and easily accessible. This includes having contact details for customer support, SLAs (Service Level Agreements), and escalation procedures in place for each vendor.
- **Regular Training for Network Engineers**: Network administrators should undergo regular training on both Cisco and non-Cisco products to stay up-to-date on features, troubleshooting techniques, and best practices. Certifications such as **Cisco CCNP** or **CompTIA Network+** are valuable for building a strong knowledge base.
- **Vendor-Led Workshops and Training Sessions**: Vendors often offer workshops and training sessions that focus on their products and best practices for integrating with other systems. Taking advantage of these opportunities ensures that the team is well-

prepared to manage a multi-vendor network.

Building a Robust Multi-Vendor Network

Designing a multi-vendor network requires careful planning, testing, and integration to ensure all devices and systems work harmoniously together. By following best practices such as using open standards, leveraging network automation, and maintaining consistency in security policies, businesses can create flexible, scalable, and secure networks that take advantage of the best technologies from multiple vendors.

While there are challenges associated with multi-vendor environments, adopting a well-thought-out network design and leveraging the right tools can mitigate these challenges and enable businesses to enjoy the benefits of enhanced flexibility, reduced costs, and greater innovation. The key is to maintain a balance between vendor-specific features and open standards, ensuring seamless operation across the network.

The Future of Network Architecture with Cisco

The Impact of IoT, 5G, and AI on Network Design

The future of network architecture is being shaped by three transformative technologies: **Internet of Things (IoT)**, **5G**, and **Artificial Intelligence (AI)**. These technologies are not only driving innovation in the way networks are designed and managed, but they are also fundamentally changing the way businesses interact with their networks, end users, and devices. As networks become more complex and demand for speed, security, and scalability increases, understanding the implications of IoT, 5G, and AI on network design is crucial for IT professionals and network architects.

In this section, we'll explore how each of these technologies is impacting the evolution of network architecture, how they will transform existing network models, and how Cisco's solutions are helping organizations adapt to these changes.

1. The Internet of Things (IoT) and Network Design

The **Internet of Things (IoT)** refers to the growing network of physical devices, vehicles, buildings, and other objects embedded with sensors, software, and network connectivity, enabling them to collect and exchange data. IoT is revolutionizing industries by enabling real-time monitoring, automation, and more informed decision-making. However, IoT also introduces new challenges for network architecture.

Challenges Introduced by IoT:

- **Massive Scale and Device Density:** IoT networks often involve a large number of devices—ranging from sensors and smart appliances to industrial machines and connected vehicles. A single IoT network can easily consist of thousands or even millions of connected devices. This scale requires new approaches to handling device connectivity, IP addressing, and data traffic management.
- **Network Congestion:** The high volume of IoT traffic can lead to network congestion and latency issues, especially when devices send frequent, small bursts of data. This can strain existing network infrastructure if not properly managed.
- **Security Concerns:** IoT devices often lack robust security mechanisms, making them vulnerable to cyberattacks. This requires the network to be designed with **strong authentication**, **encryption**, and **segmentation** to isolate IoT devices from critical systems.

Impact on Network Design:

To accommodate the IoT boom, network architecture must evolve to handle the massive scale, latency requirements, and security risks associated with IoT devices.

- **Edge Computing for IoT:** One of the most important design changes to accommodate IoT is the shift toward **edge computing**. Instead of sending all data generated by IoT devices to centralized cloud servers, edge computing allows data processing to occur closer to where the data is generated (on local devices or edge nodes). This reduces latency, improves performance, and minimizes the need for bandwidth to transmit large volumes of data back to the cloud.
- **Network Segmentation for Security:** Given the security vulnerabil-

ities of IoT devices, it's critical to segment IoT devices into their own isolated network zones. **Virtual Local Area Networks (VLANs)** and **Access Control Lists (ACLs)** are used to separate IoT traffic from critical systems, thus reducing the risk of potential security breaches spreading throughout the entire network.
- **Cisco IoT Solutions:** Cisco's **IoT portfolio**, including **Cisco IoT Gateways** and **Cisco Kinetic**, enables businesses to efficiently collect, process, and analyze IoT data while maintaining a secure, scalable, and high-performance network. Cisco also leverages its **Cisco Industrial Asset Vision (IAV)** for tracking and managing connected devices in industrial IoT environments.

2. The Rise of 5G and Its Impact on Network Design

5G, the fifth generation of mobile network technology, promises to deliver faster speeds, lower latency, and more reliable connections compared to previous generations. With the ability to support massive IoT deployments, real-time applications, and high-bandwidth activities, 5G is poised to transform network design at the core, edge, and access layers.

Challenges Introduced by 5G:

- **Low Latency Requirements:** Many 5G use cases, such as autonomous vehicles, smart cities, and real-time remote healthcare, rely on **ultra-low latency**. Network architectures must be designed to meet these stringent latency requirements.
- **Network Slicing:** 5G networks are built with the concept of **network slicing**, allowing the creation of multiple virtual networks, each tailored for specific use cases. This requires a highly flexible and programmable network architecture capable of dynamically adjusting resources to meet the needs of different services.
- **Massive Capacity and High Bandwidth:** 5G will enable high-speed data transmission with more reliable connections. As a result,

network infrastructures must be upgraded to support higher data rates and larger numbers of connected devices.

Impact on Network Design:

The deployment of 5G will require fundamental changes in network architecture to handle the increased demand for speed, scalability, and low latency.

- **Edge Computing and 5G Integration:** Just like with IoT, the integration of **edge computing** is essential to realize the full potential of 5G. With 5G, ultra-low latency and high-speed applications depend on processing data close to the user, reducing the need to send data back to centralized data centers. Cisco's **5G and Edge Computing** solutions enable operators to deploy edge nodes closer to the end-user, ensuring the necessary speed and efficiency for high-demand applications.
- **Cloud-Native and Virtualized Networks:** 5G networks require more flexible, cloud-native, and **virtualized infrastructure**. Cisco's **Network Function Virtualization (NFV)** and **SDN solutions** can create virtualized network functions that allow for flexible, dynamic management of network resources, optimizing performance and reducing costs.
- **Cisco 5G Solutions:** Cisco's **5G Core Network** solutions and **Cisco Wireless Technologies** provide the backbone for 5G deployment. With a focus on network automation, virtualized network functions, and edge computing, Cisco is helping enterprises and telecom providers design and deploy 5G networks that meet high-speed, low-latency demands while maintaining scalability.

3. Artificial Intelligence (AI) and Network Design

Artificial Intelligence (AI) is increasingly becoming an integral part of network architecture, transforming how networks are designed, optimized, and managed. AI allows for intelligent decision-making based on real-time data, automating complex processes, and improving network security.

Challenges Introduced by AI:

- **Increased Complexity:** As AI technologies become more embedded in network operations, networks become more complex and require greater computational power to process and analyze data in real time.
- **Need for Automation:** The ability of AI to automate tasks such as traffic routing, load balancing, and fault detection requires that the network be highly programmable and capable of integrating with machine learning models.
- **Data Privacy and Ethics:** AI-powered network management tools often rely on vast amounts of data. As AI takes over decision-making processes, there are concerns regarding data privacy, ethics, and transparency in how AI algorithms are trained and deployed.

Impact on Network Design:

AI's impact on network design is profound, as it changes how networks are managed, optimized, and secured. AI will drive more intelligent, efficient, and adaptive network architectures.

- **Network Automation and Self-Optimizing Networks:** AI-powered tools can automate routine network tasks, such as **configuration, monitoring,** and **troubleshooting**. With the help of **machine learning** algorithms, networks can learn from past experiences and continuously optimize themselves. Cisco's **DNA Center** uses AI-driven network automation to optimize routing, resource allocation, and troubleshooting, ensuring that networks run

smoothly and efficiently.
- **AI in Security:** AI-driven security tools can detect unusual patterns and anomalies in real time, identifying potential threats faster than human operators. Cisco's **AI-powered security tools**, such as **Cisco Stealthwatch**, leverage AI and machine learning to analyze network traffic and identify potential security risks, protecting against evolving threats.
- **Cisco AI and Machine Learning Solutions:** Cisco is at the forefront of integrating AI and machine learning into network design. Through **Cisco ACI (Application Centric Infrastructure)** and **Cisco DNA Center**, businesses can create intelligent networks that automate provisioning, monitoring, and troubleshooting, all while improving operational efficiency.

4. The Intersection of IoT, 5G, and AI in Network Design

When combined, **IoT**, **5G**, and **AI** create a perfect storm of transformative technology that demands a complete rethink of network architecture. These technologies are increasingly interconnected, with IoT generating vast amounts of data, 5G providing the high-speed, low-latency network infrastructure to support it, and AI analyzing and automating responses to that data.

Impact on Network Design:

- **Adaptive, Programmable Networks:** Networks must become more **adaptive** and **programmable** to handle the demands of IoT, 5G, and AI. With these technologies working in tandem, networks must be able to dynamically adjust bandwidth, processing power, and routing based on real-time conditions. This requires the deployment of **SDN**, **NFV**, and **edge computing** to allow for flexible and intelligent network management.
- **Massive Data Processing and Storage:** IoT and 5G will create a deluge of data that must be processed, analyzed, and stored efficiently.

AI will assist in **data processing**, but network designs must also accommodate the infrastructure to support **big data storage** and processing.
- **End-to-End Security:** With IoT devices generating data, 5G networks transporting it, and AI analyzing it, ensuring end-to-end **security** becomes even more critical. Networks must be designed with robust encryption, authentication, and anomaly detection capabilities across all three layers.

The Future of Network Architecture with Cisco

The future of network design will be shaped by the seamless integration of IoT, 5G, and AI. These technologies will drive new levels of performance, scalability, and security, but they also present unique challenges that require innovative solutions. Cisco's portfolio of network solutions—from **IoT connectivity** and **5G networks** to **AI-powered automation** and **edge computing**—offers businesses the tools needed to build resilient, high-performance networks capable of supporting the next generation of digital innovation. By understanding the implications of these technologies and leveraging Cisco's cutting-edge solutions, enterprises can position themselves to thrive in the increasingly connected, data-driven world of tomorrow.

Cisco's Role in Enabling Smart Cities and Autonomous Networks

As the world becomes more urbanized, cities are evolving into **smart cities**—urban environments that leverage technology and data to improve quality of life, increase efficiency, and reduce environmental impact. Smart cities utilize a wide range of technologies, including the **Internet of Things (IoT)**, **5G connectivity**, **Artificial Intelligence (AI)**, and **cloud computing**, to create intelligent networks that automate processes and enable real-time decision-making. At the core of these transformations is the **network infrastructure**—the backbone that connects devices, sensors, applications, and services across the urban environment.

Cisco, a leader in networking solutions, plays a pivotal role in enabling the development of **smart cities** and **autonomous networks**. By providing the necessary hardware, software, and cloud services, Cisco empowers cities to build **connected environments** that are more efficient, sustainable, and resilient.

In this section, we'll explore how Cisco is contributing to the rise of smart cities, its innovations in **autonomous networks**, and the transformative impact this has on urban life and beyond.

1. Smart Cities: The Future of Urban Living

Smart cities use digital technologies to enhance performance, well-being, and reduce costs and resource consumption across the city. The goal is to create more sustainable, livable, and efficient urban environments that improve the daily lives of their inhabitants. Cisco's solutions are at the forefront of this transformation, offering a range of products and services that enable cities to deploy, manage, and optimize their networks for smart city applications.

Key Components of a Smart City:

- **IoT Infrastructure:** Smart cities rely heavily on IoT devices—such as sensors, cameras, traffic lights, and smart meters—that generate vast amounts of real-time data. Cisco's **IoT platforms** allow cities to securely connect, manage, and analyze these devices, enabling real-time monitoring and decision-making.
- **Connected Transportation:** In smart cities, transportation systems are interconnected, enabling real-time tracking, automated traffic management, and dynamic route optimization. Cisco's **Connected Vehicle** solutions and **smart traffic management** systems use real-time data to optimize traffic flow, reduce congestion, and improve

safety.

- **Smart Utilities and Energy Management:** Smart cities also optimize utility management, including water, electricity, and waste systems, using connected infrastructure to reduce waste, ensure efficiency, and enable predictive maintenance. Cisco's **Connected Utilities** solutions help cities to automate and manage these systems more effectively.
- **Public Safety and Security:** The integration of IoT and **AI-powered security solutions** enables smart cities to respond to emergencies more rapidly. Cisco's **video surveillance**, **smart sensors**, and **real-time analytics** ensure public safety while enhancing responsiveness in times of crisis.
- **Urban Planning and Sustainability:** Cities can also leverage data-driven insights to better manage urban development, making informed decisions on zoning, housing, environmental sustainability, and infrastructure investment. Cisco's **urban planning solutions** support sustainable growth, optimize public services, and reduce the environmental footprint of cities.

Cisco's Solutions for Smart Cities:

- **Cisco Kinetic for Cities:** Cisco's **Kinetic** platform is designed to help cities securely connect IoT devices, process and analyze the data they generate, and take action in real time. It acts as the "operating system" for smart cities, providing the necessary framework for integrating devices, applications, and data to enable smart city applications.
- **Cisco Smart+Connected Communities (S+CC):** Cisco's **Smart+Connected Communities** platform enables cities to deploy a connected infrastructure for urban environments. From **smart lighting** and **digital signage** to **environmental monitoring**, S+CC helps cities deliver enhanced services, increase public safety, and reduce energy consumption.

- **Cisco DNA Center and IoT Integration:** Cisco's **DNA Center** provides a unified network management solution that supports the scalability and flexibility needed for smart city deployments. By integrating IoT devices and sensors into the network, cities can manage and automate services, optimize traffic, and monitor public spaces all from a single platform.
- **Cloud and Edge Solutions:** Cisco's **cloud-based** and **edge computing solutions** provide the scalability and low-latency processing necessary for smart city operations. With **edge computing** and **IoT gateways**, Cisco ensures that critical data can be processed locally for immediate action, while still providing the ability to store and analyze data in the cloud for long-term insights.

2. Autonomous Networks: The Next Step in Network Evolution

An **autonomous network** is one that can automatically configure, optimize, and repair itself with minimal human intervention. With the integration of **AI**, **machine learning**, and **automation**, autonomous networks are the future of networking. These networks can dynamically adjust to changing traffic patterns, detect and mitigate security threats, and self-heal when issues arise—ensuring that services are always available, secure, and efficient.

The Importance of Autonomous Networks:

- **Network Automation:** Autonomous networks use **AI-driven automation** to simplify network management. These networks can autonomously handle routine tasks, such as **provisioning, monitoring, configuring devices**, and **troubleshooting**, which reduces human errors and operational costs.
- **Self-Optimizing Networks:** With AI and **machine learning**, autonomous networks can analyze traffic patterns and dynamically optimize the flow of data, ensuring high performance and low latency across the network. These networks can automatically reroute traffic,

prioritize critical applications, and balance loads without manual intervention.

- **Security and Threat Detection:** Autonomous networks are highly adept at identifying and responding to security threats in real-time. By continuously analyzing network traffic and applying **AI algorithms**, these networks can detect anomalies, flag potential breaches, and automatically initiate security protocols to mitigate risks.

- **Network Resilience and Fault Management:** Autonomous networks are designed to be highly resilient. When network faults or failures occur, autonomous networks can automatically reroute traffic, replace faulty hardware, and adjust configurations to ensure continuous service availability.

Cisco's Role in Autonomous Networks:

- **Cisco DNA Center:** Cisco's **DNA Center** is a critical tool in the creation of autonomous networks. It provides **AI-driven network automation**, **intent-based networking**, and a **centralized management platform** that can autonomously provision, configure, and manage network devices. With **Cisco DNA Center**, businesses can ensure that their network is always optimized for performance, security, and efficiency.

- **Cisco ACI (Application Centric Infrastructure):** Cisco's **ACI** solution automates network configuration and management, using **policy-based automation** to ensure that applications always receive the necessary resources. It's an essential part of the autonomous network strategy, ensuring that application performance is consistently high and that network resources are efficiently allocated.

- **AI and Machine Learning Integration:** Cisco's **AI-powered analytics**, such as **Cisco Stealthwatch** and **Cisco Network Assurance Engine**, use machine learning to continuously monitor network behavior and predict potential issues before they affect

performance. These solutions automate the detection of security threats, performance bottlenecks, and network outages.
- **Zero-Touch Provisioning (ZTP):** Cisco's **ZTP** technology allows for the **automated deployment** of network devices with minimal human intervention. Once a device is connected to the network, it automatically receives the necessary configurations and software updates, simplifying the deployment process and reducing operational overhead.

3. How Cisco Is Enabling the Smart Cities of Tomorrow

Cisco's solutions for **smart cities** and **autonomous networks** are designed to support the growing demand for connectivity, efficiency, and security in urban environments. By providing scalable, secure, and intelligent network infrastructures, Cisco is helping cities around the world leverage **real-time data**, **edge computing**, and **AI-driven automation** to improve city services, enhance public safety, and build a more sustainable future.

Key Benefits of Cisco's Solutions for Smart Cities and Autonomous Networks:

- **Scalability and Flexibility:** Cisco's products and platforms, including **IoT solutions**, **5G technologies**, and **cloud services**, provide the scalability and flexibility required for smart cities to expand as their populations and technological needs grow.
- **Enhanced Public Safety and Security:** With **AI-driven analytics**, **IoT-based monitoring**, and **edge computing**, Cisco helps cities enhance security, detect and prevent criminal activities, and respond quickly to emergencies.
- **Sustainability and Efficiency:** Cisco's solutions enable cities to reduce energy consumption, optimize resource usage, and streamline operations, helping create more sustainable urban environments.
- **Improved Citizen Engagement:** Through **smart infrastructure**

and **real-time data**, Cisco empowers cities to better engage with their citizens, providing more responsive services and a higher quality of life.

Cisco's Vision for the Future of Smart Cities and Autonomous Networks

As cities become smarter and networks more autonomous, Cisco is at the forefront of this technological evolution. Through its comprehensive suite of solutions—including **IoT platforms**, **edge computing**, **network automation**, and **AI-driven security**—Cisco is enabling cities to build the infrastructure needed for the connected future. Whether it's improving the efficiency of urban services, enhancing public safety, or enabling the next generation of smart applications, Cisco's role in shaping the cities and networks of tomorrow is critical to achieving a sustainable and connected world.

Future-Proofing Networks with Cisco Technologies

As organizations across the globe adopt more sophisticated digital technologies, the need for future-proof network architectures has never been greater. The traditional approach to networking, which relies on fixed hardware, manual configuration, and rigid designs, is no longer sufficient to meet the demands of modern enterprises. Today's businesses require networks that are scalable, adaptable, and able to handle new innovations such as **IoT**, **5G**, **cloud computing**, and **AI**.

Future-proofing a network means designing and implementing systems that are flexible enough to support emerging technologies while also ensuring that the network can grow and evolve without requiring frequent, costly overhauls. Cisco, as a leader in networking and IT infrastructure, provides a wide range of solutions that enable organizations to future-proof their networks. By leveraging **Cisco's**

technologies, businesses can build networks that are agile, resilient, and capable of supporting the rapidly changing digital landscape.

1. The Concept of Future-Proofing Networks

Future-proofing in networking refers to creating a network infrastructure that is not only equipped to meet current demands but also designed to accommodate technological advancements and changes in business requirements in the future. It's about anticipating growth, technological shifts, and the evolving nature of IT. Future-proofing enables businesses to adapt quickly to new innovations while minimizing disruptions and optimizing their existing infrastructure.

Key characteristics of future-proof networks include:

- **Scalability**: The ability to expand without significant redesign or resource constraints.
- **Flexibility**: Support for emerging technologies and protocols, without requiring major overhauls.
- **Automation**: Automation for ease of management, configuration, and provisioning, reducing manual intervention.
- **Security**: Future-proof networks must have robust security capabilities that evolve to meet new threats.
- **Reliability**: Ensuring high availability and fault tolerance even as the network grows and diversifies.

Cisco offers a broad range of products and platforms designed specifically to meet the challenges of future-proof networking. From **cloud-managed systems** and **automation tools** to **AI-driven analytics**, Cisco's portfolio is aimed at helping businesses adapt and thrive in an increasingly connected and dynamic world.

2. Cisco's Technological Innovations for Future-Proof Networks

Cisco has long been at the forefront of networking innovation. By focusing on the evolving needs of businesses, Cisco has developed a wide array of technologies that enable organizations to future-proof their networks. These technologies encompass multiple domains, including **network automation**, **cloud computing**, **security**, **network analytics**, and **AI integration**. Let's explore some of the core innovations that Cisco is providing to future-proof network infrastructures:

a. Cisco DNA (Digital Network Architecture)

Cisco DNA is a comprehensive network architecture that enables businesses to build scalable, automated, and secure networks. It provides a foundation for **intent-based networking** and **automation**, allowing networks to dynamically adapt to changing demands.

- **Intent-based Networking**: Cisco DNA Center allows administrators to define the business intent for their network. The system automatically configures and manages the network based on this intent, simplifying management and reducing human errors.
- **Automation**: Cisco DNA automates tasks like provisioning, monitoring, and troubleshooting, freeing IT teams from repetitive manual work and improving overall network efficiency.
- **Cloud Integration**: DNA integrates with cloud environments, allowing for a seamless extension of on-premises infrastructure to the cloud, ensuring that the network can evolve as businesses adopt hybrid cloud models.

By using Cisco DNA, organizations can create adaptable and flexible networks that scale with business growth and technological advancements, ensuring that the network infrastructure can easily evolve as new requirements emerge.

b. Cisco Meraki: Cloud-Managed Networking

Cisco Meraki is a cloud-managed network solution that enables organizations to deploy, monitor, and manage networks without the need for specialized IT staff. Meraki allows businesses to easily scale their network infrastructure without adding complexity, making it ideal for organizations looking to future-proof their network by leveraging cloud technologies.

- **Cloud Management**: Meraki's **cloud dashboard** allows for centralized, real-time monitoring and management of networks, providing visibility across multiple sites without the need for on-site IT staff.
- **Scalability**: Meraki's cloud-managed approach makes it easy to add new devices and expand the network. New access points, switches, and routers can be deployed with minimal effort, and configurations can be pushed to devices from a centralized cloud platform.
- **Security**: Meraki offers built-in **security features** like **firewalls**, **intrusion detection** systems, and **content filtering** that can be updated in real time, ensuring that the network stays secure in an ever-evolving threat landscape.

Meraki's combination of ease of use, scalability, and security positions it as an ideal solution for future-proofing networks, particularly for businesses looking for simple but powerful cloud-managed systems.

c. Cisco ACI (Application-Centric Infrastructure)

Cisco **ACI** is a software-defined networking (SDN) solution that provides centralized automation, policy-based management, and visibility across the network. ACI is ideal for organizations looking to support **data center virtualization**, **hybrid cloud deployments**, and **multi-cloud environments**, all of which are critical for future-proofing the network.

- **Automation and Flexibility**: ACI automates network configurations and provisioning, enabling the network to respond dynamically to changing demands and workloads.
- **Centralized Policy Management**: ACI allows businesses to define and enforce policies across the network, ensuring that security and

performance are optimized regardless of where workloads reside.
- **Support for Hybrid and Multi-Cloud**: ACI integrates seamlessly with public and private cloud environments, ensuring that the network can evolve to support cloud-native applications, IoT devices, and multi-cloud architectures.

ACI enables businesses to deploy a network infrastructure that can grow with their digital transformation needs, making it a critical tool for future-proofing enterprise data centers and cloud environments.

d. Cisco SD-WAN (Software-Defined Wide Area Network)

Cisco **SD-WAN** simplifies the management and operation of a wide-area network by decoupling the network control plane from the physical hardware. This technology offers dynamic path selection, security features, and centralized control, making it a key component for businesses looking to future-proof their wide-area networks.

- **Cloud-First Architecture**: SD-WAN allows businesses to prioritize traffic to cloud-based applications, ensuring optimal performance even as cloud adoption accelerates.
- **Enhanced Security**: Built-in **security features** such as encryption, secure direct internet access (DIA), and automated threat detection ensure that SD-WAN provides the protection needed for modern networks.
- **Scalability**: As organizations expand globally, SD-WAN makes it easier to scale the network infrastructure without significant overhead, supporting new branches, remote offices, and cloud services.

SD-WAN is designed to optimize **cloud connectivity**, **secure branch-to-cloud communication**, and improve **application performance**, all of which are vital for businesses looking to stay ahead in an increasingly cloud-driven world.

3. Key Benefits of Future-Proofing Networks with Cisco Technologies

By leveraging Cisco's suite of networking solutions, organizations can future-proof their networks in the following ways:

a. Scalability and Flexibility

Cisco's technologies, such as **Cisco DNA**, **Meraki**, and **ACI**, allow businesses to scale their networks effortlessly. Whether it's adding new devices, expanding to new geographic regions, or integrating new technologies, Cisco ensures that your network can grow without disrupting existing operations.

b. Seamless Cloud Integration

With solutions like **Cisco Meraki** and **SD-WAN**, Cisco enables organizations to transition to **hybrid** and **multi-cloud environments** without compromising on security or performance. The integration with cloud platforms allows businesses to access resources dynamically and ensures that the network can evolve with the growing adoption of cloud-based services.

c. Security Built In

Cisco's comprehensive security offerings, from **Meraki**'s built-in firewall and security features to **SD-WAN**'s secure cloud access and **ACI's** policy enforcement, ensure that networks are protected from evolving cyber threats. As security becomes increasingly critical in the digital landscape, Cisco's solutions offer proactive defense mechanisms that grow with the network.

d. Automation and AI-Driven Insights

The future of networking is automated. Cisco's **DNA Center** and **ACI** provide advanced automation and AI-driven insights to reduce manual configurations and optimize network performance. These platforms use machine learning to predict network behavior, detect anomalies, and automate troubleshooting, reducing human error and operational costs.

e. Simplified Network Management

Cloud-managed solutions like **Meraki** provide simplified, centralized network management, which reduces the complexity of scaling operations. With cloud-based dashboards and **AI-powered network analytics**, businesses can optimize their networks and gain actionable insights in real time, helping them stay agile in the face of change.

Cisco's Role in Future-Proofing Networks

As businesses look to navigate the complexities of the digital era, **future-proofing** their networks is critical. Cisco's suite of technologies—including **IoT platforms**, **SD-WAN**, **ACI**, and **Meraki**—empowers organizations to create networks that are flexible, scalable, secure, and capable of adapting to emerging technologies. By investing in Cisco's cutting-edge solutions, businesses can ensure their networks are ready to support new innovations, drive business growth, and provide exceptional user experiences for years to come.

Through **automation**, **cloud integration**, and **AI-driven capabilities**, Cisco is not just meeting the demands of today's businesses, but actively shaping the future of networking.

Preparing for Future Trends: Machine Learning, Automation, and Beyond

The pace at which networking technologies are evolving today is unprecedented, driven by innovations in **machine learning (ML), artificial intelligence (AI), automation**, and other next-generation technologies. As businesses across industries look to stay ahead of their competitors, they must prepare for these emerging trends and integrate them into their network infrastructure. Cisco, a leader in networking technology, is uniquely positioned to enable organizations to embrace these trends through advanced network solutions that make the most of machine learning, automation, and cloud computing.

The future of network architecture will be characterized by **self-optimizing** systems, **intelligent automation**, and **predictive analytics**, all powered by **machine learning algorithms**. These technologies promise to revolutionize network management, enhance security, improve application performance, and significantly reduce human intervention. Let's explore how businesses can prepare for these trends and leverage Cisco's technologies to create intelligent, automated, and adaptable networks.

1. Machine Learning and AI in Network Management

The role of **machine learning (ML)** and **artificial intelligence (AI)** in network management is rapidly growing. Traditionally, network management required manual configuration, monitoring, and troubleshooting by IT professionals. As networks grow in complexity, with millions of connected devices and users, this hands-on approach is no longer feasible. Machine learning and AI can help address this challenge by enabling more **intelligent network operations** and **predictive capabilities**.

a. Predictive Analytics for Network Performance

Machine learning models can be used to analyze vast amounts of network data to predict potential issues before they occur. For example, Cisco's **AI-powered systems**, such as **Cisco DNA Center** and **Cisco Meraki**, leverage ML algorithms to monitor network traffic, detect anomalies, and even predict bandwidth congestion or device failures before they impact the network.

- **Network Optimization**: By analyzing historical data, ML models can automatically adjust configurations and optimize routing paths to prevent performance degradation or downtime. This predictive approach enables businesses to preemptively address issues rather than react to them after they occur, minimizing downtime and improving overall network efficiency.
- **Anomaly Detection**: Machine learning algorithms are adept at recognizing patterns in network traffic and user behavior. When unusual patterns—such as potential security threats or sudden spikes in traffic—are detected, the system can automatically flag or respond to the issue, reducing response times and minimizing human error.

b. Network Security and AI

The security landscape is also rapidly evolving with the integration of **AI** and **ML** into Cisco's security technologies. **Cisco's AI-driven security solutions**, such as **Cisco Stealthwatch** and **Cisco Umbrella**, use machine learning to detect threats in real-time, analyze the behavior of devices and users, and identify abnormal activities or potential intrusions.

- **Threat Intelligence**: ML can identify new, previously unknown threats by analyzing data from across the network and matching it against known attack patterns. Cisco's **Umbrella** platform uses AI to enhance threat intelligence and protect the network perimeter by proactively blocking malicious activity.
- **Automated Incident Response**: With AI-powered solutions, the network can detect security threats and initiate an automated response, such as isolating compromised devices, adjusting firewall rules, or

blocking malicious IP addresses, without human intervention. This automation reduces the workload on IT teams and enhances the network's ability to respond quickly to potential threats.

2. Automation: Reducing Complexity and Improving Efficiency

Automation is the key to managing the complexity of modern enterprise networks. With businesses operating in dynamic environments, where network requirements can change rapidly, automated systems are essential to maintain optimal performance and reliability. Cisco's network automation solutions simplify the process of managing and configuring network devices, allowing for faster deployments, easier scaling, and more efficient network management.

a. Automating Network Provisioning

Cisco's **DNA Center** and **Cisco Meraki** offer **automation** features that allow administrators to configure devices and deploy network services automatically, reducing the manual work required to set up new devices, configure network policies, and ensure compliance with security standards. For example:

- **Zero-Touch Provisioning**: Devices can be automatically configured as soon as they are connected to the network, reducing the need for manual intervention during deployment. This approach speeds up network rollout and ensures consistency across all devices.
- **Policy Automation**: Network policies (e.g., security, traffic prioritization, and access control) can be automatically enforced across the entire network, ensuring compliance with business rules and regulatory standards without requiring manual updates.

b. Automated Network Management

Network automation extends beyond provisioning and configuration. With Cisco's **AI-powered network management** tools, network administrators can automate routine network management tasks such as:

- **Traffic Analysis**: Network traffic flows can be monitored automatically, and policies can be adjusted dynamically to optimize performance.
- **Fault Detection and Remediation**: Automation tools can detect faults and automatically apply predefined corrective actions, such as rerouting traffic or adjusting configurations, without requiring human intervention.

This automation significantly reduces the complexity of network management, allowing IT teams to focus on higher-value tasks like strategic planning and innovation.

3. Leveraging APIs for Intelligent Network Control

The future of network management is also characterized by **increased integration** and **interoperability** through the use of **APIs** (Application Programming Interfaces). Cisco has embraced APIs as a way to enable organizations to integrate their network infrastructure with other business systems, applications, and cloud platforms. By using APIs, businesses can automate workflows, manage multiple network devices from a centralized interface, and integrate network data with business intelligence platforms.

- **API-Driven Automation**: With Cisco's **open APIs**, network administrators can create customized automation workflows that integrate with other IT systems (e.g., cloud platforms, security tools, and IT service management systems). For example, network changes triggered by business operations can automatically be implemented on the network without manual intervention.
- **Cross-Platform Integration**: Cisco's **DNA Center** and **ACI** allow businesses to leverage APIs for integrating with third-party platforms and applications. This enables businesses to build more cohesive and unified IT environments, where the network infrastructure interacts

seamlessly with other enterprise applications, from HR systems to customer-facing services.

By integrating **machine learning**, **automation**, and **APIs**, businesses can create a more agile and efficient network that responds dynamically to new demands and technologies.

4. Preparing for Emerging Technologies: 5G, IoT, and Beyond

The next phase of network evolution will be heavily influenced by **5G**, the **Internet of Things (IoT)**, and other emerging technologies. These advancements will create new opportunities, but also present new challenges in terms of network design, scalability, and performance.

a. Preparing for 5G

The rollout of **5G** networks is expected to dramatically increase network speeds, reduce latency, and enable a new generation of connected devices. Cisco is preparing businesses for the **5G revolution** by developing solutions that can handle the enormous data throughput, low-latency requirements, and increased security demands associated with 5G.

- **Edge Computing**: Cisco's **edge computing solutions**, integrated with 5G, allow data to be processed closer to the source, reducing latency and improving application performance. This is especially important for real-time applications such as autonomous vehicles, telemedicine, and augmented reality.
- **Network Slicing**: Cisco's **ACI** and **SD-WAN** solutions are already equipped to support the concept of **network slicing**, which allows businesses to create customized, isolated virtual networks on top of the physical infrastructure. This is crucial for supporting the diverse use cases enabled by 5G.

b. Supporting IoT Growth

The rapid growth of **IoT** devices will generate massive amounts of data and create complex networking challenges. Cisco's IoT solutions, like **Cisco Kinetic** and **IoT Control Center**, are designed to help businesses securely manage, connect, and scale IoT devices, ensuring that networks are ready to handle the traffic from billions of connected sensors, devices, and machines.

- **Network Capacity**: Cisco's network solutions are designed with scalability in mind, enabling businesses to expand their networks to accommodate the growing number of IoT devices and the data they generate.
- **Security**: Cisco's **security-first approach** ensures that IoT devices are securely connected to the network, with end-to-end encryption and segmentation to protect against potential vulnerabilities in an increasingly connected world.

5. The Road Ahead: Innovation and Continuous Improvement

As network technology continues to evolve, businesses must be prepared to innovate and adapt quickly to new trends. The combination of **AI**, **ML**, **automation**, **IoT**, and **5G** presents an exciting future for network architects, but it also requires a proactive approach to ensure that networks can scale and evolve in line with technological advancements.

With Cisco's advanced technologies—**AI-driven network management**, **cloud integration**, **SD-WAN**, **automation**, and **IoT solutions**—organizations are equipped to build networks that are flexible, scalable, and future-proof. The ability to harness these technologies will empower businesses to not only meet the demands of today's digital world but also capitalize on the opportunities of tomorrow.

By investing in the right tools, infrastructure, and expertise, businesses can create networks that are ready for **future technologies**, ensuring long-term success and resilience in an ever-changing landscape.

Practice Labs and Configuration Examples

Lab 1: Configuring VLANs and Inter-VLAN Routing

Virtual Local Area Networks (VLANs) and Inter-VLAN Routing are essential components of modern network design, enabling network segmentation and facilitating communication between different segments of the network. VLANs allow the isolation of traffic to improve security, reduce congestion, and enhance performance by logically grouping devices together, regardless of their physical location. Inter-VLAN Routing is required to enable communication between devices in different VLANs, typically performed by a Layer 3 switch or a router.

In this lab, we'll configure VLANs, assign them to network interfaces, and set up Inter-VLAN Routing to allow communication between devices in different VLANs. This is a crucial task for network administrators, as it forms the basis for scalable and secure network architecture in both small and large networks.

Overview of VLAN Configuration

The first step in configuring VLANs is to define the VLANs themselves on the switch. Cisco devices allow network administrators to define VLANs by specifying a unique ID and associating specific interfaces to

PRACTICE LABS AND CONFIGURATION EXAMPLES

each VLAN.

Steps to Configure VLANs:

- **Create VLANs:** Using Cisco's CLI (Command-Line Interface), VLANs are created with the vlan command followed by the VLAN ID and name.
- **Assign VLANs to Switch Ports:** After VLANs are created, you will assign switch ports to the appropriate VLANs. This is done by configuring the switch port mode to access and associating it with the desired VLAN.
- Example:

```arduino
Switch(config)# vlan 10
Switch(config-vlan)# name Sales
Switch(config)# vlan 20
Switch(config-vlan)# name HR
```

- Assigning VLANs to switch ports:

```arduino
Switch(config)# interface range fa0/1 - 10
Switch(config-if)# switchport mode access
Switch(config-if)# switchport access vlan 10
```

- **Verify VLAN Configuration:** You can verify the VLAN configuration using the show vlan brief command, which will display a list of configured VLANs along with the associated ports.

477

Configuring Inter-VLAN Routing

Once VLANs are configured, the next step is to enable communication between them. Routers are traditionally used for Inter-VLAN Routing, but Layer 3 switches with routing capabilities can also be used to route traffic between VLANs without the need for an external router.

Steps for Inter-VLAN Routing:

- **Enable Routing on the Layer 3 Switch or Router:** First, ensure that IP routing is enabled on the device that will perform Inter-VLAN Routing. On a Layer 3 switch, this can be done by entering the global configuration mode and issuing the ip routing command.

arduino

```
Switch(config)# ip routing
```

- **Assign IP Addresses to VLAN Interfaces:** Each VLAN requires a virtual interface (SVI - Switched Virtual Interface) for routing. This is typically done by assigning an IP address to each VLAN interface, making it the default gateway for devices in that VLAN.
- Example:

arduino

```
Switch(config)# interface vlan 10
Switch(config-if)# ip address 192.168.10.1 255.255.255.0
Switch(config-if)# no shutdown
```

- **Configure Routing Between VLANs:** On a Layer 3 switch or router,

PRACTICE LABS AND CONFIGURATION EXAMPLES

routing is automatically enabled once SVIs are configured with IP addresses. The device can now route traffic between VLANs.
- **Verify Routing:** After the configuration, test communication between different VLANs by pinging from a device in one VLAN to a device in another. For example, from a computer in VLAN 10, try to ping the default gateway of VLAN 20.
- Example:

```makefile
C:\> ping 192.168.20.1
```

Troubleshooting and Verification

After configuring VLANs and Inter-VLAN Routing, verifying the configuration is crucial to ensure everything is working as expected. Here are some commands to help with troubleshooting:

- **Check VLAN Configuration:**

```arduino
Switch# show vlan brief
```

- **Verify Interface Status:**

```kotlin
Switch# show ip interface brief
```

- **Check Routing Table:**

```arduino
Switch# show ip route
```

- **Ping Between VLANs:** Use the ping command from devices in different VLANs to verify that routing is working correctly.

Lab 2: Implementing QoS for Traffic Prioritization

Quality of Service (QoS) is a critical concept in network design, particularly for businesses and service providers who need to ensure that certain types of traffic are prioritized over others. QoS mechanisms allow network administrators to manage bandwidth, control latency, and optimize traffic flow across the network. By implementing QoS, administrators can guarantee the performance of essential applications like VoIP, video conferencing, or other latency-sensitive services, even in the face of network congestion.

In this lab, we will explore how to implement QoS to prioritize traffic based on its type and importance. We'll configure Cisco routers and switches to classify, mark, and queue different types of traffic, ensuring that mission-critical services receive the bandwidth they need without

PRACTICE LABS AND CONFIGURATION EXAMPLES

delay.

Overview of QoS Concepts

Before diving into the configuration, it's essential to understand the core principles of QoS. These include:

- **Traffic Classification:** The process of categorizing network traffic into different classes or types based on parameters like source/destination IP, protocol type, port number, etc.
- **Traffic Marking:** Marking packets with priority tags (e.g., Differentiated Services Code Point (DSCP) values or IP precedence) to indicate their priority level in the network.
- **Traffic Policing:** Limiting the traffic rate for certain types of traffic, ensuring that excess traffic does not impact the overall network performance.
- **Traffic Shaping:** Buffers traffic in a way that smooths out bursts of data to fit within predefined bandwidth constraints.
- **Queueing:** Organizing packets into different queues based on priority, ensuring that high-priority traffic gets processed first.

By understanding these concepts, you can implement an effective QoS strategy that aligns with the needs of your network.

Steps to Implement QoS for Traffic Prioritization

In this lab, we will configure a basic QoS setup on Cisco routers and switches using the following steps:

Step 1: Define Traffic Classes

The first step in implementing QoS is defining traffic classes based on specific criteria such as application type, protocol, or IP address. Traffic classes are typically defined using Access Control Lists (ACLs) or class maps.

- **Create a Class Map:** A class map defines the traffic type (e.g., VoIP, video, or HTTP traffic). You can use the match command to specify the criteria for traffic selection.
- Example:

```arduino
Router(config)# class-map match-any VoIP
Router(config-cmap)# match protocol rtp
Router(config-cmap)# exit
Router(config)# class-map match-any Video
Router(config-cmap)# match protocol h323
Router(config-cmap)# exit
```

This configuration creates two class maps: one for VoIP traffic (Real-time Transport Protocol or RTP) and one for video traffic (H.323).

Step 2: Create a Policy Map for Traffic Marking

Once traffic classes are defined, the next step is to create a policy map that specifies what actions to take on the classified traffic. In this case, we'll mark the traffic with DSCP values that define its priority.

- **Create a Policy Map:** A policy map can include multiple class maps and specifies what action to take for each class, such as marking, policing, or shaping traffic.
- Example:

```arduino
Rcuter(config)# policy-map QoS-Policy
Rcuter(config-pmap)# class VoIP
Rcuter(config-pmap-c)# set dscp ef
Rcuter(config-pmap-c)# exit
```

PRACTICE LABS AND CONFIGURATION EXAMPLES

```
Router(config-pmap)# class Video
Router(config-pmap-c)# set dscp af41
Router(config-pmap-c)# exit
```

In this example, VoIP traffic is marked with a DSCP value of EF (Expedited Forwarding), which is the highest priority for time-sensitive traffic. Video traffic is marked with DSCP value AF41, which provides a lower priority than VoIP but higher than best-effort traffic.

Step 3: Apply the Policy Map to Interfaces

After defining the class and policy maps, the next step is to apply the QoS policies to the appropriate network interfaces. This can be done on both inbound and outbound interfaces, depending on the type of traffic.

- **Apply the Policy Map to the Interface:** You apply the policy map to the interface to enforce traffic classification and prioritization.
- Example:

```
arduino

Router(config)# interface gigabitEthernet 0/1
Router(config-if)# service-policy input QoS-Policy
Router(config-if)# exit
```

This configuration applies the QoS-Policy to the inbound traffic on the interface GigabitEthernet 0/1.

Step 4: Configure Traffic Policing (Optional)

Policing can be applied to limit the rate of traffic for specific classes. Policing drops packets that exceed a defined rate, which helps prevent excessive traffic from consuming all available bandwidth.

- **Configure Policing for Traffic:** You can configure policing within

the policy map by specifying a maximum rate.
- Example:

```arduino
Router(config)# policy-map QoS-Policy
Router(config-pmap)# class VoIP
Router(config-pmap-c)# police 256000 312500 4000 conform-action transmit exceed-action drop
Router(config-pmap-c)# exit
```

In this example, the VoIP class is limited to 256 Kbps, and any excess traffic is dropped.

Step 5: Configure Traffic Shaping (Optional)

Traffic shaping is useful for smoothing out bursts of traffic to ensure that bandwidth is used more evenly over time. This can be particularly useful for video or other bursty traffic types.

- **Configure Traffic Shaping:** Shaping can be configured by defining a maximum bandwidth for traffic flows.
- Example:

```arduino
Router(config)# policy-map QoS-Policy
Router(config-pmap)# class Video
Router(config-pmap-c)# shape average 512000
Router(config-pmap-c)# exit
```

This configuration shapes video traffic to a steady 512 Kbps rate, preventing bursts from overwhelming the network.

Step 6: Verify the Configuration

After completing the configuration, it's important to verify that QoS is functioning correctly. Use the following commands to check the status and statistics of the QoS configuration:

- **Verify the Policy Map on the Interface:**

```bash
Router# show policy-map interface gigabitEthernet 0/1
```

- **Check the DSCP Marking:** You can check whether traffic is being marked with the correct DSCP values using the following command:

```arduino
Router# show mls qos
```

- **Monitor Traffic:** Use show commands to view traffic statistics and ensure that high-priority traffic is being properly prioritized:

```bash
Router# show policy-map interface gigabitEthernet 0/1
```

Implementing QoS in a network is essential for ensuring that critical applications receive the necessary resources to function effectively. By classifying, marking, policing, and shaping traffic, you can guarantee that voice, video, and other latency-sensitive services get the required bandwidth even during times of congestion. Through this lab, we've demonstrated how to set up QoS policies on Cisco routers, apply them to interfaces, and verify their effectiveness.

Next Steps

Once you have successfully configured basic QoS for traffic prioritization, you can explore more advanced QoS techniques, such as integrating with routing protocols like OSPF or BGP for QoS-aware routing, configuring QoS in a multi-service network environment, or combining QoS with application performance monitoring for end-to-end traffic optimization.

Lab 3: Setting Up Cisco SD-WAN

Software-Defined Wide Area Networking (SD-WAN) is revolutionizing how organizations manage their wide area networks. By decoupling the network control plane from the underlying hardware and leveraging cloud-based management, SD-WAN simplifies WAN architecture, enhances flexibility, and provides significant cost savings. Cisco's SD-WAN solution, built on its Viptela platform, offers a robust and scalable approach to managing branch offices, remote sites, and cloud applications with enhanced security and optimal performance.

In this lab, we will walk through the process of setting up Cisco SD-WAN, focusing on key steps such as deployment, configuration, and management using Cisco's vManage platform.

PRACTICE LABS AND CONFIGURATION EXAMPLES

Overview of Cisco SD-WAN

Cisco SD-WAN simplifies branch and remote-office connectivity by dynamically adjusting the path used by traffic based on real-time network conditions, such as congestion or failures. It integrates application-aware routing, end-to-end encryption, centralized policy management, and cloud optimization features, which makes it a powerful tool for organizations with distributed networks.

Key features of Cisco SD-WAN include:

- **Centralized Management:** All configuration and management are centralized through Cisco vManage.
- **Application-Aware Routing:** Ensures that critical applications like VoIP or video conferences get priority over less important traffic.
- **Secure Direct Internet Access (DIA):** Enables secure internet traffic routing directly from branch offices, bypassing the traditional backhaul to headquarters.
- **Cloud Integration:** Seamlessly integrates with cloud providers such as AWS, Microsoft Azure, and Google Cloud to optimize traffic between remote locations and cloud applications.

Steps to Set Up Cisco SD-WAN

In this lab, you will learn how to set up and configure a Cisco SD-WAN network for a small-to-medium-sized organization with several branch offices and headquarters.

Step 1: Prerequisites

Before proceeding, ensure you have the following prerequisites:

- Cisco SD-WAN vEdge routers or compatible devices.
- Cisco vManage (for centralized control and configuration).
- Cisco vSmart (for centralized control plane).
- Cisco vBond (for secure device authentication and authorization).

- Access to the SD-WAN cloud management console.
- Internet connectivity for remote devices.

Ensure that your environment is ready for SD-WAN deployment with appropriate licenses in place for all Cisco SD-WAN components (vSmart, vBond, vManage).

Step 2: Deploy Cisco vBond

The first step in setting up Cisco SD-WAN is to deploy and configure the Cisco vBond, which is responsible for authenticating and authorizing devices in the SD-WAN network.

Install Cisco vBond:

- Deploy Cisco vBond in your data center or cloud environment.
- Ensure that vBond has public IP addresses (this is required for remote devices to connect over the internet).

Configure Cisco vBond:

- Log in to the vBond web interface and configure basic settings such as management IP addresses, authentication credentials, and secure access details.
- Once vBond is configured, it will serve as the secure gateway for all device connections in the SD-WAN network.

Enable Device Registration:

- During the vBond configuration, you will also configure device registration, which allows vBond to securely validate and authorize all devices (vEdge routers, vSmart, and vManage) in the network.

Step 3: Deploy Cisco vSmart

Cisco vSmart is responsible for the centralized control plane, distributing policies, route advertisements, and application rules to all routers in

PRACTICE LABS AND CONFIGURATION EXAMPLES

the network.

Install Cisco vSmart:

- Deploy Cisco vSmart in your data center or cloud environment.
- Like vBond, ensure vSmart has access to the internet to establish secure communications with the SD-WAN routers.

Configure Cisco vSmart:

- Log in to the vSmart web interface and configure necessary settings, including the control plane certificate, authentication, and routing protocols.

Establish Connectivity:

- vSmart should establish secure communication with the vBond. This ensures that vSmart will start managing device configurations and enforcing policies across the SD-WAN fabric.

Step 4: Deploy vEdge Routers

Cisco vEdge routers serve as the data plane of the SD-WAN solution, routing traffic between branch offices, headquarters, and cloud services.

Install vEdge Routers:

- Deploy Cisco vEdge routers at each branch office and headquarters.
- Ensure that vEdge routers are connected to the internet and can communicate with the vBond and vSmart through secure tunnels.

Configure vEdge Routers:

- Power on the vEdge routers and connect them to the internet. Once connected, they will automatically initiate communication with vBond for authentication.

- vBond will authenticate the routers and establish an encrypted control plane between them and vSmart.
- Once authenticated, the routers will automatically download configuration policies from vSmart.

Step 5: Configure Centralized Policy Management Using vManage

Cisco vManage is the centralized platform for configuration, monitoring, and management of the SD-WAN network. It allows administrators to define policies, monitor network performance, and troubleshoot issues.

Install Cisco vManage:

- Install and configure Cisco vManage, either on-premises or in the cloud, based on your organization's preferences.

Configure Network Topology:

- Using the vManage interface, create and configure the network topology. This includes defining the various devices (routers, WAN connections, cloud applications), creating site information, and establishing network zones.
- The vManage dashboard allows you to visualize the entire SD-WAN network, providing insight into device status, application performance, and traffic flow.

Create Policies:

- Define application-aware routing policies using vManage. For example, you can create policies that prioritize traffic from certain applications, such as VoIP or video conferencing, while ensuring that less critical applications (like email or web browsing) receive lower priority.
- Use QoS policies to define bandwidth limits and latency thresholds,

ensuring that critical traffic flows smoothly even during periods of network congestion.

Example:

yaml

```
Application Policy:
- VoIP: Highest priority, low latency
- Video: High priority, medium latency
- Web Browsing: Low priority, acceptable latency
```

Configure Secure Direct Internet Access (DIA):

- Configure secure DIA for branch offices, allowing them to route internet-bound traffic directly from the branch to the cloud, bypassing the corporate data center. This can significantly improve performance and reduce backhaul traffic.

Monitor Network Performance:

- Use vManage's real-time monitoring tools to check network performance metrics such as latency, packet loss, and jitter. You can also check the health of the SD-WAN network by viewing the status of various devices, tunnels, and links.

Step 6: Test Connectivity and Verify Configuration

Once the configuration is complete, it's time to test and verify that the SD-WAN setup is working as intended.

Verify Device Registration:

- Ensure that all routers have successfully registered with vBond and are able to establish tunnels with vSmart. You can use the following command on the router:

```sql
show sdwan control connection
```

Test Routing and Traffic Flows:

- Test routing between branch offices, headquarters, and cloud resources. Use standard ping or traceroute commands to ensure connectivity is functional and that traffic is flowing according to defined policies.

Monitor the SD-WAN Dashboard:

- Using the vManage dashboard, confirm that the correct application traffic is being routed according to the policies. For example, VoIP traffic should be prioritized and should show lower latency compared to web browsing traffic.

Verify Security:

- Ensure that traffic is encrypted and secured using the built-in IPsec tunnels between SD-WAN devices. Use monitoring tools to verify that no unsecured traffic is traversing the network.

In this lab, you have successfully set up Cisco SD-WAN, deployed key SD-WAN components (vBond, vSmart, vManage), and configured the network for dynamic and secure traffic routing. You have learned how to create and apply policies for application-aware routing, direct internet access, and secure cloud connectivity. This SD-WAN setup provides centralized control, improved WAN performance, enhanced security, and increased flexibility for managing branch offices, remote sites, and cloud applications.

Next Steps

After completing the basic SD-WAN deployment, you can explore more advanced features such as integrating SD-WAN with cloud-based applications (AWS, Azure), adding security features like firewall integration, or optimizing traffic with WAN optimization techniques. You may also configure centralized logging and monitoring to maintain a real-time view of network performance and troubleshoot any issues that arise.

Lab 4: Configuring Redundancy with HSRP

In any enterprise network, network availability and fault tolerance are critical to ensure business continuity. One of the key technologies to achieve high availability in a network is **redundancy**. Redundant network designs ensure that if one device or path fails, traffic can be rerouted through an alternative path or device without causing a disruption in service. One of the most widely used methods for achieving this in a router environment is **HSRP** (Hot Standby Router Protocol).

HSRP is a Cisco proprietary protocol that provides high network availability by configuring two or more routers to act as a virtual router. In this lab, we will walk through the steps required to configure HSRP for redundancy in a Cisco network.

Understanding HSRP

HSRP allows you to configure a group of routers to work together to present a single virtual gateway to the network. The group of routers is called an **HSRP group**, and within this group, one router assumes the role of the **Active Router**, while another router takes on the role of the **Standby Router**. The Active Router is responsible for forwarding traffic, and the Standby Router takes over if the Active Router fails.

Key HSRP Terms:

- **Virtual Router IP (VIP):** This is the IP address that clients use as their default gateway. The VIP is shared by the Active and Standby routers, so if one fails, the other can take over seamlessly.
- **Active Router:** The router that forwards traffic on behalf of the HSRP group. It holds the VIP and is responsible for handling the traffic until it fails.
- **Standby Router:** The router that waits in the background, monitoring the Active Router. If the Active Router fails, the Standby Router takes over the forwarding role.
- **Hello Timer:** The timer used by routers to communicate their availability. If a router does not hear from the Active Router within a specified time, it assumes it has failed and triggers a failover.
- **HSRP Priority:** This is a value used to determine which router is preferred to become the Active Router. The higher the priority, the more likely it is to become the Active Router.

Steps to Configure HSRP

In this lab, we will configure a basic HSRP setup between two Cisco routers. We will configure the routers to share a single virtual IP address and ensure that traffic can still flow even if one router fails.

Step 1: Initial Setup
Physical Setup:

- You will need at least two routers for this lab (Router1 and Router2).
- Each router will be connected to the same LAN segment, which will serve as the virtual gateway for the devices in the network.

Network Configuration:

- Assign IP addresses to the interfaces on both routers that will be participating in the HSRP group. The network segment should be a standard /24 subnet.

Example Configuration:

- Router1 (R1): GigabitEthernet0/0 IP address: 192.168.1.1/24
- Router2 (R2): GigabitEthernet0/0 IP address: 192.168.1.2/24
- Virtual IP (VIP): 192.168.1.254/24 (This will be the default gateway for client devices)

Step 2: Configuring HSRP on Router1 (Active Router)
Enter Global Configuration Mode:

```arduino
Router1# configure terminal
```

Enter Interface Configuration Mode for the Interface Participating in HSRP:

```arduino
Router1(config)# interface gigabitethernet 0/0
```

Enable HSRP on the Interface:
Use the following commands to configure HSRP on the interface and assign the Virtual IP address:

```arduino
```

```
Router1(config-if)# standby 1 ip 192.168.1.254
Router1(config-if)# standby 1 priority 110
Router1(config-if)# standby 1 preempt
```

- **standby 1 ip 192.168.1.254**: Configures the virtual IP address.
- **standby 1 priority 110**: Sets the priority for this router. The default priority is 100, and higher values make the router more likely to become the Active Router.
- **standby 1 preempt**: Allows Router1 to preemptively take over as the Active Router if it becomes available after a failure.

Exit the Interface Configuration Mode:

arduino

```
Router1(config-if)# exit
```

Step 3: Configuring HSRP on Router2 (Standby Router)
   Enter Global Configuration Mode:

arduino

```
Router2# configure terminal
```

Enter Interface Configuration Mode for the Interface Participating in HSRP:

arduino

```
Router2(config)# interface gigabitethernet 0/0
```

Enable HSRP on the Interface and Configure the Virtual IP Address:

```arduino
Router2(config-if)# standby 1 ip 192.168.1.254
Router2(config-if)# standby 1 priority 100
Router2(config-if)# standby 1 preempt
```

- **standby 1 priority 100**: Sets the priority of Router2. By default, the priority is 100, so Router2 will only become the Active Router if Router1 fails or is unavailable.

Exit the Interface Configuration Mode:

```arduino
Router2(config-if)# exit
```

Step 4: Verifying HSRP Configuration

Once both routers are configured, it's important to verify that HSRP is functioning as expected.

Check HSRP Status on Router1: Use the following command to verify the status of HSRP:

```arduino
Router1# show standby
```

Output should indicate that Router1 is the Active Router with the virtual IP 192.168.1.254 assigned.

Check HSRP Status on Router2: On Router2, run the same command to verify its status as the Standby Router:

```
arduino

Router2# show standby
```

The output should indicate that Router2 is in standby mode, waiting to take over if Router1 fails.

Test Connectivity to Virtual IP: From a client device on the network, set the default gateway to 192.168.1.254 (the virtual IP). Test connectivity by pinging the virtual IP:

```
makefile

C:\> ping 192.168.1.254
```

If HSRP is correctly configured, the ping should succeed, indicating that the virtual router is operational.

Step 5: Testing Failover

To ensure that HSRP failover works as expected, you can simulate a failure of the Active Router (Router1).

Shut Down the Active Router Interface: On Router1, shut down the interface:

```
arduino

Router1# configure terminal
Router1(config)# interface gigabitethernet 0/0
Router1(config-if)# shutdown
```

This action will force Router2 to take over as the Active Router.

Verify Failover: On Router2, run the show standby command again to verify that Router2 has taken over as the Active Router:

PRACTICE LABS AND CONFIGURATION EXAMPLES

```arduino
Router2# show standby
```

Router2 should now show as the Active Router for the HSRP group.

Test Connectivity Again: From the client device, ping 192.168.1.254 again to verify that traffic is being routed through Router2.

Restore Router1 and Verify Preemption: Bring Router1 back up:

```arduino
Router1# configure terminal
Router1(config)# interface gigabitethernet 0/0
Router1(config-if)# no shutdown
```

1. If you have configured **preemption** on Router1, it will automatically take back the Active Router role once it's up and running again.
2. Verify the status on both routers to ensure that Router1 has resumed the Active Router role.

In this lab, you have configured HSRP for redundancy in a Cisco network, ensuring high availability and fault tolerance in the routing environment. By setting up an Active and Standby router pair, with a shared virtual IP address, you've ensured that traffic can seamlessly be rerouted in the event of a router failure. HSRP is a critical tool for ensuring that networks remain resilient and available, providing business continuity even in the face of device failures.

This configuration is ideal for environments where uptime is critical, such as in data centers, enterprise offices, and cloud environments. With HSRP, organizations can achieve a fault-tolerant and highly available network, helping to prevent service disruptions and maintain consistent application performance.

Lab 5: Implementing Security Policies with Cisco ASA

In modern network architectures, security is paramount, especially at the network perimeter where traffic enters and leaves the network. **Cisco ASA (Adaptive Security Appliance)** is a comprehensive security solution that provides firewall protection, VPN support, and intrusion prevention for both small and large enterprises. This lab focuses on configuring and implementing security policies using Cisco ASA, ensuring that your network is protected from external threats and that internal traffic is properly managed.

In this lab, we will go through the steps to configure a Cisco ASA firewall, define security policies, and set up basic rules to protect the network.

Understanding Cisco ASA Security Policies

The Cisco ASA provides a wide range of security features, including:

- **Stateful Inspection**: This monitors the state of active connections and ensures that traffic conforms to security policies.
- **Access Control Lists (ACLs)**: ACLs are used to permit or deny traffic based on specified criteria, such as source and destination IP, protocol, or port.
- **NAT (Network Address Translation)**: ASA devices provide dynamic or static NAT to hide internal IP addresses from external users.
- **VPN Support**: Cisco ASA also provides secure remote access via IPSec and SSL VPNs.
- **Intrusion Prevention**: ASA devices can detect and prevent attacks on the network through predefined signatures and anomaly detection.

PRACTICE LABS AND CONFIGURATION EXAMPLES

This lab will focus primarily on configuring ACLs, defining NAT policies, and setting up basic firewall rules to secure the network perimeter.

Lab Setup

Network Setup:

- **Cisco ASA Device**: This will serve as the firewall between the internal network and the external network (e.g., the Internet).
- **Internal Network (Inside)**: The inside network is the trusted network where internal resources (e.g., servers, workstations) reside.
- **External Network (Outside)**: The outside network typically refers to the Internet or an untrusted network.
- **DMZ (Optional)**: A demilitarized zone (DMZ) can be configured for publicly accessible services, such as web servers.

Network Diagram:

- **Inside Network (192.168.1.0/24)**
- **DMZ Network (192.168.2.0/24)**
- **Outside Network (Internet, 203.0.113.0/24)**
- **ASA Firewall (192.168.1.1 on Inside, 203.0.113.2 on Outside)**

Step 1: Initial Configuration of the Cisco ASA

Access the ASA Device: Connect to the Cisco ASA device via console cable, SSH, or through the ASDM (Adaptive Security Device Manager) GUI.

- Using the CLI:

```
arduino

ASA# configure terminal
```

Assign IP Addresses to the Interfaces: Assign the appropriate IP addresses to the ASA's interfaces, which connect to the Inside, Outside, and DMZ networks.

```scss
ASA(config)# interface ethernet0/0
ASA(config-if)# nameif outside
ASA(config-if)# security-level 0
ASA(config-if)# ip address 203.0.113.2 255.255.255.0
ASA(config-if)# no shutdown
ASA(config-if)# exit
ASA(config)# interface ethernet0/1
ASA(config-if)# nameif inside
ASA(config-if)# security-level 100
ASA(config-if)# ip address 192.168.1.1 255.255.255.0
ASA(config-if)# no shutdown
ASA(config-if)# exit
```

Enable Routing: Ensure that routing between the ASA's interfaces is properly configured for internal and external communication.

```scss
ASA(config)# route inside 0.0.0.0 0.0.0.0 192.168.1.1
ASA(config)# route outside 0.0.0.0 0.0.0.0 203.0.113.1
```

Step 2: Configuring Basic Access Control Policies

1. **Define Security Levels**: In Cisco ASA, interfaces are assigned security levels (ranging from 0 to 100). The inside network typically has a higher security level than the outside network. By default,

traffic from a higher-security interface to a lower-security interface is allowed, while traffic from lower to higher security is denied.
2. **Create an Access Control List (ACL) for Traffic Filtering**: An ACL is used to define which traffic is allowed to pass through the firewall. In this example, we will allow internal users to access the Internet but block external access to the internal network.

- Create an ACL for outbound traffic (Inside to Outside):

```arduino
ASA(config)# access-list outside_access_in extended permit ip 192.168.1.0 255.255.255.0 any
```

- Apply the ACL to the Inside interface:

```scss
ASA(config)# access-group outside_access_in in interface inside
```

- Create an ACL to block inbound traffic (Outside to Inside):

```arduino
ASA(config)# access-list outside_access_in extended deny ip any 192.168.1.0 255.255.255.0
```

This will allow all traffic from the Inside network to the Outside network (Internet), while blocking any direct access from the Outside network to the Inside network.

Verify the ACL Configuration: Use the following command to verify the applied ACLs:

```arduino
ASA# show access-list
```

Step 3: Configuring NAT (Network Address Translation)

NAT is commonly used in firewalls to modify the source or destination IP addresses of packets to ensure proper routing and to hide internal IP addresses from the outside world.

Configure Dynamic NAT: To allow internal devices to access the Internet using the public IP of the ASA's Outside interface, configure dynamic NAT.

```scss
ASA(config)# object network obj_any
ASA(config-network-object)# subnet 192.168.1.0 255.255.255.0
ASA(config)# nat (inside,outside) dynamic interface
```

In this configuration, the ASA will translate the internal IP addresses to the ASA's own Outside interface IP (203.0.113.2) when accessing the Internet.

Configure Static NAT (Optional for DMZ Services): If you want to make a specific internal server accessible from the outside, configure static NAT to map a public IP to an internal IP.

Example: If a web server in the DMZ (192.168.2.10) needs to be accessed from the Outside network, configure static NAT:

PRACTICE LABS AND CONFIGURATION EXAMPLES

```scss
ASA(config)# object network obj_web_server
ASA(config-network-object)# host 192.168.2.10
ASA(config)# nat (outside,dmz) static 203.0.113.3
```

Now, external clients can access the web server using the IP address 203.0.113.3.

Step 4: Configuring VPN (Optional)

If remote access is required, you can configure a VPN (either IPsec or SSL). For simplicity, let's configure a basic **Remote Access VPN** using SSL.

Create a VPN Pool for Clients:

```scss
ASA(config)# ip local pool vpn_pool 192.168.100.1-192.168.100.50 mask 255.255.255.0
```

Configure SSL VPN:

```arduino
ASA(config)# webvpn
ASA(config-webvpn)# enable outside
ASA(config-webvpn)# ssl-dh min 2048
ASA(config-webvpn)# anyconnect image disk0:/anyconnect-win-4.x.x-k9.pkg 1
ASA(config-webvpn)# anyconnect enable
```

Assign VPN Group Policy:

```
arduino

ASA(config)# group-policy VPN_Policy internal
ASA(config)# group-policy VPN_Policy attributes
ASA(config-group-policy)# vpn-tunnel-protocol ssl-client
```

Step 5: Verifying and Monitoring Security Policies

Once the configuration is completed, it is important to verify the security policy implementation and ensure that the network is secure.

Show Access Control Lists: Verify the applied ACLs:

```
arduino

ASA# show access-list
```

Check NAT Rules: Verify that NAT is correctly configured:

```
arduino

ASA# show nat
```

Check Active Connections: Monitor the active connections to ensure that traffic is flowing correctly:

```
arduino

ASA# show conn
```

Monitor VPN Status: If a VPN is configured, monitor the status of VPN connections:

```
arduino

ASA# show vpn-sessiondb
```

In this lab, you have configured basic security policies on a Cisco ASA firewall, including access control lists (ACLs), NAT, and VPN settings. This setup ensures that your internal network is secured from external threats, and your internal users can access the Internet without exposing internal systems to the outside world.

Cisco ASA firewalls offer robust security features, and with the appropriate configurations, you can tailor your security policies to meet your specific network requirements, whether it's for a small business or an enterprise network.

Lab 6: Automating Network Configurations with Cisco DNA Center

In today's fast-paced IT environments, network automation has become essential for reducing operational complexity, enhancing network agility, and ensuring consistency across network devices. **Cisco DNA Center** is a powerful platform that allows network administrators to automate and manage network configurations through a centralized dashboard. It leverages the principles of Software-Defined Networking (SDN) to simplify network provisioning, troubleshooting, and policy enforcement.

In this lab, we will focus on configuring network devices, deploying templates, and automating network policies using **Cisco DNA Center**, offering practical insights into how automation can streamline network management.

Understanding Cisco DNA Center

Cisco DNA Center is an intent-based networking platform that automates the provisioning, monitoring, and management of network infrastructure. It enables a proactive approach to network management, ensuring that network policies are automatically applied to devices across the network, improving both efficiency and security.

Key features of Cisco DNA Center include:

- **Network Automation**: Automates configuration deployment, compliance checks, and device provisioning.
- **Policy-Based Management**: Ensures that security and access policies are consistently enforced across the network.
- **Analytics and Insights**: Provides deep visibility into network performance and health, using machine learning to identify trends and potential issues.
- **Zero-Touch Provisioning**: Facilitates plug-and-play deployment of network devices without manual configuration.
- **Intent-Based Networking**: Translates business intent into network policies that are automatically implemented on the devices.

Lab Setup

Devices to be Managed:

- **Cisco Catalyst Switches** (e.g., Catalyst 9300 Series)
- **Cisco Access Points** (e.g., Cisco Aironet or Meraki APs)
- **Cisco Routers** (e.g., Cisco ISR or ASR routers)

Cisco DNA Center:

- A pre-configured **Cisco DNA Center** server is needed to orchestrate the automation process. For this lab, assume that the Cisco DNA

Center instance is already set up and can communicate with the network devices.

Network Topology:

- **Core Network**: Cisco Catalyst switches and routers.
- **Access Layer**: Cisco access points and endpoint devices.
- **Network Services**: DHCP, DNS, and other necessary network services.

Step 1: Initializing Cisco DNA Center

Access the Cisco DNA Center Dashboard: To begin the automation process, log into the Cisco DNA Center interface using a web browser.

- **URL**: https://<DNAC_IP_Address>
- **Username/Password**: Use your admin credentials provided by the network administrator.

Verify Device Reachability: Once logged in, navigate to the **Provision** tab and ensure that Cisco DNA Center is able to communicate with the network devices. Devices such as switches, routers, and access points should be listed under the "Devices" section.

Add Network Devices to DNA Center: To automate the configuration, the devices must first be added to the DNA Center inventory.

- Go to **Provision → Devices → Add Devices**.
- Select the device type (e.g., Switch, Router, Wireless Access Point).
- Input the device's IP address, SNMP credentials, and login credentials for the device.
- Select **Add** to register the device with Cisco DNA Center.

Step 2: Configuring Templates for Device Provisioning

Create a Device Template: Device templates allow for bulk configuration of multiple devices based on predefined settings. In this step, we'll create a configuration template for a Cisco Catalyst switch.

- Navigate to **Design → Network Profiles → Device Templates**.
- Click on **Create Template** and select the **Device Type** (e.g., Cisco Catalyst 9300).
- Specify the desired configuration settings for the switch, such as interface VLANs, IP addressing, and routing protocols.

Use the Template to Configure Multiple Devices: Once the template is created, it can be applied to multiple devices for uniform configuration. This ensures consistency across the network.

- Go to **Provision → Devices** and select the devices you want to configure.
- Apply the created device template to all selected devices by choosing **Provision → Push Configuration**.

Verify Configuration: After applying the template, verify the configuration on the devices to ensure that the settings have been successfully applied. You can use the **CLI** or the device's web interface to check the configuration.

```arduino
show running-config
```

The configuration should reflect the settings from the DNA Center template.

PRACTICE LABS AND CONFIGURATION EXAMPLES

Step 3: Automating Policy Enforcement

Create a Network Policy: Policies are essential for maintaining network security and operational consistency. Using Cisco DNA Center, you can define policies for access control, Quality of Service (QoS), and security.

- Navigate to **Policy → Intent**.
- Define the policies you want to enforce. For example:
- **Access Control**: Define roles for devices based on their function (e.g., user, server, admin).
- **QoS**: Create rules for traffic prioritization based on application type (e.g., VoIP, video conferencing).

Apply Policies to Devices: Once the policies are defined, apply them across your network devices to ensure that network traffic is managed according to the specified criteria.

- In the **Policy** section, assign policies to devices, users, or specific network segments.
- For example, apply a **QoS policy** to ensure that video conferencing traffic is prioritized over regular web browsing traffic.

Verify Policy Application: To confirm that policies have been applied successfully, use the **Monitoring** tab to check policy enforcement status across your network. You can view the compliance status of each device and identify any policy violations.

- Go to **Monitor → Network Insights**.
- Check if the configured policies are being enforced, and if there are any exceptions or issues.

Step 4: Zero-Touch Provisioning (ZTP) for New Devices

One of the most powerful features of Cisco DNA Center is its ability to provide **Zero-Touch Provisioning (ZTP)**. This feature automates the process of deploying new devices into the network with minimal manual intervention.

Enable ZTP on Cisco DNA Center:

- Navigate to **Provision → Devices** and click on **Add Device**.
- Select **ZTP Mode** and specify the device's model and the image version required for provisioning.
- The new device should automatically reach out to Cisco DNA Center for configuration upon bootup.

Deploy a New Switch Using ZTP:

- When a new Cisco Catalyst switch is physically connected to the network, it will automatically communicate with Cisco DNA Center.
- Cisco DNA Center will apply the correct configurations and policies to the device, ensuring it is properly provisioned and ready for use without manual intervention.

Step 5: Monitoring and Troubleshooting

Monitor Device Health and Performance: Once the network is configured and running, you can monitor the performance of your devices using Cisco DNA Center's built-in monitoring tools.

- Go to **Monitor → Devices** to see real-time status and health metrics for each device.
- Cisco DNA Center provides a dashboard with visibility into device performance, interface status, and network health.

Troubleshoot Network Issues: In case of network issues, Cisco DNA Center provides troubleshooting tools to identify and resolve problems quickly. For instance:

- Use **Network Insights** to detect abnormal traffic patterns or device behavior.
- Check the **Event Logs** for errors or issues that might be impacting network performance.

In this lab, you have learned how to automate network configurations and policy enforcement using **Cisco DNA Center**, a powerful tool that enhances the efficiency, security, and scalability of enterprise networks. By creating device templates, applying policies, and using Zero-Touch Provisioning, you can drastically reduce the time and effort needed for network management while ensuring consistent, secure, and compliant configurations across your devices.

Cisco DNA Center is a cornerstone of modern network management, enabling organizations to embrace **intent-based networking** and **automation** to deliver faster, more reliable, and more secure network experiences. By integrating this automation into your workflows, you can ensure that your network evolves in alignment with the business goals, improving operational efficiency and user satisfaction.

Troubleshooting and Network Optimization

Troubleshooting Network Connectivity Issues

Network connectivity issues are a common challenge in modern IT environments, affecting everything from individual user devices to entire data centers. Efficient troubleshooting is essential for minimizing downtime, maintaining business operations, and ensuring a smooth user experience. Identifying the root causes of connectivity problems requires a structured approach, methodical diagnostic tools, and a solid understanding of the underlying network architecture.

This section will provide a comprehensive guide on how to troubleshoot network connectivity issues systematically. We will cover common causes of connectivity problems, introduce a troubleshooting methodology, and explore key tools and techniques used to diagnose and resolve issues in enterprise networks.

1. Understanding Network Connectivity Issues

Before diving into troubleshooting, it is essential to understand the different types of network connectivity problems that can occur. Connectivity issues typically fall into one of the following categories:

a) **Physical Layer Issues**

- **Cable Problems**: Faulty, damaged, or loose cables (Ethernet, fiber optic, etc.) can disrupt connectivity.
- **Hardware Failures**: Network interface cards (NICs), switches, routers, or other physical devices can malfunction or fail.
- **Port Configuration Issues**: Incorrect port settings or inactive ports can cause devices to be unable to connect.

b) **Link Layer (Data Link) Issues**

- **MAC Address Conflicts**: Two devices on the same network having identical MAC addresses can cause issues with data packet delivery.
- **Ethernet Frame Errors**: Collisions, bad frames, or excessive retransmissions can impact connectivity.
- **Switch Configuration Problems**: VLAN misconfigurations, port security violations, and spanning tree loops can create disruptions.

c) **Network Layer (Layer 3) Issues**

- **IP Addressing Conflicts**: Duplicate IP addresses or incorrect subnetting can cause devices to be unreachable or to conflict with other network nodes.
- **Routing Problems**: Misconfigured static routes, issues with routing protocols, or broken routes can prevent packets from reaching their destination.
- **Subnetting Errors**: Incorrect subnetting can isolate devices within the same physical network, making them unable to communicate.

d) **Transport Layer Issues**

- **Port Blocking**: Firewalls or security policies may block specific ports required for applications (e.g., HTTP, SSH).
- **TCP/IP Stack Issues**: Misconfigured TCP/IP settings (e.g., incorrect DNS, gateway, or subnet mask) can prevent communication.

e) **Application Layer Issues**

- **DNS Resolution Problems**: Incorrect DNS server settings can prevent devices from resolving domain names to IP addresses.
- **Application Configuration**: Some connectivity problems are application-specific, such as misconfigured VPN clients or incorrect database connection strings.

2. Troubleshooting Methodology

To troubleshoot network connectivity issues effectively, you should follow a systematic process that helps isolate the root cause. The following methodology will guide you through this process.

a) **Step 1: Gather Information**

Before jumping into diagnostics, gather as much information as possible about the problem:

- **User Reports**: Are other users experiencing similar issues, or is it isolated to one device?
- **Time of Occurrence**: When did the issue start? Is it intermittent or constant?
- **Network Impact**: Is it affecting the entire network or just specific devices or segments?

Use network monitoring tools like **Cisco Prime Infrastructure** or **SolarWinds Network Performance Monitor** to get real-time insights into your network health. These tools can show affected devices, interfaces, or segments.

b) **Step 2: Identify the Scope**

- **Check for Local or Global Issue**: Determine if the issue is localized to a specific device or user, or if it's affecting the broader network (e.g., entire VLAN or subnet).

- **Ping Tests**: Run basic **ping tests** from the affected device to various network components (e.g., gateway, DNS server, and other devices) to narrow down the scope of the issue.

c) **Step 3: Physical Layer Verification**

- **Check Hardware Connections**: Ensure all physical connections (e.g., cables, ports, devices) are intact. Look for any loose cables, damaged ports, or disconnected equipment.
- **Replace Faulty Components**: If any cables or NICs are suspected to be faulty, replace them to see if the issue resolves.

Use **link lights** on switches and routers to check if devices are physically connected. If there are no link lights, the issue is likely related to physical connections.

d) **Step 4: Link Layer Verification**

- **Verify MAC Addresses**: Check for MAC address conflicts by using commands like show mac address-table (on Cisco switches) to identify and resolve any conflicts.
- **Check VLAN Configuration**: Ensure that the device is in the correct VLAN and that VLANs are properly configured across the switches. Use show vlan brief on switches to verify VLAN membership.
- **Verify Port Status**: Use commands like show interface status to check the operational state of switch ports. Look for any errors or down interfaces.

e) **Step 5: Network Layer Verification**

- **Check IP Addressing**: Ensure that the device has a valid IP address, correct subnet mask, and default gateway.
- Use ipconfig (Windows) or ifconfig/ip a (Linux) to verify IP configuration on the local device.

- Check for duplicate IP addresses using ping <IP> or network management tools.
- **Routing Configuration**: Verify routing tables on routers and layer-3 switches to ensure routes to the destination network are correct. Use show ip route on Cisco devices.
- **Traceroute**: Use **traceroute** or **tracert** to track the path packets take across the network. This can help pinpoint where the issue occurs.

f) **Step 6: Transport Layer Verification**

- **Check for Port Blockage**: Use tools like telnet or nc (Netcat) to test connectivity on specific ports. For example:

```php
telnet <hostname> <port>
```

- If the connection fails, it's likely that the port is blocked by a firewall or device security policy.
- **Verify TCP/IP Stack**: On the local device, verify that the TCP/IP stack is correctly configured and that there are no issues with the DNS, DHCP, or gateway settings.

g) **Step 7: Application Layer Verification**

- **DNS Resolution**: If the issue is related to accessing websites or services by name, check DNS resolution using nslookup or dig.
- Verify that the DNS servers are correctly configured and reachable.
- Test the DNS server's response times and status.
- **Check Application Logs**: If the issue is application-specific (e.g., a web server, database, or VPN client), review application logs for

errors or misconfigurations.

h) **Step 8: Perform Network Diagnostics**

Use advanced network diagnostic tools to gather more detailed data:

- **Wireshark**: Use packet capturing software like Wireshark to capture network traffic and analyze it for anomalies, retransmissions, or errors.
- **Cisco's Embedded Event Manager (EEM)**: Cisco devices offer EEM to automate network troubleshooting and alerts. Use EEM to configure triggers and actions based on network events.

i) **Step 9: Resolve and Test**

After identifying the cause of the issue:

- **Apply Fixes**: Apply necessary configuration changes (e.g., update IP addresses, change routing settings, replace faulty cables).
- **Test the Solution**: After making changes, test the connection to ensure the issue is resolved. Ping test, traceroute, and application access should work as expected.

3. Common Tools for Network Troubleshooting

- **Ping**: Used to check connectivity between devices on a network. It can help identify if a device is reachable.
- **Traceroute**: Helps determine the path that packets take to reach their destination, identifying where delays or failures occur.
- **Show Commands**: Use commands like show ip route, show interfaces, show vlan brief, and show mac address-table to inspect router and switch configurations.
- **Wireshark**: Captures and analyzes packets to diagnose detailed connectivity issues.
- **Cisco DNA Center**: A centralized management tool that provides

insights into network health and performance, simplifying troubleshooting.

4. Preventative Measures and Best Practices

Once the connectivity issue is resolved, it is essential to take steps to prevent future occurrences:

- **Network Documentation**: Maintain up-to-date network diagrams and documentation to help identify configuration issues quickly.
- **Automate Monitoring**: Use network monitoring tools to alert administrators of potential issues before they become critical.
- **Regular Software Updates**: Ensure that firmware and software on network devices are kept up to date to avoid bugs and vulnerabilities.
- **Implement Redundancy**: Design networks with redundancy (e.g., redundant links, devices) to ensure high availability and minimize the impact of future issues.

Troubleshooting network connectivity issues requires a structured approach, from gathering information and identifying the scope of the problem to using the right diagnostic tools. By systematically analyzing the physical, link, network, transport, and application layers, network administrators can efficiently pinpoint and resolve connectivity issues.

A proactive approach—combining real-time monitoring, regular updates, and network documentation—will help minimize the occurrence of connectivity problems in the future, ensuring that enterprise networks remain reliable and performant.

TROUBLESHOOTING AND NETWORK OPTIMIZATION

Optimizing Network Performance with Cisco Tools

Optimizing network performance is critical for ensuring that applications, services, and communication across your infrastructure run efficiently. With Cisco's suite of tools, network administrators can monitor, analyze, and fine-tune network configurations to maintain high performance, minimize downtime, and ensure that user and business needs are met. Cisco provides a comprehensive set of solutions for proactive network management, real-time diagnostics, and optimization.

In this section, we will cover some of the key Cisco tools and techniques for optimizing network performance, including how they work, their benefits, and best practices for using them.

1. Cisco DNA Center

Cisco Digital Network Architecture (DNA) Center is an advanced platform that simplifies the management of Cisco networks while optimizing performance, security, and automation. It allows network administrators to manage, monitor, and optimize the entire network infrastructure from a single, centralized interface. DNA Center integrates with other Cisco tools and devices to provide end-to-end visibility and performance insights.

Key Features and Benefits of Cisco DNA Center for Optimization:

- **Automated Network Assurance**: DNA Center automatically ensures that network configurations and policies are adhered to, continuously optimizing network performance without requiring manual intervention.
- **Performance Monitoring and Analytics**: It collects detailed metrics about network performance, such as traffic patterns, device utilization, and application performance, allowing administrators to identify bottlenecks and inefficiencies.
- **Intelligent Path Control**: Cisco DNA Center uses machine learning

algorithms to intelligently optimize network paths, ensuring that traffic flows through the most efficient route based on real-time performance data.
- **Software-Defined Access (SDA)**: By integrating Cisco DNA with SDA, administrators can dynamically allocate network resources and optimize bandwidth utilization based on traffic needs.
- **Segmentation and Security**: It enables fine-grained network segmentation to prevent performance degradation from unnecessary traffic, optimizing security and performance at the same time.

2. Cisco Prime Infrastructure

Cisco Prime Infrastructure provides comprehensive lifecycle management of your Cisco network, offering end-to-end visibility, monitoring, and troubleshooting capabilities. It helps streamline the management of devices across the network, while optimizing their performance through data-driven insights.

Key Features and Benefits of Cisco Prime Infrastructure:

- **Network Performance Monitoring**: Cisco Prime monitors network performance and provides historical data and trends on traffic usage, device performance, and application health, helping to identify underutilized or overburdened network segments.
- **Troubleshooting and Diagnostics**: Integrated diagnostic tools help administrators quickly identify performance bottlenecks and pinpoint network issues, reducing troubleshooting time and minimizing downtime.
- **Capacity Planning**: Prime Infrastructure offers insights into future network demands, helping organizations forecast capacity needs and optimize resource allocation.
- **Configuration Automation**: By automating configuration changes and policy enforcement, Prime Infrastructure reduces human error and ensures that the network remains aligned with best practices,

optimizing overall performance.

3. Cisco Network Assurance Engine (NAE)

Cisco Network Assurance Engine (NAE) uses AI-driven analytics to ensure that network configurations and policies are being correctly enforced and optimized. NAE provides visibility into the network's health and performance by continuously analyzing the entire network and providing proactive insights.

Key Features and Benefits of Cisco NAE:

- **Proactive Monitoring**: NAE constantly monitors the network's health, identifying potential issues before they affect performance.
- **Predictive Analytics**: The tool can predict performance issues, such as network congestion or failure, based on historical data and patterns.
- **Policy Compliance**: It ensures that network configurations adhere to organizational policies, helping to optimize security and performance simultaneously.
- **Network Visibility**: NAE provides deep insights into how the network is functioning, making it easier to pinpoint performance issues and optimize device configurations.

4. Cisco ThousandEyes

Cisco ThousandEyes is a powerful network performance monitoring and visibility tool that offers end-to-end visibility into the performance of your network, applications, and services. It provides real-time insights into how applications and network infrastructure interact, ensuring that you can optimize performance for end users.

Key Features and Benefits of Cisco ThousandEyes:

- **Application and Network Visibility**: ThousandEyes monitors both

the network and application layer, giving administrators detailed data on how network issues affect application performance, such as delays, packet loss, and round-trip time.
- **Cloud and WAN Monitoring**: It offers visibility into cloud environments, remote offices, and WAN connections, allowing you to optimize traffic between on-premises and cloud infrastructure.
- **Alerting and Reporting**: ThousandEyes provides custom alerts and reports, so you can proactively address performance degradation, optimizing both the network and user experience.
- **Root Cause Analysis**: By identifying the root cause of network and application issues, ThousandEyes helps minimize downtime and improve performance by guiding corrective actions.

5. Cisco Prime and Meraki Dashboard Integration

Cisco Meraki provides a cloud-based solution for managing networking hardware like routers, switches, and wireless access points. With the **Meraki Dashboard**, administrators can manage their networks, monitor performance, and optimize operations with real-time data insights.

Key Features and Benefits of Cisco Meraki for Performance Optimization:

- **Cloud-Based Management**: Meraki provides an intuitive cloud interface that allows administrators to manage the entire network infrastructure remotely, optimizing network performance without the need for on-site presence.
- **Real-Time Analytics**: The dashboard offers insights into network traffic, device performance, and wireless health, helping administrators make data-driven decisions to improve performance.
- **Automatic Firmware Updates**: Meraki devices can automatically update their firmware, ensuring that they are always running the latest software optimized for performance and security.
- **Load Balancing**: The Meraki Dashboard allows for load balancing of

TROUBLESHOOTING AND NETWORK OPTIMIZATION

wireless access points, ensuring that traffic is distributed efficiently across devices and preventing network congestion.

6. Cisco NetFlow and sFlow for Traffic Analysis

Cisco NetFlow and **sFlow** are network traffic monitoring technologies that provide deep insights into network performance. Both tools enable administrators to track traffic flows in real time and optimize network performance by identifying bandwidth usage patterns, top talkers, and traffic anomalies.

Key Features and Benefits of Cisco NetFlow and sFlow:

- **Traffic Flow Analysis**: NetFlow and sFlow enable administrators to analyze traffic at a granular level, understanding which devices, applications, or users are consuming the most bandwidth.
- **Anomaly Detection**: These tools can help identify unusual traffic patterns, such as sudden spikes in traffic, which can indicate potential performance problems or security threats.
- **Usage Reporting**: By generating traffic reports, administrators can optimize the allocation of network resources based on actual usage patterns, improving efficiency and reducing waste.
- **Scalability**: Both NetFlow and sFlow are designed to scale across large networks, enabling monitoring and analysis even in complex, distributed environments.

7. Cisco Application Visibility and Control (AVC)

Cisco Application Visibility and Control (AVC) is a feature set that provides application-level monitoring and optimization for both on-premises and cloud-based applications. AVC allows administrators to understand the impact of network performance on application behavior, enabling the optimization of application traffic.

Key Features and Benefits of Cisco AVC:

- **Application Performance Metrics**: AVC provides real-time application performance metrics, helping to identify delays, jitter, and packet loss that impact end-user experience.
- **Application-Aware Routing**: With AVC, you can implement intelligent routing policies based on application performance data, ensuring that critical applications get the necessary bandwidth while optimizing less-sensitive traffic.
- **End-to-End Visibility**: AVC delivers insights into application performance from the network edge to the data center, helping you optimize application delivery and improve user experience.

8. Best Practices for Network Optimization with Cisco Tools

To optimize network performance effectively, administrators should follow a set of best practices when using Cisco tools:

- **Continuous Monitoring**: Use tools like Cisco DNA Center, Prime Infrastructure, and ThousandEyes to continuously monitor the health of your network. Set up alerts to proactively address potential issues.
- **Automate Routine Tasks**: Leverage the automation features in Cisco DNA Center and Meraki Dashboard to reduce manual errors and optimize configuration management.
- **Performance Baselines**: Establish performance baselines for your network. Compare current performance data against these baselines to identify performance degradation over time.
- **Traffic Shaping and Load Balancing**: Implement traffic shaping and load balancing to ensure that critical applications get the necessary bandwidth, preventing congestion and ensuring efficient use of available resources.
- **Network Segmentation**: Use VLANs and QoS policies to segment traffic, ensuring that sensitive or high-priority applications get optimal resources while preventing low-priority traffic from consuming bandwidth.

- **Keep Software Up-to-Date**: Regularly update software and firmware to ensure that your network devices and tools are running the latest features, optimizations, and security patches.

Optimizing network performance is essential for delivering a high-quality user experience, supporting business operations, and maintaining a robust IT infrastructure. With Cisco's suite of tools, network administrators can proactively monitor, analyze, and optimize their networks to ensure peak performance. By utilizing platforms like Cisco DNA Center, Prime Infrastructure, ThousandEyes, and Meraki, network managers can address issues in real-time, predict future network behavior, and maintain the scalability and reliability of their network.

Using Cisco's Prime Infrastructure for Monitoring and Troubleshooting

Cisco **Prime Infrastructure** is a comprehensive solution for managing, monitoring, and troubleshooting network infrastructure. It integrates various network management functions—such as performance monitoring, configuration management, and troubleshooting—into a single, intuitive platform. Prime Infrastructure offers a unified view of your network, making it easier to detect issues, optimize network performance, and ensure smooth operation across devices and applications.

In this section, we will explore how Cisco Prime Infrastructure can be used for effective monitoring, diagnostics, and troubleshooting of network issues, ensuring that the network is optimized for performance and reliability.

1. Centralized Network Monitoring

Prime Infrastructure provides a **centralized dashboard** that allows network administrators to monitor the entire network from a single interface. This visibility enables administrators to track key performance metrics, identify potential issues, and gain insights into network health.

Key Features for Monitoring:

- **Device and Interface Health**: Prime Infrastructure tracks the health of network devices (routers, switches, access points) and interfaces, providing real-time information about their status, availability, and performance.
- **Performance Metrics**: It collects metrics such as bandwidth utilization, packet loss, latency, and CPU/memory usage, allowing administrators to monitor the network's overall performance and identify performance degradation.
- **Event Correlation**: Prime Infrastructure aggregates events from different network components and correlates them, helping administrators identify the root cause of network problems. The event viewer filters through alarms, presenting them in a manageable format.
- **Historical Data and Trend Analysis**: By capturing historical data on traffic patterns, device performance, and other key metrics, Prime Infrastructure helps administrators identify trends and make data-driven decisions to optimize performance.

2. Fault Detection and Diagnostics

Prime Infrastructure includes advanced **fault management** capabilities, allowing network administrators to quickly identify and troubleshoot network issues. The system uses event correlation, automated alerts, and detailed diagnostics to ensure that problems are resolved promptly before they affect network performance or user experience.

Key Fault Detection Features:

TROUBLESHOOTING AND NETWORK OPTIMIZATION

- **Automatic Fault Detection**: Prime Infrastructure uses SNMP polling and other monitoring protocols to automatically detect device failures, interface issues, and connectivity problems. It continuously scans the network and alerts administrators about any significant events or errors.
- **Root Cause Analysis**: By correlating events from different network devices, Prime Infrastructure helps administrators perform root cause analysis (RCA). For example, if a network outage occurs, it will highlight which devices, interfaces, or links are involved in the failure and provide diagnostic information to pinpoint the source of the problem.
- **Performance Degradation Alerts**: Prime Infrastructure can generate alerts based on thresholds such as high CPU usage, excessive bandwidth utilization, or network congestion. These proactive alerts allow administrators to take action before the issue affects end-users.

3. Proactive Troubleshooting with Cisco Prime

Prime Infrastructure offers several tools that enable **proactive troubleshooting** of network issues. These tools help administrators identify, isolate, and resolve network problems more effectively.

Key Troubleshooting Tools:

- **Interactive Topology View**: Prime Infrastructure provides an interactive map or topology view of the network, showing the status of devices, connections, and links. This view allows administrators to identify failed links, misconfigured devices, or potential points of failure quickly.
- **Network Health Score**: The health score feature aggregates device health, traffic, and error statistics to provide an overall network health score. If a device or network segment has a poor health score, it indicates an area that may need troubleshooting or optimization.
- **Device and Interface Logs**: Prime Infrastructure collects and

displays logs from network devices. These logs provide detailed information on device status, configuration changes, and interface errors, which can help administrators troubleshoot and diagnose issues.

- **Packet Capture**: Cisco Prime integrates with **Cisco Packet Capture** to analyze traffic at the packet level. Packet capture is essential for diagnosing complex issues such as latency, packet loss, and application performance problems.
- **Configuration Auditing**: Prime Infrastructure can also monitor configuration changes across the network. It detects configuration inconsistencies and helps prevent network issues caused by manual misconfigurations.

4. *Configuration Management and Optimization*

Prime Infrastructure is not only useful for monitoring and troubleshooting but also plays a vital role in **configuration management**. With its ability to manage network devices centrally, administrators can make configuration changes and push policies across multiple devices simultaneously, streamlining network management.

Configuration Management Features:

- **Configuration Backup and Restore**: Prime Infrastructure provides centralized backup of network device configurations, ensuring that configurations can be restored quickly in the event of a failure or misconfiguration. This ensures business continuity and minimizes downtime during recovery.
- **Compliance and Best Practices**: The platform allows administrators to ensure that devices adhere to industry best practices and compliance requirements. By using predefined templates and configuration policies, Prime Infrastructure helps maintain consistency across network devices and prevent performance or security issues caused by improper configurations.

- **Change Management**: Prime Infrastructure tracks and logs configuration changes, making it easy to audit and roll back to previous configurations if necessary. It also allows for policy-based enforcement to ensure that devices are correctly configured according to network standards.

5. Performance Optimization with Cisco Prime

Prime Infrastructure offers several features aimed at **optimizing network performance** by fine-tuning configurations and ensuring that devices operate efficiently. Performance optimization ensures that the network remains responsive and capable of handling increasing demands, especially in enterprise environments.

Key Performance Optimization Features:

- **Traffic Analysis**: Cisco Prime collects traffic data from all layers of the network. By analyzing this data, administrators can identify network congestion, latency, or packet loss, allowing them to take corrective actions such as adjusting QoS policies or rerouting traffic.
- **QoS Configuration and Monitoring**: Prime Infrastructure supports Quality of Service (QoS) policies, allowing administrators to prioritize traffic based on business requirements. It helps in configuring QoS for time-sensitive applications like VoIP and video conferencing, ensuring that high-priority traffic gets the necessary bandwidth.
- **Application Monitoring**: Prime Infrastructure offers application-level visibility to ensure that business-critical applications are running efficiently across the network. By monitoring application performance, administrators can address any issues that affect application delivery.
- **Bandwidth Utilization Reports**: Prime Infrastructure generates reports on bandwidth utilization across the network, helping to identify underutilized or overburdened links. This information

enables administrators to optimize network resources and improve overall performance.

6. Customizable Reporting and Alerts

Prime Infrastructure provides **customizable reports and alerts** that help network administrators stay informed about the network's health, performance, and any issues that arise. These reports can be scheduled, automated, and shared with stakeholders to ensure transparency and better decision-making.

Key Reporting and Alerting Features:

- **Customizable Dashboards**: Prime Infrastructure offers customizable dashboards that display key performance indicators (KPIs), health metrics, and traffic data in real-time. These dashboards provide an at-a-glance overview of the network's status and performance.
- **Scheduled Reports**: Administrators can schedule reports on network performance, traffic utilization, device health, and more. These reports can be generated in various formats (PDF, Excel, etc.) for distribution to stakeholders.
- **Event Notification and Alerts**: Prime Infrastructure can send real-time alerts about network events via email, SNMP traps, or other notification methods. Alerts are fully customizable to ensure that administrators are notified of only the most critical events.

7. Integration with Other Cisco Tools

Prime Infrastructure integrates seamlessly with other Cisco solutions, providing a unified approach to network monitoring and troubleshooting. Some integrations include:

- **Cisco DNA Center**: For enhanced automation and network assurance.

TROUBLESHOOTING AND NETWORK OPTIMIZATION

- **Cisco Stealthwatch**: For advanced network monitoring and security analytics.
- **Cisco Meraki**: For managing Meraki devices alongside Cisco infrastructure in a single interface.
- **Cisco Umbrella**: For integrating cloud security with network management.

These integrations ensure that Cisco Prime Infrastructure provides comprehensive visibility and control over the entire network, from the data center to the edge, optimizing both performance and security.

Cisco Prime Infrastructure is an invaluable tool for network administrators looking to optimize, monitor, and troubleshoot their network infrastructure. By offering a unified view of network performance, proactive troubleshooting tools, and configuration management capabilities, it allows administrators to ensure that the network operates efficiently and meets organizational needs. With its real-time diagnostics, performance optimization features, and seamless integration with other Cisco solutions, Prime Infrastructure is an essential part of any Cisco-powered network, driving both operational efficiency and network reliability.

Troubleshooting SD-WAN and Cloud Networking Issues

As businesses increasingly adopt **Software-Defined Wide Area Networking (SD-WAN)** and move applications to the **cloud**, network architects and administrators face new challenges in troubleshooting. SD-WAN and cloud networking introduce complexities such as dynamic paths, multi-cloud environments, and advanced traffic management, making traditional troubleshooting techniques insufficient. This section explores the common issues in SD-WAN and cloud networking, and how to effectively troubleshoot these environments using Cisco's advanced tools and methodologies.

1. Common SD-WAN Issues

SD-WAN allows for more efficient routing of traffic by leveraging multiple WAN connections such as MPLS, broadband internet, and LTE. While SD-WAN enhances network flexibility and agility, it introduces new challenges, particularly around configuration, performance, and path selection.

a. Connectivity and Path Issues

SD-WAN dynamically selects the best path based on real-time metrics, such as latency, jitter, and packet loss. However, issues such as **incorrect path selection**, **unreliable links**, or **link flaps** can occur.

Troubleshooting Steps:

- **Check Path Utilization and Performance Metrics**: Use Cisco's SD-WAN dashboard to view the health of all WAN links and identify whether the wrong path is being selected due to poor link performance.
- **Verify SLA Policies**: SD-WAN uses SLA-based routing policies. Ensure that your SLA thresholds are appropriately configured for latency, jitter, and packet loss to avoid improper path selection.
- **Link Failover Analysis**: In case of path failure, SD-WAN should reroute traffic to the next best path. Ensure failover configurations are correct and review logs for any issues with automatic failover or manual configurations.

b. Overlay and Underlay Network Issues

SD-WAN creates an **overlay network** that runs over an **underlay network** (MPLS, broadband, etc.). Troubleshooting overlay issues often requires understanding both layers.

TROUBLESHOOTING AND NETWORK OPTIMIZATION

Troubleshooting Steps:

- **Verify Underlay Connectivity**: Before focusing on the SD-WAN overlay, ensure the underlay network (physical connections and routing) is stable. Use Cisco tools like **Cisco vManage** to verify the status of the underlay.
- **Check Tunnel Establishment**: SD-WAN relies on secure tunnels between devices. Check for any tunnel establishment issues in the **vSmart** or **vBond** components, and verify tunnel configuration consistency across all devices.
- **Monitor Control Plane Traffic**: Verify that the control plane (managed by **vSmart**) is properly distributing routing information and policies to SD-WAN devices. Control plane connectivity issues may prevent traffic routing from being updated correctly.

c. **QoS and Traffic Prioritization Problems**

SD-WAN enables dynamic path selection based on traffic types, but **incorrect QoS configurations** or **misconfigured traffic prioritization** can impact application performance.

Troubleshooting Steps:

- **Check QoS Configurations**: Review the QoS settings applied on SD-WAN routers and ensure they match application requirements. Use tools like **Cisco vManage** to verify policies and traffic markings.
- **Monitor Application Performance**: Identify whether specific applications are being deprioritized or experiencing delays by using **Cisco vAnalytics** or **NetFlow** data.
- **Traffic Flow Analysis**: Review the traffic flow, including any potential **bottlenecks** or suboptimal routing decisions that may be causing poor performance. Look for dropped packets or congestion in the network paths.

2. Common Cloud Networking Issues

Cloud networking brings several benefits but also creates challenges related to **hybrid cloud environments**, **multi-cloud architectures**, and the **complexity of cloud-to-on-premises connectivity**.

a. **Connectivity Issues Between On-Premises and Cloud Environments**

Many organizations use a hybrid cloud strategy where resources are distributed across on-premises data centers and public clouds. Issues with cloud connectivity can arise from **VPN tunneling, poor bandwidth utilization**, or **misconfigured routing**.

Troubleshooting Steps:

- **Check VPN Connectivity**: Ensure that the VPN tunnels between on-premises and the cloud are properly established and the required routes are being advertised correctly. Use tools like **Cisco Cloud Services Router (CSR)** to monitor the VPN connections.
- **Cloud Peering and Transit Gateways**: Verify that your cloud networking service (e.g., AWS Direct Connect, Azure ExpressRoute) is correctly set up and that routing between different cloud regions or on-premises networks is functioning.
- **Review Cloud Gateway Configurations**: For multi-cloud environments, ensure that the cloud gateways (e.g., **Azure VPN Gateway, AWS Transit Gateway**) are properly configured and route traffic correctly between clouds and on-premises networks.

b. **Latency and Performance Degradation in Cloud Applications**

Cloud-hosted applications rely heavily on the underlying network. **Increased latency, packet loss**, and **jitter** can degrade application performance, especially for real-time applications like VoIP or video conferencing.

Troubleshooting Steps:

- **End-to-End Latency Measurement**: Use **Cisco vAnalytics** to monitor latency between the user and cloud-hosted applications. If latency is higher than expected, identify whether the bottleneck is occurring in the SD-WAN layer, the cloud provider's network, or the last-mile connectivity.
- **Bandwidth Utilization Monitoring**: Analyze whether network congestion is limiting the available bandwidth for cloud applications. This can be done through **Cisco Meraki Dashboard** or **Cisco Prime Infrastructure**, which helps monitor bandwidth consumption and identify potential areas of congestion.
- **Cloud Optimization**: Use tools like **Cisco SD-WAN** and **Cisco CloudCenter** to optimize cloud connectivity and ensure that traffic is routed over the best path. Implementing cloud-native optimization techniques, such as caching and compression, can also reduce performance degradation.

c. **Security Misconfigurations in Cloud Networks**

Cloud networks are more exposed to security risks due to their public nature. Issues such as **misconfigured firewalls, lack of encryption**, and **poor segmentation** can create vulnerabilities.

Troubleshooting Steps:

- **Cloud Security Audit**: Perform a security audit using **Cisco Umbrella** or **Cisco Meraki Security Appliance** to ensure proper segmentation between cloud workloads and on-premises systems. Review access control lists (ACLs) and firewall rules.
- **Encryption Protocols**: Verify that encryption is applied end-to-end for both data in transit and at rest in cloud environments. Ensure that **SSL/TLS**, **IPsec**, or other encryption mechanisms are being used to secure communications.
- **Access Control and Identity Management**: Ensure that proper identity and access management (IAM) policies are in place in the cloud environment. Review **IAM roles** and **permissions** to ensure

only authorized entities can access resources.

3. Cloud Monitoring and Management Tools

Cisco offers several tools to help troubleshoot cloud networking issues:

- **Cisco vManage**: The SD-WAN management platform offers real-time monitoring, troubleshooting, and diagnostics for SD-WAN deployments. It can be used to track tunnel status, view performance metrics, and analyze SLA violations.
- **Cisco vAnalytics**: This tool provides **network performance analytics** for SD-WAN and cloud environments. It can generate insights into network latency, application performance, and identify bottlenecks that affect cloud connectivity.
- **Cisco DNA Center**: Cisco's **DNA Center** provides automated network management, assurance, and monitoring, which is crucial when dealing with cloud and SD-WAN infrastructure. It offers real-time troubleshooting capabilities and analytics for cloud-connected devices.
- **Cisco Umbrella**: A cloud-native security platform that integrates with SD-WAN to provide visibility and security for cloud-bound traffic, helping to troubleshoot and mitigate security issues in cloud environments.

4. Best Practices for SD-WAN and Cloud Networking Troubleshooting

- **Establish Baselines**: Define performance baselines for SD-WAN and cloud traffic. Having an established benchmark will help detect anomalies and avoid false alarms when troubleshooting.
- **Proactive Monitoring**: Implement **continuous monitoring** using Cisco's SD-WAN and cloud tools to ensure that network issues are detected and addressed before they affect users.

- **Regular Updates and Patches**: Keep SD-WAN and cloud networking devices up-to-date with the latest firmware, patches, and software releases to avoid issues caused by outdated configurations or vulnerabilities.
- **Collaborate Across Teams**: Troubleshooting SD-WAN and cloud networking often requires collaboration between networking, cloud, and security teams. Establish clear communication channels and incident response workflows to speed up the diagnosis and resolution of complex issues.

Troubleshooting SD-WAN and cloud networking issues requires specialized knowledge of the technologies and tools involved. By leveraging Cisco's robust suite of management, monitoring, and diagnostic tools such as **vManage**, **vAnalytics**, and **Prime Infrastructure**, administrators can quickly detect, diagnose, and resolve network issues. Proactive monitoring, performance tuning, and security best practices will help ensure that SD-WAN and cloud environments deliver optimal performance, availability, and security.

Best Practices for Ongoing Network Health and Optimization

Ensuring ongoing network health and optimization is vital for maintaining a reliable, efficient, and secure network. In today's fast-paced, interconnected world, where businesses rely on high-performance networks for daily operations, regular monitoring, proactive maintenance, and continuous optimization are key to preventing disruptions and ensuring a positive user experience. This section explores best practices for maintaining and optimizing network health in dynamic environments like **SD-WAN**, **cloud networking**, and traditional enterprise networks.

1. Regular Network Monitoring and Performance Metrics

Continuous monitoring is foundational to maintaining optimal network health. It helps detect issues early, prevents outages, and ensures that performance meets organizational expectations.

Best Practices:

- **Implement Proactive Monitoring**: Utilize tools like **Cisco Prime Infrastructure**, **Cisco DNA Center**, and **Cisco vManage** to monitor network health in real-time. These tools offer visibility into network performance, device status, and traffic flow.
- **Monitor Key Metrics**: Track essential performance indicators (KPIs) such as **latency**, **jitter**, **packet loss**, and **bandwidth utilization** to ensure that applications and services are performing optimally. Use **Cisco vAnalytics** to gain deep insights into network traffic patterns and performance trends.
- **Set Up Alerts and Thresholds**: Define performance thresholds and set up alerts for key metrics like high latency or unusual packet loss. Alerts can be integrated with automated workflows to quickly resolve issues before they impact users.

- **Analyze Traffic Patterns**: Regularly review traffic patterns to identify bandwidth hogs, bottlenecks, and underutilized links. This helps prevent congestion and ensures that resources are being used efficiently.

2. Capacity Planning and Scaling

Network capacity planning is a critical aspect of ongoing network optimization. As organizations grow and add new users, devices, and applications, the network must be able to scale to meet increasing demands without degrading performance.

Best Practices:

- **Forecast Network Growth**: Use data from monitoring tools and performance analytics to forecast future network needs. Plan for traffic increases, device expansions, and higher service-level expectations by understanding both current and future demands.
- **Scale with SD-WAN**: In SD-WAN environments, scale by adding additional devices and network paths as needed. SD-WAN allows organizations to easily add new branches or locations without significant reconfiguration.
- **Optimize Resource Allocation**: Make sure bandwidth is appropriately allocated to high-priority applications. Use **Quality of Service (QoS)** policies to ensure critical applications (e.g., VoIP, video conferencing) receive the necessary resources.
- **Consider Cloud Expansion**: For organizations leveraging the cloud, ensure that cloud networking and services can scale with demand. Use **Cisco CloudCenter** or cloud-native network optimization techniques to optimize cloud resource allocation.

3. Redundancy and Fault Tolerance

Designing for redundancy and fault tolerance is essential to maintaining network availability. Networks should be able to recover quickly from failures or disruptions to minimize downtime and ensure continuous service.

Best Practices:

- **Design for High Availability**: Use **High Availability (HA)** architectures with redundant network devices and paths to eliminate single points of failure. For example, employ **HSRP**, **VRRP**, or **GLBP** for router redundancy in Cisco environments.
- **Dual-Path Connectivity**: Ensure that network devices are connected to at least two separate physical paths (e.g., internet links or MPLS) for failover. This ensures that if one link fails, traffic can be rerouted over the second link without interruption.
- **Monitor Redundancy Status**: Regularly verify the health of redundant components using monitoring tools. Make sure that failover processes are working correctly and that redundant systems are not sitting idle.
- **Test Failover Scenarios**: Periodically test failover mechanisms to ensure they function correctly when needed. Schedule maintenance windows to simulate failures and evaluate the performance of recovery processes.

4. Regular Security Audits and Updates

Network security is an ongoing process. Security threats evolve continuously, and networks need to stay protected from vulnerabilities. Regular security audits and updates are crucial for maintaining a secure network environment.

Best Practices:

- **Conduct Security Audits**: Perform periodic security audits to identify and address vulnerabilities. Use tools like **Cisco Umbrella** for cloud security and **Cisco ASA** or **Cisco Firepower** for network perimeter security.
- **Keep Systems Updated**: Regularly apply firmware updates and patches to all networking devices, including routers, switches, firewalls, and SD-WAN appliances. Automation tools like **Cisco DNA Center** can streamline patch management and firmware upgrades across large networks.
- **Enforce Access Control**: Regularly review and update user and device access control policies. Use **Cisco Identity Services Engine (ISE)** for role-based access control (RBAC) to enforce least-privilege access policies and prevent unauthorized access.
- **Implement Zero Trust**: Adopt a **Zero Trust Architecture** for network security, which assumes that no one (internal or external) should be trusted by default. Use **Cisco TrustSec** and **ISE** to enforce network segmentation and least-privilege access.

5. Traffic Optimization and Load Balancing

Network optimization goes beyond performance monitoring—it also involves ensuring that traffic is efficiently routed and distributed. Optimizing network traffic flow can improve user experience and reduce latency for critical applications.

Best Practices:

- **Implement Traffic Shaping**: Use **traffic shaping** techniques to smooth traffic flows and ensure bandwidth is distributed effectively. This can help manage burst traffic and prevent network congestion during peak times.
- **Leverage Load Balancing**: For large-scale applications or data centers, implement **load balancing** mechanisms to distribute traffic evenly across multiple servers or network links. Cisco's **Application**

Centric Infrastructure (ACI) and **Cisco SD-WAN** provide robust load-balancing features that help optimize resource utilization.
- **Use WAN Optimization**: For WAN traffic, employ **WAN optimization** tools that reduce latency and bandwidth consumption for remote users. Cisco's **WAN Optimization Solution** and **Meraki SD-WAN** offer advanced features like **compression**, **caching**, and **protocol acceleration** to improve performance.

6. *Automation and Orchestration for Efficiency*

Automation reduces human error and ensures network configurations remain consistent across large environments. It also increases operational efficiency and agility, which is critical in maintaining and optimizing network health.

Best Practices:

- **Automate Network Configuration**: Use **Cisco DNA Center** or **Cisco ACI** to automate network configuration, provisioning, and management. This reduces manual intervention, speeds up deployment, and ensures consistency in network configurations.
- **Implement Network Orchestration**: Orchestrate network workflows to automate routine tasks such as device provisioning, software updates, and policy enforcement. **Cisco SD-WAN** and **Cisco Meraki** allow for simplified orchestration that can be integrated with IT operations.
- **Use AI/ML for Automation**: Leverage **AI/ML** tools to optimize network performance. Cisco's **DNA Center** and **vAnalytics** use machine learning to analyze historical data, predict traffic spikes, and automatically adjust network resources to ensure optimal performance.

7. User Experience and Application Performance Monitoring

In today's business landscape, ensuring that end-users have a positive experience when using networked applications is essential. Monitoring application performance ensures that users are getting the expected service levels, regardless of where they are or how they connect to the network.

Best Practices:

- **Monitor Application Performance**: Use **Cisco AppDynamics** and **Cisco vAnalytics** to gain insights into application performance and user experience. Monitor metrics like application response times, latency, and transaction volumes to ensure optimal performance.
- **Define Service-Level Agreements (SLAs)**: Set clear **SLAs** for critical applications and services to ensure that performance standards are met. Use **Cisco SD-WAN** or **ACI** to enforce these SLAs across the network.
- **Test User Experience**: Regularly test end-user experience by simulating real-world traffic patterns. Ensure that network configurations, including load balancing and QoS, are optimized to meet application performance expectations.

8. Documentation and Knowledge Management

Effective network documentation and knowledge management are essential for ongoing network health and troubleshooting. Detailed records help teams quickly identify configurations, understand network topology, and resolve issues more efficiently.

Best Practices:

- **Maintain Accurate Network Maps**: Use tools like **Cisco Prime Infrastructure** or **Cisco DNA Center** to create and maintain updated network topology maps. These maps provide a visual

representation of the entire network and help troubleshoot issues faster.
- **Document Configuration Changes**: Keep detailed logs of all configuration changes and updates. Use version control for configurations to ensure that changes can be tracked and rolled back when necessary.
- **Centralized Knowledge Base**: Create a knowledge base that contains troubleshooting guides, best practices, and network policies. This allows team members to access solutions quickly and reduces downtime during incidents.

Ongoing network health and optimization require continuous effort and the use of best practices in monitoring, maintenance, and performance management. By implementing proactive monitoring, automating tasks, ensuring redundancy, and continuously optimizing traffic flow, organizations can ensure their networks remain robust, scalable, and secure. Leveraging advanced Cisco tools and technologies like **Cisco DNA Center**, **Cisco SD-WAN**, and **Cisco vAnalytics** can streamline network operations, improve performance, and reduce operational costs, ensuring that the network can scale effectively with growing business demands.

Appendices

A: Glossary of Key Terms

A comprehensive glossary of key terms is essential for understanding the various concepts and technologies discussed in network architecture, design, and management, especially in the context of Cisco solutions. This glossary defines the most important terms related to networking, security, cloud technologies, SD-WAN, and other critical areas in the modern network landscape.

1. **Access Control List (ACL)**

A set of rules used to control the flow of network traffic, typically implemented on routers and switches. ACLs can be used to permit or deny traffic based on IP addresses, subnets, and protocols. They are often used for security purposes to filter traffic at network boundaries.

2. **Application Centric Infrastructure (ACI)**

A Cisco solution for data center networking that provides a holistic, software-defined approach to managing and automating network operations. ACI integrates hardware and software with application policies, making networks more agile and efficient.

3. **Bandwidth**

The maximum rate of data transfer across a network or communication channel, typically measured in bits per second (bps). Bandwidth determines the amount of data that can be transmitted at once, affecting network speed and capacity.

4. Cloud Access Security Broker (CASB)

A security policy enforcement point that sits between cloud service users and cloud service providers to enforce corporate security policies. CASBs can provide visibility into cloud activity, data encryption, and threat protection for cloud services.

5. Cloud-Managed Networking

A model where network devices (e.g., routers, switches, and access points) are centrally managed and monitored from the cloud. Cisco Meraki is an example of a cloud-managed network solution that provides ease of use and scalability through cloud-based dashboards.

6. Content Delivery Network (CDN)

A geographically distributed network of servers designed to deliver content (e.g., web pages, videos, and software) to users based on their geographic location. CDNs improve performance by caching content closer to the user, reducing latency and load times.

7. Data Center Interconnect (DCI)

The technology that enables the connection of multiple data centers, facilitating seamless data transfer, load balancing, and redundancy. DCI solutions are crucial for organizations with distributed data centers across various locations.

8. Deep Packet Inspection (DPI)

A form of data inspection where the entire content of data packets (rather than just the header) is analyzed for security, performance, or policy enforcement purposes. DPI is often used in firewalls, intrusion detection/prevention systems (IDS/IPS), and QoS applications.

9. Edge Computing

A decentralized computing model in which data processing and storage are done closer to the location where it is needed, such as on devices at the edge of the network, rather than in a centralized cloud data center. This approach reduces latency and bandwidth usage.

10. Ethernet

A widely used local area network (LAN) technology for connecting devices, typically using coaxial cables or fiber optics. Ethernet is based on a system of packet-switching and operates on both wired and wireless networks.

11. **Firewall**

A network security device that monitors and controls incoming and outgoing network traffic based on predetermined security rules. Firewalls can be hardware-based or software-based, providing a critical barrier between trusted internal networks and untrusted external networks.

12. **Global Load Balancing**

The process of distributing traffic across multiple geographically dispersed data centers or servers to ensure the best performance and redundancy for end users. It helps balance the load on different network paths to avoid congestion and ensure high availability.

13. **High Availability (HA)**

A design principle aimed at ensuring that systems and services are continuously operational and available with minimal downtime. HA architectures typically use redundancy, failover mechanisms, and load balancing to prevent service interruptions.

14. **Intrusion Prevention System (IPS)**

A network security technology that monitors network traffic for malicious activity or violations of policy and takes action to block or prevent such activities in real time. IPS is often integrated with firewalls and other security devices to enhance overall network defense.

15. **Latency**

The time it takes for data to travel from the source to the destination, usually measured in milliseconds (ms). Low latency is crucial for applications like VoIP and video conferencing, where delays can negatively affect user experience.

16. **Load Balancer**

A device or software application that distributes network traffic across multiple servers or resources to ensure optimal resource utilization, minimize response time, and prevent server overload. It helps ensure high availability and redundancy.

17. **Network Access Control (NAC)**

A security solution that enforces policies to control device access to a network based on security posture, user identity, and compliance with security policies. Cisco ISE (Identity Services Engine) is a popular NAC solution.

18. **Network Function Virtualization (NFV)**

A technology that virtualizes network services traditionally run on proprietary hardware. NFV allows the deployment of network functions (such as firewalls, load balancers, and routers) as software instances on virtual machines, improving flexibility and scalability.

19. **Network Monitoring**

The process of continuously observing network activity and performance to ensure that it is operating correctly. Network monitoring tools can alert administrators to issues like performance degradation, congestion, or security threats.

20. **Network Segmentation**

The practice of dividing a network into smaller, isolated segments to improve security and performance. Segmentation limits the spread of malicious traffic, provides better control over traffic flows, and optimizes network resources.

21. **Next-Generation Firewall (NGFW)**

A type of firewall that goes beyond traditional packet filtering by incorporating additional features such as application awareness, intrusion prevention, advanced malware detection, and content filtering.

22. **SD-WAN (Software-Defined Wide Area Network)**

A network architecture that uses software to control the management and operation of WAN connections. SD-WAN decouples network hardware from control functions, enabling dynamic, policy-based traffic routing and cost-effective management of wide-area networks.

23. **Software-Defined Networking (SDN)**

A network architecture that allows for centralized control of network resources through software applications. SDN separates the control plane from the data plane, enabling more flexible, programmable, and automated network management.

APPENDICES

24. **Quality of Service (QoS)**

A network management technique that prioritizes traffic based on its type, importance, or bandwidth requirements. QoS is used to ensure that critical applications (such as voice or video conferencing) receive priority over less-sensitive traffic (such as file downloads).

25. **Virtual Local Area Network (VLAN)**

A logical subdivision of a physical network that groups devices into a broadcast domain regardless of their physical location. VLANs help reduce broadcast traffic and improve network security by isolating sensitive data.

26. **Virtual Private Network (VPN)**

A secure, encrypted connection between a user or device and a network over the public internet. VPNs are commonly used to securely connect remote users or branch offices to a corporate network.

27. **WAN Optimization**

A set of techniques used to improve the speed and performance of a Wide Area Network (WAN). WAN optimization involves compressing data, caching frequently accessed data, and optimizing protocols to reduce latency and increase throughput.

28. **Zero Trust Security Model**

A security approach that assumes no one—whether inside or outside the network—should be trusted by default. It enforces strict verification of every device, user, and application attempting to access network resources, ensuring robust access control and reducing potential attack surfaces.

This glossary provides a foundational understanding of key networking terms and technologies, helping users navigate the complexities of modern network design and management. Whether for deploying **SD-WAN**, ensuring **security**, or optimizing **network performance**, familiarity with these terms is essential for network administrators and architects to build, maintain, and scale robust, efficient, and secure networks.

B: Cisco Certifications and Further Learning Resources

Cisco certifications are a valuable asset for network professionals looking to deepen their expertise in network architecture, management, and security. Cisco's certification programs provide structured learning paths, hands-on experience, and recognition of skill development, offering opportunities for both beginners and experienced professionals. In addition to Cisco certifications, a range of learning resources—online courses, study materials, and community forums—can support continuous learning in the fast-evolving world of network technology.

Cisco Certifications

Cisco offers a broad range of certifications aimed at various skill levels, from foundational knowledge to advanced networking concepts. Cisco certifications are globally recognized and are often considered a benchmark for network professionals.

Cisco Certified Technician (CCT)

- **Overview**: The CCT certification is an entry-level certification for network professionals looking to develop hands-on skills in network troubleshooting and support.
- **Focus Areas**: Basic network troubleshooting, Cisco router and switch maintenance, and understanding networking fundamentals.
- **Target Audience**: Those new to networking or technicians responsible for supporting Cisco devices in enterprise environments.

Cisco Certified Network Associate (CCNA)

- **Overview**: The CCNA certification provides a solid foundation in networking, covering key concepts such as IP addressing, routing and switching, and network security.
- **Focus Areas**: Routing and switching, IP addressing, network security, and the fundamentals of wireless networking and automation.

- **Target Audience**: Entry-level network engineers or technicians seeking to understand basic network design, configuration, and management.

Cisco Certified Network Professional (CCNP)

- **Overview**: CCNP is an intermediate-level certification designed for network engineers who wish to advance their knowledge in areas such as routing, switching, and troubleshooting in complex enterprise networks.
- **Focus Areas**: Advanced routing and switching, network security, VPNs, and performance optimization.
- **Target Audience**: Network engineers or IT professionals with foundational knowledge looking to enhance their skill set in areas such as routing, security, and network design.

Cisco Certified Internetwork Expert (CCIE)

- **Overview**: The CCIE certification is one of the most prestigious network certifications available, aimed at network professionals with expert-level knowledge in networking and network troubleshooting.
- **Focus Areas**: Deep networking knowledge and skills in areas like routing, switching, network security, and design. Specializations include enterprise infrastructure, security, data center, and service provider.
- **Target Audience**: Experienced network engineers or architects who want to demonstrate their ability to design, implement, and troubleshoot the most complex network infrastructures.

Cisco Certified Design Associate (CCDA) and Cisco Certified Design Professional (CCDP)

- **Overview**: These certifications focus on the design aspect of

networks. CCDA is an entry-level certification, while CCDP is aimed at those with more experience in designing large-scale networks.
- **Focus Areas**: Network design, IP addressing, routing protocols, and LAN/WAN design principles.
- **Target Audience**: Network architects and designers involved in the planning and development of network infrastructures.

Cisco Certified CyberOps Associate and Professional

- **Overview**: CyberOps certifications focus on network security operations. The associate level focuses on the basics, while the professional level dives deeper into security operations centers (SOC), threat detection, and incident response.
- **Focus Areas**: Security operations, monitoring, and incident handling. The professional-level certifications also cover advanced security measures, threat analysis, and incident response.
- **Target Audience**: Network security professionals looking to specialize in security operations and response to threats.

Cisco Certified DevNet Associate, Professional, and Expert

- **Overview**: Cisco DevNet certifications are designed for professionals looking to integrate networking and software development skills. These certifications emphasize automation, programming, and software development in network management.
- **Focus Areas**: Automation, network programmability, APIs, and cloud technologies. The Expert level covers the most advanced software networking solutions and automation strategies.
- **Target Audience**: DevOps engineers, software developers, and network automation professionals interested in the convergence of networking and software development.

Further Learning Resources

In addition to formal certification programs, there are numerous resources available for ongoing learning in network architecture and management. These resources can help both beginners and seasoned professionals expand their knowledge and stay up to date with the latest industry trends and technologies.

Cisco Networking Academy

- **Overview**: Cisco's official educational platform offers self-paced online courses, labs, and resources for learners at all levels. The Networking Academy offers specialized courses such as CCNA, CCNP, and CCIE, alongside learning materials for other Cisco products and technologies.
- **Features**: Interactive simulations, hands-on labs, and video tutorials. It is an excellent resource for anyone aiming for Cisco certification or simply seeking to deepen their networking knowledge.

Cisco Press Books

- **Overview**: Cisco Press is the official publisher of books and study materials for Cisco certifications and networking topics. Books cover a wide range of topics, from basic networking concepts to advanced network design and security principles.
- **Recommended Titles**: *CCNA Routing and Switching 200-125 Official Cert Guide, CCNP and CCIE Enterprise Core ENCOR 350-401 Official Cert Guide, Cisco Networking Simplified,* and *Network Security Essentials.*

Cisco Learning Network

- **Overview**: Cisco's Learning Network provides an online community for networking professionals. It includes discussion forums, study groups, video tutorials, webinars, and exam resources. The platform is an excellent place to connect with other learners and experts.
- **Features**: Practice exams, study material sharing, and virtual labs for

hands-on practice. It's a collaborative environment where members can ask questions, share experiences, and seek advice.

Cisco DevNet

- **Overview**: For professionals interested in network automation and software development, Cisco DevNet is a great resource. It provides tutorials, sandboxes, APIs, and other tools for learning about Cisco technologies and integrating networking with software development.
- **Features**: Sandbox environments for testing applications, automation tools, programming resources, and webinars. DevNet also offers certifications such as DevNet Associate and DevNet Professional for software developers and network engineers.

YouTube Channels and Webinars

- Many industry leaders, including Cisco, share educational content and tutorials through YouTube channels. Cisco's official channel and other community-run channels offer a wide variety of free resources.
- **Recommended Channels**: *Cisco Networking Academy, Cisco Press, NetworkChuck,* and *The Networking Nerd* offer video content ranging from certification tutorials to networking best practices.

Online Learning Platforms

- Several platforms offer comprehensive network-related courses and tutorials. Websites like Udemy, Pluralsight, LinkedIn Learning, and Coursera offer on-demand courses that cover a wide range of Cisco technologies and certifications.
- **Recommended Courses**: "Cisco CCNA 200-301," "Cisco CCNP Enterprise ENCOR 350-401," and "Cisco CCIE Enterprise Infrastructure" are popular courses that offer in-depth content for Cisco certification aspirants.

Cisco Live!

- Cisco Live! is Cisco's annual event where professionals and experts gather to share the latest network technologies, best practices, and solutions. Cisco Live! includes technical sessions, workshops, hands-on labs, and product demos.
- **Features**: Access to exclusive technical sessions, keynote addresses, and the opportunity to network with Cisco engineers and other industry experts. Cisco Live! is a fantastic opportunity for professionals to stay ahead of the curve.

Vendor-Specific Communities and Forums

- In addition to Cisco-specific resources, professional forums such as Stack Overflow, Reddit's /r/networking, and Spiceworks provide platforms for networking professionals to discuss solutions, troubleshoot problems, and share experiences.
- **Features**: Community-driven support, troubleshooting, advice on configuration issues, and a chance to collaborate with others on networking challenges.

Cisco certifications, along with the additional learning resources and tools mentioned above, offer valuable opportunities for network professionals to expand their skill set and deepen their expertise. Whether aiming for a foundational certification like CCNA, an advanced qualification such as CCIE, or expanding into network automation through DevNet, there is a wealth of resources available to guide learners at every stage of their careers. Continuous learning and certification are essential for staying current with evolving technologies, such as SD-WAN, cloud computing, IoT, and security, and for driving career growth in the dynamic field of networking.

C: Recommended Tools and Software for Network Architects

In the modern landscape of network design and management, network architects rely on a range of tools and software to streamline tasks, improve efficiency, and ensure scalability, security, and performance. These tools help network architects plan, configure, monitor, and troubleshoot network infrastructures, enabling them to build resilient and efficient network systems. The tools listed in this section are widely used by professionals in the field and cater to different aspects of network architecture, from design and configuration to monitoring, analysis, and automation.

Network Design and Simulation Tools

Cisco Packet Tracer

- **Overview**: Cisco Packet Tracer is a powerful network simulation tool designed for network design and training. It allows network architects to model complex network topologies, configure network devices, and test configurations without needing a physical network.
- **Key Features**:
- Simulation of a wide range of Cisco devices (routers, switches, firewalls, etc.).
- Support for various network protocols and routing technologies.
- Visualized network topology for easy configuration and troubleshooting.
- **Use Cases**: Ideal for design testing, training, and simulating network behaviors before deploying actual hardware.

GNS3 (Graphical Network Simulator)

- **Overview**: GNS3 is an open-source network simulation software that allows network engineers and architects to design and simulate

APPENDICES

complex network topologies with real Cisco IOS images, virtual devices, and third-party network devices.
- **Key Features**:
- Supports multiple vendors' devices.
- Integrates with virtual machines and real devices for more accurate simulations.
- High-performance simulations for larger networks and topologies.
- **Use Cases**: Suitable for advanced network design, testing, and certification preparation (e.g., CCNA, CCNP, CCIE).

SolarWinds Network Topology Mapper

- **Overview**: SolarWinds Network Topology Mapper is a network diagramming tool that automatically discovers and maps your network topology, providing detailed insights into your network's structure and connectivity.
- **Key Features**:
- Automatic discovery of network devices and topology.
- Generates real-time network diagrams and reports.
- Supports Layer 2 and Layer 3 mapping.
- **Use Cases**: Useful for creating and maintaining network diagrams and for visualizing complex network infrastructures.

Cisco Design Zone

- **Overview**: Cisco Design Zone provides network architects with reference architectures, best practices, and design guides tailored to Cisco solutions and technologies. It is an invaluable resource for creating and deploying Cisco-based network infrastructures.
- **Key Features**:
- Access to Cisco's validated designs for a wide range of technologies (e.g., LAN, WAN, wireless, data centers).
- Comprehensive documentation and step-by-step guides.

- Best practices for scaling and securing Cisco networks.
- **Use Cases**: Primarily used to reference Cisco's best practices and to speed up the design process for Cisco-based solutions.

Network Configuration and Management Tools

Cisco DNA Center

- **Overview**: Cisco DNA Center is an advanced network management platform that automates network operations, integrates multiple Cisco devices, and enables software-defined networking (SDN) through a centralized, unified interface.
- **Key Features**:
- Full lifecycle management of network devices.
- Automation of network configuration, monitoring, and troubleshooting.
- AI-driven insights for predictive network analytics and optimization.
- **Use Cases**: Best for managing and automating large enterprise networks with a focus on software-defined networking, security, and network assurance.

Ansible

- **Overview**: Ansible is an open-source automation tool that enables network architects to automate tasks, manage configurations, and orchestrate network operations across various devices and systems.
- **Key Features**:
- Simple, human-readable automation scripts (YAML).
- Supports a wide range of networking vendors (including Cisco) and devices.
- Automates repetitive tasks such as configuration management, software updates, and device provisioning.
- **Use Cases**: Ideal for network automation, configuration management, and integration in multi-vendor environments.

APPENDICES

Cisco Prime Infrastructure

- **Overview**: Cisco Prime Infrastructure is a network management platform that provides tools for monitoring, managing, and troubleshooting network devices across LAN, WLAN, and WAN environments.
- **Key Features**:
- Centralized monitoring and management for Cisco devices.
- Simplified network provisioning and policy enforcement.
- Performance monitoring and troubleshooting.
- **Use Cases**: Suitable for large enterprises that require centralized control over their Cisco network infrastructure, including detailed performance analytics and automated configuration management.

SolarWinds Network Configuration Manager

- **Overview**: SolarWinds Network Configuration Manager is a network configuration management tool that enables users to automate network device backups, configuration changes, and policy enforcement.
- **Key Features**:
- Automated backup of network device configurations.
- Change management and auditing.
- Configuration compliance checks.
- **Use Cases**: Ideal for managing configurations, ensuring compliance, and minimizing network downtime through automation.

Network Monitoring and Performance Tools
SolarWinds Network Performance Monitor

- **Overview**: SolarWinds Network Performance Monitor (NPM) is a comprehensive network monitoring tool that provides real-time visibility into network performance, uptime, and traffic flow.

- **Key Features**:
- Real-time network monitoring and alerting.
- Network performance dashboards and reports.
- Detailed analytics and root cause analysis.
- **Use Cases**: Best suited for proactive monitoring of network health, identifying issues early, and optimizing network performance.

Wireshark

- **Overview**: Wireshark is an open-source network protocol analyzer that captures and inspects network traffic at various layers, making it a powerful tool for troubleshooting and analyzing complex network issues.
- **Key Features**:
- Real-time traffic capture and packet inspection.
- Supports hundreds of protocols and protocols dissection.
- Filters and statistics for in-depth network analysis.
- **Use Cases**: Perfect for network troubleshooting, protocol analysis, and identifying issues like latency, packet loss, and misconfigurations.

PRTG Network Monitor

- **Overview**: PRTG Network Monitor is a powerful and flexible monitoring tool that helps network architects monitor network devices, traffic, and performance metrics to ensure optimal network operation.
- **Key Features**:
- Real-time monitoring of bandwidth, availability, and performance.
- Supports SNMP, WMI, NetFlow, and other protocols.
- Customizable dashboards and alerting.
- **Use Cases**: Ideal for smaller to mid-sized networks that require comprehensive monitoring, bandwidth analysis, and fault detection.

APPENDICES

NetFlow Analyzer

- **Overview**: NetFlow Analyzer by ManageEngine is a traffic analytics tool that uses NetFlow and IPFIX data to provide visibility into network traffic and bandwidth usage.
- **Key Features**:
- Flow-based traffic analysis (supports NetFlow, sFlow, IPFIX).
- Bandwidth monitoring and capacity planning.
- Security monitoring and anomaly detection.
- **Use Cases**: Perfect for analyzing traffic patterns, optimizing bandwidth usage, and improving network security through anomaly detection.

Network Security Tools

Cisco Umbrella

- **Overview**: Cisco Umbrella is a cloud-based security solution that protects users from online threats by blocking malicious websites and controlling internet access.
- **Key Features**:
- DNS-layer security to block harmful sites and protect against phishing attacks.
- Secure web filtering and content control.
- Cloud-delivered security with no hardware requirements.
- **Use Cases**: Ideal for protecting enterprise networks from internet-based threats, particularly in distributed environments or remote offices.

Firepower Management Center (FMC)

- **Overview**: Cisco Firepower Management Center provides centralized management of Cisco Firepower security appliances, offering advanced threat detection, real-time monitoring, and policy enforce-

ment.
- **Key Features**:
- Centralized threat analysis and policy management.
- Deep packet inspection and intrusion prevention.
- Real-time visibility and reporting for network security.
- **Use Cases**: Best suited for organizations that require advanced threat protection and unified management for their Cisco Firepower devices.

Splunk

- **Overview**: Splunk is a comprehensive data analytics platform used to monitor, search, and analyze machine-generated data, including network security logs.
- **Key Features**:
- Real-time event monitoring and alerts.
- Integration with Cisco security devices for log management and analysis.
- Advanced machine learning capabilities for anomaly detection.
- **Use Cases**: Ideal for large enterprises that need centralized log management, advanced security monitoring, and incident detection.

The tools and software mentioned in this appendix are crucial for network architects in designing, configuring, managing, and securing enterprise networks. From simulation and design tools like Cisco Packet Tracer and GNS3 to network monitoring solutions like SolarWinds and Wireshark, these resources allow network professionals to optimize performance, ensure security, and improve network resilience. By leveraging the right set of tools, network architects can streamline their workflows, enhance network efficiency, and tackle the growing complexity of modern network infrastructures.

APPENDICES

D: Cisco Resources and Communities

As a network architect, staying up-to-date with the latest Cisco technologies, best practices, and troubleshooting techniques is essential for success. Cisco offers a wide range of resources and community-driven platforms that can assist professionals in navigating the complexities of network design, configuration, and optimization. Whether you are looking for educational content, product documentation, troubleshooting help, or networking opportunities, these resources can provide valuable insights and support.

Cisco Support and Documentation

Cisco Support Community

- **Overview**: Cisco Support Community is a vast online forum where Cisco customers, engineers, and experts can discuss products, share solutions, and seek advice. It's a great place to find answers to technical questions, discover best practices, and troubleshoot network issues.
- **Key Features**:
- User-driven Q&A and discussions.
- Cisco experts provide detailed answers and solutions.
- Access to troubleshooting guides, software updates, and release notes.
- **Use Cases**: Ideal for finding solutions to specific network issues, discovering product updates, and connecting with other network professionals.

Cisco TechDocs

- **Overview**: Cisco TechDocs is Cisco's official online documentation portal, where you can access detailed guides, configuration examples, release notes, and installation instructions for all Cisco products and solutions.
- **Key Features**:

- Searchable knowledge base with product manuals and configuration guides.
- Detailed information on software and hardware releases, updates, and patches.
- Access to troubleshooting tools and diagnostic support.
- **Use Cases**: Essential for configuring Cisco products, troubleshooting network issues, and staying informed about product updates and patches.

Cisco Live

- **Overview**: Cisco Live is Cisco's flagship annual conference, providing access to cutting-edge technology briefings, training, workshops, and live sessions from Cisco experts. It covers a wide range of Cisco technologies and offers deep dives into networking, security, cloud, and more.
- **Key Features**:
- Live sessions with industry experts and thought leaders.
- Hands-on labs and training sessions.
- Access to recorded sessions and keynotes after the event.
- **Use Cases**: Great for gaining deeper insights into Cisco's latest technologies, networking with peers and industry leaders, and participating in technical workshops and labs.

Cisco Learning Network

- **Overview**: Cisco Learning Network is an online educational platform that offers a variety of training materials, resources, and certification preparation tools. It helps network professionals prepare for Cisco certifications (e.g., CCNA, CCNP, CCIE) and stay updated on Cisco technologies.
- **Key Features**:
- Certification exam preparation resources and practice tests.

APPENDICES

- Community-driven discussion forums for certification support.
- Access to Cisco's training content, including video lessons and interactive learning modules.
- **Use Cases**: Perfect for individuals pursuing Cisco certifications or looking to stay up-to-date with Cisco technology through learning resources.

Cisco Documentation Portal

- **Overview**: The Cisco Documentation Portal is a centralized location for all Cisco product documentation, including configuration guides, deployment guides, software specifications, and hardware manuals.
- **Key Features**:
- Comprehensive product documentation for all Cisco solutions.
- Searchable knowledge base with configuration examples and step-by-step instructions.
- Product lifecycle support information, including end-of-life (EOL) details.
- **Use Cases**: Essential for network architects configuring Cisco devices, managing network resources, and troubleshooting complex issues.

Cisco User Groups and Communities

Cisco User Groups (CUGs)

- **Overview**: Cisco User Groups (CUGs) are local and regional communities of Cisco customers and users who meet to share knowledge, discuss new technologies, and network with peers. CUGs are organized by geography or specific technologies, and they provide a platform for exchanging insights and best practices.
- **Key Features**:
- Regional events, meetings, and webinars.
- Access to community discussions on Cisco products and solutions.

- Opportunities for collaboration and learning from Cisco professionals and peers.
- **Use Cases**: Ideal for professionals looking to connect with local peers, share knowledge, and participate in events and technical discussions specific to their geographic region.

Cisco Champions Program

- **Overview**: The Cisco Champions Program is a community of highly engaged Cisco customers who are recognized for their expertise and contributions to the community. These individuals are selected based on their active participation in online discussions, knowledge sharing, and technical leadership.
- **Key Features**:
- Early access to Cisco products, technologies, and beta releases.
- Direct engagement with Cisco product teams and engineers.
- Invitations to exclusive events and forums, including virtual meetings with Cisco executives.
- **Use Cases**: Perfect for seasoned Cisco professionals and network architects who want to stay ahead of the curve and influence Cisco's technology development.

Cisco Developer Network (CDN)

- **Overview**: Cisco Developer Network is a community that provides resources and tools for developers working with Cisco technologies. It supports developers who are integrating Cisco's solutions, APIs, and SDN frameworks into custom applications and services.
- **Key Features**:
- Access to Cisco's developer tools, SDKs, and APIs.
- Online forums and resources for developing applications on Cisco platforms.
- Collaboration opportunities with other developers and Cisco engi-

neering teams.
- **Use Cases**: Ideal for developers looking to build applications using Cisco APIs or integrate Cisco's SDN, IoT, or cloud services into custom solutions.

Cisco Security Community

- **Overview**: The Cisco Security Community is a specialized group within Cisco's overall support and community structure that focuses on network security. It provides resources, tools, and a forum for discussing the latest security technologies, threat intelligence, and best practices.
- **Key Features**:
- Discussions on security threats, vulnerabilities, and Cisco's security solutions.
- Access to expert-led webinars and security updates.
- Collaboration with Cisco engineers on security technologies.
- **Use Cases**: Ideal for network architects focused on network security, threat detection, and incident response, and looking to collaborate with other security professionals.

Online Learning and Training Platforms
Cisco Networking Academy

- **Overview**: Cisco Networking Academy offers a comprehensive online learning platform with courses and certifications designed to help network professionals acquire skills in networking, security, IoT, automation, and more.
- **Key Features**:
- Online courses and certifications for foundational to advanced networking skills.
- Hands-on labs and real-world learning scenarios.
- Global access and collaboration with students and instructors.

- **Use Cases**: Ideal for network professionals looking to build a foundational understanding of networking concepts or expand their skills in specialized areas like cybersecurity or IoT.

Pluralsight

- **Overview**: Pluralsight is an online technology training platform that offers comprehensive courses in Cisco technologies, networking, cloud computing, and cybersecurity. Cisco-certified professionals and experts create the courses, ensuring high-quality, up-to-date content.
- **Key Features**:
- Video-based courses on Cisco technologies and network architecture.
- Skill assessments and learning paths for specific certifications.
- Access to real-world scenarios and practice labs.
- **Use Cases**: Excellent for professionals looking to enhance their Cisco skills or pursue certifications like CCNA, CCNP, or CCIE through expert-led online courses.

CBT Nuggets

- **Overview**: CBT Nuggets is another top-tier platform for online IT training, offering Cisco-specific courses focused on networking, security, and cloud technologies. It features practical labs and access to a community of learners.
- **Key Features**:
- Cisco certification training (CCNA, CCNP, etc.).
- Hands-on labs and practice tests.
- Interactive study tools and community support.
- **Use Cases**: Perfect for professionals who prefer structured training modules and hands-on labs to prepare for Cisco exams and deepen their network architecture skills.

APPENDICES

The Cisco resources and communities listed in this section provide network architects with a wealth of knowledge, training, and professional support to enhance their expertise in network design, configuration, troubleshooting, and security. From official documentation and training platforms to community-driven user groups and forums, Cisco offers a comprehensive ecosystem of resources that allow professionals to stay ahead in a rapidly evolving technology landscape. Engaging with these resources not only helps improve technical skills but also fosters collaboration and knowledge sharing among peers and experts.

www.ingramcontent.com/pod-product-compliance
Lightning Source LLC
Chambersburg PA
CBHW082243220526
45469CB00009B/2855